Praise for

MAKERS AND TAKERS

"A masterly account of the disproportionate power that the financial sector exercises in the economy and the disastrous consequences this has for society as a whole."

—Forbes.com

"A credible explanation for the rise of economic populism in the 2016 U.S. presidential race. Anyone seeking to truly understand the resonance of the anti–Wall Street vitriol of Bernie Sanders and Donald Trump could do worse than to start here."

—Fortune.com

"Foroohar demystifies the decline in America's economic prominence, showing that the competitive threats came not from the outside—migration or China—but from within our borders. She explains how finance has permeated every aspect of our economic and political life, and how those who caused the financial crisis wound up benefiting from it."

—Joseph E. Stiglitz, Nobel laureate in economics and former head of the Council of Economic Advisors

"A fast-paced, exciting, and well-researched tale that brings alive the shady dealings that have been part of the recent rise of finance (the takers). Wall Street has prospered beyond measure by consuming far too much of the value created by the real economy (the makers). Readers will be shocked by the shenanigans that are revealed, and then eager to help fix what has been so badly broken."

—John C. Bogle, founder and former CEO, Vanguard

"In this well-written, refreshing, and provocative book, Rana Foroohar analyzes how Wall Street went from an enabler of prosperity to a headwind to growth and a contributor to inequality. This is a must-read for those looking to better understand how, why, and when financial engineering went too far, and what to do about it."

—Mohamed A. El-Erian, chief economic adviser, Allianz; former CEO, PIMCO

"A powerful book about how financial manipulation has spread beyond the financial sector itself to colonize the American economy, to the enormous detriment of real, productive activities. Foroohar sheds light on almost everything we now see, from the inequality debate to presidential politics to America's global competitiveness. A phenomenal achievement."

—Charles Ferguson, producer, *Inside Job*

"One of the most important questions being asked right now is what is wrong with the American economy—and what can be done to fix it. Foroohar's book is required reading for this. With deft storytelling and clear analysis, she explains how America's economy has become stealthily "financialized"—and why this process has been so debilitating for American growth, not to mention the lives of ordinary people. Politicians—and voters—should take note."

—Gillian Tett, US managing editor, *Financial Times*, author of *The Silo Effect*

"There is no bigger question in public policy than whether the emergence of an ever-larger financial sector has made for a smaller and less equal society. *Makers and Takers* provides an intellectually compelling, and beautifully written, answer to that question, one which policy makers cannot and should not duck."

—Andy Haldane, chief economist and executive director of monetary analysis and statistics at the Bank of England

"A sometimes maddening, thoroughly fascinating look at the financial sector's outsized role in the US economy and what it means for America's future. This is a critical story that speaks directly to the ways in which banks are stripping businesses of their potential—and to the income inequality that increasingly defines our times."

—Ian Bremmer, founder and head of Eurasia Group

"A compelling case for how businesses have come to focus more on engineering their finances than engineering good products, and the negative effect this has on US growth and productivity."

—Ruchir Sharma, chief macroeconomist and head of emerging markets, Morgan Stanley Investment Management

MAKERS

— AND —

TAKERS

HOW WALL STREET
DESTROYED MAIN STREET

RANA FOROOHAR

CROWN
BUSINESS
NEW YORK

All rights reserved.
Published in the United States by Crown Business,
an imprint of the Crown Publishing Group,
a division of Penguin Random House LLC, New York.
crownpublishing.com

CROWN BUSINESS is a trademark and CROWN and the Rising Sun colophon
are registered trademarks of Penguin Random House LLC.

Originally published in hardcover in the United States by Crown Business,
an imprint of the Crown Publishing Group, a division of
Penguin Random House LLC, New York, in 2016.

Crown Business books are available at special discounts for bulk purchases for
sales promotions or corporate use. Special editions, including personalized covers,
excerpts of existing books, or books with corporate logos, can be created in large
quantities for special needs. For more information, contact Premium Sales at
(212) 572-2232 or e-mail specialmarkets@penguinrandomhouse.com.

Library of Congress Cataloging-in-Publication Data is available upon request.

ISBN 978-0-553-44725-5
Ebook ISBN 978-0-553-44724-8

PRINTED IN THE UNITED STATES OF AMERICA

Cover design by Alison Forner
Cover photograph by Kevin B. Moore / Moment Open / Getty Images

10 9 8 7 6 5 4 3 2 1

First Paperback Edition

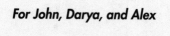

For John, Darya, and Alex

CONTENTS

AUTHOR'S NOTE
JUNE 2017

IF HERMAN Melville were writing his famous last novel, *The Confidence-Man*, today, there's little doubt who his model for the titular rapscallion would be: Donald Trump. One of the great powers of the confidence man is his ability to embed nuggets of truth in a welter of lies. His victims have no idea where the facts end and the fiction begins. That's the power of the con.

President Trump has sold the American people on any number of falsehoods—that immigrants are the reason for our economic woes, that we can turn back the clock on globalization, even that tax cuts for the nation's wealthiest citizens and its most profitable corporations will miraculously fuel growth and prosperity, though all evidence has shown the contrary over the last twenty years.

Yet he has also given voice to some important truths—most notably the fact that our economic "recovery," the financial crisis, is built on shaky ground. Months before his election, Trump proclaimed that there was a "big bubble" in the market fueled by "cheap money" that could cause a "massive recession" when it bursts. When stripped of their Trumpian embellishments, these statements are fact. Corporate debt and leverage *are* at record levels. Wall Street stock prices *are* at record highs, and yet wages have only just begun to tick slowly upward. Technically, America has been in a recovery since 2009. But it's a recovery that Main Street hasn't felt. This isn't sentiment; it's statistical fact. Data compiled by economists Thomas Piketty, Emmanuel Saez, and Gabriel Zucman show that not only has inequality risen dramatically over the last four decades, but also the top 1 percent have captured 52 percent of total real income growth in America since 2009.[1]

Of course, that's exactly what propelled President Trump's victory. He (and, to a lesser extent, Bernie Sanders) was able to convince the public that only an "outsider" could fix a system that was so clearly rigged in favor of Wall Street. And on that score, he has a point, one that is reflected in the moment that led me to write *Makers and Takers*. It was back in 2013, and I was sitting in an off-the-record briefing with a former Obama administration official who had been a key player in the financial crisis of 2008. A group of journalists, mostly financial beat reporters, had been gathered together in New York to hear this former official's post-game analysis of the crisis, part of the administration's efforts to bring closure to the most painful economic event in seven years in this country (as well as to tie a neat bow around the Obama team's handling of it).

At one point, a reporter pressed the former official on whether he thought that the Dodd-Frank bank reform regulation, which was still only half finished at the time, had been unduly influenced by Wall Street's lobbying efforts. The official insisted that this wasn't the case. I was taken aback—I had recently done a column citing academic research showing that 93 percent of all the public consultation on the Volcker Rule, one of the most contentious parts of the Dodd-Frank regulation, had been taken with the financial industry. Wall Street, not Main Street, was clearly the primary voice in the room as the regulation was being crafted. I raised my hand and shared the statistic, and then asked why so many such meetings had been done with bankers themselves, rather than a broader group of stakeholders. The official looked at me in an honest befuddlement, and said, "Who else should we have taken them with?"

That moment captured for me how difficult it is to grapple with the role of finance in our economy and our society. Finance holds a disproportionate amount of power in sheer economic terms. (It represents about 7 percent of our economy but takes around 25 percent of all corporate profit, while creating only 4 percent of all jobs.) But its power to shape the thinking and the mind-set of government officials, regulators, CEOs, and even many consumers (who are, of course, brought into the status quo market system via their 401(k) plans) is even more important. This "cognitive capture," as academics call it, was a crucial reason that the policy decisions taken post-2008 resulted in large gains for the financial industry but losses for homeowners, small businesses, workers, and consumers. It's also the reason that the rules of our capitalist system haven't yet been rewritten in a way that would force the financial markets to do what they were set up to do: support Main Street. As the aforementioned conversation shows, when all the people in charge of deciding how market capitalism should operate are themselves beholden to the financial industry, it's impossible to craft a system that will be fair for everyone.

Sadly, despite President Trump's rhetoric, we shouldn't count on him to have the interests of Main Street Americans at heart. While it's easy to understand why the American public might look to a political outsider for change, the truth is that President Trump has been a consummate creature of Wall Street for decades. He made his money as any high-stakes financier would—with little equity down; lots of leverage; and a heads-I-win, tails-you-lose modus operandi. His cabinet is filled with financiers and those who profit from a Wall Street–centric view of the world (seventeen of his earliest appointees, including various Goldman alumnae, have a greater net worth than the bottom third of the country). One of his first executive acts was an attempt to dismantle what little financial regulation *was* actually crafted post 2008. The only reason Trump knows so much about the gap between the 1 percent and the 99 percent is because he's one of the guys who helped widen it. He's not a businessman who'll bring back US jobs; he's a branding expert adept at making money mainly for himself. Still, his ability to spin a fable about "draining the swamp," and taking the power out of the hands of the "elites," resonated with the day-to-day experience of Main Street, where the recovery has felt like anything but. Of course, it didn't hurt that he ran against a candidate whose husband's administration was responsible for breaking down barriers between risky trading and commercial lending on Wall Street, cutting trade deals that benefited large corporations but helped hollow out the Rust Belt, and deregulating derivatives, those "weapons of mass financial destruction" that resulted in the 2008 crisis. President Trump was able to use all of this to deflect from the fact that he himself was a key beneficiary of the financialization of our economy over the last forty years.

This battle between Wall Street and Main Street, a battle still ragging eight years on from the worst financial crisis in seventy years, is the subject of this book. The view from Wall Street has over the past four years or so become the conventional view of how our market system and our economy should operate. And yet, it's a view that is highly biased and distorted. While we think about the financial industry as the grease for the wheels of our capitalist system, the interests of Wall Street have come to trump—no pun intended—those of American businesses, American consumers, and American workers.

Finance has become a headwind to economic growth, not a catalyst for it. As it has grown, business—as well as the American economy and society at large—has suffered. The crisis of 2008 was followed by the longest and weakest economic recovery of the post–World War II era. While the top tier of society is now thriving, most everyone else is still struggling. The solution isn't isolationism or turning back the clock on globalization (something that isn't really possible anyway), but a dramatically different balance of power between finance and the real economy—between the takers and the makers—to ensure better and more sustainable growth. It's a conversation that has been hard to have, given how much control finance has in our economy and our society. But it's crucial if we are to have an economic system that truly serves all Americans, not to mention curbing the sort of Hobbsian hopelessness among the general population that propelled Trump (and any number of other autocrats globally) into power. This book is an attempt to start that conversation—to illustrate how takers came to dominate makers in our economy, and how we can craft a better future.

INTRODUCTION

IT WASN'T the way Steve Jobs would have done it.

In the spring of 2013, Jobs's successor as CEO of Apple Inc., Tim Cook, decided the company needed to borrow $17 billion. Yes, borrow. Never mind that Apple was the world's most valuable corporation, that it had sold more than a billion devices so far, and that it already had $145 billion sitting in the bank, with another $3 billion in profits flowing in every month.

So, why borrow? It was not because the company was a little short, obviously, or because it couldn't put its hands on any of its cash. The reason, rather, was that Apple's financial masters had determined borrowing was the better, more cost-effective way to obtain the funds. Whatever a loan might normally cost, it would cost Apple far less, thanks to a low-interest bond offering available only to blue-chip companies. Even better, Apple would not actually have to touch its bank accounts, which aren't held someplace down the street like yours or mine. Rather, they are scattered in a variety of places around the globe, including offshore financial institutions. (The company is secretive about the details.) If that money were to return to the United States, Apple would have to pay hefty tax rates on it, something it has always studiously avoided, even though there is something a little off about a quintessentially American firm dodging a huge chunk of American taxes.

So Apple borrowed the $17 billion.

This was never the Steve Jobs way. Jobs focused relentlessly on creating irresistible, life-changing products, and was confident that money would follow. By contrast, Cook pays close attention to the money and to increasingly sophisticated manipulations of money. And why? Part of the reason is that Apple hasn't introduced any truly game-changing technology since Jobs's death in 2011. That has at times depressed the company's stock price and led to concerns about its long-term future, despite the fact that it still sells a heck of a lot of devices. It's a chicken-and-egg cycle, of course. The more a company focuses on financial engineering rather than the real kind, the more it ensures it will need to continue to do so. But right now, what Apple does have is cash.

Which gets us to that $17 billion. Apple didn't need that money to build a new plant or to develop a new product line. It needed the funds to buy off investors by repurchasing stock and fattening dividends, which would goose the company's lagging share price. And, at least for a little while, the tactic worked. The stock soared, yielding hundreds of millions of dollars in paper wealth for Apple board members who approved the maneuver and for the company's shareholders, of whom Cook is one of the largest. That was great for them, but it didn't put much shine on Apple. David Einhorn, the hedge fund manager who'd long been complaining that the company wasn't sharing enough of its cash hoard, inadvertently put it very well when he said that Apple should apply "the same level of creativity" on its balance sheet as it does to producing revolutionary products.[1] To him, and to many others in corporate America today, one kind of creativity is just as good as another.

I'll argue differently in this book.

The fact that Apple, probably the best-known company in the world and surely one of the most admired, now spends a large amount of its time and effort thinking about how to make more money via *financial* engineering rather than by the old-fashioned kind, tells us how upside down our biggest corporation's priorities have become, not to mention the politics behind a tax system that encourages it all. This little vignette also demonstrates how detached many of America's biggest businesses have become from the needs and desires of their consumers—and from the hearts and minds of the country at large.

Because make no mistake, Apple's behavior is no aberration. Stock buybacks and dividend payments of the kind being made by Apple—moves that enrich mainly a firm's top management and its largest shareholders but often stifle its capacity for innovation, depress job creation, and erode its competitive position over the longer haul—have become commonplace. The S&P 500 companies as a whole have spent more than $6 trillion on such payments between 2005 and 2014,[2] bolstering share prices and the markets even as they were cutting jobs and investment.[3] Corporate coffers like Apple's are filled to overflowing, and America's top companies will very likely hand back a record amount of cash to shareholders this year.

Meanwhile, our economy limps along in a "recovery" that is tremendously bifurcated. Wage growth is flat. Six out of the top ten fastest-growing job categories pay $15 an hour and workforce participation is as low as it's been since the late 1970s.[4] It used to be that as the fortunes of American companies improved, the fortunes of the average American rose, too. But now something has broken that relationship.

That something is Wall Street. Just consider that only weeks after Apple announced it would pay off investors with the $17 billion, more sharks began circling. Corporate raider Carl Icahn, one of the original barbarians at the gate who attacked companies from TWA to RJR Nabisco in the 1980s and 1990s, promptly began buying up Apple stock, all the while tweeting demands that Cook spend billions and billions more on buybacks. With each tweet, Apple's share price jumped. By May 2015, Icahn's stake in Apple had soared 330 percent, to more than $6.5 billion, and Apple had pledged to spend a total of $200 billion on dividends and buybacks through March 2017. Meanwhile, the company's R&D as a percentage of sales, which has been falling since 2001, is creeping ever lower.[5] What these sorts of sugar highs portend for Apple's long-term future is anyone's guess, but one thing is clear: the business of America isn't business anymore. It's finance. From "activist investors" to investment banks, from management consultants to asset managers, from high-frequency traders to insurance companies, today, *financiers dictate terms to American business, rather than the other way around.* Wealth creation within the financial markets has become an end in itself, rather than a means to the end of shared economic prosperity. The tail is wagging the dog.

Worse, financial *thinking* has become so ingrained in American business that even our biggest and brightest companies have started to act like banks. Apple, for example, has begun using a good chunk of its spare cash to buy corporate bonds the same way financial institutions do, prompting a 2015 Bloomberg headline to declare, "Apple Is the New Pimco, and Tim Cook Is the New King of Bonds."[6] Apple and other tech companies now anchor new corporate bond offerings just as investment banks do, which is not surprising considering how much cash they hold (it seems only a matter of time before Apple launches its own credit card). They are, in essence, acting like banks, but they aren't regulated like banks. If Big Tech decided at any point to dump those bonds, it could become a market-moving event, an issue that is already raising concern among experts at the Office of Financial Research, the Treasury Department body founded after the 2008 financial crisis to monitor stability in financial markets.[7]

Big Tech isn't alone in emulating finance. Airlines often make more money from hedging on oil prices than on selling seats—while bad bets can leave them with millions of dollars in losses. GE Capital, a subsidiary of the company launched by America's original innovator, Thomas Alva Edison, was until quite recently a Too Big to Fail financial institution like AIG (GE has spun it off in part because of the risks it posed). Any number of Fortune 500 firms engage in complicated Whac-A-Mole schemes to keep their cash in a variety of offshore banks to avoid paying taxes not only in the United States but also in many other countries where they operate. But tax avoidance and even "tax inversions" of the sort firms like the drug giant Pfizer have done—maneuvers that allow companies to skirt paying their fair share of the national burden despite taking advantage of all sorts of government supports (federally funded research and technology, intellectual property protection)—are only the tip of the iceberg. In fact, American firms today make more money than ever before by simply moving money around, getting about five times the revenue from purely financial activities, such as trading, hedging, tax optimizing, and selling financial services, than they did in the immediate post–World War II period.[8]

It seems that we are all bankers now.

It's a truth that is at the heart of the way our economy works—and doesn't work—today. Eight years on from the financial crisis of 2008, we are finally in a recovery, but it has been the longest and weakest recovery of the postwar era. The reason? Our financial system has stopped serving the real economy and now serves mainly itself, as the story above and many others in this book, along with copious amounts of data, will illustrate. Our system of market capitalism is sick, and the big-picture symptoms—slower-than-average growth, higher income inequality, stagnant wages, greater market fragility, the inability of many people to afford middle-class basics like a home, retirement, and education—are being felt throughout our entire economy and, indeed, our society.

DIAGNOSING THE PROBLEM

Our economic illness has a name: financialization. It's a term for the trend by which Wall Street and its way of thinking have come to reign supreme in America, permeating not just the financial industry but all American business. The very type of short-term, risky thinking that nearly toppled the global economy in 2008 is today widening the gap between rich and poor, hampering economic progress, and threatening the future of the American Dream itself. The financialization of America includes everything from the growth in size and scope of finance and financial activity in our economy to the rise of debt-fueled speculation over productive lending, to the ascendancy of shareholder value as a model for corporate governance, to the proliferation of risky, selfish thinking in both our private and public sectors, to the increasing political power of financiers and the CEOs they enrich, to the way in which a "markets know best" ideology remains the status quo, even after it caused the worst financial crisis in seventy-five years. It's a shift that has even affected our language, our civic life, and our way of relating to one another. We speak about human or social "capital" and securitize everything from education to critical infrastructure to prison terms, a mark of our burgeoning "portfolio society."[9]

The Kafkaesque story of Apple described above is just one of the many perverse outcomes associated with financialization, a wonky but apt moniker picked up by academics to describe our upside-down economy, one in which *Makers*—the term I use in this book to describe the people, companies, and ideas that create real economic growth—have come to be servants to *Takers*, those that use our dysfunctional market system mainly to enrich themselves rather than society at large. These takers include many (though certainly not all) financiers and financial institutions, as well as misguided leaders in both the private and the public sector, including numerous CEOs, politicians, and regulators who don't seem to understand how financialization is undermining our economic growth, our social stability, and even our democracy.

The first step to tackling financialization is, of course, understanding it. This immensely complex and broad-based phenomenon starts with, but is by no means limited to, the banking sector. The traditional role of finance within an economy—the one our growth depends on—is to take the savings of households and turn it into investment. But that critical link has been lost. Today finance engages mostly in alchemy, issuing massive amounts of debt and funneling money to different parts of the financial system itself, rather than investing in Main Street.[10] "The trend varies slightly country by country, but the broad direction is clear: across all advanced economies, and the United States and the UK in particular, the role of the capital markets and the banking sector in funding new investment is decreasing. Most of the money in the system is being used for lending against existing assets," says Adair Turner, former British banking regulator, financial stability expert, and now chairman of the Institute for New Economic Thinking, whose recent book, *Between Debt and the Devil*, explains the phenomenon in detail.[11] In simple terms, what Turner is saying is that rather than funding the new ideas and projects that create jobs and raise wages, finance has shifted its attention to securitizing existing assets (like homes, stocks, bonds, and such), turning them into tradable products that can be spliced and diced and sold as many times as possible—that is, until things blow up, as they did in 2008. He is right. Academic research shows that only a fraction of all the money washing around the financial markets these days actually makes it to Main Street businesses. As recently as the 1970s, the majority of capital coming from financial institutions would have been used to fund business investments, whereas today's estimates indicate that figure at around 15 percent. The rest simply stays inside the financial system, enriching financiers, corporate titans, and the wealthiest fraction of the population, which hold the vast majority of financial assets in the United States and, indeed, the world.[12]

The unchecked influence of the financial industry is a phenomenon that has played out over many decades and in many ways. So what is so urgent about it now? For one, the fact that we are in the longest and weakest economic recovery of the post–World War II period, despite the trillions of dollars of monetary and fiscal stimulus that our government has shelled out since 2008, shows that our model is broken. Our ability to offer up the appearance of growth—via low interest rates, more and more consumer credit, tax-deferred debt financing for businesses, and asset bubbles that make us all feel richer than we really are, until they burst—is at an end. What we need isn't virtual growth fueled by finance, but real, sustainable growth for Main Street.

To get there, we need to understand the key question, which is really quite simple: How did finance, a sector that makes up 7 percent of the economy and creates only 4 percent of all jobs, come to generate almost a third of all corporate profits in America at the height of the housing boom, up from some 10 percent of the slice it was taking twenty-five years ago?[13] How did this sector, which was once meant to merely *facilitate* business, manage to get such a stranglehold over it? That is the question this book will strive to answer, in particular by examining just how the rise of finance has led to the fall of American business, a juxtaposition that has rarely been explored. Many of the perverse trends associated with financialization, such as rising inequality, stagnating wages, financial market fragility, and slower growth, are often (rightly) spoken about in social terms and in highly politicized ways—with polarizing discussions of the 1 percent versus the 99 percent, and Too Big to Fail banks versus profligate consumers and rapacious investors.

All these things are part of the story. But none of them captures the full picture of how our financial system has come to rule—rather than fuel—the real economy, the one that you and I actually live and work in. By looking at the effect of our dysfunctional financial system on *business* itself, an area that I have covered as a journalist for twenty-three years, I will move beyond sound bites into real analysis of the problem and illustrate how the trend of financialization is damaging the very heart of our economy and thus endangering prosperity for us *all*.

This is a book that will speak to average Americans, who have yet to be given a full or understandable explanation about what has happened to our economy over the last several years (not to mention the last several decades), and why many of the financial regulations promised us in the wake of the 2008 crisis never came to pass. But it will also speak to policy makers who still have a chance to fix our system—a chance that has so far been missed in the post-financial-crisis era. It's an opportunity that must be seized, because, as I will explore in this book, our financial apparatus has collapsed under its own weight multiple times in the last several decades, and without changes to our system, it's only a matter of time before it does again, taking us all down with it.

THE LIFEBLOOD OF FINANCE

Our shift to a system in which finance has become an end in and of itself, rather than a helpmeet for Main Street, has been facilitated by many changes within the financial services industry. One of them is a decrease in lending, and another is an increase in trading—particularly the kind of rapid-fire computerized trading that now makes up about half of all US stock market activity.[14] The entire value of the New York Stock Exchange now turns over about once every nineteen months, a rate that has tripled since the 1970s.[15] No wonder the size of the securities industry grew fivefold as a share of gross domestic product (GDP) between 1980 and mid-2000s while ordinary bank deposits shrunk from 70 to 50 percent of GDP.[16]

With the rise of the securities and trading portion of the industry came a rise in debt of all kinds, public and private. Debt is the lifeblood of finance; it is where the financial industry makes its money. At the same time, a broad range of academic research shows that rising debt and credit levels stoke financial instability.[17] And yet, as finance has captured a greater and greater piece of the national pie—its share of the US economy has tripled in the postwar era[18]—it has, perversely, all but ensured that debt is indispensable to maintaining any growth at all in an advanced economy like the United States, where 70 percent of output is consumer spending. Stagnating wages and historically low economic growth can't do the trick, so debt-fueled finance becomes a saccharine substitute for the real thing, an addiction that just gets worse and worse.[19] As the economist Raghuram Rajan, one of the most prescient seers of the 2008 financial crisis, argued in his book *Fault Lines*, credit has become a palliative to address the deeper anxieties of downward mobility in the middle class. As he puts it sharply, "let them eat credit" could well summarize the mantra of the go-go years before the economic meltdown.[20]

This balloon of debt and credit has not gone away since. Private debt, as most of us know, increased dramatically in the run-up to 2008.[21] But now public debt too is at record levels, thanks to the economic fallout from the crisis (and hence the fall in tax revenue) and the government stimulus spending that went along with it.[22] That the amount of credit offered to American consumers has doubled since the 1980s, as have the fees they pay to their banks—along with the fact that the largest of these banks are holding an unprecedented level of assets—is proof positive of the industry's monopoly power.[23] In sum, financial fees are rising, even as financial efficiency *falls*.[24] So much for efficient markets.[25]

STEALING THE SEED CORN OF THE FUTURE

But as credit and fees have risen inexorably, lending to business—and in particular small business—has come down over time. Back in the early 1980s, when financialization began to gain steam, commercial banks in the United States provided almost as much in loans to industrial and commercial enterprises as they did in real estate and consumer loans; that ratio stood at 80 percent. By the end of the 1990s, the ratio fell to 52 percent, and by 2005, it was only 28 percent.[26] Lending to small business has fallen particularly sharply,[27] as has the number of start-up firms themselves. In the early 1980s, new companies made up half of all US businesses. By 2011, they were just a third,[28] a trend that numerous academics and even many investors and businesspeople have linked to the financial industry's change in focus from lending to speculation.[29] The wane in entrepreneurship means less economic vibrancy, given that new businesses are the nation's foremost source of job creation and GDP growth. As Warren Buffett once summed it up to me in his folksy way, "You've now got a body of people who've decided they'd rather go to the casino than the restaurant" of capitalism.

In lobbying for short-term share-boosting management, finance is also largely responsible for the drastic cutback in research and development outlays in corporate America, investments that are the seed corn for the future. Indeed, if you chart the rise in money spent on share buybacks and the fall in corporate spending on productive investments like R&D, the two lines make a perfect X.[30] The former has been going up since the 1980s, with S&P 500 firms now spending $1 trillion a year on buybacks and dividends—equal to more than 95 percent of their net earnings—rather than investing that money back in research, product development, or anything that could contribute to long-term company growth.

Indeed, long-term investment has fallen precipitously over the past half century. In the 1950s, companies routinely set aside 5–6 percent of profits for research. Only a handful of firms do so today. Analysis funded by the Roosevelt Institute, for example, shows that the relationship between cash flow and corporate investment began to fall apart in the 1980s, as the financial markets really took off.[31] And no sector, even the most innovative, has been immune. Many tech firms, for example, spend far more on share-price boosting than on R&D as a whole. The markets penalize them when they don't. One case in point: back in March 2006, Microsoft announced major new technology investments, and its stock fell for two months. But in July of that same year, it embarked on $20 billion worth of stock buying, and the share price promptly rose by 7 percent.[32] It's a pattern that's being repeated more recently at a record number of companies, including Yahoo, where CEO Marissa Mayer, backed by hedge fund titan Daniel Loeb, began boosting the firm's share price several years ago by handing back cash to investors who hadn't been persuaded by Yahoo's underlying growth story. (Mayer later found herself under pressure from yet more "activists" looking to dissuade her from using a cash hoard from the proposed spin-off of Yahoo's core search business for acquisitions rather than buybacks.[33]) She's certainly not alone. The year 2015 set a new record for buybacks and dividend payments, as well as demands for even greater payouts issued by activist investors like Loeb, Icahn, Einhorn, and many others.[34]

What's more, though many of us don't know it, we ourselves are part of a dysfunctional ecosystem that fuels all this short-term thinking. The people who manage our retirement money—fund managers working for firms like Fidelity and BlackRock—are typically compensated for delivering returns over a year or less.[35] That means they use their financial clout (which is really ours) to push companies to produce quick-hit results, rather than to execute longer-term strategies. Sometimes our pension funds even invest with the "activists" who are buying up the companies we might be working for—and then firing us. All of it erodes growth, not to mention our own livelihoods. And yet, so many Americans now rely on the financial markets for safety in their old age that we fear anything that might have a chilling effect on them, a fear that the financial industry expertly exploits. After all, who would want to puncture the bubble that pays for our retirement? We have made a Faustian bargain, in which we depend on the markets for wealth and thus don't look too closely at how the sausage gets made.

Given this kind of pressure for short-term results, it is not surprising that business dynamism, which is at the root of economic growth, has suffered. The number of new initial public offerings (IPOs) is about a third of what it was twenty years ago. Part of this is about the end of the unsustainable, Wall Street–driven tech stock boom of the 1990s. But another reason is that firms simply don't want to go public. That's because an IPO today is likely to mark not the beginning of a new company's greatness, but the end of it. According to a Stanford University study, innovation tails off by 40 percent at tech companies after they go public, often because of Wall Street pressure to keep jacking up the stock price, even if it means curbing the entrepreneurial verve that made the company hot in the first place.[36] A flat stock price spells doom. It can get CEOs canned and turn companies into acquisition fodder, which dampens public ardor and often leaves once-dynamic firms broken down and sold for parts. Little wonder, then, that business optimism, as well as business creation, is lower than it was thirty years ago.

It is perhaps the ultimate irony that large and rich companies like Apple and Pfizer are most involved with financial markets at times when *they don't need any financing.* As with Apple, top-tier American businesses have never enjoyed greater capital resources; they have a record $4.5 trillion on their balance sheets—enough money to make them the fourth-largest economy in the world. Yet in the bizarro realm that is our financial system, they have also taken on record amounts of debt to buy back their own stock, creating what may be the next debt bubble to burst in our fragile, financialized economy.[37]

THE END OF GROWTH, AND THE GROWTH OF INEQUALITY

While there are other countries that have a larger banking sector as a percentage of their overall economy, no country beats the United States in the size of its financial system as a whole (meaning, if you tally up the value of all financial assets).[38] In the first half of 2015, the United States boasted $81.7 trillion worth of financial assets— more than the combined total of the next three countries (China, Japan, and the United Kingdom).[39] We are at the forefront of financialization; our financiers and politicians like to brag that America has the world's broadest and deepest capital markets. But contrary to the conventional wisdom of the last several decades, that isn't a good thing.[40] All this finance has not made us more prosperous. Instead, it has deepened inequality and ushered in more financial crises, which destroy massive amounts of economic value each time they happen. Far from being a help to our economy, finance has become a hindrance. More finance isn't increasing our economic growth—it is slowing it.[41]

Indeed, studies show that countries with large and quickly growing financial systems tend to exhibit *weaker* productivity growth.[42]

That's a huge problem, given that productivity and demographics together are basically the recipe for economic progress. One influential paper published by the Bank for International Settlements (BIS) put the issue in quite visceral terms, asking whether a "bloated financial system" was like "a person who eats too much," slowing down the rest of the economy. The answer is yes—and in fact, finance starts having these kinds of adverse effects when it's only *half* of its current size in the United States.[43] Other reports by groups like the Organisation for Economic Co-operation and Development (OECD)[44] and the International Monetary Fund (IMF)[45] have come to a similar conclusion: the industry that was supposed to grease the wheels of growth has instead become a headwind to it.

Part of this adverse impact stems from the decrease in entrepreneurship and economic vibrancy that has gone hand in hand with the growth of finance. Another part is about the mounting monopoly power of large banks, whose share of all banking assets has more than tripled since the early 1970s. (America's five largest banks now make up half its commercial banking industry.)[46] That growing dominance means that financial institutions can increasingly funnel money where they like, which tends to be toward debt and speculation, rather than productive investment on which it takes longer to reap a profit. Power—in terms of both size and influence—is also the reason the financial sector's lobby is so effective. Finance regularly outspends every other industry on lobbying efforts in Washington, D.C.,[47] which has enabled it to turn back key areas of regulation (remember the trading loopholes pushed into the federal spending bill by the banking industry in 2014?) and change our tax and legal codes at will. Increasingly, the power of these large, oligopolistic interests is remaking our unique brand of American capitalism into a crony capitalism more suited to a third-world autocracy than a supposedly free-market democracy.[48] Thanks to these changes, our economy is gradually becoming "a zero-sum game between financial wealth-holders and the rest of America," according to the late Wallace Turbeville, a former Goldman Sachs banker who also ran a multiyear project on financialization at the nonprofit think tank Demos.[49]

Indeed, one of the most pernicious effects of the rise of finance has been the growth of massive inequality, the likes of which haven't been seen since the Gilded Age. The two trends have in fact moved in sync. Financial sector wages—an easy way to track the two variables' relationship—were high relative to everyone else's in the run-up to the market crash of 1929, then fell precipitously after banking was reregulated in the 1930s, and then grew wildly from the 1980s onward as finance was once again unleashed.[50] The share of financiers within the top 1 percent of the income distribution nearly doubled between 1979 and 2005.[51]

Rich bankers themselves aren't so much the reason for inequality as the most striking illustration of just how important financial assets have become in widening America's wealth gap. Financiers and the corporate supermanagers whom they enrich represent a growing percentage of the nation's elite precisely because they control the most financial resources. These assets (stocks, bonds, and such) are the dominant form of wealth for the most privileged,[52] which actually creates a snowball effect of inequality. As French economist Thomas Piketty explained so thoroughly in his 696-page tome, *Capital in the Twenty-First Century*, the returns on financial assets greatly outweigh those from income earned the old-fashioned way: by working for wages.[53] Even when you consider the salaries of the modern economy's supermanagers—the CEOs, bankers, accountants, agents, consultants, and lawyers that groups like Occupy Wall Street rail against—it's important to remember that somewhere between 30 and 80 percent of their income is awarded not in cash but in incentive stock options and stock shares.

This type of income is taxed at a much lower rate than what most of us pay on our regular paychecks, thanks to finance-friendly shifts in tax policy in the past thirty-plus years. That means the composition of supermanager pay has the effect of dramatically reducing the public sector take of the national wealth pie (and thus the government's ability to shore up the poor and middle classes) while widening the income gap in the economy as a whole. The top twenty-five hedge fund managers in America make more than all the country's kindergarten teachers combined, a statistic that, as much as any, reflects the skewed resource allocation that is part and parcel of financialization.[54]

This downward spiral accelerates as executives paid in stock make short-term business decisions that might undermine growth in their companies even as they raise the value of their own options. It's no accident that corporate stock buybacks, which tend to bolster share prices but not underlying growth, and corporate pay have risen concurrently over the last four decades.[55] There are any number of studies that illustrate this type of intersection between financialization and the wealth gap. One of the most striking was done by economists James Galbraith and Travis Hale, who showed how during the late 1990s, changing income inequality tracked the go-go NASDAQ stock index to a remarkable degree.[56] The same thing happened during the stock boom of the last several years, underscoring the point that commentators like journalist Robert Frank have made, that wealth built on financial markets is "more abstracted from the real world" and thus more volatile, contributing to a cycle of booms and busts (which of course hurt the poor more than any other group).[57] As Piketty's work so clearly shows, in the absence of some change-making event, like a war or a severe depression that destroys financial asset value, financialization ensures that the rich really do get richer—a lot richer—while the rest become worse off. That's bad not only for those at the bottom, but for all of us. Research proves that more inequality leads to poorer health outcomes, lower levels of trust, more violent crime, and less social mobility—all of the things that can make a society unstable.[58] As Piketty told me during an interview in 2014, there's "no algorithm" to predict when revolutions happen, but if current trends continue, the consequences for society in terms of social unrest and economic upheaval could be "terrifying."[59]

There are plenty of conservative academics, policy makers, and businesspeople (along with liberals who've bought into the trickle-down approach) who will dispute the details of such analysis. True, one can argue that precise and irrefutable causalities between finance and per capita GDP growth are difficult to isolate because of the tremendous number of variables at play. But the depth and breadth of correlations between the rise of finance and the growth of inequality, the fall in new businesses, wage stagnation, and political dysfunction strongly suggest that finance is not just pulling ahead, but is also actively depressing the real economy. On top of this, it's quantitatively increasing market volatility and risk of the sort that wiped out $16 trillion in household wealth during the Great Recession.[60] Evidence shows that the number of wealth-destroying financial crises has risen in tandem with financial sector growth over the last several decades. In their book *This Time Is Different: Eight Centuries of Financial Folly,* academics Carmen Reinhart and Kenneth Rogoff describe how the proportion of the world affected by banking crises (weighed by countries' share of global GDP) rose from some 7.5 percent in 1971 to 11 percent in 1980 and to 32 percent in 2007.[61] And economist Robert Aliber, in updating one of the seminal books on financial bubbles, the late Charles Kindleberger's *Manias, Panics, and Crashes: A History of Financial Crises,* issued a grave warning in 2005, well before the 2008 meltdown: "The conclusion is unmistakable that financial failure has been more extensive and pervasive in the last thirty years than in any previous period."[62] This is a startling illustration of how finance has transitioned from an industry that encourages healthy risk taking to one that simply creates debt and spreads unproductive risk in the market system as a whole.

THE ROOT CAUSES

It didn't have to be this way. In the period following the Great Depression, banking was a cornerstone of American prosperity. Back then, banks built the companies that created the products that kept the economy going. If you had some initiative and a great idea, you went to a bank, and the bank checked out your business plan, tracked your credit record, and, with any luck, helped you build your dream. Banks funded America—that's what we grew up to believe. And that's what we were told in 2008, when our government pledged some $700 billion of taxpayer money (enough to rebuild the entire Interstate Highway System from scratch and then some) to bail out the American financial system. The resultant Troubled Asset Relief Program, or TARP, was meant to quell the subprime mortgage crisis, brought on, of course, by colossal malfeasance by some of the very banks being saved. But, no surprise, that hasn't fixed the problem. Wall Street is not only back, but bigger than it was before. The ten largest banks in the country now make up a greater percentage of the financial industry and hold more assets than they did in 2007, nearly two-thirds as much as the entire $18-trillion US economy itself. Main Street, meanwhile, continues to struggle.

Pundits and politicians will give many superficial reasons for this: we have suffered from a lack of business confidence; we are dragged down by the continuing debt crisis in Europe; we are paralyzed by the slowdown in China; we are victims of Washington's political dysfunction; we are hurt by increased federal regulation and its attendant red tape. While these issues have some peripheral effect, they don't explain the fact that productivity and growth in our underlying economy have been slowing since the 1990s, regardless of which political party was in power, what policies were in place, or which countries were doing well or poorly on the global stage.

There are more serious conversations to be had about the effects that things like globalization and technology-driven job destruction have had on growth. It is true that jobs have been outsourced to places where labor is cheaper, that increasingly even middle-class work is being done by software, and that these factors have played a role in our slowed recovery. But the financialization of the American economy is the third major, unacknowledged factor in slower growth, and it engages with the other two in myriad destructive ways. Finance loves outsourcing, for example, since pushing labor to emerging markets reduces costs. But financiers rarely think about the risks that offshoring adds to supply chains—risks tragically evidenced in events like the 2013 collapse of the Rana Plaza textile manufacturing center in Bangladesh, which killed more than a thousand garment workers who spent their days stitching T-shirts and jeans for companies like Walmart, Children's Place, and JCPenney in buildings that weren't up to code. Finance also loves the cost savings inherent in technology. Yet high-tech financial applications like flash trading and computer-generated algorithms used in complex securities have resulted in repeated market crashes, wiping out trillions of dollars of wealth. Meanwhile, Big Tech firms have become some of the most rapaciously financialized businesses of all.

PASSING THE BUCK

The hugely complex process of financialization is often aided and abetted by government leaders, policy makers, and regulators—the very people who are supposed to be in charge of keeping market crashes from happening. Greta Krippner, the University of Michigan scholar who has written one of the most comprehensive books on financialization,[63] believes this was the case in the run-up to the 1980s, when financialization began its fastest growth—a period often called the "age of greed."[64] According to Krippner, that shift, which would come to encompass Reagan-era deregulation, the unleashing of Wall Street, the rise of the ownership society, and the launch of the 401(k) system, actually began in the late 1960s and early 1970s. It was during that period that the growth that America had enjoyed following World War II began to slow, inflation began to rise, and government was forced to confront the challenge of how to allocate resources that were becoming more scarce (the "guns versus butter" debate). Rather than make the tough decisions themselves, politicians decided to pass the buck to finance under the guise of a "markets know best" approach. Little by little, from the 1970s onward, the Depression-era regulation that had served America so well was rolled back, and finance grew to become the dominant force that it is today. The key point is that the public policy decisions that aided financialization didn't happen all at once, but were taken incrementally, creating a dysfunctional web of changes in areas like tax, trade, regulatory policy, corporate governance, and law. It's a web that will take time and tremendous effort to dismantle.

Financialization is behind the shifts in our retirement system and tax code that have given banks ever more money to play with, and the rise of high-speed trading that has allowed more and more risk and leverage in the system to serve up huge profits to a privileged few. It is behind the destructive deregulation of the 1980s and 1990s, and the failure to reregulate the banking sector properly after the financial crisis of 2008. Individuals from J.P. Morgan and Goldman Sachs may (or, more often, may not) go to jail for reckless trading, but the *system* that permitted their malfeasance remains in place. The problems are so blatant, in fact, that even a number of Too Big to Fail bankers themselves, including former Citigroup chairman Sandy Weill, have admitted that the system is unsafe, that finance needs much stricter reregulation, and that big banks should be broken up.[65]

It won't happen anytime soon. Even now, finance continues to grow as a percentage of our economy. Leverage ratios are barely down from where they were in 2007—it's still status quo for big banks to conduct daily business with 95 percent borrowed money.[66] Assets of the informal lending sector, which includes shadow banking, grew globally by $13 trillion since 2007, to a whopping $80 trillion in 2014.[67] Less than half of all derivatives, those financial weapons of mass destruction that poured gasoline on the crisis, are regulated, even after the passing of the Dodd-Frank financial reform legislation in 2010.[68] We may have gotten past the crisis of 2008, but we have not fixed our financial system.

What's more, regulators are ill-equipped to handle future crises (and history shows they are happening more and more frequently) when they come. Bankers exert immense soft power via the revolving door between Wall Street and Washington. Just look at how many top positions in the Treasury Department, the Securities and Exchange Commission (SEC), and other regulatory bodies are filled by former executives from Goldman Sachs and other major financial institutions. These are the people who've advocated for tax and regulatory "reforms" that have, since the early 1980s, decreased capital gains taxes, prevented risky securities from being regulated, and allowed for the boom in share buybacks. Not only are many regulators disinclined to police the industry, but they are also woefully underpaid, understaffed, and underfunded. Consider the Commodity Futures Trading Commission (CFTC), which has about the same staff size today as it did in the 1990s, despite the fact that the swaps market it oversees has ballooned to more than $400 trillion.[69] It's not easy for regulators on five-figure salaries, with modest research budgets and enforcement assets, to stay ahead of the algorithmic misdeeds of traders making seven figures. And that's a shame, because a 2015 survey of hundreds of high-level financial professionals found that more than a third had witnessed instances of malfeasance at their own firms and 38 percent disagreed that the industry puts a client's best interests first.[70]

THE THEATER OF FINANCIALIZATION

Of course, there are other theories about why financialization occurs. Nobel Prize winner Robert Shiller has described the "irrational exuberance" that he believes is a natural human tendency. The fact that we go repeatedly from boom to bust throughout history, moving like lemmings toward the New New Thing—be it tulips or collateralized debt obligations (CDOs)—points to the idea that there are strong psychological forces at work. (The neuroscience of traders' brains, which respond to deal making similarly to how addicts' brains respond to cocaine, is in itself a fascinating area of scholarly inquiry.)[71] Other academics, like University of Michigan scholar Gerald Davis, focus on the importance of new management theories such as our notion of shareholder value that puts the investor before everyone and everything else in society, including customers, employees, and the public good.[72]

The changes in the financial system have gone hand in hand with changes in business culture. Apple is hardly alone in its financial maneuvering. Companies as diverse as Sony, Intel, Kodak, Microsoft, General Electric, Cisco, AT&T, Pfizer, and Hewlett-Packard have been worked over by the ambassadors of finance, sacrificing their long-term interest for short-term gains. This may happen by choice, by force, or even unconsciously. As I will explore in this book, Wall Street's values and culture have been so fully imbibed by business leaders that the Street's idea about what's good for the economy has come to be the conventional wisdom within business, and even society at large. To that point, much of the corrosive effect of Wall Street on corporate America can be measured not in terms of raw malfeasance but in the new dominance of short-term thinking. The culture of finance looks for growth *now,* starting this morning, in time to show results for the next quarterly profit filings. That pressure leads companies into all sorts of bad decisions, such as hasty mergers and acquisitions that look great on PowerPoint before the headaches set in and the layoffs start. (And they usually do—studies show that up to 70 percent of the mergers pushed by Wall Street end in disappointment.)[73]

Davis likens financialization to a "Copernican revolution" in which business has reoriented its orbit around the financial sector. There's also an entire body of anthropological research that explores the way in which Wall Street *culture* has come to dominate society and the economy, providing yet another theater for financialization. The anthropologist Karen Ho's book *Liquidated: An Ethnography of Wall Street,* for example, looks at how Wall Street's own labor practices, characterized by volatility and insecurity, have become status quo for the rest of the country.[74] "In many ways investment bankers and how they approach work became a model for how work should be conducted. Wall Street shapes not just the stock market but also the very nature of employment and what kinds of workers are valued," says Ho, who worked in banking before becoming an academic. "What [Wall Street values] is not worker stability but constant market simultaneity. If mortgages aren't the best thing, it's, 'Let's get rid of the mortgage desk and we'll hire them back in a year.' People [in finance are] working a hundred hours a week, but

constantly talking about job insecurity. Wall Street bankers understand that they are liquid people."[75] Now, as a consequence, so do
we all.

Moreover, financialization has bred a business culture built
around MBAs rather than engineers and entrepreneurs. Because
Wall Street salaries are 70 percent higher on average than in any
other industry, many of the best minds are drawn into its ranks and
away from anything more useful to society.[76] At the same time, business education itself is overly focused on finance.

COLLATERAL DAMAGE

The deep political economy of financialization was first outlined by
Karl Marx, who considered it to be the last stage of capitalism, one
in which a system based primarily on greed would eventually collapse.[77] The fact that it hasn't yet done so is not necessarily an indictment of Marx.[78] As academics like Piketty as well as the famous
Marxist scholar and Harvard economist Paul Sweezy have noted,[79]
our financialized system creates its own momentum, ensuring that
the dysfunctional relationship between finance and the real economy can last a very long time.

The truth is that all of these theories tell us something important
about financialization; you can find elements of each in play during
nearly every period of financial boom and bust in American history.
Flawed incentives, dysfunctional political economy, and simple bad
management and poor regulation were all part of the market crash
of 1929 and the Great Depression, just as they were part of the crisis of 2008 and the Great Recession. There are the causes of the
problem, of course, and then there are the symptoms, which are
sometimes equally pernicious. Financialization has resulted not only
in big-picture, destructive trends like slower growth, inequality, and
market fragility, but also in any number of secondary symptoms that
are part of the core illness. We need to treat them now, before it's
too late. This book intends to be a road map for how.

FIXING THE SYSTEM

And so, the divide between the markets and the real economy, be-tween Wall Street and Main Street, grows. All of these distortions have given a scary boost to the risks inherent in our financial sys-tem. With so much money and power concentrated in the hands of so few, ours is a top without a bottom. Rising inequality, falling pro-ductivity, and distorted incentives have created a world in which vir-tual enterprises prosper while real ones, with real workers, struggle. Innovation is falling to cash management, long-term plans to short-term tricks. Risk in the financial system continues to rise, even as risk capital to real businesses declines. These trends are choking off our growth as a nation. There is a long and fascinating history to the rise of financialization in America, which I will outline in many of the chapters to follow. But the deepest concern of this book lies not with the past, but with the present and the future.

The Trump administration would like to roll back what little reg-ulation and reform of the financial sector has been done since the 2008 crisis. It's a dangerous moment. And yet there are bright spots on the horizon. Despite the lobbying power of banks and the vested interests in both Washington and on Wall Street, there's a growing popular push to put the financial system back in its rightful place as a servant of business, rather than a master. Surveys show that the majority of Americans would like to see our tax system reformed, our government taking more direct action on poverty reduction, and inequality addressed in a meaningful way.[80] Indeed, two of the most pernicious effects of financialization—the decline of the middle class and wage stagnation—were front and center as issues in the 2016 presidential campaign. Trump wasn't the solution, but his vic-tory has further illuminated the problem.

We have the tools to fix our system, and thankfully there is a dedicated group of public officials, academics, and regulators who want to move us far beyond the current watered-down Dodd-Frank financial regulation and truly put the financial sector back in service to business and society. But the key to reforming our current system is making *the American public* understand just how deeply and profoundly things *aren't* working for the majority of people in this country and, just as important, *why* they aren't working. Re-mooring finance in the real economy isn't as simple as splitting up the biggest banks, although that would be a good start. It's about dismantling the hold of financial-oriented thinking on every corner of corporate America. It's about reforming business education, which is still filled with academics who resist challenges to the false gospel of efficient markets in the same way that medieval clergy dismissed scientific evidence that challenged the existence of God. It's about changing a tax system that treats one-year investment gains the same as longer-term ones and induces financial institutions to push overconsumption and speculation, rather than healthy lending to small businesses and job creators. It's about rethinking retirement, crafting smarter housing policy, and restraining a money culture filled with lobbyists who violate the essential principles of democracy.

This book is about connecting those dots and the complex phenomenon that connects them: financialization. It's a topic that has traditionally been the sole domain of "experts"—those academics, financiers, and policy makers who often have a self-interested perspective to promote, and who do so with complicated language that keeps outsiders from the debate. But when it comes to finance, as in so many things, complexity is the enemy. The right question here is in fact the simplest one: Are financial institutions doing things that provide a clear, measurable benefit to the real economy? Sadly, the answer is mostly no.

Explaining how the rise of finance has caused the fall of American business, and how that's jeopardizing the American Dream, is the primary purpose of this book, because to fix things we need to first tell ourselves the correct story about how we got here. Financialization is easily the least studied and least explored reason behind our inability to create shared prosperity—despite our being the richest and most successful nation in history. And the fact that the phenomenon itself is so poorly understood is in many ways the problem. While I've interviewed many a rapacious capitalist in my

nearly three decades in journalism, the truth is that the vast majority of bankers, businesspeople, and economic policy makers aren't
venal—far from it. They are simply part of a very large, complex,
and (for them) lucrative system, one that has unfortunately become
so dysfunctional that it actively prevents us from making the best
and fairest use of our nation's resources. Fixing that dysfunction
is the challenge at hand. Change begins with understanding, and I
wrote this book to provide some.

In an effort to engage the lay reader and avoid the soporific tone
of many academic and business volumes that have tackled elements
of this problem over the years, I have structured *Makers and Takers*
as a series of stories about the companies and the people at the
heart of financialization over the past hundred years. They are by no
means the only representatives of the tectonic shift that's been going
on, but they are among the best and most colorful. My hope is that
by focusing on the real people and companies whose lives have been
touched by financialization—usually for the worse—I can bring our
thinking about this phenomenon down to earth in a way that will
forward a healthier debate.

Chapter 1 will explain the rise of finance itself. How did an industry that represents only 4 percent of jobs come to account for a
quarter of all corporate profits? It's a story that will be told through
the lens of the country's original Too Big to Fail bank, Citigroup.

Chapter 2 will examine how financial thinking came to dominate American corporate life by telling the story of General Motors
and of former secretary of defense Robert McNamara and the Whiz
Kids, whose obsession with numbers decisively contributed to the
loss of the Vietnam War, the decline of the American auto industry,
and the ultimate spread of financialized thinking into every corner
of American business today.

Chapter 3 will delve deeply into the history of US business education and examine how and why it came to focus on balance sheet
manipulation to the exclusion of real managerial skills.

Chapter 4 will deconstruct our conventional wisdom around

shareholder value by looking at how activist investors like Carl Icahn now call the shots at the country's largest and most successful firms—such as Apple—at the expense of innovation and job creation.

Chapter 5 will show how much of corporate America has come to emulate banking—how we're all glorified bankers now—by tracking the history of General Electric, which is one of the great American innovators, but which became the country's fifth-largest bank before trying to reclaim its roots in industry.

Chapter 6 will focus on one of the most dangerous areas of the financial sector, derivatives, and show via the tale of Goldman Sachs and its manipulation of the commodities market how banks have come to control the natural resources that companies and consumers depend on—and what that means for the prices of goods the average American consumes every day.

Chapter 7 will tell the story of how one of the richest and most opaque areas of finance, private equity, has come to dominate the most important sector of our economy, housing—making the American Dream of owning a home an elusive fantasy for so many middle-class American families.

Chapter 8 will look at how privatizing our retirement system enabled asset management—the fastest-growing sector of finance—to grow rich on unnecessary fees, and how the mutual fund business is essentially gambling away our nest eggs.

Chapter 9 will lay out how and why we came to have a tax system that privileges corporations over individuals, encourages debt over equity, and allows firms like Pfizer to engage in financial engineering as a business strategy.

Chapter 10 will analyze how the money culture and the revolving door between Wall Street and Washington have made it so hard to turn back the tide of financialization, and why so many of the reforms promised after the 2008 meltdown have yet to come to pass.

But while turning back the tide of financialization may be hard, it is far from impossible. Chapter 11 will lay out policy solutions—

informed by interviews with people at the highest rungs of industry, academia, and government—about how finance might be put back into the service of the real economy.

And throughout this book, I'll sketch stories not only of takers but also of makers, as well as the lessons the rest of us can take from companies and leaders who are getting things right. Through these stories we'll see that we *can* create for ourselves a new New Normal—one that loosens the crushing grip of finance on American business and leads to a more prosperous, sustainable future for American workers, families, and the economy at large. My hope is that this book will help show how.

CHAPTER 1

THE RISE OF FINANCE

IF THERE is a Godfather of modern finance, it must be Sanford "Sandy" Weill, the former CEO of one of the world's largest financial institutions, Citigroup. A kid from Bensonhurst, Brooklyn, who grew up to become the world's most powerful banker, he started his career with $30,000 and rose through Wall Street ranks to lead the megabank that came to epitomize the Too Big to Fail era.

The creation of Citigroup—a merger between Weill's own Travelers Group (an insurance and investment firm) and Citicorp back in 1998—was a seismic moment in the story of financialization that created the planet's biggest-ever financial conglomerate. Not only that, but it was also the nail in the coffin of Glass-Steagall, the Depression-era banking legislation that had kept consumers relatively safe from exploitation by financial interests since the 1930s. Weill called the merger "the greatest deal in the history of the financial services industry" and "the crowning of my career."[1] It was a transaction that would allow the newly formed company to offer pretty much every financial service ever invented, from credit cards to corporate IPO underwriting, high-speed trading to mortgages, investment advice to the sale of any complex security you could imagine, in 160-plus countries, twenty-four hours a day. As with the British Empire in a former era, the sun never set on Citigroup.

So it was quite a moment when, in mid-2012, the emperor had an ideological abdication. Weill, who stepped down as Citi CEO in 2003 and has recently undergone something of an existential crisis over his role in the worst financial crash in eighty years, went on CNBC and declared that pretty much everything he'd believed about the bank, and about finance, was wrong. In fact, he said, if he were to do it over again, Citigroup itself would probably never have come to be. What's more, the business model that financial institutions have fought to preserve through billions spent on funding campaigns and lobbying Congress had saddled American depositors and taxpayers with unacceptable risks. "What we should probably do is go and split up investment banking from [commercial] banking," Weill said. "Have banks be deposit takers. Have banks make commercial loans and real estate loans. Have banks do something that's not going to risk the taxpayer dollars, that's not going to be Too Big to Fail."[2]

As conversions go, Weill's was positively biblical. It came four years after a long chain of disastrous decisions by Citigroup and the rest of the Too Big to Fail banks had landed them at the epicenter of the financial crisis, with hundreds of billions of dollars of exploding securities on their books and worried customers on the verge of mass panic that threatened to throw the country into another Great Depression. The crisis ultimately required $1.59 trillion in government bailouts (and another $12 trillion worth of federal guarantees and loans) and even with that, it shaved more off the American economy than any other downturn since the 1930s.[3]

But that wasn't all.

As the dust settled on the crisis and the American recovery continued to be lackluster, particularly in relation to recoveries past, some policy makers, academics, and rank-and-file consumers began to suspect that something was wrong at a deeper level—namely, that although the financial industry had been set up to support business and to provide the liquidity that firms and individuals needed to prosper, it no longer seemed to serve that function. As Stephen Roach, the former chief economist of Morgan Stanley, put it to me in an interview right after the fall of Lehman Brothers, "finance has simply moved too far from its moorings in the real economy."[4]

Indeed, as the banks got bailed out and swiftly recovered, things in the real economy grew worse. Bank profits reached record heights, yet loans to businesses and consumers shrank. Corporate earnings were high, yet few companies wanted to invest their cash in Main Street. Instead, managers beholden to the markets disgorged it mainly to rich investors and Wall Street.[5] Meanwhile, America's largest financial institutions remained as focused as ever on securities trading, the "casino" part of the banking business, since there was no reason not to be. Regulators had yet—and still have yet—to prohibit bankers from eschewing this more profitable type of business in favor of boring, old-fashioned lending. The very riskiest portion of the markets, derivatives trading, actually grew following the crisis. Globally, it was 20 percent bigger in late 2013 than in late 2007 (and US regulators are trying to police it with budgets that haven't increased much since then).[6]

And that's just what we can see. Shadow banking, the portion of the financial industry that remains largely unregulated (and includes hedge funds, money market funds, and financial arms of big companies like GE), has grown like kudzu: swelling by more than $1.3 trillion per year since 2011 and reaching $36 trillion today.[7] Through it all, low interest rates set by the Federal Reserve, which were supposed to help individuals, ended up making the rich richer by inflating the stock market rather than improving the ability of real people to refinance their homes. (Most of the housing recovery has been led by investors, as will be covered in chapter 7.)

A POST-TRAUMATIC NATION

Of course, plenty of people will ask why, if finance is having such a dampening effect on the economy, America is in recovery. I would argue that it's simply not much of a recovery. Indeed, consumer confidence and spending continue to be volatile in the wake of the crash.

As Starbucks CEO Howard Schultz put it to me in 2015, even in the midst of economic recovery American consumers remain "fragile," almost as if they have suffered a kind of trauma. Schultz and many other executives believe that skittishness has become a generational imprint, meaning that today's generation of American consumers, who are still counted on to fuel the world's growth engine, may be so traumatized they can't perform that traditional role anymore.

Meanwhile, the deep structural dysfunction in our economy, emanating from the financial system, remains in place. The size of the sector itself is still close to record highs (as measured by its share of overall employment), though that may wax and wane as the impact of digital technology on job growth becomes more pronounced. But what's quite clear is that the reorientation of our economy toward finance and the dominance of financial *thinking* in daily management of nonfinancial firms have warped the way both business and society work. The sway of the markets over the real economy has skewed the playing field and created growing inequality and capture of resources at the top of the socioeconomic pyramid. It has also led to dramatic inefficiencies in resource allocation that may be a cause, rather than a symptom, of slower economic growth.[8]

These aren't new observations, but rather old warnings that have been pushed aside or forgotten. The great liberal economist John Maynard Keynes, for one, worried that market capitalism might be able to function quite well without actually employing many people, particularly if money went to speculation rather than productive investment. (He called on the government to boost long-term investment through special incentives.) Other thinkers, like Hyman Minsky, Harry Magdoff, and Paul Sweezy, took that idea further, arguing that finance itself creates bubbles and draws money away from the real economy as a matter of course. As Minsky put it, "capitalism is a flawed system in that, if its development is not constrained, it will lead to periodic deep depressions and the perpetuation of poverty."[9] He also believed that the government would be forced to act as a lender of last resort during such periods, a position that would become untenable as public debt levels rose, leading to more public pressure to allow more speculation, which would unleash renewed instability, and so on. This story of a "symbiotic embrace" between finance and underlying economic malaise, one that the markets can't stave off forever, finds resonance in the fact that every recovery of the post–World War II period has been longer and weaker than the one before.[10]

What's new and important now is the growing body of data that supports these ideas. Consider the 2015 paper by BIS senior economist Enisse Kharroubi and Brandeis University professor Stephen Cecchetti, who examined how finance affected growth in fifteen countries. They found that productivity—the value that each worker creates in the economy, which, along with demographics, is basically the driver of economic progress—declines in markets with rapidly expanding financial sectors. What's more, the industries most likely to suffer are those, like advanced manufacturing, that are most critical for long-term growth and jobs. That's because finance would rather invest in areas like real estate and construction, which are far less productive but offer quicker, more reliable short-term gains (as well as collateral that can be sold in crisis or securitized in boom times).[11] No wonder twin booms in credit and real estate were a defining characteristic of many economies worst hit by the 2008 financial crisis.[12]

Government has a huge role to play in all this. Deregulation from the 1970s onward encouraged banks to move away from their traditional role of enabling investment, and toward embracing speculation. It also paved the way to the so-called shareholder revolution, which enriched investors but pushed corporations into debt and toward short-term decision making. Both trends have redirected capital to less socially useful areas of the economy and created a vicious cycle that's increasingly difficult to break via the usual methods like monetary policy. Witness the fact that despite the $4.5 trillion the Fed injected into the economy and six years of historically low interest rates, corporations are reinvesting just 1–2 percent of their assets into Main Street.[13] Much of the rest is going straight into the pockets of the richest 10 percent of the population—mostly in the form of rising asset prices—and those people are unlikely to spend as much of it as the middle and working classes would.

That our market system has been corrupted in a way that's thwarting growth is something Adam Smith himself would have agreed with. His theory of how markets worked evolved at a time when small family-owned firms operated largely on level playing fields with equal access to information. Today financial capitalism is fraught with special interests, corporate monopolies, and an opacity that would have boggled Smith's mind. Let me be clear: despite my criticism of our existing model of financial capitalism, this book isn't anticapitalist. I am not in favor of a planned economy or a turn away from a market system. I simply don't think that the system we have now *is* a properly functioning market system. We have a rentier economy in which a small group of vested interests take the cream off the top, to the detriment of overall growth. I agree with economists like Joseph Stiglitz, George Akerlof, Paul Volcker, and others who believe that markets prudently regulated by governments are the best guarantee of peace and prosperity the world has ever known. Until we make more progress toward that goal, we won't have the kind of recovery we deserve.

THE HIGH PRICE OF COMPLEXITY

The first step in this process is understanding how the financial sector, which is the pivot point for all of this, came to play such an outsize role. Finance isn't just banking. It includes securities dealers, insurance companies, mutual funds, pension funds, hedge funds, traders, credit derivative product companies, real estate firms, structured investment vehicles, and commercial paper conduits, among others. All of them "can fit together like Russian dolls," as Paul Tucker, the former head of markets for the Bank of England, once put it.[14]

Yet at the heart of all this is the Too Big to Fail bank. The very same one-stop-shop bank model that Weill once heralded as the future of the industry—and of American competitiveness—proved to be its downfall. Yes, customers around the world could do everything at Citi, an institution with assets implicitly underwritten by the US government, thanks to FDIC insurance and Fed protection. But that also meant that financial shocks could migrate quickly through the bank's interconnected global operations. Not only could problems in Iceland ricochet within seconds to Iowa, but the connections themselves were too complicated even for the bank's own risk managers, not to mention their leaders, to comprehend in real time. "Do CEOs of large, complex financial institutions today know everything that's on their balance sheet? It's not possible to know," former Goldman Sachs partner and former head of the Commodity Futures Trading Commission Gary Gensler told me in 2014. "There are just too many things going on for their operations now in the markets for them to know."[15]

That complexity creates tremendous risk. But complexity is also where banks make their money. The financial industry is the world's ultimate power and information hub, the tiny middle portion of an hourglass that represents the larger global economy. All the money in the world, and all the information about who's making and taking it, passes through that tiny middle. Financiers sit in what is the most privileged position, extracting whatever rent they like for passage. It's telling that technology, which usually decreases industries' operating costs, has failed to deflate the costs of financial intermediation. Indeed, finance has become *more* costly and *less* efficient as an industry as it deployed new and more advanced tools over time.[16]

It's also telling that during the last few decades financiers have earned three times as much as their peers in other industries with similar education and skills.[17] As Thomas Piketty put it in *Capital in the Twenty-First Century*, financiers are, in some ways, like the landowners of old. Instead of controlling labor, they regulate access to things even more important in the modern economy: capital and information. As a result, they represent the largest single group of the richest and most powerful people on earth.

THE INSIDER ADVANTAGE

As such, financiers get lots of special perks, including preferred access to policy makers. Perhaps the key reason that our Too Big to Fail problem is nowhere near being solved is that finance, the largest US corporate lobby (if you count together banking, insurance, asset management, and mortgage finance), has spent so much time and money watering down Dodd-Frank over the last few years. In 2013, even as Citigroup was paying billions of dollars in fines for selling toxic mortgage-backed securities, Citi lobbyists helped draft a new rule, which eventually got tucked into the 2015 federal spending bill. The rule effectively rolled back one of the most important bits of post-crisis regulation: the ban on trading taxpayer-insured derivatives, those "financial weapons of mass destruction," as Warren Buffett famously called them, that sparked the 2008 crisis to begin with. Thanks to the hard work of bank lobbyists and top financiers, including Weill's onetime protégé, JPMorgan Chase CEO Jamie Dimon, the ban is now history. Banks will keep on trading, capitalizing profits and socializing risk, just as they have been since Weill made the final blow to Glass-Steagall with the creation of Citigroup in 1998. (That event got a rubber stamp by then–Treasury secretary Robert Rubin, who shortly afterward would go on to become the cochair of Citi.)

Public officials are so beholden to the industry—a phenomenon known in academic circles as "cognitive capture"—that most of them don't really see much wrong with any of this. The Obama administration has spent the last couple of years trying to tie a bow around its handling of the crisis, assuring everyone that bailing out the banks was necessary to avoid a depression, and that the system is now safe. The first part of the story is true; the bank bailouts were necessary to avoid another Great Depression.[18] But the second part of the story is absolutely not. Unlike in the aftermath of the 1929 crash, policy makers did not use the opportunity presented by the crisis to properly reregulate the financial industry—far from it. Rather, they allowed the market system itself to set the terms of regulation, often with Washington's full complicity, per the anecdote in my author's note at the beginning of this book. To many in Washington, regulating finance is a job that should be done by insiders. That might work in theory, but when those insiders' priorities are not aligned with what's good for the general public, then we have a problem. Indeed, the careful cultivation and protection of that group of technocrats by both Wall Street and Washington is one reason the discussion around financialization and its perverse effects on our economy has become so muddled. As the anthropologist David Graeber, one of the key participants in the Occupy Wall Street movement, has pointed out, bureaucracy of this kind is the enemy. Incomprehensible rules crafted and controlled by a small cadre of insiders, discussed in a language that only they find comprehensible, is one of the key ways that elites maintain power—in finance and elsewhere.[19]

Financiers claim that their disproportionate privilege is a reward for the responsibilities they assume for lubricating the economy. This underscores a false notion that began to take root in the 1980s— namely, that finance is a business unto itself, rather than *just* a catalyst to other industries. Both the Left and the Right bought into the idea; indeed, it has informed most economic policy decisions from the Kennedy administration onward. It's easy to understand why, given that it's exactly what's taught in most financial theory classes at major business schools (a subject to which I return in chapter 4). Yet the data shows the opposite. For several decades now, "the main function of the financial system with respect to corporate America has not been raising funds for investment, but compelling corporations to 'disgorge the cash' in the form of payments to shareholders," says economist J. W. Mason, who studies financialization at the Roosevelt Institute.[20]

This shift spells bad news for the average worker. Over the last forty years, as finance has grown, the traditional relationship between productivity and wages has gone out the window. Conventional economic wisdom holds that as productivity grows, so too should wages. But during the time that finance has been ascendant, since the late 1970s on, even as productivity per worker doubled, real wages have stalled.[21]

How did things get this unbalanced? How did an industry that was supposed to lubricate growth begin choking it off instead? The history of Citigroup itself is a good place to start searching for answers. The Too Big to Fail behemoth has been at the center of nearly every big shift in finance and every major crisis in American history. The revolving door from Wall Street to Washington was practically created by Citi and the institutions it evolved from. The men who led them funded the Union side of the Civil War and the building of the Panama Canal. They were instrumental in crafting the current structure of the Fed and were behind the market collapse of 1929. They invented investment banking and complex securitization, introduced credit cards and ATMs, and came up with the first complex security (the certificate of deposit, or CD) to be traded by commercial banks in the post–World War II era. Citi was the first billion-dollar bank. It pioneered emerging market lending, brought trading and commercial banking together under one roof, and stood at the heart of the Enron and WorldCom scandals, as well as the dot-com bust, the housing bubble, and of course the crisis of 2008.

Citi certainly wasn't the only institution at fault in these crises. But it was the major player in America's forty-year shift from a highly regulated, simpler Depression-era system of banking to a riskier, more globalized, high-tech system that breeds global volatility. At every juncture in which the seeds of financial chaos—debt, leverage, and a dysfunctional political economy—were planted, Citi was there, too. If you want to understand how an industry that creates only 4 percent of the jobs in this country came to represent 7 percent of the economy and take almost 25 percent of all corporate profits, there's no better place to start than with the history of Citigroup.

THE BIRTH OF THE MODERN BANKER

As Vincent Carosso sketches out in his seminal history, *Investment Banking in America*,[22] the modern financier was born of the economic need of industrial makers. Americans had always been skeptical about powerful banks. In the early days of the republic, founding father Thomas Jefferson, who represented the interest of small farmers, and Alexander Hamilton, who stood for the urban elites, argued over what the country's system of finance should look like. Jefferson and the populist agrarians were nervous about concentrating financial power in New York City, which is of course exactly what Hamilton wanted. The two split the difference, with a system of state-chartered banks in which solvency varied wildly. This is one key reason that finance in America has always been more crisis-prone than, say, that in Canada, which has a strong and consolidated network of national bank branches yet also keeps lending separate from risky trading.[23]

By the nineteenth century, though, pressure to change the old system was growing. Industrialists needed capital to build the railroads and the businesses that were making the Industrial Revolution possible. Before the 1850s, funding for business ventures had been supplied either by firms themselves, from their own savings, or by a motley crew of speculators, merchants, and loan contractors, as well as a few domestic agents of big foreign banking houses like Rothschild. America was still small potatoes for those venerable firms, but American family businesses were growing and starting to reorganize themselves as public corporations.[24] They needed greater amounts of funding from more secure domestic sources to finance that growth, as did the US government itself. Private banking firms like Goldman Sachs and J.P. Morgan as well as commercial banks like the National City Bank of New York—the predecessor of today's Citigroup—evolved to serve them.

This transition in American capitalism, from family-owned and family-funded firms to bank-funded corporations, got a powerful boost in the Civil War—a shift that illuminated the traditional embedded relationship between finance and the government (which depends on bankers to fund its endeavors).[25] Abraham Lincoln's administration had a terrible time trying to sell bonds and raise funds for the war on its own, so it turned to big banks in New York, Boston, and Philadelphia to do the job. Thus investment banking, as well as its ties to government, began to grow. So did banking's relationship with middle America. Then, as now, there were no rules dividing traditional lending from the sale of securities, and so banks did both. This predictably resulted in a number of market crises, including the so-called Black Friday crash of 1869, which bankrupted a number of high-profile financial firms that had, like so many institutions today, been trying to push the risky securities of companies with which they did business.[26]

Nevertheless, financiers' relationship with both government and business only got tighter. Bankers became a big source of campaign contributions for politicians and sat on the boards of companies for which they increasingly helped issue and sell securities, many of them of dubious quality.[27] There were a few major corporations that chose to expand the old-fashioned way—by actually reinvesting their earnings. One of those was Standard Oil, whose founder, John D. Rockefeller, was skeptical of depending on the banking sector for corporate well-being. "I think a concern so large as we are should have its own money and be independent of the 'Street,'" he once said.[28] But not many companies agreed, or could afford to feel that way. Stock offerings for growing American companies began to proliferate. Even the Rockefellers eventually got on board, as Henry Huttleston Rogers and William Rockefeller (two leading Standard Oil executives) teamed up with the National City Bank to launch the Amalgamated Copper Company; it owned, among other properties, the soon-infamous Anaconda copper mines.[29]

The Anaconda mine scandal involved a financial trick that anyone familiar with the crisis of 2008 will know well: bankers knowingly selling clients and the general public financial products that were essentially junk, while marketing them as the next big thing. It was also the culmination of nearly three decades of financial sector growth, loosening of banking standards, attempts to better regulate a banking industry that was perceived as being increasingly risky and out of control, and vigorous pushback from the industry itself, which spent millions of dollars trying to avoid being constrained. If this sounds familiar, it should. The crash of 1929 and the Great Depression, like the crisis of 2008 and the Great Recession, didn't happen overnight. They happened over decades during which risk, debt, and excess credit built up in the financial system, unchecked by policy makers who were increasingly beholden to the sector—the very same one that was instrumental in financing both the expansion of the US economy (via railroad IPOs, real estate loans, and the sale of securities to a burgeoning middle class) and, eventually, World War I. Then, as now, financiers used their privileged position to argue that if they were stymied in their attempts to make increasingly large profits, the capitalist system itself would collapse.[30] It eventually did, of course—not in spite of finance, but because of it.

It's no accident that the size of the financial sector today as a percentage of GDP is at levels equaled only on the eve of the Great Depression. Like the decade leading up to the financial crisis of 2008, the Roaring Twenties were marked by not only financial boom and technological wonder, but also massive income inequality. Worker wages stagnated and those of the upper classes grew, bolstered in large part by stock prices. Another similarity was a rise in debt, both public and private, which was used to mask the declining spending power of the lower and middle classes and its dampening effect on GDP growth. Then, as now, when people couldn't afford to buy, they borrowed—Americans in the 1920s bought more than three-quarters of major household items on credit. Moreover, lured by aggressive advertising campaigns by banks and the proliferation of war bonds, which had been pushed by a government eager to raise funds, the American public began investing for the first time en masse in the securities markets. As Harvard economic historian Edwin Gay put it, millions of people who had never done anything with their money but save it were suddenly borrowing and investing in securities. "They were not ... educated in the use of credit; they simply received a new vision of its possibilities. The basis was thus laid for the vast and credulous post-war market for credit which culminated in the portentous speculation of 1928 and 1929."[31]

Sound familiar?

CHARLES MITCHELL, FERDINAND PECORA, AND THE CRISIS OF 1929

The run-up in debt and consumer credit aren't the only similarity between the periods leading up to the Great Depression and the Great Recession. Everyone remembers Senator Carl Levin, who cochaired the Senate investigation into the roots of the 2008 financial crisis, grilling the heads of Wall Street institutions like Washington Mutual, Moody's, and Goldman Sachs over the subprime debacle. But hardly anyone knows that there was a precedent for these spectacles seventy-seven years earlier, in 1932, when the Senate conducted the Pecora hearings, named for chief investigator Ferdinand Pecora, on the reasons for the stock market crash of 1929. The first banker on the hot seat back then was Charles "Sunshine Charley" Mitchell, the chairman of Citi's predecessor, the National City Bank of New York.

National City had actually started the crisis on a good footing. Like most major New York banks, it was holding around 20 percent equity capital on its balance sheets—ten times more than the 2–5 percent average for large institutions today (and a target that many contemporary advocates of banking reform would like to see reinstated).[32] When the panic of 1929 began, National City was flush enough to pump $25 million into the system, which held off the crash for about six months.[33] But as the Pecora investigations eventually uncovered, National City itself was one of the main causes of the stock market crash. Like the Too Big to Fail institutions of the twenty-first century, this bank and many others had knowingly sold bad securities to their customers without disclosing hidden interests in the transactions. Banks had, in essence, shorted their own clients, trading against them in order to make money for the house. For example, in the run-up to the crash of 1929, National City aggressively peddled its holdings in Anaconda Copper to clients as soon as the price of copper began dropping, while continuing to recommend the stock as a sound investment. No wonder that Senator Carter Glass said in 1929 that Mitchell "more than any 50 men is responsible for this stock crash."[34] But like the bankers of today, Mitchell got off without jail time. He continued to work on Wall Street after his public shaming, even though he left National City in disgrace just days after taking the stand and paid government officials (with whom he'd done many cozy deals) $1.1 million in back taxes.[35]

The crisis had one big upside, though. Senator Glass, along with Congressman Henry Steagall, crafted the Glass-Steagall Act to separate commercial and investment banking in the United States. For more than six decades afterward, the law helped to ring-fence commercial lending from risky proprietary trading. Glass-Steagall also created the Federal Deposit Insurance Corporation (FDIC), which insured bank depositors up to $5,000 each, reducing the risk of bank runs and assuring the general public that it would be safe in case of a financial crisis. Finally, the legislation put limits on the amount of interest that banks could offer savers to attract their money. This measure, known as Regulation Q, was designed in part to prevent banks from competing too vigorously with one another for deposits by offering higher and higher interest rates, which might in turn push them into the sort of risky investments that had precipitated Black Tuesday in 1929. The idea behind all of it was to make banking a safe, boring utility, something that facilitated business rather than disrupted it or competed with it for investment.

And it worked, at least for a few decades. The period between the Great Depression and the 1960s was one in which banking was held largely in check, providing mostly plain-vanilla services to average people. Think of the 1946 movie *It's a Wonderful Life*, in which Jimmy Stewart's character, George Bailey, stems a bank run with a famous monologue explaining the local building and loan as the glue holding the community together: "The money's not here. Your money's in Joe's house that's right next to yours. And in the Kennedy house and Mrs.

Macklin's house and a hundred others." Bankers of the time thought of themselves not as dealmakers but as stewards of individual wealth and lubricators of industry. They were people who turned savings into investments. They made mostly conservative loans to conservative people and businesses. Indeed, in the wake of the Pecora hearings, National City Bank replaced its discredited chairman, Charles Mitchell, with James Perkins, a man who "looked like and acted like a New England farmer." Trading was verboten, and no loan could be made without the sign-off of three officers.[36] Things were sleepy, for sure. But the fact that finance was tightly moored to the real economy during this period is one reason, according to Piketty, that inequality was also historically low.[37] Finance had finally been tamed, and the economy was less risky because of it. Or at least that's the way it was until Walter Wriston came on the scene.

THE MILLION-DOLLAR BANKER

National City Bank, like all commercial banks after Glass-Steagall, had become a safe, predictable, boring place to work. But Walter Wriston, a returning GI with a graduate degree in foreign affairs from Tufts who took an entry-level job with the bank in 1946, would change all that. Wriston was a child of privilege; his father, a successful academic who eventually became president of Brown University, had argued against the government planning of the New Deal and idolized Adam Smith and his "invisible hand."[38] (No matter that Smith only mentioned the hand a few times, briefly, in a couple of his works, or that this Scottish economist who came to emblematize laissez-faire economic thinking had built his ideas at a time when the economy was mostly small, family-owned businesses rather than large and growing corporations.) Smith's core belief—namely, that markets worked better than government planning only when all players enjoyed equal footing and complete price transparency—had already been lost to the "markets know best" and "selfishness is good" simplification of his theories.

Wriston bought into the CliffsNotes version of the Smith doctrine wholeheartedly. What's more, he believed that banking should no longer play second fiddle to industry in America. He wanted to find a way to make finance a more fun and glamorous business, one that could be even more profitable than the sectors to which it was supposed to be in service. Wriston eventually brought to First National City Bank (the firm's new name after it merged with First National Bank in 1955) a host of new ideas about how to challenge old regulatory regimes, use technology to grow operations, expand in both national and international markets, and offer up more credit to companies and to the individual consumer, the latter having been largely ignored by big commercial banks. In many ways he was the model for Sandy Weill, a man who once believed that globalization, technology, and consumer culture could drive the financial industry to new heights if only it could be freed from the post-Depression regulatory regime.[39]

Wriston wanted to find a way to lure deposits, which had been falling, via higher interest rates, thus earning the bank more profits, which could then be invested in the more glamorous ventures he dreamed of. This involved pushing hard against barriers like Regulation Q, as well as others that made it difficult for banks to expand across states or internationally. Like Weill several decades later, Wriston would act first and ask questions of regulators second. He aggressively sought out areas of finance with higher profit margins and made inroads into new instruments once considered quite risky, like shipping loans.[40] Such complicated financial maneuvering soon began to backfire in big and unexpected ways. By pioneering the use of ship charters as collateral, for example, Wriston expedited the decline of the American-flag tanker fleet, since the Greeks built for half the price and would domicile ships in places like Liberia and Panama, where owners paid almost no taxes.[41]

But by then, Wriston and his bank were moving into new and increasingly elaborate financial products. In the early 1960s, in a foreshadowing of the kind of "innovation" that would come to characterize the modern banking industry, Wriston developed an ingenious way around the Glass-Steagall rules. His solution, the first to blur the line between lending and trading, became known as the negotiable certificate of deposit, or the CD. These securities were inspired by a Greek shipping tycoon who wanted a place to stash his funds away from his personal bank accounts, where the IRS could tap them.[42] Negotiable CDs began to function as special time-limited savings accounts with higher-than-normal interest rates for companies and rich people (you needed $100,000 to buy one).[43] Deposits poured in, and First National City began another, even more profitable business: buying and selling the CDs on a secondary market. Everyone thought that the new strategy, which involved lending to other financial entities that would then trade investors' products, probably broke the Glass-Steagall rules. But the government and the Fed, eager to keep banks solvent, did not stop the music. Within a year, $1 billion worth of negotiable CDs had been issued, and the market continued to grow as the securities were offered in smaller denominations, allowing average investors into the party.

Wriston had also begun to focus on American consumers who, hit by rising inflation that ate away at their returns, were unsatisfied with their traditional savings and checking accounts and were looking for ways to extend their buying power. Wriston gave it to them in 1967 with the introduction of the first credit card. Slowly, regulations around interest rates and the price of credit began to fall away. Money was becoming not a limited commodity but something you could buy—at the right price, anyway. By the mid-1970s, all of these inventions and many others had made First National City the most profitable financial institution in America—and Wriston, now the CEO, was quite the player, driving around New York in a red Corvette. He was well on his way to becoming the first commercial banker since the Great Depression to earn more than $1 million in one year.[44] He had also made powerful friends in Washington, as an adviser to the Kennedy and Nixon administrations. (A few years later, under President Ronald Reagan, Wriston would sit on the president's Economic Policy Advisory Board and help craft some of his infamous "trickle-down" economic policies.)

The success of the CD and other Wriston-led innovations was more that just a windfall for First National City, which changed its name to Citibank in 1976. It also set off an industry-wide chain re-action, as other financial institutions began searching for more and more high-yield products. Smaller thrift banks with fewer rate re-strictions invented the mutual fund. Bankers at Salomon Brothers, which would later be acquired by Citi, started experimenting with packaging mortgages into securities. Financial institutions started to try out derivatives, in the form of futures trading. It was hard for regulators to resist the growth of all this securitization, since every time interest rates went up, money would flow out of the banks, who would then demand a hike in the Regulation Q interest rate ceiling, and the Fed, frightened of capital flight, would comply.

It was a vicious cycle, but no one in Washington had the resolve to slow it down—and, to be fair, it wasn't completely clear at that point what was happening. Besides, the end goal of all this nipping and tucking of the rules, which had been to encourage more credit to flow to individuals and businesses, was failing. Even the govern-ment's own effort to create more mortgage financing, by develop-ing a market for mortgage-backed securities via the Government National Mortgage Association (GNMA, which would come to be known as Ginnie Mae) did not improve things. In the end, it only pulled money away from thrifts, which supplied most of the mort-gage lending, since deposits could now get better yields on the trad-able products.[45] Finance was gradually becoming an end in and of itself, rather than a facilitator for real business. In many ways, the creation of the CD and the secondary market for trading it marked a turning point for banking in the postwar era. The size of the sector began to grow, as did its focus on coming up with ways to game the system to make more money—two trends that fed on each other. Banking was no longer a utility. Just as Wriston had hoped, it was increasingly a high-speed, high-stakes business.

Buoyed by his successes, Wriston told the Street that he wanted his bank's earnings to grow at 15 percent a year, rather than the usual single digits; this would necessitate keeping less capital on hand and taking on more leverage.[46] To encourage employees to do whatever it took to hit that target, Citi also changed its compensation structure and began awarding stock options based on the value of its shares (which of course encouraged even greater risk taking and creative accounting to hide bad assets on income statements).[47] None of it worried Wall Street's million-dollar banker. Wriston had a dream—one that Sandy Weill would realize many years later. He wanted his institution to become a one-stop shop that would supply any financial product—from mortgages to securities to deposit accounts to trading platforms—to businesses and individuals. That goal would come with many unintended consequences.

INFLATION AND ITS DISCONTENTS

The CD market and the growth of more complex securities had actually contributed to a cycle of rising inflation that was already well under way thanks to the Vietnam War and the growing number of social programs being offered to offset some of the pain of the slowing economy. This is where the rebound in finance intersected with the political economy in ways that would once again foreshadow many of the crises of the future, including the one in 2008. Since the end of World War II, the country had come to expect more and more affluence. In order to keep Americans buying color TVs and shiny new cars, capital needed to flow more freely. But the 1933 rules, in particular Regulation Q, acted as an emergency break. That wasn't accidental; the whole purpose of the regulation had been to deter unbridled credit growth—which led to speculation, bubbles, and, often, financial crises and subsequent slowdowns—by limiting credit via interest rate ceilings.

One of the unfortunate side effects of Regulation Q, however, was that it tended to hit average individuals harder than it did companies. Firms and very wealthy people could always find clever ways to get cash and make higher returns (often via the methods devised by bankers like Wriston, who much preferred to lend to large, wealthy borrowers rather than average Joes). But ordinary people who needed mortgages were the first to feel the effects of credit crunches. During one such crunch, in the summer of 1973, a Texas homemaker named Vivian Cates wrote to her congressman complaining that her family could not find a bank to give them a mortgage, even though they had a 25 percent cash down payment and her husband was gainfully employed. "I can feed my family meatless meals and more rice and beans, we can buy less clothing, wash it more often, and wear it longer, but we cannot postpone having a place to live," she said.[48]

Such public reaction was obviously a political conundrum. But then, as now, it would have been politically difficult to prioritize lending to individuals over corporations, since the latter represented such an important lobbying block. So, rather than tell people like Vivian Cates that things simply weren't going to be quite as good as they had been in the past, at least until the economy could get back on its feet, the Nixon, Ford, and Carter administrations tried to pass the buck to the Fed. In a sense, they left it to central bankers to make the big decisions on how much capital American banks could move around the economy. In 1970, Andrew Brimmer, a Federal Reserve Board member, suggested an idea that's actually back on the discussion table today—namely, that the Fed should set reserve requirements in a way that would force financial institutions engaging in speculative activities to hold more money on their balance sheets, while allowing providers of simple Main Street credit to hold less. But the Fed's chairman at the time, Arthur Burns, rejected the proposal along with the entire notion that the Fed should take on the political hot potato of setting social priorities. (Never mind that this was already happening, via the prevailing system of regulation, even if nobody wanted to admit it outright.) So the Fed decided to fall back on the "markets know best" argument and let a laissez-faire attitude rule.[49] The upshot was that CDs were allowed to grow, as were other submarkets that were at least one step removed from the job of lending, like Eurodollar trading, which First National City also came to dominate. Securitization, rather than plain-vanilla lending, was becoming the business of banks. Slowly, the financial community began to claw back power over where and how capital flowed, funneling more and more of it away from middle-class Americans and toward finance itself.

A seminal moment in the rise of finance came in 1974, when Wriston convinced Secretary of the Treasury George Shultz that commercial banks, rather than government-backed institutions like the IMF or World Bank, should be in charge of helping recycle the petrodollars from oil-rich nations into emerging markets hungry for cash. Some of those petrodollars were already parked at Citi; one of Wriston's first overseas deals had been with the shah of Iran. Pushing the "markets know best" approach, Wriston argued that Wall Street could do this lending much better and more efficiently than government. He convinced Shultz to overturn a law that forbade US commercial institutions to make such loans to risky nations, and banks started lending to countries like Mexico, Brazil, Argentina, Zaire, Turkey, and many others. Within five years, foreign loans to developing countries by private banks had risen from $44 billion to $233 billion.[50] Plenty of the deals were dicey, but inflation, which remained high thanks in part to all the complex deal making at a global level, helped keep these risky countries solvent for a while, by making their debt payments less onerous.

It was a bubble, one that was destined to pop. By the late 1970s, Wriston and other US bankers were lending emerging markets money just so they could pay back the interest they owed on their existing obligations. Risky loans that Wriston had made both in the United States and overseas started going bad. In 1977, for the first time since the Depression, Citi posted a loss. By early 1982, both Standard & Poor's and Moody's had downgraded its credit rating. In August of that year, Mexico went into default, one of the first in a series of emerging market debt crises predicated on bad lending by US commercial banks. Fed chairman Paul Volcker helped put together a $1.5-billion bailout package for the country, in large part because he feared that Mexico's default would sink a number of large American banks, in particular Citi, that were holding so much of that bad debt. Volcker, who'd been wary of the growing clout of banking and finance, hated bailouts, but he felt they were necessary to avert a broader recession. In some way, Volcker was the first to declare these institutions Too Big to Fail.[51]

Yet just like the financiers who in 2008 successfully argued that banks must be bailed out during crises, so that they could lubricate the economy, Wriston found a way to turn disaster into opportunity. Volcker's strategy of combating runaway inflation with higher interest rates had once again made it hard for banks and thrifts to attract deposits, since they couldn't offer competitive rates. Wriston became the leader of a cross-industry lobbying effort to overturn Regulation Q once and for all. Along with big commercial institutions, he cleverly brought together diverse interest groups, such as smaller banks that wanted to grow, mortgage brokers that wanted to expand into other areas of finance, and individuals who wanted to access higher-yielding investments, not to mention ensure that they could get the mortgages they needed. Even the Consumer Federation of America and consumer advocates like Ralph Nader were persuaded that repealing Regulation Q would be a good thing. The Gray Panthers, a group advocating for retirees, filed a suit arguing that Regulation Q discriminated against small-time savers.[52] There were of course concerns that without the cap on rates and limits on how much credit could flow around freely, unexpected shifts in the economic climate could ruin livelihoods. What would, say, a steelworker or a schoolteacher with a fluctuating rate on a thirty-five-year mortgage do when the rate changed? The answer, according to the financial industry, was more consumer education about issues like credit and responsible spending (no matter that such campaigns had been conducted at the state level with no success). It's a diversionary tactic that is still used today, via calls for "financial literacy" in lieu of a secure retirement system (a topic we will return to in chapter 8).

Of course, politicians and policy makers could have decided to recraft rules to support the economy more broadly, making sure that businesses and individuals deserving of capital got priority over speculators. Instead they opted for the easy way out: deregulation. Little by little, the financial industry chipped away at the Glass-Steagall regulatory framework. In 1980, Wriston got his ultimate prize when President Jimmy Carter deregulated interest rates and banks were allowed to offer whatever rates they liked to attract funds. Regulation Q was history. The door was open to a whole new world of variable-rate mortgages, ever more complex securities, derivatives to hedge them all, and the rapidly swelling financial institutions that would make vast fortunes on them, wreaking havoc on the country's economic stability in the process.

REAGANOMICS AND THE RISE OF FINANCE

The financialization of the economy was turbocharged in the 1980s, fueled by the laissez-faire policies of the Reagan era that strongly favored Wall Street. The 1981 tax reform, for example, dramatically lowered the capital gains tax (Wriston played a part in crafting it), and a 1982 measure allowed companies to start buying back their own shares.[53] While Reagan has a reputation as having been a fiscal conservative, he was really anything but; he accompanied tax cuts with increased government spending, a cycle that deepened the national deficit.[54] That in turn had the effect of encouraging inflation, which Volcker continued to manage with higher interest rates. Traditional economic theory held that as interest rates got higher, companies and individuals would eventually stop borrowing, which would become a check on inflation, bubbles, and an overheated economy. But it didn't happen that way. In large part that was because the rise of information technology and the forces of globalization interacted with financialization in a way that led to the current financial era—a time that former Clinton labor secretary Robert Reich has called "supercapitalism"—creating a market system that exists mainly to serve the market itself.[55]

To be fair, it was impossible at that point to predict that these emerging trends would change the way monetary policy worked. Volcker's strategy of using nosebleed interest rates to try to tame the financialization of the economy made sense in many ways; he feared that Reagan's deficit spending would set back his fight against inflation, and so he refused to lower rates and allow that inflation to curb the debt. The Fed chiefs who succeeded him have rarely shown such conviction in the face of political pressure. But high rates turned out to be irresistible bait to foreign investors, who could now get superhigh yields in the United States. The Japanese, and later the Chinese and other emerging-market investors, became huge purchasers of US Treasury bills. This inflow of foreign capital allowed the cycle of financialization to continue, bolstering assets of all kinds and making people eager to engage in more and more speculative ways with the financial markets.

Foreign cash had the additional effect of raising the value of the dollar, which, perversely, hurt the US economy by suppressing demand for US goods. In 1982, the Business Roundtable, led by Caterpillar Tractor chairman Lee Morgan, began to complain about this.[56] Unfortunately the solution they proposed—deregulating global financial markets further to try to push capital back to places like Japan—didn't work. Treasury didn't mind, though. The influx of foreign capital was allowing the Reagan administration to maintain large deficits, even as it was pushing up asset prices to record highs.

The technology revolution that began in the mid-1980s did nothing to democratize this increasingly dysfunctional system—in fact, it had the opposite effect. In 1984, the Nobel Prize–winning economist James Tobin, a former member of Kennedy's Council of Economic Advisers and mentor to current Fed chair Janet Yellen, gave a talk on the "casino aspect of our financial markets," in which he lamented both the trend of financialization and the way in which technology was facilitating it, rather than actually strengthening the economy as a whole. "I confess to an uneasy Physiocratic suspicion . . . that we are throwing more and more of our resources, including the cream of our youth, into financial activities remote from the production of goods and services, into activities that generate high private rewards disproportionate to their social productivity," he said. "I suspect that the immense power of the computer is being harnessed to this 'paper economy,' not to do the same transactions more economically but to balloon the quantity and variety of financial exchanges. For this reason perhaps, high technology has so far yielded disappointing results in economy-wide productivity."[57]

This witch's brew of globalization, technology-driven trading, and the growth of finance boiled over in the October 1987 stock market crash, during which the Dow lost 22.6 percent of its value in a single day. It was just one of many crises that would follow. Through the 1980s, every few years saw the classic stages of boom and bust depicted by Charles Kindleberger in his famous book, *Manias, Panics, and Crashes*. A novel offering (be it the CD, the adjustable-rate mortgage, or a hot new IPO) would be followed by credit expansion, then speculative mania, distress, and ultimately a meltdown (usually followed by frantic government efforts to stem panic). By the time Volcker's successor, Alan Greenspan, took over control of the Fed in 1987, the government had gotten into the habit of lowering interest rates to jump-start markets each time they weakened. It was kerosene for finance, adding both reward and risk.

"What happens when you give a bunch of financiers easy money and zero interest rates is that they go out and try to make more money. That's what they are wired to do," says Ruchir Sharma, head of emerging markets for Morgan Stanley Investment Management and chief of macroeconomics for the bank. (He is just one of many experts who worry about the market-distorting effects of the Fed's unprecedented program of asset buying and low interest rates, which reached an apex in the wake of the 2008 crisis.) "Easy money monetary policy is the best reward in the world for Wall Street. After all, it's mainly the rich who benefit from a rising stock market."[58]

Although markets boomed under Greenspan, they also went bust more than ever before. The crash of 1987, the S&L crisis of 1989, the Mexican peso collapse of 1994, the Asian financial crisis of 1997, the larger emerging-market crisis of 1998, and the dot-com boom and bust all happened on his watch. Each time the economy faltered as a result, Greenspan would lower rates to boost lending. (He used this tactic so reliably, in fact, that Wall Street bankers began calling it the "Greenspan put"—a caustic term that encapsulated their belief that the Fed would bail them out no matter what.) But these policies never changed the underlying problems in the economy. Rather, they served to cover up its deep structural cracks with a monetary blanket that made people feel more prosperous on paper, even as their jobs were being outsourced and their companies were being weakened by short-term market-driven decision making. By the 2000s, underlying investment in the American economy was less as a percentage of GDP than in any other decade since World War II.[59] The casino, not the restaurant, was firmly in charge.

DEBT AND CREDIT: THE OPIATE OF THE MASSES

Surging assets prices in the 1980s and '90s were the root of a debt-fueled consumption boom that turned Americans into the "buyer of last resort" for the global economy.[60] At the start of the 1980s, personal savings as a percentage of GDP was about 12 percent; by 1999 it had free-fallen to near 2 percent,[61] as people took on second mortgages, home equity loans, more credit card debt, and other kinds of personal credit lines to fuel consumption. The growth in asset values, though based more on financial wizardry than real economy metrics, enabled another major change in the financial markets: the shift from a fixed corporate pension system to a market-driven 401(k) system. Such a system was, of course, relatively easy to sell in an era when all market boats were rising. In the 1950s, when retirement money was property, savings, or company-run pensions rather than private 401(k)s, fewer than one in ten households directly owned shares in corporations. Back then, investing was for stockbrokers and financial wizards, not the common man. But by 1983 one in eight families held stock, and by 2001 it was half. Today, 44 percent of Americans are in the market via a 401(k) or 403(b) plan, while only 18 percent have fixed pensions, a shift that has actually made retirement less secure (see chapter 8).[62] The result, according to sociologist Gerald Davis, who wrote extensively about this shift in his 2009 book, *Managed by the Markets*, was that "the bonds between employees and firms have loosened, while the economic security of individuals is increasingly tied to the overall health of the stock market."[63] Suddenly we all had a stake in the money game. With these changes, individuals have come to rely not on companies or government for their well-being, but on the markets—a dangerous proposition, given that stock gains benefit mostly the top tenth of the population, which holds most of these assets.

Instead of worrying about labor's ever-decreasing share of the pie, which began shrinking in the late 1970s (thanks to the same toxic combination of globalization, technology-related job destruction, and financialization), households hoped for market hikes. Over time, they came to rely on the value of their stock portfolios and their homes—which had themselves become financial assets—rather than on salary raises. Personal debt and business debt have grown at two and a half times the rate of Americans' total income over the past forty years.[64] We are only now beginning to grapple with the full ramifications of these shifts, as stagnant wages become a major dampener on economic recovery.

The political and cultural environment has reflected the market's rise in prestige. Bill Clinton's lead strategist, James Carville, joked in 1993 about wanting to be reincarnated as the bond market, a nod to Alan Greenspan's market-friendly policies. Later, George W. Bush tried to institutionalize the transition to an "ownership society" by trying to privatize Social Security (thankfully, that plan was unsuccessful) and increase home ownership by lowering lending standards, which was of course one of the factors that precipitated the housing market collapse in 2007. And throughout the entire period, public obsession with the markets grew. The financial media burgeoned. Traders became stars, shareholder value became the guiding force for corporate America, and, as Gordon Gekko put it so famously in the 1987 movie *Wall Street*, greed was good. Our economic orbit has been realigned.

TOO BIG TO FAIL

It was a revolution that benefited financiers the most. Even though Wriston's blunders in the emerging markets haunted Citi balance sheets for years, requiring the sort of government interventions that Wriston deplored for other industries,[65] he retired on a high note in 1984. His successor, John Reed, continued many of the same risky lending practices, giving easy money to leveraged buyout kings, real estate developers, and cash-hungry governments around the world.

He also championed a new wave of high-tech finance, which relied more heavily on complex algorithms that promised to predict future trends from shallow historical data—an assumption that would come back to bite Citi during the crash of 1987 and the bursting of the dot-com bubble in 2000 and the housing bubble in 2007. Many underlying problems in the bank's business model were papered over by rising asset prices in the 1980s and '90s, relatively low interest rates, and ample profits from corporate mergers and acquisitions. (Bankers cashed in on both ends of these deals, of course, by putting them together and then breaking them back apart, despite the fact that only about half of them ever succeeded, even when judged solely by share price.)

But inevitably, it all blew up again. By the late 1990s, the world was in the midst of yet another emerging-market crisis, this time brought on by the further deregulation of global capital flows orchestrated by the Clinton administration. (Treasury secretary Rubin and his deputy and then successor, Lawrence Summers, were principal architects of these measures, and finance lobbied vigorously for them.) Too much money had flowed into the markets too quickly, ending up in speculative projects that were now going bust. Dominos were falling in Asia, Brazil, Russia, and the West, eventually toppling an infamous hedge fund, Long-Term Capital Management (LTCM), which nearly tanked the US financial system. Citigroup alone lost half its quarterly profit, year over year, as a result. The Fed was once again left to pick up the pieces—though in that case, unlike with the bailouts of 2008, the banks themselves had to take responsibility for their losses.

All of this underscored just how complex the system and its most powerful institutions had become. Amazingly, though, instead of widespread criticism for their choices, Greenspan, Rubin, and Summers got a love letter in the form of a 1999 *Time* cover story entitled "The Committee to Save the World." So fully were the media and the government enthralled with finance that nobody seemed to raise an eyebrow when Citibank's Reid and Travelers Group's Sandy Weill announced the creation of the world's largest financial institution—Citigroup—in the midst of a crisis that showed just how risky such entities could be. The two CEOs had followed the strategy of acting first and asking questions later and moved ahead with their deal even though it was unclear whether the Fed and regulators would approve it. Yet the *New York Times* heralded the merger with a fawning editorial that could only have been written in the go-go nineties: "Congress dithers, so [Reed and Weill] grandly propose to modernize financial markets on their own."[66]

In their retroactive attempts to get the Fed to sign off on the merger, which dealt the final blow to the dividing wall between commercial and investment banking, Reed and Weill employed another time-tested strategy, telling government that banks needed more room to roam precisely *because* of the problems in the market. If banks kept hurting in the wake of LTCM's collapse, Reed and Weill argued, the broader economy would, too. Banking had to get *bigger* in order to thrive. This line, coupled with vigorous personal lobbying, yielded the ultimate triumph for finance: in November 1999, Clinton abolished Glass-Steagall, eliminating the last vestiges of Depression-era regulation. A month earlier, Rubin (fresh off his Treasury job) became cochairman of Citigroup, a move that would net him $15 million and 1.5 million shares of stock in his first year.[67]

BRIGHTNESS FALLS

Weill made plenty of money, too, thanks in large part to the symbiosis between the high-tech boom and banking. Until 2001, before the dot-com crash, Citi was one of the most aggressive players in the high-tech IPO market. The bank made huge fees helping firms go public (and even bigger money trading shares in those companies via early and preferential access). At the same time, it performed research for investors, advising them on the growth potential of various companies. These "buy" and "sell" functions within banks are very different and were supposedly insulated from one another. The people selling clients on IPOs weren't supposed to be in cahoots with the people publishing research, the risk of course being that the latter would otherwise be under pressure to create glowing reports to get their customers to buy whatever stocks the firm was selling.

But that's exactly what happened. In fact, it was one of the core triggers for scandals such as Enron and WorldCom: investors were told a completely false story by the companies' own bankers—of which Citi was one.[68] Analysts created positive reports about the companies that traders were hawking, enticing clients to buy more stock, which pushed up stock prices, which made the firm more money, and so on and so forth in a whirl of cash and exuberance that never seemed to end. One colorful misdeed involved a telecom analyst named Jack Grubman, who in 1999 worked for Salomon Smith Barney, then a division of Citi. Grubman, who had previously propped up the WorldCom stock with positive reports,[69] conveniently upgraded his negative rating on AT&T stock after Weill asked him to "take a fresh look" at the company. Grubman raised his rating and AT&T chose Citi as one of three underwriters on a huge sale of its wireless subsidiary's shares five months later, netting the bank $45 million in fees.[70] And, in an only-in-New-York twist, Weill helped Grubman get his twins accepted into one of Manhattan's most prestigious nursery schools.[71] Of course, it all ended in tears. New York attorney general Eliot Spitzer took Grubman and Weill down. Grubman was fined $15 million and barred from the industry for life, and Weill had to agree to never again speak with his own analysts one-on-one without a company lawyer present. Citi and nine other banks signed new rules barring their analysts from participating in any effort by outside firms to solicit investment-banking business, especially during IPOs. They also paid $1.4 billion in fines, which was supposed to be a way of making sure everyone stuck to it (which they didn't).

Still, those were the halcyon days for Citi. Very soon afterward, things really began to go south, thanks to Citi and other major banks' role as key players in the overheating of the housing market between 2000 and 2007, and the biggest holders of toxic assets following the implosion. Many of the spliced-and-diced securities were now held off banks' balance sheets altogether, in quasi-shell entities known as structured investment vehicles, which Citibank had invented two decades earlier to circumvent capital requirement rules.[72] The upshot was that in the midst of the crisis, it was difficult for bankers themselves to know where the next tranche of exploding debt would come from.

We know how that story ends, of course. I won't recount the details of the 2008 financial crisis here, since many excellent books have already done so.[73] Suffice it to say that all the elements of financialization were in play in 2008: a skewed playing field that led policy makers to put the interest of bankers above that of taxpayers and to absolve the financial industry of most of the responsibility for the debt; extreme levels of leverage and complexity; and a false narrative about who was to blame. The culprit certainly wasn't the spendthrift homeowner, but you wouldn't know that from the story Wall Street was telling. The elites kept more than their money following the bailout; they also kept control of the narrative. "I think that's the heart of the problem," says Senator Elizabeth Warren, the fiercest financial reform advocate of recent years. "The economic elite decided they had their own theory of the case. But it wasn't the right story. And without the right story about what went wrong, we won't fix what needs to be fixed."[74]

That's a big reason not much has changed in our financial system since the Great Recession. In 2014, two years after Sandy Weill issued his mea culpa, the US Financial Industry Regulatory Authority fined ten major banks, including Citi, $43.5 million for breaking Spitzer's rules and allowing their supposedly independent analysts to push positive research during a planned IPO of Toys 'R' Us. Yet the fines were minuscule compared to the windfall the banks hoped to make from fees and trading; flouting the rules was a risk clearly worth taking. This calculus has held true in nearly all other areas of finance—witness the $139 billion in fines paid by the industry between 2012 and 2014,[75] for everything from Libor interest rate rigging, to insider trading, to knowingly selling bad mortgages to unsuspecting clients. Rather than deterring rule breaking, the occasional penalty was considered a mere cost of doing business.

CAPITAL IN THE TWENTY-FIRST CENTURY

The scariest part of it all is that finance has yet to be properly re-regulated in the wake of the crisis. While it's true that some institutions have since offloaded risk, our system is most decidedly not safer. In fact, the exercise in public theater that is the banking stress tests is actually counterproductive, since it makes people think that new rules have been introduced to protect them from the next meltdown—which might be the case, if only these rules could be enforced, and if they could encompass the complexity of the financial system, which tends to morph too quickly for regulators to keep up. But in reality, the clean bill of health for the financial sector presented to the American public is false. In fact, I'd argue that the complexity of the Dodd-Frank rules—itself a result of vigorous industry lobbying—makes it as easy as ever to continue to hide risk, as long as you have a smart team of traders and lawyers.

What we need are simpler banking rules that would re-moor finance in the real economy, and there are other countries that provide models for how this might be done (a topic I will return to later). And it's a task that must begin now. Because, as the rest of this book will show, the triumph of financial capitalism is taking a toll on our businesses and our livelihoods that we can no longer afford.

CHAPTER 2

THE FALL OF BUSINESS

Bean Counters Versus Car Guys—Frederick
Winslow Taylor, Robert McNamara, and
the Financialization of Industry

GENERAL MOTORS CEO Mary Barra was, appropriately enough, in her car when she heard the news that the company she'd been appointed to run a few weeks before, in December 2013, was about to plunge into the worst product-safety crisis in recent memory. It was at the end of a cold, dark, midwestern winter day, and her chauffeur-driven Cadillac Escalade was tooling down the highway from the sprawling GM headquarters in downtown Detroit to her affluent suburban home, when one of her lieutenants, product development head Mark Reuss, called with some very, very bad news. It was about the ignition switch problem that would eventually lead to the recall of 2.6 million GM vehicles. "He said he'd just learned we had this problem with the vehicles and that we had to do a recall, and that it was large," she recounts.[1] "And then I literally can't remember [what happened next], because there was a period of probably 30 days where—I don't want to say it was a blur—but things were happening so quickly as we started to look through what we needed to do."

The to-do list was long, and urgent. Initial reports indicated that the problem related to the ignition switches in Chevy Cobalts and Pontiac G5s built between 2005 and 2007. It seemed that under certain conditions, the ignition switch could turn off, locking the wheel and disabling the air bag, an issue that had resulted in a number of injuries and even deaths. Recalls began, hundreds of thousands at first, then even more, as Barra gathered a tight war room team of top GM leaders to manage the growing crisis, which eventually totaled at least 124 deaths, hundreds of injuries, four grueling congressional testimonies by Barra, and a criminal penalty of $900 million—on top of at least $575 million GM paid to settle private lawsuits.[2] "We began meeting daily," she says. "And initially, I was just trying to understand . . . why? You know, how did this happen, and what caused it?"

The answer to that question was both simple and incredibly complex. At the surface level, GM's ignition switch disaster was the result of some seriously bad decisions on the part of individuals. Ray DeGiorgio, the engineer in charge of the faulty part (which he'd nicknamed "the switch from hell"), had decided, after years of struggling with a fix, to redesign but *not* renumber it. By creating a new part but not giving it a new number, which is how auto manufacturers recognize that a design has been changed, DeGiorgio essentially covered up the original problem—while throwing staff who were investigating the switch malfunctions off the correct trail.

That's the easy explanation, the one GM wanted people to focus on. But the mischaracterization of the switch problem early on as a "customer convenience" issue rather than a safety one obscured a much bigger problem—a management structure dominated by corporate silos in which information wasn't being shared and people were afraid to pass bad news up the ladder. What's more, these silos, outlined in detail in a now-famous report written by former US attorney Anton Valukas (who'd also been the bankruptcy examiner of Lehman Brothers), were the result of an even deeper and more tangled problem: the evolution of GM over decades from a company focused on making cars to one focused on making money and pleasing the financial markets.

THE RISE OF THE BEAN COUNTERS

The Valukas report is about as interesting a document as a corporate crisis report written by a team of lawyers can be. In 315 pages, it outlines a culture in which silence, obfuscation, and buck passing had been raised to an art form, resulting in an ignition switch crisis that many employees had known about but no one had taken the steps to prevent, despite numerous opportunities to do so. It's a problem starkly reflected in references to corporate tics like the "GM nod" (everyone nods yes to some action plan in a meeting, then leaves and does nothing) and the "GM salute" (arms crossed, finger pointed at the other guy).

The report reveals that GM's culture was a culture of unaccountability in which "no single person owned any decision."[3] Across every division of the company, one with more than 200,000 employees, few people actually spoke to one another—even if they were working on the same problem. That's why the engineers who designed an airbag that wouldn't deploy in a vehicle that was turned off (to avoid smothering passengers) didn't realize that the switch designers had made an ignition switch that sometimes shut off while the car was moving—meaning the airbag wouldn't deploy even if it was needed. As the Valukas report put it, the "critical factor in GM personnel's initial delay in fixing the switch was their failure to understand, quite simply, how the car was built." The switch guys weren't talking to the airbag guys, who weren't speaking to the legal department, which was getting an increasing number of complaints from passengers involved in switch-related accidents in which airbags didn't deploy.

The silence in Detroit was in large part the result of noise from Wall Street. All this noncommunication was happening at a time when GM and other automakers were under more pressure than ever from financial institutions to cut costs and rein in spending. Between 2001 and 2007, GM's global market share for automobiles had declined from 15 percent to 13.3 percent.[4] The Street wasn't happy, and it demanded belt tightening, not just at GM, but also from the entire industry. The 2000s was a time of extraordinary budget slashing, and the top leadership at GM was focused 100 percent "on the need to control costs." One engineer stated that cost control "permeates the fabric of the whole culture" at the company. Keeping projects on time and on budget was the paramount concern. In many cases, quality—and safety—took a backseat.[5]

That hierarchy of priorities had a perverse ripple effect throughout the firm. Supply choices were based on what was cheapest, not what was best. And if a division in charge of a particular car wanted to make an improvement that would add significantly to the development or manufacturing price of the vehicle, it was responsible for the costs of that change across the entire company—one reason that DeGiorgio might not have wanted to alert GM to his switch part revamp. Who wanted to be the guy who was responsible for slowing down the line and adding millions of dollars to the budget?

In the end, the Chevy Cobalts and other GM vehicles that ultimately resulted in the deaths of at least 124 people, including several who perished after fiery crashes, were being produced as "cost-conscious" vehicles on "slim margins."[6] The company was selling the cars in bulk, with steep discounts, to big fleet buyers like car rental companies—never a good sign. CEO Barra insisted that employees absolutely would have put their hands up if the switch problem had been properly understood to be a safety issue, but thanks to the institutionalized siloing of information, it wasn't. Once the switch problems were put into the "customer convenience" basket rather than the "safety" basket, each decision in the process of addressing the problem was predicated on cost control.

Wall Street pressure to cut costs and "make the numbers" was a big part of the ignition switch crisis, but in some ways it was merely a symptom of the deeper issue of silos and, more important, of the financial thinking that spawned them.[7] GM had a leadership dominated by "bean counters" and not "car guys." Those are the words used by many in Detroit, including former GM vice chairman Bob Lutz, who laid out some of the problems associated with this culture in his book *Car Guys vs. Bean Counters: The Battle for the Soul of American Business.* The book, which is both hilarious and tragic, is filled with stories of how financially oriented, MBA-toting managers at GM and other automakers trumped engineers, leading to a culture in which financial metrics mattered more than products. The results ranged from sobering (managers signing off on inferior products because customers "had no other choice" in that particular product category) to side-splitting (Cadillac ashtrays that wouldn't open because of senseless corporate mandates that they be designed to function at minus 40 degrees Fahrenheit).[8] It's all too easy to envision Lutz, a "car guy" known for going off corporate message, removing his mirrored shades and shouting to his cowering line manager, "Well, customers in North Dakota will be happy. Too bad nobody else will!"

But while it's easy to make fun of the bean counters, the fact is that you can draw a direct line between the problems at GM today and the ascendency of financial thinking within the company—and so many companies like it. As Lutz told me in an interview in August 2014, he believes that the silos that caused GM's switch crisis were absolutely the result of a management focused on financial metrics rather than overall quality and customer satisfaction. Putting finance in charge actually leads inexorably to corporate silos, says Lutz, "because bean counters believe greatly in suboptimization and keeping things small enough to where they can be controlled." From the point of view of the accountants, siloing is great, since it makes the various parts of a company easier to tally on a balance sheet and thus manage from the top down. "It's all part of the financial control mentality," says Lutz. "Anytime they [the bean counters] see a strategy or a philosophy where something risks slipping out of their grasp, they get worried."

It's a view that many management experts share. And certainly, you could see the effects of that limited thinking on the corporate structure of GM. The company had a culture in which, as Barra herself acknowledged to me in an interview, you have employees who "were expert in this or that without recognizing people don't buy this or that—they buy a car, and we've got to pull it together, and people have to talk." Yet the entire structure of GM was set up in a way that almost ensured that nobody talked. People who made airbags just did airbags; those who focused on switches did switches. That made it easier for bean counters to tally cost inputs and outputs from various divisions, but it also created what Barra calls "transactional" thinking, in which everyone colors inside the lines of their own precise job description without thinking more holistically about problems or solutions.

GM is rife with stories of workers so infantilized and unwilling to leave the comfort zone of their corporate boxes that they fail to speak up about problems—and of managers too fearful of making a mistake to challenge them. Not all of those decisions lead to something as tragic as GM's ignition switch crisis. But the reluctance to question metrics or think outside of corporate boxes is at the root of nearly all of the company's major missteps—everything from being behind the curve on electric cars (which were considered too expensive and too risky to overall profit margins to roll out early on) to launching products that were not rooted in what customers actually wanted.

One of the more famous examples of the triumph of the bean counters at GM involves the development of the Pontiac Aztek, a concept car introduced in the early 2000s. As one executive put it at the time, it was a "horrible, least-common-denominator vehicle" that reflected all that was wrong with GM's design process.[9] The financial decision makers (who knew very little about how the cars were actually made) insisted costs be kept low, and so it was decided that the new car would be built on an already existing minivan platform. Never mind that this resulted in a frame that was too big, while also limiting the freedom of designers to alter any major components. The result was an engine with a sickly wheeze, and a design that only a bean counter could love. As the journalist Justin Hyde of the widely read Motoramic blog put it, "tight budgets and boardroom dominance of manufacturing over design meant the underlying bits of the Aztek were set in stone before stylists ever lifted a pencil."[10] Says Lutz, who was brought in to try to bolster GM's design department in the wake of such disasters: "[The Aztek] was atrociously ugly, with featureless, flat body panels offset in front by what appeared to be one lower and one upper grille opening. I remember staring at it in disbelief. . . . I could not imagine that a group of professional automobile designers and executives had green-lighted this Quasimodo of crossovers."[11]

The triumph of the bean counters isn't limited to the auto industry, of course. Corporate America is filled with examples of big and small disasters resulting from the linear thinking that financially driven management encourages. Part of the story can be told in numbers. American companies have been cutting capital investments at home for decades now, but the effects have been particularly pronounced in recent years. Between 2000 and 2010, capital investment in things like R&D, equipment, new factories, and so on declined in manufacturing businesses by more than 21 percent. The decrease was particularly steep in certain industries, like motor vehicles—a sector in which investment plummeted by 40 percent.[12] But the cuts were made across the board and can be illustrated with stories of decline across nearly every sector. Consider Kodak's decision not to invest in digital cameras in order to preserve its profit margins on film, or AT&T's resistance to Internet telephony, or the way in which traditional media companies have been so slow to adapt to the digital age, since they are focused on preserving the profits of their old models.

When you read stories about companies destroying billions of dollars in long-term value to save a few million in the short term, you have to wonder how any corporation could make such obvious mistakes. Why didn't people raise their hands and wave them around until the decision makers took notice? Sometimes, as in the case of GM's ignition switch crisis, employees are so well trained to stay in their boxes that they simply don't raise the alarm. Other times they just can't swim against the tide of profit. The decline of the once-great technology firm Hewlett-Packard is a good example of a culture of innovation destroyed by bean counters. HP was the original Silicon Valley start-up, founded in a garage by two Stanford engineering students. Originally its culture, like Google's today, was focused on engineering and innovation and was very entrepreneurial. Its structure was flat rather than hierarchical. Workers were given great freedom and good benefits; layoffs, even in down times, were mostly used as a last resort. The firm was a regular on *Fortune*'s list of "Most Admired Corporations" and was a top performer in many areas.

Things started to change when longtime CEO Lewis Platt retired in 1999 and Carly Fiorina was brought in to replace him. She made it clear very quickly that she wasn't about superior technology, but about branding, marketing, and cost cutting. She was happy to shell out $200 million for a new marketing campaign but cut worker salaries, even as she gave herself an exorbitant (at least by HP standards) $3 million signing bonus and a $65 million stock package. (She even requested that the board pay the cost of shipping her fifty-two-foot yacht from the East Coast to San Francisco.)[13] One of her first moves was, not surprising, a merger with Compaq, which resulted in the loss of 15,000 jobs and a new culture that was more focused on sales and services than on engineering and innovation. By 2004, though, it was clear that while the merger had cut costs, it hadn't increased profits. Fiorina was eventually forced out by the board, but HP never really recovered. Under its next CEO, Mark Hurd, it continued cutting R&D and froze worker pension benefits. Another desperate attempt to bolster margins via a merger (rather than investments in innovation), this time with Electronic Data Systems, was a disappointment. Today, HP is a struggling also-ran in the technology business that it practically invented.[14]

IF YOU CAN MEASURE IT, YOU CAN MANAGE IT

These missteps, like GM's switch crisis, are all part of a very long-term shift in corporate America toward balance-sheet-driven management. This transformation began in the first half of the twentieth century, when a change in thinking about business gave rise to a seminal new idea: if you could measure it, you could manage it. It was a shift that put markets before business, capital before labor, and profits before anything else. And it was a shift that would ultimately undermine real growth and innovation within American business itself.

This change can be traced all the way back to Alfred P. Sloan Jr., the storied CEO of General Motors from 1923 to 1946, who proclaimed that his goal was "to make *money,* not just to make motor cars."[15] The statement summed up a new conventional wisdom about the purpose of business and foreshadowed the banking sector's ideas about shareholder value, which hold that the chief mission of a corporation is to maximize returns to shareholders and put their interests above those of any other group—be it customers, founders, laborers, or the community at large. It was an idea that had only recently been enshrined in law, in the 1919 Michigan Supreme Court case *Dodge v. Ford Motor Co.,* which established that "a business corporation is organized and carried on primarily for the profit of the stockholders."

The case centered on a disagreement between Henry Ford, the founder and majority shareholder of Ford Motor Company, and two automaker brothers—John Francis Dodge and Horace Elgin Dodge (the founders of Dodge Brothers car company). Henry Ford had been making a killing on his Model T car, cutting prices on the vehicle as economies of scale increased, while also very publicly increasing the wages of his workers, in part so that they would have enough money to buy his products—a strategy that came to be known as Fordism. The company had accumulated quite the cash trove: around $52 million, or $1.1 billion today. The Dodge brothers, who were minority shareholders in the firm, wanted Henry to pay back some of that money in the form of dividends. But Ford wanted to put the money to work building more factories, so that he could sell more cars. "My ambition," he said, "is to employ still more men, to spread the benefits of this industrial system to the greatest possible number, to help them build up their lives and their homes. To do this we are putting the greatest share of our profits back in the business."[16]

The courts didn't see it that way. They ruled for the Dodge brothers, the stock dividend was duly boosted, and the pair quickly invested their payout in their own car company that was competing with Ford (yet another reason Ford had been wary of paying out dividends). Dodge Brothers would eventually be merged into Chrysler, and Ford continued expanding despite the setback, eventually building its River Rouge plant into the world's largest integrated factory. But the case reverberated throughout American business and is still a key legal precedent in the area of corporate governance. The ruling enshrined in law the idea that companies had a legal obligation to maximize profits for investors, and that their interests trumped those of anyone else.

Indeed, "shareholder value" has become the rallying cry of many a financially oriented manager making decisions that boost a company's share price at the expense of longer-term growth. And it has also become the justification for "activist" investors who, in a clever semantic trick, have today been rebranded from their previous incarnation as "corporate raiders"—people like Carl Icahn, Bill Ackman, and Daniel Loeb, who have pushed American companies to pay back their record $2 trillion cash hoard in the form of dividends and share buybacks, rather than pay higher wages or make investments in factories, infrastructure, or worker training.[17] And they've been quite successful at forcing companies to do just that. In 2015 alone, American firms have paid a record $1 trillion back to investors in the form of buybacks and dividends, more than ever before in history, even as wages have remained stagnant and business investment in capital goods, factories, worker training, and other growth-enhancing things has flagged.

Dodge v. Ford not only established a legal justification for shareholders' rights above anyone else's; it also set a terrible precedent for labor relations that would haunt American business. It was a precedent that chimed with another major business idea of the era: Taylorism.

THE PRINCIPLES OF SCIENTIFIC (MIS)MANAGEMENT

Even before Henry Ford was battling the Dodge brothers, Frederick Winslow Taylor, a mechanical engineer from Philadelphia, was gaining fame and fortune for his ideas about how to improve American industry. Those ideas, which came to be known as "efficiency theory" or, as critics put it, "Taylorism," were laid out in his seminal work, *The Principles of Scientific Management,* published in 1911. Like the Dodge brothers, Taylor didn't think much of labor. His theories were built around the notion that workers were a lazy and rather stupid bunch who needed to be managed closely if the American economy was to become more efficient. His book laid out his disdain for labor in ways that are hard to imagine any business leader openly articulating today. "One of the very first requirements for a man who is fit to handle pig iron as a regular occupation is that he shall be so stupid and so phlegmatic that he more nearly resembles in his mental make-up the ox than any other type," wrote Taylor. "The man who is mentally alert and intelligent is for this very reason entirely unsuited to what would, for him, be the grinding monotony of work of this character. Therefore the workman who is best suited to handling pig iron is unable to understand the real science of doing this class of work."[18]

It's easy to see, in reading this, how Taylor's ideas were eventually used to justify racist philosophies like eugenics. But around the turn of the century and for the three decades that followed, Taylorism was considered the state of the art in business theory (Taylor himself had a stint teaching the ideas at Harvard Business School). His teachings spread like wildfire in firms eager to become faster, more efficient, and more profitable. Doing so, according to Taylor, involved putting workers in much more rigidly defined boxes, and keeping a tight lid on them. His "time and motion" studies became the basis for new job categorizations in which workers would do one very specific task in a very specific way. Using a stopwatch, Taylor famously stood over factory workers doing the component parts of a job and timed them—down to the hundredth of a minute. One of his most infamous studies involved measuring the most efficient load for a shovel (twenty-one pounds) and deducing the exact way in which the worker should hold it to move the most amount of material in the least amount of time (never mind the repetitive stress injuries). Taylor claimed that such efficiency would reduce working hours but was never able to prove it. As workers began to be paid by the piece, they simply worked harder, and longer.

Capitalists, of course, were the main beneficiaries of all this; their factories were making more parts, and more money. But as tasks were broken down, new chains of reporting were built up. Shovel wielders now needed a spate of shovel measurers and managers to oversee their work. That added people and costs, which created demand for more profit via producing more efficiency. Oddly, this growing bureaucracy was something that Taylor, who explicitly favored the transfer of power from workers to management, actually lauded. As he put it, "the most marked outward characteristic of functional management lies in the fact that each workman, instead of coming in direct contact with the management at one point only . . . receives his daily orders and help from eight different bosses," including route clerks, instruction card men, cost and time clerks, gang bosses, speed bosses, inspectors, repair bosses, and the shop disciplinarian.[19]

None of these people were encouraged to speak to one another— only to do the tasks that they'd been assigned by top brass, which was increasingly removed from the shop floor. Top management spent its time processing all the information that was being churned out: the operating and cost statistics, the transport and distribution data, and of course the financials. Corporate leadership became a numbers job. Workers and engineers in the factories made parts, and managers made money. In this environment, the controller (whom we today call the chief financial officer) became the board of directors' indispensable man.[20] He alone had access to everyone and everything. Indeed, his role was that hole in the hourglass through which all corporate information flowed.

Chief financial officers proliferated in the 1920s. They went from being pretty much unheard-of at the turn of the century to being so ubiquitous as to establish their own professional institute just a few years later.[21] Moreover, managers themselves were increasingly drawn from the accounting profession, something of which Taylor (who died in 1915) would have heartily approved, since he didn't think there was much difference in the skills needed to run an auto factory, an oil company, or an advertising firm. If you could measure it, you could manage it—a motto that McKinsey, the global business consulting giant, would eventually pick up and adopt as its unofficial slogan decades later. A managerial high caste was being born, one separate from owner-entrepreneurs. It was focused mainly on financial metrics and adversarial to labor, which was increasingly being de-skilled, thanks to Taylorist ideas of rigid, limited job descriptions.

But if workers were being de-skilled, so were managers. As firms became more financialized, managers became less and less knowledgeable about the actual products their companies were creating, even as they knew more about their financial performance. As control of production got decentralized, financial decision making, the most important power node in the company, was being ever more centralized and crucial to corporate strategy. That fact in and of itself supported greater financialization. As communication between corporate divisions became harder, numbers—and the absolute truth they were perceived to hold—became increasingly important, the only real information that firms could marshal to make decisions.

No company better exemplified this than GM. While Henry Ford had incorporated Taylorist notions of job precision into his factories, which was one of the reasons he could churn out so many Model Ts, it was GM that first combined both the practical details of mass-market automation with the intellectual underpinnings of efficiency theory, by adopting the Taylorist philosophy of completely separating labor and management. As Sloan himself said at the time, he didn't *want* high-level managers to know too much about the products the company was producing; their job was simply to look at the spreadsheets and, in a rational way, make decisions about which divisions were working well and which ones weren't, based solely on accounting data. Only the top-line numbers mattered. Everything else—quality, customer satisfaction, and certainly worker satisfaction—was background noise.

All this was the beginning of the financially driven silos that would lead GM to its ignition switch disaster many decades later. But this phenomenon wasn't confined to GM, or even to automakers. In many industries at the end of the 1930s, most corporations had adopted some aspects of the numerical religion that was efficiency theory. Taylor himself had, interestingly, come in for a fair bit of criticism along the way. Laborers in factories using his methods were increasingly unhappy, and a particularly volatile strike at the Watertown Arsenal in Massachusetts in 1911 resulted in a congressional investigation into his methods, which were eventually labeled too brutal and banned at the factory.

Yet even as Taylor the man became less popular, his quantitative approach to business was about to get a huge boost in influence, as it was picked up and repopularized in a new form by a much more powerful prophet. Taylor's famous quip that "in the past the man has been first; in the future the system must be first"[22] would inform an entirely new field of financially oriented research—the field of systems analysis. It was a field that would change the economic and political shape of our world.

THE BEST AND THE BRIGHTEST

The last several decades of economic history might have been quite different if not for that prophet: Robert F. McNamara, a cerebral, tightly wired colossus of a figure who, as secretary of defense under President John F. Kennedy and later Lyndon Johnson, was largely responsible for the failure of US strategy in Vietnam. His obsession with systems analysis—in which data about every aspect of the war effort, from bombs to defoliants to fatalities to the number of enemy vehicles disabled per air strike megaton, was collected in order to maximize efficiency—blinded Washington to the overall flaws in its conduct of the war. Since it was impossible to argue with numbers, it was difficult to question McNamara's thinking, a topic well described in books like David Halberstam's *The Best and the Brightest*.[23]

But a less-known aspect of McNamara's legacy was his bringing of financial efficiency theory to corporate America, introducing a culture of management by numbers that eventually undercut productivity in top US corporations. Before leading America into Vietnam, McNamara launched an attack of a different sort—on Ford Motor Company, where he developed a mania for squeezing fractions of pennies out of the cost of front-wheel lug bolts while ignoring the creative side of the business. This strategy eventually led the automaker, along with the rest of the American car industry, to lose its global dominance.

The streamlining of Ford was orchestrated by a team of number-crunching analysts known as the Whiz Kids, who came out of the Pentagon's statistical analysis department, and of whom McNamara was the best known. McNamara had always been enamored of numbers. In his youth, he'd studied business administration at Harvard and become a proponent of the sort of decentralized management and financially driven decision making already seen at GM, which would eventually become the gold standard for financialized firms, lauded by the father of management consulting, Peter Drucker, in his management tome *Concept of the Corporation*. (Both Drucker and McNamara were big fans of Taylor.)[24] McNamara, though, wasn't just interested in numbers; he also sought power and prestige. Following a brief stint on the West Coast at the accounting firm Price Waterhouse, McNamara quickly returned to Cambridge to imbue other impressionable minds with a love of data points as a professor at Harvard Business School.

McNamara was teaching accounting at Harvard in 1942 when Charles "Tex" Thornton, head of the US Army Air Forces' Office of Statistical Control, visited the university on a mission to find "the best and the brightest" minds to help him form a new statistics analysis group at the War Department. His idea was to help ramp up the military effort by using quantitative analysis to figure out which targets to bomb, how to transport troops, and, ultimately, how to win the war.[25] The Whiz Kids would, as John Byrne wrote in his book of the same name, "serve the role of corporate controllers, their reports flowing up to Air Force headquarters through a parallel and largely independent command structure headed by Tex."[26] That independent structure made a lot of veteran military people mad, in large part because it put little stock in the personal experience, intuitions, and emotions of men on the ground. Command and control was the management method, and statistics were the only information that mattered. The Stat Control group, in which McNamara became a star player, squeezed more flying hours out of planes and figured out the most efficient way to move equipment from point to point. But it also recommended cost-cutting maneuvers like getting rid of fighter escorts on bombing missions, based on number crunching that estimated an 80 percent survival rate for pilots without escorts. Never mind the remaining 20 percent doomed by the algorithm, or the intangible, morale-dampening effect of sending pilots into a war zone without wingmen. When General Curtis LeMay, one of the top air force leaders at the time (and later George Wallace's vice presidential candidate), read the recommendations in that particular Whiz Kid report, he scrawled an expletive across it before throwing it in the trash.[27]

As history shows, it was just as well. While the Whiz Kids were lauded after the US victory in World War II, later research found that it was unclear whether their analysis actually helped or hurt the war effort. Despite the hype, their numbers weren't magical—indeed, key metrics that determined major war decisions were often chosen not because they were the best, but because they were easiest to calculate.[28] One military report on the bombing effort following the war found that Stat Control methods had been an "overall disappointment." Even the RAND Corporation, the shadowy, pseudomilitary institution that actually developed the systems analysis techniques later deployed by McNamara at the War Department, issued a self-critical report in 1950, saying its methods had been too rigid and reactive. This internal report, authored by a RAND engineer, noted that "the great dangers inherent in the systems analysis approach ... are that factors which we aren't yet in a position to treat quantitatively tend to be omitted from serious consideration. Even some factors we can be quantitative about are omitted because of limits on the complexity of structure we have learned to handle. Finally, a system analysis is fairly rigid, so that we have to decide six months in advance what the ... problem is we are trying to answer—frequently the question has changed or disappeared by the time the analysis is finished."[29] It turned out that while systems analysis was pretty good at increasing efficiency around *known* goals, it was terrible at helping people figure out what the goals should actually be, especially when there were a lot of sticky variables at play, like human motivations and emotions.

FROM WASHINGTON TO DETROIT

But nobody was thinking about these pitfalls following America's World War II triumph. The Whiz Kids, McNamara in particular, could do no wrong; they knew what was important to know. If they thought management by numbers was the way forward, then that was that. And so, in 1946, the Whiz Kids, hired by Henry Ford II himself, began their overhaul of the Ford Motor Company. Recruited as a team, they decamped from Washington to Detroit, where they set about transforming American business from the top down, just as they'd transformed the air force strategy: with numbers and facts.

Ford certainly needed the help. It was hemorrhaging money at a rate of around $9 million a month, having lost market share to GM during the intrawar period. Henry Ford II took a two-pronged approach to the problem. He hired as many GM executives as he could woo away from the larger automaker, and he hired the Whiz Kids to come lead the new management efforts.[30] Enter McNamara. One of the first things he did, of course, was to order an audit. The result indicated, predictably, that Ford needed more precise financial metrics and a bigger staff of accountants to track them. Almost immediately the financialization of Ford began, with McNamara and his team of bean counters bringing order, but also cold rationality and logic, to the company, creating a culture in which there was no room for emotion—only for numbers. This was quite a change in Detroit, where car companies were typically run by "car guys" who believed automobiles were a highly emotional purchase. Yet McNamara, ever the rationalist, believed they were a commodity and should be treated like one. Designers and engineers were put on shorter leashes and given tighter budgets. Where finance had once been nearly nonexistent within Ford, it quickly became the control hub of the firm. "Bob McNamara was behind the effort to install profit centers throughout the corporation so they could take the pulse of each operation. The men went beyond the traditional control of manufacturing costs, to include control over everything, from marketing to purchasing," writes Byrne.[31]

Over the next few years, the MBAs wrested control of the entire company from the car guys in the engineering and design departments, who resented them and scoffed at their lack of knowledge about how products were made and what customers actually wanted. "The coming of the Whiz Kids [to Ford] was an important moment, for it reflected a major change about to take place in many American companies. These eager, able young men were not car men. They were not, like those who had gone before them, rooted in the business itself, lured to it by love of mechanical devices or by the excitement of making something. Nothing, indeed, could have been more alien to them," wrote David Halberstam in his 1986 book, *The Reckoning.* This transition—which can be called the Whiz Kidding of the American auto industry—underscored in his view a larger corporate malaise taking hold in the country, one in which finance was coming to dominate business. Accountants were replacing tradesmen, and making money was slowly but surely replacing the goal of making great products. In short, financialization loomed. "The Whiz Kids were the forerunner of the new class in American business," Halberstam wrote. "Their knowledge was not concrete, about a product, but abstract, about systems—systems that could, if used properly, govern any company. Their approach was largely theoretical, their language closer to that of the business school than the auto assembly line."[32]

The Ford finance department, headed by McNamara, who eventually became the company controller, would pay lip service to quality but promote people—particularly themselves—by the numbers. The Whiz Kids filled some of the highest positions at Ford through the 1980s, along with other upstarts who came out of the finance department, many of them armed with MBAs.[33] (And, in a foreshadowing of the staggeringly unequal pay structures brought about by financialization, their salaries grew at a rate some 50 percent higher than those of executives who held only undergraduate degrees.)[34] For a while, this management by numbers actually worked. As the Whiz Kids shaved millions off Ford's balance sheet, profits nearly doubled, going from $94 million to $177 million between 1948 and 1949 alone.[35] The share price of the company rose, too, as did the stock of McNamara and his team.

Of course, the biggest factor in the company's rebound in the 1950s, the significance of which is clear only in retrospect, is that America was going through an economic boom of unprecedented proportions at the time. This was the height of the baby boom, as returning GIs started families and began buying cars, homes, appliances, and everything else. The government was spending more than $40 billion on the new Interstate Highway System. Demand was so huge that automakers couldn't help succeeding. GM, which had overtaken Ford in the 1930s as the largest car manufacturer, was on its way to becoming the first-ever company to earn more than $1 billion in a year.[36] In such an environment, the Whiz Kids' strategy of putting finance first could continue unimpeded for some time. Its innovation- and growth-dampening effects simply weren't noticed amid the postwar boom—at least not immediately.

Ford's IPO in 1956 bought more time, and money, to implement McNamara's strategies. The Ford family after World War II was "both rich and impoverished," Halberstam writes, since old Henry

Ford had bequeathed most of his money to the Ford Foundation, which he'd set up less as a charity than as a tax dodge. (He loathed taxes and couldn't stand the idea of a large chunk of his wealth going to estate taxes.)[37] Unfortunately for his family, which was used to living in a mansion in Grosse Pointe, Michigan, with a surplus of servants, this made it tough to continue the high life while also leaving enough money to fund corporate growth. The obvious solution was to take Ford public.

The IPO was done by none other than the country's leading investment bank, Goldman Sachs. One of the junior partners on the deal, John Whitehead (who'd eventually come to lead Goldman—one of the last pure investment bankers to do so before the traders took over), later said that Ford's IPO represented the democratization of capitalism. Up until then, stockholding among the masses wasn't common; people held their wealth largely in bonds and property. But everyone knew who Ford was, and what Ford made, and everyone wanted a piece of this company, which more than any other seemed to represent the American dream of freedom and entrepreneurial possibility. The offering was a huge success, and the stock price soared well beyond what was expected, like the hot technology offerings of today. So it was that the Ford family got 300,000 new corporate owners from Main Street. And by taking the firm public rather than cashing out their stake privately, they got to avoid $300 million in inheritance taxes while also keeping control of the company.[38]

The money that flowed into Ford's coffers fueled the expansion necessary to meet demand within the postwar economy, but it also ensured that from then on, the corporate focus would be mostly on keeping the stock price up—while avoiding any risks that might bring it down. As a large body of research shows, public companies are almost always more conservative in this way than private ones, because the former are under pressure from Wall Street to make quarterly earnings and keep shareholders happy, whether or not that involves decisions that are good for long-term growth. Private companies, for example, invest about twice as much as equivalent public firms do in things like factories, worker training, R&D, and other long-term investments[39] (something that belies a claim made by many large public firms today—namely, that a lack of investment into the US economy is the result of high tax rates). It's interesting to note that some of the deep-seated problems that have plagued the American auto industry for generations, such as unsustainable pay deals with unions, began after companies went public.

This shift from private to public also engendered shifts in the company's labor and compensation policies. Ford wanted at all costs to avoid margin-killing strikes, so the firm tended to cut deals with unions that increased pay, while refusing to adopt the more collaborative methods of production that were already being employed in postwar Europe. There, companies like Daimler had adopted a "codetermination" style of management in which labor actually sat on the corporate board and helped make decisions about how the firm was run and how cars were made—a model that ultimately proved more productive and globally competitive. But in the United States, the traditionally Taylorist approach meant management was inclined not to collaborate with labor but to pacify it. Workers got raises but little control, in a Faustian bargain that ultimately backfired decades later as jobs and skills were sent abroad to Asia, where things could be made more cheaply.

Adversarial is perhaps the best word to describe relations between management and labor in America, not only at GM but also in most of the auto industry and, indeed, in US corporations as a whole. One of the many reasons that American auto manufacturers are still struggling to implement the sort of collaborative approaches to production that have made some Asian and European companies so successful is that doing so requires a profound mental reset. For example, back in the 1980s and '90s—when GM and other firms tried to put into place a Japanese-style "andon cord" system that would allow any worker to stop the line if something went wrong— American workers would regularly be yelled at by bosses for actually pulling the cord. They were, some managers thought, just trying to get themselves a free work break.[40] The idea that they might take pride in their products and want them to be top-notch seemed an imaginative leap too far.

Even when bosses were actually willing to create more collaboration, their efforts were subject to Wall Street approval and the fluctuations of market conditions. Back in 1991, for example, when Robert Stempel, then CEO of GM and a respected "car guy," tried to roll out lean production methods throughout the firm, he was unable to persuade his board or the analysts on the Street that it was worth the effort. They wanted the company to beat their quarterly numbers now, and so Stempel eventually had to revert to the usual way of doing so. He announced plans to close twenty-one plants and cut 74,000 workers—moves that boosted the company's stock price but cost it trust with labor, which was of course subsequently less interested in negotiating compromises in compensation in exchange for control over the production process. While there has been some incremental improvement, the basic lack of trust in these relationships, which has been largely broken by financialization, persists to this day.

All of it resulted in an increasingly dysfunctional business model, one that discouraged all manner of innovation and long-term thinking. Managers used the fact that they were paying higher salaries to justify cuts in R&D spending. Profits were increasingly bolstered not with truly new products and technologies, but by nipping and tucking costs. "The Ford Motor Company was becoming a stagnant place at which to work," writes Halberstam in The Reckoning.[41] "The impulse of product, to make the best and most modern cars possible, was giving way to the impulse of profit, to maximize the margins and drive both the profit and the stock up. It did not happen overnight. It had begun with McNamara and his systems."

Keeping stock prices up meant keeping costs down, and no one was better at that than the Whiz Kids. Yet even before McNamara was named president of Ford in 1960, his strategy of putting finance ahead of design and engineering was having a major effect on quality. It's no surprise, then, that the Edsel, the most notorious flop in all of automotive history, happened under the watch of his team. The

Edsel had been designed in the middle of turf fights between bean counters and engineers within the firm, and it had a fraught birth. It was supposed to be a midpriced car that would help Ford capitalize on the rising middle class, but instead it became an overhyped stylistic mishmash (one reviewer likened the Edsel's front grille to "an Olds sucking a lemon") with numerous design problems. While McNamara himself hadn't green-lighted the car, he was the executive to debut it, and, worst of all, his own quality control system failed to catch its flaws. Under his system, defects in a car were assigned a point value, and no car could be delivered to a dealer if it had more than 35 points' worth. But auditors measured only a sample of vehicles coming off the line—and as long as that sample averaged within the acceptable limits, the whole lot of cars produced that day would ship.

That meant thousands of cars with mismatching upholstery, loose hubcaps, and faulty transmissions made their way into customers' garages. Complaints mounted, and it wasn't long before Johnny Carson, Bob Hope, and Milton Berle were harpooning the car in their television comedy shticks. Well before McNamara pulled the plug on the vehicle in 1959, Ford had started shipping the Edsel to dealers with repair instructions tied to the steering wheel.[42]

Yet to the Whiz Kids, customer satisfaction was ultimately less important than the corporate balance sheet and the company share price. In their minds, the priority of an auto executive—or any kind of executive—wasn't to be passionate about your product. It was to make money, just like GM's Alfred Sloan had admonished years earlier. McNamara and his team had "contrived not to improve but in the most subtle way to weaken each car model, year by year," explains Halberstam in *The Reckoning*.[43] A cheaper metal here, a quicker drying paint there ... Pennies saved added up to dollars, which added up to thousands of dollars, which added up—you get the picture. McNamara even tried to eliminate providing a spare tire in each trunk, on the basis that neither he nor anyone he knew ever used them. Happily, an aide intervened, reminding him that the vehicles of industry executives were generally replaced every six months.

Predictably, McNamara was the first of the auto industry executives to begin talking about outsourcing the production of component parts to countries where labor was cheaper, in order to bolster corporate profit margins further.[44] Wall Street, of course, loved the idea, and there was little to no thought about how it might erode the manufacturing knowledge base in America and thus undermine longer-term growth.

UP IN FLAMES

But the focus on balance sheets over quality couldn't last forever. The strategy of penny-pinching and undercutting investment in product development finally exploded, literally, in the 1970s, when the Pinto, a low-cost subcompact Ford car, was found to burst into flames during rear-end collisions. Worse, reports soon surfaced that Ford engineers had actually known about these risks, but chose to send the Pinto into production anyway because they had already tooled the assembly line for it. The disaster would ultimately cost Ford millions in payouts and lost market share. The Pinto, cheap and deadly, became a potent symbol for the problems plaguing the American automotive business and the decline of the US manufacturing industry itself. And, as Andrea Gabor writes in her book *The Capitalist Philosophers*, although the car was introduced in the 1970s, its problems could be traced directly back to the cost-benefit analyses established by the Whiz Kids.

"The Pinto's problem was due to the placement and configuration of the gas tank, a design flaw that could have been solved by, for example, sheathing the inside of the gas tank with a rubber lining," Gabor explains.[45] But the potential cost of adding those liners—$137 million—far exceeded Ford's original estimate of what it would cost to compensate customers for burn-related injuries and deaths: $49.5 million. "Since the price of avoiding burn accidents ... was nearly triple the benefit of doing so," Gabor says, "the company never authorized the change."

McNamara did not have to answer for the Pinto tragedy. Shortly after being named president of the company in 1960, he was tapped for an even higher calling, to be secretary of defense under the newly elected president John F. Kennedy. He seemed the perfect fit for this young, technocratic, rational administration—a can-do type who would bring mathematical precision and quantitative analysis to the complex business of the Vietnam War. But McNamara's relentless focus on measurables blinded him to the overall pointlessness of the war itself. As Halberstam wrote in *The Best and the Brightest*, "this man, whose only real experience had been in dealing with the second largest automotive empire in the world, producing huge Western vehicles, was the last man to understand and measure the problems of a people looking for their political freedom. Yet he was very much a man of the Kennedy Administration. He symbolized the idea that it could manage and control events, in an intelligent, rational way."[46] Taking on a guerrilla campaign was like directing a production line—"you brought your systems to it."

The system of top-down decision making in which only number-toting managers had power would not only lose the war in Vietnam; it would also cost American automakers their preeminent place in the industry that they had invented. All of the US car giants suffered setbacks from the 1970s onward, losing market share and revenue to better-run European companies as well as Asian upstarts, both of which put the focus on engineering quality over short-term profit making. A famous *Harvard Business Review* article by Robert H. Hayes and William J. Abernathy, published in 1980, looked at the problem not only in the auto business, but throughout American industry.[47] It found that US firms' research and development spending had been falling since the mid-1960s, even as the percentage of company leaders coming out of finance, relative to any other area, had been increasing. Money spent on mergers amounted to nearly two-thirds of the entire amount of R&D spending by American industry. Companies were hoarding cash rather than investing, and executives spent the majority of their time on "sophisticated and exotic techniques used for managing their cash hoard," treating "technological matters simply as if they were adjuncts to finance or marketing decisions." The article, which was entitled "Managing Our Way to Economic Decline," could have been written today; the only difference would be that the numbers supporting its thesis would be more striking. No wonder it was re-released in 2007 to popular acclaim.

The legacy of the Whiz Kids ensured that the top-down, financialized approach to management became the de facto approach at most firms, a misguided practice that still plagues many American companies. This is in large part because the Whiz Kids themselves took over so many top firms in the years following their revamping of Ford. By the early 1980s there were more than 250 Ford alums, most from the finance division, in positions of vice president or above at major US corporations. And at least sixteen Ford finance executives had gone on to become presidents and chairmen of other firms including Firestone, Rockwell International, Prudential, Zenith, Reynolds Metals, Navistar, and Bell & Howell.[48]

At Xerox, the disciples of McNamara turned one of the country's great research companies into a firm focused on cost cutting over innovation. Inventions like the point-and-click interface, the mouse, and the laser printer had come out of Xerox's research labs, which were the envy of Silicon Valley. But in the late 1960s, two former Ford executives went to Xerox and started subjecting the company to "the same minute financial analysis that the Whiz Kids had brought to Ford," making cost-cutting suggestions like replacing high-quality metal hinges with plastic ones on the firm's top-selling copiers, Gabor writes.[49] From the 1970s onward, the company that had owned 80 percent of the copier market went into permanent decline, losing more than half its market share and selling off assets piece by piece.[50]

Yet the growth-killing legacy of the Whiz Kids in corporate America simply wasn't recognized until years later. And even now, many of the top business schools in the country, a number of which were funded by major grants from the Ford Foundation, continue to teach the tenets of financialization imparted by McNamara and his disciples. American business education, as I will explore further in chapter 3, remains largely a study of finance rather than industry.

In the auto industry itself, GM perhaps more than any other company has embodied the bitter legacy of Taylor, McNamara, and the triumph of bean counters over car guys. While both Ford and Chrysler have been successfully made over in recent years by product-oriented leaders who took the reins from the finance department, GM is only now starting to make those much-needed corrections, as Mary Barra, a career engineer, tries to revamp the once-iconic firm. To be fair, it's a job that involves making deep shifts in the DNA of the company. GM has been divided and sectioned in ways that worked for the bean counters, if not for anyone else, for the past several decades. Up until 1984, product development was managed by three separate divisions within the firm, each of which made protecting its own balance sheet the priority, rather than developing in a collaborative manner the products that customers actually wanted. Costly consultants supporting the bean counters have been rife, and the firm struggled unsuccessfully to implement Asian-style lean manufacturing methods that depended on minute-by-minute collaboration between workers and managers. No wonder—such collaboration necessitated trust, and one of the legacies of a top-down, systems-oriented approach popularized by Taylor and later the Whiz Kids was that no one except the guys at the top were trusted to make decisions.

Barra recognizes that making the company successful will require moving to a new paradigm and creating a workforce full of employees who can step outside their boxes and contribute in creative ways to corporate success. Already she has streamlined the corporate structure in ways that allow different divisions to communicate more freely. She's also rewritten the corporate mission statement to explicitly put the customer first (the fact that this counts as a major breakthrough tells you how far GM has to go). But creating a culture of makers that supports collaboration and a commitment to product excellence rather than financial metrics is a long, slow slog. It requires focusing not on numbers, but on products and the people who make them—the exact opposite of what Taylor or Mc-Namara would have done. It's about building strong teams, rather than manufacturing balance sheets that look good to investors. Indeed, there's a large and growing body of research showing that great teams, not all-powerful leaders, are the connective tissue of companies that perform better over the long haul, and that financialization and team building are antithetical.[51]

Barra, who is the first engineer to head GM after a long line of bean counters, is trying hard to effect those kinds of changes. On a muggy summer day in 2014, I watched her walk the line at a plant in Burton, Michigan, where factory laborers were piecing together revamped ignition switch packages. She stood alongside an hourly employee, who was wearing a World War II–era "We Can Do It" T-shirt, and worked the line herself, dropping parts at first, then picking them back up and recalibrating her hand movements until she was able to keep pace. At one point she stopped near a worker using a small magnetic tool to lift tiny parts and move them into place more precisely. "That's so interesting. I've never seen that tool before," Barra said. The worker, a middle-aged African American woman, told her she had picked it up herself at a dollar store. Barra beamed. "What a clever idea. That's so creative."

Later, in a meeting with senior staff, Barra recounted the event, lauding it as an example of how she wants people to problem-solve for themselves. It's a small moment, but one that, if replicated at scale, could have enormous consequences for the firm. Instead of imparting received wisdom from the bean counters about how work should be done, a line worker in one factory told her CEO how it might be done better. It's something that neither Taylor nor McNamara nor any of their disciples who are still rife in the American business world would have advocated. But it's exactly the sort of shift that will help GM move from being a taker, to a maker.

CHAPTER 3

WHAT AN MBA WON'T TEACH YOU

*How Business Education Is Failing
American Businesses*

IF ADAM SMITH had a mind meld with Charles Darwin, Andrew Lo—a man who has brought evolutionary theory to economics— might result. A professor at the Massachusetts Institute of Technology's Sloan School of Management, Lo is known for his multidisciplinary approach to finance, using everything from statistical analysis to neuroscience to better understand the markets. A few years back, he was given the biggest research challenge of his life, when his beloved mother, a Chinese immigrant who had left a difficult husband to raise Lo and his two siblings alone in New York City, was diagnosed with lung cancer.

Eager to understand her prognosis and make sure she was getting the best care, Lo went straight into research mode. A colleague at the university introduced him to the chief scientific officer of a biotech firm in Cambridge, one that was developing an experimental drug for exactly the type of cancer his mother had. The CSO and the chief financial officer, who had studied Lo's work in grad school, agreed to meet with the professor and discuss the trajectory of their treatments and whether they might help his mom. "During that conversation, I asked what I thought was an innocent question," says Lo. "What influence does your source of financing have, if any, on your scientific agenda?" The two executives looked at each other and laughed ruefully. Then the CSO turned back to him and gave an answer that left him speechless: "Influence? Finance *drives* our research agenda."

As the son of a patient depending on the company's treatment to save her life, Lo found that answer outrageous. "What do stock market volatility, interest rates, and Fed policy have to do with whether you can cure cancer by angiogenesis or immunotherapy?" he asks. "Nothing. But it drove their agenda. And this was a *successful* company, not a struggling one."

Lo began to dig deeper into the economic model of the pharmaceutical industry. And what he found horrified him. While the decoding of the human genome has presented incredible new opportunities for breakthrough drugs and therapies in everything from cancer to dementia, investment into early-stage biotech and pharmaceutical research and development was actually *decreasing*. The number of new firms being started was declining. And the number of venture capitalists investing in the area was going down, too—from 201 firms in 2008 to a mere 137 by 2013. Why was this happening? Because even as genomic research has made more potential drug targets available, it made it harder and harder to pick winners, due to the multitude of possibilities out there. Opportunity was increasing, in other words, but so were complexity and risk—both of which were things that business programs teach corporate leaders to studiously avoid. A typical CFO, for example, looks at a new drug investment and sees that there's only a 5 percent chance it will become a blockbuster—so he chooses to invest in something already in development, or to sit on the cash altogether. The result? "The really innovative stuff doesn't get funded," says Lo.[1]

That's certainly the case at Pfizer, one of the largest drug manufacturers in the world, which in mid-2015 had more than $30 billion worth of cash on its balance sheet.[2] Pfizer provoked ire from politicians and the public alike in 2015 by acquiring a Dublin-based firm, Allergan, as a way to domicile itself abroad to avoid paying US tax rates (a huge irony given how much the firm has benefited from taxpayer money in the form of National Institutes of Health funding for the basic research that made many of its breakthroughs possible).[3] Yet even beyond this politically left-footed action, Pfizer behaves more like a taker than a maker. The money in its corporate coffers isn't being used to fund the sort of R&D that led to the creation of past blockbuster medications like Lipitor and Viagra. Rather, says Lo, Pfizer is using the cash "the way their investors want them to, which is focusing on acquisitions that will improve their stock multiple." That means spending on mergers (many of which have failed) rather than on the early-stage research that creates new wonder drugs.

Naturally, it's a tendency that Wall Street has wholeheartedly supported. One resonant 2010 Morgan Stanley report called for the pharmaceutical industry to "exit research [meaning the search for new drugs] and create value," by throwing cash back to shareholders or buying up companies that could create short-term revenue streams, if not longer-term profits.[4] Of course, the term *value* has a different meaning for shareholders than for patients. Consider the story of another pharmaceutical company, Valeant, which is a classic example of how to create faux, financially driven growth rather than the real kind. Until 2015, this Canadian-based company was one of the world's fastest-growing drug developers, buying up firm after firm, ratcheting up drug prices above industry norms, and using legal but dubious accounting standards to make its earnings look better on paper—all the while cutting back R&D. But investors eventually found out what was behind the company's growth facade, and its stock fell like a stone: it lost $60 billion in value between August and November 2015.[5]

Valeant might be a particularly unscrupulous drug firm, but much of Big Pharma has taken Wall Street's advice and used mergers and acquisitions (M&A) and other financial strategies, rather than true innovation, to buoy growth. Pharmaceutical executives could have bucked the trend; companies like Pfizer don't need any cash from the public markets right now. But many of the people who run these companies have MBAs from the top business schools in the country. And they are doing exactly what Finance 101 classes at such schools tell them to do—which is to minimize the amount of cash at risk and increase shareholder value, at all costs. That meant cutting nearly 150,000 jobs across the pharma sector, most of which were in R&D, between 2008 and 2013.[6] It also meant outsourcing more research and turning formerly great pharmaceutical innovators into entities that look suspiciously like portfolio management companies—a group of disparate firms operating separately and trying to make as much money as quickly as possible, with little thought to the long-term impact of their decisions. Even as the pharmaceutical industry was getting less and less funding, drug firms themselves were starting to look more and more like giant financial institutions that sucked out value but created little in return.

It's ironic that the very financial courses taught at a typical MBA program that would advise CEOs to make such cuts would also insist that markets are efficient. Finance 101 teaches that capital will go where it's most needed to create the products and services that consumers want. Yet, clearly, in the pharmaceutical industry (not to mention any number of other industries) that isn't happening. It's just one of many examples of how business education doesn't prepare our future business leaders for the reality of what happens in actual firms and in the capital markets. Instead of turning the finest business minds into innovators and job creators, it's turning the people who will run the next generation of American businesses into glorified number crunchers. Business education, it turns out, is failing business.

A FAILING GRADE

After the financial crisis of 2008, many people predicted that there would be a crisis of capitalism. The best and the brightest would forgo careers filled with financial ledgers and become teachers or engineers, or start small businesses. Needless to say, that didn't happen. In fact, getting an MBA has never been a more popular career path. The number of MBAs graduating from America's business schools has skyrocketed since the 1980s. But over that time, the health of American business has decreased by many metrics: corporate R&D spending,[7] new business creation,[8] productivity,[9] and the level of public trust in business in general.[10]

There are many reasons for this, most of which will be covered in various chapters of this book. But one key factor is that the basic training that future business leaders in this country receive is dictated not by the needs of Main Street but by those of Wall Street. With very few exceptions, MBA education today is basically an education in finance, not business—a major distinction. So it's no wonder that business leaders make many of the finance-friendly decisions illustrated in this book. MBA programs don't churn out innovators well prepared to cope with a fast-changing world, or leaders who can stand up to the Street and put the long-term health of their company (not to mention their customers) first; they churn out followers who learn how to run firms by the numbers. Despite the financial crisis of 2008, most top MBA programs in the United States still teach standard "markets know best" efficiency theory and preach that share price is the best representation of a firm's underlying value, glossing over the fact that the markets tend to brutalize firms for long-term investment and reward them for short-term paybacks to investors. (Consider that the year Apple debuted the iPod, its stock price fell roughly 25 percent, yet it rises every time the company hands cash back to shareholders.)[11]

This dysfunction is reflected at both a philosophical and a practical level. Business schools by and large teach an extremely limited notion of "value," and of who corporate stakeholders are. Many courses offer a pretense of data-driven knowledge without a rigorous understanding and analysis of on-the-ground facts (one of Andrew Lo's pet peeves, as we will see). Students are given little practical experience but lots of high-altitude postulating. They learn complex mathematical models and ratios, but these are in many cases skills that are becoming somewhat devalued. As Nitin Nohria, dean of the Harvard Business School, admits, "anyone can teach you how to read a P&L [profit-and-loss statement] or value a derivative; those kinds of things have become commoditized."[12] The bigger challenge is to teach America's future business leaders how to be curious, humane, and moral; how to think outside the box about problems like funding the research for a new blockbuster drug. And how to be strong enough to stand up to Wall Street when it demands the opposite.

Sadly, most business schools in America aren't doing that. What's more, unlike those in many other countries, they aren't so much teaching the specifics of the industries students want to enter, or even broader ideas about growth and innovation, as they are training future executives to manage P&Ls. It is very telling that Finance 101 is always a mandatory MBA course, while most others are not.[13] But finance isn't taught in a way that is rigorous, or truly representative of the real world. Financial risk modeling, one of the basic concepts taught in business schools, is an inexact science at best; many people feel it's more like rune reading. After all, it involves throwing thousands of variables about all the bad things that could happen into a black box, shaking them up with the millions of positions taken daily by banks, and extrapolating it all into a simple, easy-to-understand number about how much is likely to be lost if things go belly-up. What could possibly go wrong, especially when you're relying on past assumptions ("the sovereign debts of the United States and Europe will never be downgraded!") and don't account for the fact that market-moving events often create their own momentum?[14] Yet the notion that financial models can reveal truth is still taken as fact in most business schools—that was, of course, one of the key factors that fueled the great financial crisis of 2008. "The premise of financial theory [taught in MBA programs] is bogus," says Robert Johnson, an economist and former quantitative trader for George Soros's Quantum fund who now heads the Institute for New Economic Thinking, an influential group that, among other things, is trying to broaden the nature of economics and business education. "That's why we end up living with very thin margins of safety—because of the pretense of knowledge and precision about the future which does not exist."[15]

Meanwhile, the social, moral, and even larger macroeconomic consequences of corporate actions are largely ignored in the case studies students pore over. Even after the financial crisis, a survey of the world's one hundred top business schools (most of them in the United States) found that only half of all MBA programs make ethics a required course, and only 6 percent deal with issues of sustainability in their core curriculum,[16] despite the fact that a large body of research shows that firms that focus on these issues actually have higher longer-term performance.[17] Instead, students are taught that what matters most is maximizing profits and bolstering a company's share price. It's something they carry straight with them to corporate America.

People do keep heading to business school, though—in large part because business, and in particular the business of finance, is where the money is. A full quarter of American graduate students earn a master's degree in business, more than the combined share of master's degrees sought in the legal, health, and computer science fields (business is also far and away the most popular undergraduate degree).[18] The greatest percentage of those who receive an MBA degree end up not in industry, but in some area of finance. Although figures have dropped somewhat since the financial crisis of 2008, the financial conglomerate—banking, insurance, hedge funds, investment management, and consulting firms—is still the largest single block of MBA employers, along with the accounting and finance departments of Fortune 500 companies. Given that the quickest path to being a CEO these days is through a finance track, many of the top decision makers in the largest and most powerful firms not only have an MBA, but come from one of a handful of elite programs, like Harvard, Chicago, Columbia, and Wharton. "[Within] the first three months of your MBA program, you're surrounded by people in suits," says one 2015 graduate of Columbia Business School. "It's not peer pressure, but there's definitely a social element to feeling like you want to revert back to mainstream [areas of employment] with job security."[19] She, like most of her peers, is planning to work for a consulting firm, an investment bank, or a private equity shop upon graduation. Given the six-figure cost of an MBA education, that's not so much a choice for many students as it is a financial necessity.

Yet ironically, many business leaders, even those who have MBAs themselves, have begun to question the value of these programs. "I went to business school before I knew any better, kind of like sailors get tattoos," jokes former GM vice chairman Bob Lutz, whose book *Car Guys vs. Bean Counters* decries the rise of the MBAs. The problem with business education, according to him, is that students are taught not what happens in real business—which tends to be unpredictable and messy—but a series of techniques and questions that should take them to the right answers, no matter what the problem is. "The techniques, if you read the Harvard Business School cases, they are all about finding efficiencies, cost optimization, reducing your [product] assortment, buying out competitors, improving logistics, getting rid of too many warehouses, or putting in more warehouses. It's all words, and then there's a sea of numbers, and you read it all and analyze your way through this batch of charts and numbers, and then you figure out the silver bullet: the problem is X. And you're then considered brilliant." The real problem, says Lutz, is that the case studies are static—they don't reflect the messy, emotional, dynamic world of business as it is. "In these studies, annual sales are never in question. I've never seen a Harvard Business School case study that says, 'Hey, our sales are going down and we don't know why. Now what?'"[20]

As we read in chapter 2, Lutz believes this kind of approach was one of the things that tanked the American automobile industry and manufacturing in general from the 1970s onward. He's not alone. Many of America's iconic business leaders believe an MBA degree makes you less equipped to run a business well for the long term, particularly in high-growth, innovation-driven industries like pharmaceuticals or technology, which depend on leaders who are willing to invest in the future.

MBAs are everywhere, yet the industries where you find fewer of them tend to be the most successful. America's shining technology and innovation hub—Silicon Valley—is relatively light on MBAs and heavy on engineers. MBAs had almost nothing to do with the two major developments in the American business landscape over the last forty years: the Japanese-style quality revolution in manufacturing and the digital revolution.[21] Indeed, the top-down, hierarchical, financially driven management style typically taught in business schools is useless in flat, nimble start-up companies that create the majority of jobs in the country. Moreover, when that style *is* imposed on Silicon Valley firms, they typically falter (think of John Sculley, the Wharton MBA who made the ill-fated decision to oust Steve Jobs after his first tenure at Apple, or the reign of Carly Fiorina at HP, during which that company's stock lost half its value). One of the scariest trends in business these days is the increased movement of MBAs and finance types into the technology industry. They now are bringing their focus on financial engineering and balance sheet manipulation to firms such as Google, Apple, Facebook, Yahoo, and Snapchat—a shift that, if history is any indicator, doesn't bode well for the future of such firms.

Why has business education failed business? Why has it fallen so much in love with finance and the ideas it espouses? It's a problem with deep roots, which have been spreading for decades. It encompasses issues like the rise of neoliberal economic views as a challenge to the postwar threat of socialism. It's about an academic inferiority complex that propelled business educators to try to emulate hard sciences like physics rather than take lessons from biology or the humanities. It dovetails with the growth of computing power that enabled complex financial modeling. The bottom line, though, is that far from empowering business, MBA education has fostered the sort of short-term, balance-sheet-oriented thinking that is threatening the economic competitiveness of the country as a whole. If you wonder why most businesses still think of shareholders as their main priority or treat skilled labor as a cost rather than an asset—or why 80 percent of CEOs surveyed in one study said they'd pass up making an investment that would fuel a decade's worth of innovation if it meant they'd miss a quarter of earnings results[22]—it's because that's exactly what they are being educated to do.

HOW BUSINESS EDUCATION CAME TO SERVE FINANCE

Business wasn't always taught the way it is today. For a long time it wasn't taught at all; corporate leaders were people who operated more on instinct than training, as evidenced by the fact that only one-fifth of them even had a college degree at the turn of the century, let alone an MBA.[23] Wharton, the school founded to teach the topic in the late nineteenth century, offered classes that were primarily vocational and dedicated to growing local business ecosystems. The same was true of many other institutions. The Eastman Schools, founded by the father of George Eastman, the creator of Kodak, had divisions in St. Louis and three upstate New York cities; E. G. Folsom's Commercial College, connected to the merchant community of Cleveland, focused on the Midwest.[24] Just as business is still taught in places like Germany or France today, there was a focus on industry-specific expertise and the practical problems of real firms in the real world. Students had to understand each sector from the ground up, and there was substantial focus on areas like labor relations, government relations, and engineering. Classes on ethics flourished. Joseph Wharton, the Philadelphia industrialist and devout Quaker who founded his namesake school, felt that commerce had a crucial role to play in solving the social problems of the day, namely growing inequality, job disruption, and urbanization. "No country," he argued, "can afford to have this inherited wealth and capacity wasted for want of that fundamental knowledge which would enable the possessors to employ them with advantage to themselves and to the community."[25]

The role of business in society began to change following the Great Depression, though, in part because business itself was very much on the defensive. The 1929 market crash and the dark days that followed had led to a sense that capitalism had failed. Titans of industry felt the need to hunker down in their bunkers of commerce and find new ways to justify themselves, as well as to fight off what was already seen as a rising political challenge from the Soviet Union. This created strong resistance to any kind of more expansive labor relationships of the kind practiced in Germany (where the state, business, and workers have always collaborated) and strengthened the focus on number crunching and cash management. By the 1950s, business schools in the United States were teaching the sort of data-driven operations and systems research popularized by RAND and taken up so vigorously by policy makers and executives like Robert McNamara.[26]

All of it was facilitated by the rise of a more mathematically focused economics, powered by giant new computers. The machines tallied reams of data from which practitioners of business education could spin strategies that, whether or not they worked in the real world, would certainly sound convincing to the public at large. (RAND itself funded a number of fellowships for graduate students interested in using their methodology at institutions like Harvard, Stanford, Yale, Chicago, and Columbia.)[27] Convincing people that American-style business was working, and working well, was crucial to a conservative elite worried about communism. "We face a long continuing struggle throughout the world for men's minds and indeed for men's souls. . . . The best way to preserve our system is to make it work," said Harvard Business School dean Donald K. David in a speech to a group of leading business executives in 1948. "To me the brightest ray of hope in these troubled times is my firm belief that the business men can and will measure up to the task."[28]

America's capitalists, along with their philanthropies, soon went into overdrive to create a new kind of business education to support this campaign. The Ford and Carnegie foundations in particular, but also others like the Walgreen Foundation (established by the communist-hating drugstore titan Charles Walgreen), began giving donations to support an approach to business that would make it seem more serious and weighty, a "real science" to be contended with. Business and economics education began to develop a notion of itself as a hard science. One of the watershed moments for this new school of thought was the publication in 1947 of economist Paul Samuelson's *Foundations of Economic Analysis*, which laid out the case for a new approach to economic thinking—one that resembled the abstract, hyperrational field of physics much more than the messy reality of the social sciences.

Indeed, the language of the time makes it clear that the elites were a bit embarrassed about any ties that business education might have to actual factory floors. "The day of the truly professional general management man isn't here yet, but it's not far away. That man will be trained for management in general, rather than in any one phase of business. He'll learn his technique in school, rather than on the job," proclaimed a 1952 issue of *BusinessWeek* that looked at the rise of this new paradigm.[29]

It was the era of the rational manager, after all. Just as Frederick Winslow Taylor had used numerical efficiency to whip factory production and workers into shape, business schools using the same operational research methodology employed by the Defense Department would make management "scientific" and churn out the cadres of corporate followers so famously captured by William H. Whyte in his 1956 book *The Organization Man*. These managers were loyal and hardworking but learned to never rock the boat or question those above them. Some experts were concerned that business schools were simply producing a bunch of capitalist sheep. The management guru Peter Drucker, in particular, worried that "business schools no longer see themselves as social instruments. They want to be 'respectable,' as say mathematics departments are respectable. But this is wrong. Professional schools are not intellectual institutions but social institutions. Old-timers at the business schools had one great strength; they knew what they were talking about."[30]

Given their underdog complex in relation to either the liberal arts or the hard sciences, business schools increasingly began employing PhDs who specialized in neoclassical economics—a field that was gaining prestige thanks to the increased focus on mathematical modeling and data analysis. This is still largely true today. Never mind that these models often had little to do with real-world business and were always theoretical; the belief was that such modeling made economics and business educators more like their peers in the math or physics departments, which was a step up in terms of academic status. The epicenter of all this free-market, mathematical, model-oriented thinking was the University of Chicago. It was, after all, the home of Milton Friedman, the economist known perhaps more than any other for the "markets know best" argument. Educated at both Chicago and Columbia, Friedman gained exposure to the McNamara-style systems analysis via a stint at the US Navy–sponsored Statistical Research Group (which operated at Columbia during the war). Two other young economists he worked with there, George Stigler and W. Allen Wallis, also went on to become professors at Chicago. Together they developed what became known as the Chicago School of economics. Its antigovernment, antiregulation, fanatically pro-market ideology has dominated American economics and business education ever since.

With the support of major business foundations like Ford, Chicago began pulling in the biggest economic names in the field. The Walgreen Foundation, which had been a longtime supporter of the school, shifted its financial grants to the business program. (Charles Walgreen had earlier removed his niece from the university on the grounds that she was being taught "communistic views"; his foundation aimed to counterbalance those with ideas that would "foster greater appreciation of American life and values.")[31] Chicago became the center of an increasingly vigorous push for deregulation and support for large corporations. The laissez-faire theories were supported by reams of data produced by giant computers on the university premises (Chicago had some of the top technology at the time, thanks to its Defense Department ties). The result was a very finance-driven approach to business education, in which the central questions were no longer about companies, but about markets—a way of thinking that one recent account describes as "free-market-oriented and interested only in the predictive power of theory, irrespective of the realism of assumptions."[32] This new approach may have been more theoretical than practical, but it was quickly embraced and became de rigueur for anyone who wanted a career in corporate America or the finance industry.

MAXIMIZE VALUE—BUT FOR WHOM?

The key assumption of the Chicago School, one that Milton Friedman himself upheld devoutly, was that the purpose of the corporation was to maximize financial value. As Friedman famously said back in 1970, "the social responsibility of business is to increase its profits."[33] This went hand in hand with another idea, which was that the share price of a firm always perfectly reflected all known information, and thus stock prices were the best overall measure of corporate value. This idea, known as the "efficient-market hypothesis," eventually won its creator, another Friedman disciple and Chicago academic, Eugene Fama, the Nobel Prize.

Ironically, Fama won it jointly in 2013 with Robert Shiller, a Yale economist whose work basically said the opposite—that markets, and asset values, were influenced by a variety of things (emotions, biases, bad habits, and pure chance) that had little to do with efficiency, and that they didn't always work well, or predictably.[34] The joint prize to the two men, one representing the past and the other the future, expresses as well as anything the existential crisis that has beset the economics profession. Like physics with its complex yet unproven string theory, economics and business education has become prisoner to the received wisdom of efficient-market theory and neoliberal thought. Business schools continue to teach it, and probably will keep doing so until the current generation of academics is eclipsed by a younger one (as the physicist Max Planck so aptly put it, "science progresses funeral by funeral"). Yet new research shows just how much of what happens in our economy and society is irrational, unpredictable, and better thought of in terms of fluid human experience than rigid mathematical modeling.

Indeed, the most vibrant area of study today is behavioral economics, a field that takes all of this into account, and for which Shiller won his Nobel. He points out that while behavioral economics is often thought of as "soft" science, in comparison to classical thinking, it's behaviorists who actually go out into the field and collect *real* data about what's happening on Main Street. Despite all the complex financial modeling done by neoliberal economists, "a lot of [economics and business school professors] don't collect and plot real data from the real world and look at it as part of their research," says Shiller. "They consider it a bit beneath them."[35] MIT professor Andrew Lo, whose research builds on many of Shiller's ideas, agrees. He remembers a colleague once walking in on him while he was analyzing some technical data. "He looked at me and said, 'Jeez, why are you doing that?' It was like I was reading a porn magazine or something!"[36]

The idea that what happens on Main Street isn't worthy of the attention of "real economists" will eventually change—many of the top talents in economics and business education are being drawn into behavioral work. But change in academia moves at a snail's pace. And back in the late 1970s, behavioral economics was a nascent idea, while efficient-markets theory ruled. Its ascension eventually led another pair of Chicago-educated academics, Michael Jensen and William Meckling, to develop a management framework that would further reshape both business education and the corporate landscape: agency theory, or the notion that managers should be treated like owners, and paid in stock, to boost corporate performance. It's a framework that is still front and center in MBA curriculums. Jensen and Meckling were, not surprisingly, disciples of Friedman and Eugene Fama. And ironically, given the damage it would do to any number of firms, their idea was a response to a growing worry, sparked in the 1970s, that American business actually wasn't really all that healthy at its core. Despite the confidence of the "organization man" and the large, global enterprises that he ran, a series of events—from oil shocks to higher inflation to swift advances into manufacturing being made by emerging economies like China and

India—made people fear that the United States was losing ground. Postwar prosperity, which had always been taken as a given, was no longer guaranteed. The poverty rate was rising, inequality was on the upswing, and the hollowing out of American manufacturing had begun: that sector's contribution to GDP dropped from 24 percent to around 17 percent in the mid-1970s.[37] The term *Rust Belt* was invented to describe the collapse of once-great industrial cities like Buffalo, Pittsburgh, Cleveland, and Detroit. Sociologists found that trust in business was declining, and workers at big companies like GM were regularly turning up late or not at all. Unions, CEOs, consumers—pretty much any constituency you could think of—were lobbying for change in the business and regulatory environment (this deep dissatisfaction helped trigger, among other things, the push for deregulation, as we saw in chapter 1).

There was a particular concern that large, complex, and diversified organizations had given rise to a divergence of interests between managers and shareholders; indeed, many economists considered that gap to be the root of America's declining competitiveness. While the former, who were basically trained to be pliant company men, could take it easy and be guaranteed lifetime employment in large corporate bureaucracies, the latter were losing ground as profits and shares fell. The solution: align the incentives of the two better by rating managers on a very specific set of financial metrics, and pay a greater percentage of their salaries in stock options. Boards would watch over the managers, making sure they did whatever was designed to boost share price. Never mind that these theories were cooked up in college classrooms and on computers rather than in real businesses.

Agency theory took hold quickly. Jensen and Meckling's ideas were lauded in the *Wall Street Journal* and the *Harvard Business Review* and used as fuel in the legislative fight to increase limits on executive stock options, as well as justification for corporate raiders and greenmailers, such as T. Boone Pickens. Like many takeover titans, Pickens thought CEOs were mostly lazy, self-interested, and insulated. "US executives . . . look at takeovers as a threat to their salaries and their perks," said Pickens at the time. "And the reason they perceive it this way is that they generally own very little stock in their own companies. They don't relate to the shareholders' interests, because they aren't substantial shareholders themselves."[38] Indeed, academics like Jensen believed that people like Pickens were "inventors" who brought needed discipline to America's large and sloppily run corporations. In this line of thinking, Pickens, Carl Icahn, Henry Kravis, and other "barbarians at the gate" weren't predators but rather protectors of capitalism, in the sense that they would swoop in and clean out the dead wood from firms. It's a rationale that's still being used by activist investors like Icahn today; as he once put it to me, boards are typically made up of friends of the CEO, usually ones who are less clever than he, and who tend to act in their own interests. "Many businesses in this country are terribly run," Icahn said. "While there are a number of good board members, you've got some board members making four hundred thousand dollars a year that are actually counterproductive. They're not going to go against their buddy [the CEO] who put them there."[39]

That's often true, but the real reason that corporate governance in this country isn't stronger is that all the incentive structures for board members and CEOs alike are working against long-term decision making. It's an issue called the "principal-agent problem" in academic circles. The collusion isn't so much between the CEO and his golf buddies as it is between corporate executives and financiers. CEOs today have every reason to bolster short-term share price value, as the Street wants them to, because it will also result in higher compensation for *them*, since most executives receive the bulk of their compensation in stock options. Wall Street analysts, whose ratings help dictate the value of firms in the marketplace, typically look at only the yearly cash flow projections of a firm. (Never mind that McKinsey data shows that between 70 and 90 percent of the real value of any corporation tends to be tied to revenues three years or more out.)[40] The result is that business leaders paid mostly in stock race to hit the numbers rather than simply making the best decisions for their businesses for the long term. "This is one reason why, when finance is wrecking the performance of corporate America, it doesn't lead to a rebellion at the US Chamber of Commerce," says Johnson of the Institute for New Economic Thinking.[41]

This phenomenon puts American businesses at a terrible disadvantage compared to overseas competitors, like family-owned emerging-market firms or European companies in which there's a broader stakeholder model of governance that helps mitigate such pressures. "This is one of the things that constantly hits me when I travel in Asia," says McKinsey head Dominic Barton, who has written on the topic of short-termism in American business for the *Harvard Business Review*. "[Foreign firms] are just working with timeframes of a totally different order. They simply don't have the same short-term pressure that many American businesses do."[42] Indeed, emerging-market firms, particularly in Asia, often think in terms of decades rather than quarters.

The idea that companies should be explicitly managed for the benefit of shareholders, and shareholders alone, to the exclusion of anyone or anything else, is an odd system in the global context. Most firms in Germany, China, France, and Scandinavia, along with many others in countries like India and Brazil, aren't primarily managed this way. Indeed, it took quite a while for American business leaders to buy into the idea, despite the fact that it was being pushed vigorously in both business schools and the markets. As recently as 1990, the Business Roundtable, a group of CEOs from America's largest and most powerful companies, said in its mission statement that it was "the directors' responsibility to carefully weigh the interests of all stakeholders as part of their responsibility to the corporation or to the long-term interests of its shareholders." Seven years later, though, the group had finally caved, rewriting the statement to say that "the paramount duty of management and of boards of directors is to the corporation's stockholders; the interests of other stakeholders are relevant as a derivative of the duty to stockholders."[43] Today, whether they believe it or not, it's rare to find a CEO of a public company who doesn't publicly buy into the idea of shareholder value. Indeed, the only leaders who can openly question this notion and get away with it tend to be high-profile founder-owners who have a certain cult of personality (Alibaba's Jack Ma and Starbucks's Howard Schultz are two who regularly accomplish that feat).

Yet, sadly, if you sit in a Finance 101 class at any top business school today—Harvard, Wharton, Stanford, and the like—you'll learn pretty much what you would have learned three or four decades ago: that shareholder value comes before anything else. You'll also hear some of the core teachings in such classes, which are mandatory for MBA students: that people are guided by rational self-interest to make the best economic decisions; that the purpose of business is to make money and provide value to investors; and that a firm's share price, rather than its underlying technologies, innovative capacity, human resources, or social benefit, is the measure of its success. Bolstering it by whatever means necessary, MBA programs teach, is the raison d'être of the managing class. It's a guiding purpose that has not only led firms to undercut their long-term prospects and put enormous pressure on leaders themselves (CEOs today have a shelf life of less than ten years[44]), but has created a business managing class that, unlike peers in professions such as medicine, or law, or many parts of the arts, are cut off from any larger commitment to bettering society as a whole.

One Aspen Institute survey that followed a group of MBA students throughout their schooling found that their values changed, and not for the better, during the course of their time on campus.[45] The students began their studies in what the survey called "customer mode," believing that corporations should be run for the benefit of a large group of stakeholders, from workers to customers to society as a whole. By the end of their second semester, however, students shifted to "business manager mode," placing more emphasis than before on maximizing shareholder returns and less on producing high-quality goods and services—a change that, the survey said, reflected "the powerful place shareholders occupy in the first-year curriculum." Business schools teach, quite literally, that greed is good, and that rational self-interest is economically and socially beneficial. But if there is anything that the last few years of economic crisis, recession, and slow painful rebound have taught us, it's that the conventional economic wisdom doesn't always work.

THE MORALITY OF BUSINESS EDUCATION

An increasing number of business educators at top schools are concerned not only that MBA programs are churning out number crunchers without consciences, but that the programs themselves no longer uphold the mission of America's top universities, which has always been to preserve, create, and transmit knowledge to advance the public good. That's exactly the concern voiced by Harvard Business School professor Rakesh Khurana, whose book *From Higher Aims to Hired Hands* tracks the evolution of business education in America over the last century. Khurana makes a powerful case that the paradigm of business education must become more inclusive, broad-based, and socially responsible if we are to avoid Thomas Piketty's predictions of growing inequality, political dysfunction, and social instability.

It's a moral shift that can't come soon enough. One of the most corrosive effects of Chicago School thinking and teaching on American business education is that it detached the latter from its roots in morality and social responsibility, the very Calvinist foundations on which it was built in the late nineteenth century. The Whiz Kids' Cold War–era approach to management may have been too ideological, but agency theory and common assumptions about the ingrained efficiency of markets left business leaders with no moral basis on which to operate at all. In fact, the theories basically espoused a selfish view of the world, in which everyone was out to get what they could, and nobody could be trusted. In this world, which was first and foremost about profit making for a small group of people, everything was and should be transactional. It's perhaps no wonder, then, that MBA students and American managers themselves evolved to take this cool and calculating perspective on things. As Harold Leavitt, the late Stanford management psychologist, once put it, "the new professional MBA-type manager" has begun "to look more and more like the professional mercenary soldier—ready and willing to fight any war and to do so coolly and systematically, but without ever asking the tough pathfinding questions: Is this war worth fighting? Is it the right war? Is the cause just? Do I believe in it?"[46]

Before the financial crisis, business schools did very little to address public concerns about things like inequality, the growing number of corporate scandals, or executive malfeasance. Had things like the insider trading revelations of the 1980s, the accounting debacles of the 1990s, or the subprime crisis been happening in other industries, it would certainly have provoked more soul searching. (Imagine how medical schools might respond if 80 percent of doctors said they'd do long-term harm to patients in order to get paid immediately.) While there was a hope after the 2008 meltdown that business schools might lead the charge toward a new and more sustainable kind of capitalism, academic leaders in the field have been largely silent, their efforts focused mostly on more marginal issues like promoting more corporate social responsibility or diversity within boardrooms. A few years ago at the World Economic Forum in Davos, Switzerland, I interviewed Harvard Business School dean Nitin Nohria, who was at that point hoping to orchestrate a major post-financial-crisis shift in the MBA curriculum at Harvard. It's been a slow process; the school is only just beginning to develop a curriculum that moves beyond efficiency theory and into more behavioral approaches to business. Classes that deal with the morality and structure of finance, or question our current system of capitalism, are growing in popularity but are still few and far between. Nohria admits that most Harvard business students are still drawn to finance, although more of them now go into venture capital and private equity than investment banking (not surprising, given that's where the big money now is). The percentage of students starting new businesses upon graduation has shot up, but, at 9 percent, it's still less than a third of the share that go into finance.[47]

Clearly, change isn't happening fast enough. And, to be honest, few business professors or students are storming the ramparts and demanding more. This is perhaps to be expected given that the intellectually limited and increasingly commercial nature of business education has resulted in a situation where academics "are hampered by their own lack of a frame of reference within which even to consider the questions now being asked about them," as Khurana puts it.[48] "The ecosystem of business education is sick, yet there's a total sense of powerlessness about changing any of this, even amongst the most powerful people in the world," he adds.[49] The MBA degree has become less a source of valuable education than an exclusive club and passport to wealth for a privileged few. The selfishness inherent in that threatens not only how business is run, says Khurana, but also the academic degree itself, which many believe has become an overpriced commodity.

RESEARCH FOR HIRE

Indeed, academics themselves have in some ways become products that can be bought and sold to the highest bidder. Much of the funding for academic research at top-tier economics departments and business schools comes from the financial industry and people and institutions close to it. In 2011, Gerald Epstein, a professor at the University of Massachusetts Amherst, and his colleague Jessica Carrick-Hagenbarth published a paper on conflict-of-interest issues in academia after the financial crisis. They looked at the media writings, public appearances, and published research of nineteen academic financial economists who belonged to influential groups that advanced recommendations on financial regulation and reform. The authors then analyzed how these economists described their affiliations (with their public academic institutions and, in many cases, private financial firms). The paper concluded that most of the time the economists did not reveal possible conflicts of interest or private industry affiliations when they should have.[50]

One of the more shocking examples of such conflicts of interest was unveiled in the Oscar-winning 2010 documentary *Inside Job*,[51] which examined the policy decisions that led to the financial crisis. Filmmakers profiled Columbia University economist and business school dean Glenn Hubbard, formerly the chief economic adviser to the George W. Bush administration, interviewing him about his role in financial deregulation as well as various private sector associations that may have encouraged him to take a more finance-friendly view to policy issues. These associations included, among others, working as a $1,200-an-hour consultant for Countrywide Financial (a mortgage lender that was deeply involved in the subprime crisis and had to be bailed out by the Fed) and getting paid $100,000 to testify in the defense of Ralph Cioffi and Matthew Tannin, two Bear Stearns hedge fund managers who were prosecuted (and later acquitted) for fraud.[52] Hubbard had also coauthored a Goldman Sachs report in 2004, entitled "How Capital Markets Enhance Economic Performance and Facilitate Job Creation," in which he said that credit derivatives were protecting banks from losses by redistributing risk. He did not disclose how much he was paid to write the report, and in *Inside Job*, he lost it on camera when asked about his consulting clients.[53] The episode eventually led Columbia and a number of other institutions to tighten up their policies around academic conflict of interest.

In fact, schools themselves have become mere products in a marketplace. Academics no longer do research merely on the basis of their personal passions or interests or even the questions they believe to be most important in the world; they now take into account what will "sell" to students and the people who will ultimately hire them (who are, in many ways, the end consumers). Schools market themselves vigorously as "brands" to these prospective "shareholders," with full-page ads in the *Wall Street Journal* and *Financial Times* publicizing their "value proposition." There is little talk of a mission, or the type of education that students might receive from such programs, but there is plenty of "market signaling" about how students can get rich quick if they come to one school or the other. As Khurana lays out, these schools have advertising campaigns to rival the Fortune 500 clients they serve. "Want a hard-working investment?" boomed one advertisement for an MBA program in an in-flight magazine, before boasting of pre- and post-degree salary comparisons. "We don't just teach you how to make and manage solid investments, we'll be one." Another ad proclaims the "high ROI," or return on investment, associated with a degree from the school.[54]

RISE OF THE QUANTS

Bought-and-paid-for academics (and students) are just one systemic problem that is distancing MBA education from the skills required to run real-world businesses. Another is the role that MBA programs have played in destabilizing the financial system itself. Eight years after the 2008 financial crisis, many MBA programs continue to churn out traders who create the kinds of financial weapons of mass destruction that wrecked the financial system in 2008. While American business schools largely missed big-picture shifts like the Japanese-led quality revolution of the 1970s and the PC boom of the late 1970s and '80s (not to mention the rise of massive networking and mobile technologies a decade later), they have led the way in mathematical finance, which became the basis of the shift in banking from lending to trading. These business schools also spurred the growth of the "portfolio society" in which everything—from stocks and bonds to hospital beds and even human lifespans—has a market price. The key early player in this area was Harry Markowitz, another Chicago student who had worked for RAND in the 1950s and did his PhD under Friedman. Markowitz's quantitative finance methodology won him the Nobel Prize and became the basis of the first computerized arbitrage-trading program, which would eventually take over the markets. Today 70–80 percent of all trading is done by computers, much of it using flash programs designed to trade on fractional price changes over split-second time intervals, reducing the average holding period of a stock from about eight years in the 1960s to just four months by 2012.[55]

Emanuel Derman, a quantitative mathematician and physicist who pioneered some of those trading models at Goldman and now teaches financial engineering at Columbia, believes that the focus on mathematical economics in both finance and business education has gone way too far. Indeed, in 2012, he published a mea culpa for his own work in the twentieth-anniversary issue of the *Journal of Derivatives*. "Models of all kinds, ethical and quantitative too, have been behaving very badly," he wrote. The problem, he believes, is that practitioners of quantitative finance have come to believe that it can in fact have the predictive power of physics, when in reality financial modeling will always be fallible, because it's a discipline based on human behavior. "To confuse a model with the world of humans is a form of idolatry—and dangerous."[56]

Yet that danger is only increasing. At places like Harvard, the percentage of MBA students going into finance as a whole has dropped slightly from its peak (31 percent today versus 39 percent before the crisis), but the share who are bringing skills like mathematical finance to areas such as private equity, venture capital, and high tech is increasing.[57] Indeed, at many of the country's top MBA programs, students report that recruitment fairs are still dominated by financiers and financial institutions, whether they be traditional banks and consulting firms or small boutique companies.

This underscores yet another of the most corrosive effects of financialization, which is the brain drain from more productive areas of the economy. Finance is now scooping up the country's brightest people, diverting them from careers that would move our economy forward in more productive ways. Before the 1980s, banking was boring and not nearly as lucrative. But now PhDs who might once have crafted new engines at Boeing or come up with new polymers for Dow can make four to five times those former starting salaries at a hedge fund, where they can busy themselves creating twelve-dimensional computerized trading models. Eleven percent of the undergraduate class at MIT, for example, now goes to Wall Street, and despite the 2008 crisis, financial engineering is the fastest-growing field at many of the country's best engineering schools.[58] "Not only are these people not making scientific progress," says Greg Smith, the former Goldman Sachs quantitative trader who famously published his resignation letter in the *New York Times*, "but the complex derivatives products they create are being sold to unsuspecting public pension funds and investors [who don't know any better]. So there is actually an argument to be made that diverting our smartest PhDs to finance is a waste, at best, and detrimental to [overall economic growth] at worst."[59]

It's an argument that even some of the financial engineers themselves would agree with. Derman, who runs the financial engineering program at Columbia, says that despite the blowback against risky Wall Street trading in the wake of the financial crisis, demand for his classes is as strong as ever. The only thing that's changed, says Derman, "is that students today aren't content to be just traders at a bank; they want to be principals [meaning, heads of their own hedge funds]." Indeed, he says that self-tracking for a career of this kind now begins even earlier than was the case before the crisis. "It used to be that people would come here after a physics or math degree, but now they are coming straight from economics-focused math programs [at the undergraduate level]. It's become a trajectory."

Derman, who himself left a job at Bell Labs to make more money on the Street, understands the lure of a high-paid algorithmic trading job for students who will often end up with hundreds of thousands of dollars in college and graduate school loan debt—a Wall Street career is often the only quick way to financial solvency. But unlike many finance professors, he also tries to engender in his students a sense that algorithmic trading models are just one tool in the banker's toolbox and shouldn't be overrelied upon. Whether the students are listening is another question. It's telling that about 80 percent of Derman's students are now Asian, many of them Chinese, who are bringing the game of financial speculation to their own economies. Much of the latest volatility in commodities trading markets has come from Chinese hedge funds like Shanghai Chaos, which in 2015 helped trigger and exploit a plunge in copper, and Chinese shadow banks responsible for things like the distortion of the global soybean markets.[60]

HUMAN CAPITAL OVER CASH

It's ironic that even as business schools continue to teach linear, traditional, finance- and math-oriented thinking to their students, what American businesses desperately need is not executives who understand only balance sheets, but those who understand people. "Business schools are still teaching that you should run your company the way people did decades ago: marshal your capital, and treat labor like an expendable cost," says Mark Bertolini, the CEO of the health insurance giant Aetna. "But the world has completely changed. We're awash in capital, but there's a shortage of skilled labor out there. Business schools are still using the same old teaching models," despite the fact that we're now "in a world that's so complex, it can't be modeled."[61]

Indeed, in early 2015, Bertolini did something that no business school management course would have recommended: he voluntarily raised the minimum wage in his firm to $16 an hour. Not only was it more than double the amount of the federal minimum wage, but it was also a dollar more than the most generous proposals being bandied about by congressional liberals at the time. The decision was the result of a forensic data dive within his own company. Bertolini had started an internal blog by which he communicated with employees (another thing that nobody is taught to do in business school—executives are supposed to stay in their silos) and quickly began receiving many complaints from workers about how they found it difficult to live and work on the wages and benefits that they were receiving. Bertolini asked managers for more information about these workers, many of whom were on the front lines of customer service in call centers, and discovered to his surprise that basic economic data about the workforce either wasn't being tallied or wasn't readily available. Despite all the spreadsheets being used to calculate costs and profits, nobody knew much about the people who made up Aetna's business. Thus ensued a yearlong journey of data collection. Bertolini discovered that of the 7,000 people interacting with customers on a daily basis, 81 percent were women, most were single moms, and many had children on Medicaid benefits. That's when he began to agitate for higher wages. Despite pushback from his board, he succeeded. "There's a creeping dumbness in being a CEO," says Bertolini. "You have to get behind the numbers, behind the spreadsheets and the sort of thing you are taught to look at in business school. You have to understand problems in human terms."

For Bertolini, raising wages was just good business, despite the fact that it bucked conventional economic and business wisdom. He knows that the health industry, along with nearly every other business, will be using more complex technology in the future and will need to become a more direct-to-consumer business, requiring higher-level skills and superior thinking from employees, even those at entry levels. Increasingly, companies would be in competition for the best workers, and Bertolini wanted to be ready for that with attractive wages and an upward path for his employees. His firm had plenty of cash on hand. What he couldn't find so easily was the kind of worker who could help his business succeed in a more and more complex world. "The day it all went public in the *Wall Street Journal*," says Bertolini, "we began getting lots of calls from other CEOs asking how we'd done this, how we'd made it work." As part of that journey, he is now involved in a working group of other CEOs and academics, the Center for Higher Ambition Leadership, which aims to find ways to humanize business curriculums and build case studies of how to run more economically inclusive and sustainable businesses.

That's a big deal, because when Bertolini first posed the idea of his wage hike to a group of Harvard Business School professors whom he regularly consulted with, they responded negatively. The

CEO, who grew up working class in Detroit and worked a welding line for years before going to college on scholarship, has continued to push forward his agenda within Aetna; in 2015 he gave all his top executives something that's not yet on the typical MBA reading list—a copy of Thomas Piketty's *Capital in the Twenty-First Century*. Companies, says Bertolini, shouldn't just be moneymaking machines. They also have to invest in people, the real economy, and society as a whole if they want to succeed in the long term. "Capital is the resource that we often manage well, but in my opinion, the scarce resource is a talented and engaged workforce." Creating that requires thinking bigger, looking at people as assets, not just costs on a balance sheet, and knowing how to think beyond the quarter. "One of my goals as CEO is to help reestablish the credibility of corporate America," says Bertolini. "That means leaning into the recovering economy and working to bring everyone along, not just a few."

THE FUTURE OF BUSINESS EDUCATION

The sense of value, defined only as economic value without higher moral or social purpose, is what most enraged MIT Sloan School professor Andrew Lo when he began investigating the business model of the pharmaceutical industry. Fortunately, as a business school professor himself, he was in a position to do something about it. While most economists still uphold the efficient-market hypothesis, which posits that all available information is reflected in a stock's price and that investors are rational, Lo believes that markets are less like rule-based physics and more like messy biological systems. In fact, he's come up with an entirely new way of teaching finance—it's called the adaptive-markets hypothesis. In Lo's world, market participants aren't coldly rational creatures but squirmy, evolving species interacting with one another in a primordial sludge of money.

By tracking the data trails left by this Darwinian process, we might be able to get a better picture of how markets really work. Lo's teaching involves not just modeling the abstract, but analyzing the real—what people, companies, regulators, and market participants really do on Main Street. And although he uses many of the tools of quantitative finance in his work, one assumption he never makes is that markets are rational. "Practice without theory is not very effective. And theory without practice can be dangerous," says Lo. "Economics has had physics envy, but ultimately, economics is all about human behavior." Some behavior we can model. But many other times, the directions of the markets and the participants are totally unexpected. By teaching students that, and pushing them to become more curious about the hows and whys of business, Lo hopes he can start changing the way both business education and the markets themselves work. "When I teach introductory finance now, I always include my own theories about adaptive markets; ten years ago, it would have been anathema to try and bring that into the curriculum," he says.

Adaptive-markets hypothesis, which is taught not just by Lo but by an increasing number of professors around the country, is providing a new framework for academics to break down disciplinary silos. Economics and business education is slowly but surely starting to incorporate ideas from psychology, biology, neuroscience, anthropology, sociology, and many other disciplines. As for Lo himself, he has helped start the Office of Financial Research, a forensic-analysis group that sits within the US Treasury Department and came out of the ashes of the financial crisis. It is dedicated to bringing these new tools and insights to the study of financial crises, so that we can better understand them and craft regulation and market structures to prevent them. Perhaps most important to Lo, he has brought some fresh thinking to how both government and business might better support cutting-edge drug development. "We tend to focus in finance on a very narrow set of decisions. But we forget that our own business decisions are happening in the context of a much broader social and economic framework," he says. In his search to find a cure for his mom, Lo realized that pharmaceutical companies had plenty of money—but they were too frightened, because of market pressures and the slim chance of finding breakthrough drugs, to invest it. If he could find a way to help spread that risk, he might be able to encourage more early-stage research and development.

The solution? Not turning pharmaceutical companies into portfolio managers, but creating giant superfunds to support drug research. Lo has come up with a proposal for how to bolster funds for drug development by pooling the resources of individual investors just as mutual funds do, to spread risk by funding not one drug at a time, but 150 drugs. With this level of funding, rather than a 5 percent probability of success, the odds of finding a successful drug among the many being trialed go up exponentially. Lo recently finished working with researchers at the National Institutes of Health, running his model on the portfolio of drugs for rare and neglected diseases that they are currently researching. He found that with an investment of just a few hundred million dollars, private investors (including not only institutions but mom-and-pop types putting in a few thousand dollars) would get a 21.6 percent rate of return on their contributions—and the additional funding would push drug development timelines ahead by many years.

Lo's idea is a case study on how, by stepping outside the realm of conventional wisdom, business educators and business education might actually generate ideas of real economic and social value. Sadly, his epiphany didn't come early enough for his mother, who died of cancer in 2011. But it may help others. His new paradigm for funding research was recently put forward legislatively in Congress by Representative Juan Vargas as a new way of supporting basic science research in the United States. It is also under consideration by a number of private sector firms who are enthusiastic about the new funding model. Once you jettison rigid notions about how finance and business should work, says Lo, "all sorts of new ideas and methodologies" become possible.[62] It's an idea that America's business educators—and the MBA students who'll someday lead the country's top firms—would do well to embrace.

CHAPTER 4

BARBARIANS AT THE GATE

Apple, Carl Icahn, and the Rise of
Shareholder Activism

CARL ICAHN, the richest man on Wall Street and perhaps the most feared corporate raider in the world, has an unexpected talent. He's a terrific mimic. He does dead-on imitations of everyone from the Kansas oil tycoon who tried to give him the boot in his early days as an options dealer ("Cahhhl, I love yah, but I gotta leave yah—mah cousin's in this business now") to the aristocrat whom Icahn helped unload a block of Texaco shares when his cash was tight ("So I say, 'Sir Robert, I hear you got some problems,' and he says, 'Quite correct, quite correct,'" Icahn mocks with a perfect lockjaw), to the trophy wife who complains about people on welfare while entertaining at her Hamptons megamansion, to his own mother. But when I once asked him to do Apple CEO Tim Cook, he declined. "Nah, I can't do Cook. I can only do crazies."[1]

Of course, some people say Cook is crazy to listen to Icahn, who has spent the last several years trying to persuade him to give back more and more of Apple's $200 billion cash hoard to investors in the form of massive share buybacks, instead of investing it back in R&D or product development. This had the effect of pushing up the price of Apple's stock while conveniently increasing the value of Icahn's $7 billion in Apple holdings along with those of all the other Apple investors. In April 2015, Icahn's efforts paid off, bigger than even he could have imagined. Flush with revenues from iPhone sales in China, Apple increased its dividend by 10.6 percent, the largest bump-up for a nonfinancial firm in history, and announced the most massive corporate payout ever: between 2015 and 2017, it would hand back more than $200 billion in the form of dividends and share buybacks to investors like Icahn. Markets, not surprisingly, jumped with joy at this news, as did the billionaire himself, who was, until recently, Apple Inc.'s seventh-largest shareholder. He made $112 million in a single evening of after-hours trading following the announcement, which was in addition to the $125 million he made during regular trading hours. Apple CEO Tim Cook, who in January 2015 owned 950,767 shares of the technology giant, made a pretty penny, too.[2]

Icahn is part of an increasingly powerful wave of opinionated investors who call themselves "shareholder activists"—a clever rebranding of those who used to be known as corporate raiders back in the 1980s. In addition to Icahn, who was around from the start, today's prominent activists include people like Bill Ackman, Daniel Loeb, David Einhorn, and Nelson Peltz. They all have different styles and somewhat different methods for goosing share prices of the companies they get involved with. But the common thread is that they are taking on some of America's most high-profile firms. In addition to Apple, in the past few years, these activists have targeted such large and successful companies as Dell, Yahoo, Dow, JCPenney, GM, DuPont, Sears, and Hewlett-Packard. It's no accident that as the activists have become more and more active, buybacks and dividend payments have reached record levels.

Activist investors like Icahn often get involved in companies when they don't trust the management and want the firm to go in a different direction strategically. But Apple is different. Icahn has said he didn't consider his buyback push and the subsequent payouts an indictment of Cook, who has been at Apple's helm since Steve Jobs died in 2011. "Tim Cook is doing a good job with the business," Icahn told me back in 2013. "I think he's good at running the business whether he does what I want or not. I'm not against the management of this company. . . . They've just got too much money on their balance sheet," he said. "But Apple is not a bank."

It's a statement that has more truth and resonance than even Icahn, the original wolf of Wall Street, might imagine. True, Apple isn't a bank—at least not in name. But in many ways, it acts just like one. The most profitable company in history has, over the last few years, engaged in quite a few banklike activities, including lending money to other firms via the corporate bond market and implicitly backing new debt offerings with the power of its cash hoard, just like an investment bank.[3] Interestingly, though, it's not *regulated* like a bank—which means that in some ways there's even less transparency when Apple does such deals, especially if they are done by private placement rather than in public markets. (Either way, an economist at the Office of Financial Research, the Treasury body set up to monitor financial stability following the 2008 crisis, told me that it was nearly impossible to figure out from public documents what kinds of corporate debt Apple was holding, an issue that becomes worrisome if you consider that should Apple dump such debt, it could have a market-moving effect.)[4]

It has also hoarded cash in overseas bank accounts like it's going out of style, and it engages in the public markets not to raise money for real investments (Apple hasn't needed any risk capital since 1980 when it did its $97 million IPO) but for the purposes of financial wizardry.[5] From August 2012 through March 2015, Apple "returned" more than $112 billion to investors, namely people like Icahn and Cook and the corporate C-suite. Yes, some of those gains went into the coffers of pension funds and average individuals, but stock gains disproportionately enrich the wealthiest tenth of Americans, who own 91 percent of all equities.[6]

It is important to note here that most of those investors, many of them large hedge and private equity funds, have never put a penny into Apple's original technology or productive assets. They certainly didn't invest in the underlying innovations that enriched the firm; most of that was done by the federal government, which came up with the bulk of the technologies that make smartphones smart, including touch screens, GPS, voice activation, and the Internet it-self.[7] Activist investors also had nothing to do with engineering or assembling the final devices that have become the ultimate technology status symbol. That work was done by groups of engineers in Silicon Valley and low-paid factory laborers in Asia. Yet the investors are the ones reaping the vast majority of the rewards from the world's most profitable firm. In 2013 Apple announced it would double its capital-return program to $100 billion, including the largest single share-repurchase authorization in history. It raised the stakes to $130 billion in 2014, then bumped them up again to a record-breaking $200 billion in April 2015.

What's amazing is that despite having 10 percent of corporate America's liquid assets on hand, Apple has *borrowed* most of the money needed to do these massive investor payouts, at the lowest rates in corporate history, in order to avoid taking money out of offshore tax havens and paying the US corporate tax rate on it. Not only does issuing debt in order to hand over cash to investors save Apple billions, it almost always boosts its share price—since buybacks artificially decrease the amount of shares on the market, without actually changing the real value of the company via true strategic investments, like research and development, worker training, or anything else that might bolster the underlying long-term prospects of the firm.

Apple is hardly the only company engaging in this kind of financial engineering. Since 2004, American firms have spent a stunning *$7 trillion* buying back their own stock—the equivalent of half their profits.[8] Historically, when buybacks peak, they are followed by slower growth, a warning sign for today's economy. But buyback wizardry also underscores one of the great ironies of American business today: the country's biggest, richest companies have more contact with investors and capital markets than ever before, yet they don't actually *need* any capital.

And so Apple, one of the most admired firms in the world, now spends as much time and energy thinking about financial engineering, and how to create value with it, as it does about the real kind.

It's an uncomfortable truth that many economists have begun to suspect has a lot to do with our permanently slow-growth economy. "The Icahn/Apple situation is a great example of how financial markets are no longer about raising money for investment, but for arbitrage," the Nobel Prize–winning economist Joseph Stiglitz told me.[9] Money is stuck in all the wrong places and flowing to all the wrong people and things. Corporate winners like Apple accumulate vast amounts of cash, yet rather than paying their taxes or giving workers a pay hike (which would also bolster our consumption-oriented economy), they simply turn over cash to investors, who are unlikely to spend it in a way that creates real growth. There are only so many pairs of designer jeans and luxury handbags that the 1 percent can buy, after all. Stock markets go up as a result of these payouts, but the real economy stagnates.

It's an issue that's thankfully front and center in our national political debate today. Leaders from Massachusetts senator Elizabeth Warren to former presidential candidate Hillary Clinton have decried buybacks as harmful to American competitiveness. In a 2015 speech, Clinton said she wanted to take a "hard look" at the vast amounts of money that companies are pouring into buybacks, a trend that "doesn't leave much money to build a new factory or a research lab, or to train workers, or give them a raise."[10] Warren has gone further, invoking the fact that until 1982, buybacks were considered unlawful market manipulation. It's a key point, particularly given that in the United States, corporations don't have to declare buybacks for a full quarter (in Hong Kong and the UK, they must be disclosed within a day), meaning that firms have plenty of time to use buybacks to bolster their stock and allow executives to cash out before the rest of the market knows what's happening, or why. Then there's the fact that buybacks get preferential tax treatment, and that they often happen at exactly the wrong time—at the top of the market rather than at the bottom—a terrible waste of corporate funds that could go to more productive uses.[11] Most important, the wealth represented by buybacks stays within a closed loop of the financial markets and the asset portfolios of the richest Americans. In other words, buybacks don't facilitate a sharing of America's broadly created business wealth; they promote a hoarding of corporate value within the financial system itself. Buybacks are in most cases the very definition of financialization.

Of course, some would say that the enrichment of corporate titans does create value, in the sense that these capitalists start and invest in companies that create jobs. But the idea that the majority of financiers and C-suite executives (entrepreneurs excluded) are the true "makers" in our economy is clearly a myth, as evidenced by the research cited in the introduction. Apple and the rest of America's export-oriented corporate giants may make plenty of cash, but as a group they have created almost no net new jobs since at least 1990, according to an influential study done for the Council on Foreign Relations.[12] That is largely due to the fact that despite ebbs and flows in economic growth, corporate earnings, and the credit environment in the United States over the last dozen years, America's largest firms taken as a whole haven't invested more than 1–2 percent of their total assets per year into the real economy—real jobs, real goods, real services—over that time.[13]

This lack of productive investment has nothing to do with bank lending, GDP figures, the rise of China, the failure of Europe, increased government regulation, or partisan politics at home. The biggest economic conundrum of our age—why American companies aren't investing the $2 trillion in cash they have sitting on their balance sheets (most of which is held overseas) in factories, workers, and wages—turns out to have an easy answer: they are using it to bolster markets and enrich the 1 percent instead.

This isn't just a matter of social justice. You don't have to view inequality as a moral issue to appreciate that this consolidation of wealth isn't good for growth—countless data shows that affluent people, like companies, tend to hoard cash (in bank accounts, stocks, bonds, etc.) rather than spend it. When money goes mainly to the 1 percent, it stays in that closed circuit of financial markets that was described earlier. By and large, it doesn't (despite claims to the contrary) trickle down into the sort of *new* investments—in businesses, factories, and jobs—that create real economic growth. That's not the way financial markets were supposed to work. They were supposed to funnel money to *new* assets and ventures. The great irony of financialization is that it produces bad finance.

How did we get to a place in which financial markets have become an insulated system that enriches mainly the wealthy? It's all part of a shift from a system in which corporations retain their earnings and reinvest to one in which firms distribute profits almost entirely to shareholders and downsize everything else—people, pay, growth-enhancing capital investments, and tax contributions. It's a shift that is partly enabled by job-displacing technology and globalization but is fundamentally about the pervasiveness of short-term and balance-sheet-oriented thinking throughout the economy. "Financialization has polluted the entire physical investment process, the labor markets, and the innovation cycle of firms," says Andrew Haldane, the chief economist of the Bank of England and one of the deepest thinkers on the topic of financialization today. "The damage it inflicts on investments in physical and human capital [meaning factories and workers] is hugely important, because that's what slows down growth."[14]

THE RISE OF CREATIVE ACCOUNTING

Shareholder activism by people like Carl Icahn and the sort of buybacks being done by Apple and other large public firms are currently one of the best windows into the rise of finance. Back in the 1960s and '70s, companies invested about 40 percent of each additional earned or borrowed dollar into the real economy.[15] All that changed in the Reagan era. "Since the mid-1980s, in aggregate, corporations have funded the stock market rather than vice versa," says William Lazonick, a University of Massachusetts Lowell professor who has done extensive research on buybacks.[16] The legislative change that allowed this destructive shift happened in 1982, which was a crucial year for all kinds of market deregulation. The Supreme Court struck down a key antitakeover law in Illinois—and, by implication, similar laws in all other states. The Justice Department relaxed limits on concentration within industries, making it possible for large, more monopoly-oriented firms to emerge. The floodgates were opened for corporate raiders, who came to be known as "barbarians at the gate," after the title of a book by Bryan Burrough and John Helyar chronicling the leveraged buyout of RJR Nabisco in 1988.[17] That purchase was a megadeal done with megadebt—the sort that came to epitomize the era. Icahn was a major figure on that scene, embarking on hostile takeovers of firms like the aging air carrier Trans World Airlines (whose assets he sold off piecemeal to pay for the deal) and demanding asset sales in exchange for billions' worth of dividend payments and share buybacks at Texaco, where he owned a major stake.

Meanwhile, the stage was set for the buyback boom in 1981, when a vice chairman of the stock brokerage firm E. F. Hutton, John Shad, was appointed to head the SEC. He was among the first Wall Street executives to back Reagan for president and had led his fundraising campaign in New York. Not since Joseph P. Kennedy became chair of the SEC in 1934 had a Wall Street type headed the agency. Shad's tenure brought another crucial shift: regulations allowing firms to buy back their own shares, something that had previously been considered market manipulation, were dramatically loosened. On November 10, 1982, the SEC sanctioned massive open-market repurchases, up to 25 percent of a company's previous four weeks' average daily trading volume, despite complaints from long-serving SEC commissioner John Evans that this measure essentially legalized market manipulation. Market volatility rose following the rule change. No matter. Shad knew that buybacks would raise share prices, and he felt that would be good for shareholders—and what was good for them was good for America. The real-world turn toward the University of Chicago model of corporate governance, in which companies were run explicitly to "maximize shareholder value," had begun.[18]

Shad made buybacks legally possible. But today's trend, in which buybacks are a key part of a dysfunctional system of skyrocketing corporate pay and bad corporate decision making, was enabled by steps taken during the Bill Clinton years (quite an irony given Hillary Clinton's new stand against buybacks). Indeed, Clinton-era legislation that favored the markets over the real economy, and that was often a result of the revolving door between Wall Street and Washington, was a key means of turning the markets into the casino that they have become. Stock compensation and buybacks have been rising since the 1980s, but they really took a leap in the 1990s, when "new economy" tech firms began lobbying against efforts to introduce new accounting standards that would have forced companies to mark down the value of stock options on their books. One of the reasons that buybacks have burgeoned is that firms have been letting C-suite executives "buy company stock at below-market prices—and then pretending that nothing of value had changed hands," as Stiglitz once pointedly remarked. It's a mark of how strong the financial and tech lobbies are that their efforts were supported by key Democrats, such as California senators Barbara Boxer and Dianne Feinstein, as well as most conservatives.[19]

The Clinton administration itself was supportive, too. Robert Rubin (who served as both Treasury secretary and head of the National Economic Council) and Lawrence Summers (his deputy, who succeeded Rubin at Treasury) famously favored many rules allowing greater corporate compensation and tax breaks for the rich. To be fair, many Clinton-era officials were also concerned about income inequality back in the early 1990s, as the rising divide between CEO pay and what the majority of American workers took home stirred debate in Washington. The administration introduced rules that would cap tax-deductible CEO pay at $1 million, but granted an exception for "performance-based" pay over $1 million. Stiglitz, who also worked in the Clinton administration, as head of the president's Council of Economic Advisers, says it was one of the more problematic legacies of Bill Clinton's tenure.

"When they pushed through the tax exemption for performance pay," which opened the door to higher bonuses delivered as stock options, he says, "they made no effort to ensure that the increase in stock prices was in any way related to performance. The favorable treatment was granted whether the increase in stock prices was a result of the efforts of the manager or the result of a lowering of interest rates or a change in oil prices." The tax code, which was gradually relaxed to favor corporate debt over equity, only encouraged it (corporate margin debt is today at record highs thanks to the tax benefits of borrowing). The tax provision gives firms more incentives to manipulate their share prices with buybacks. Such policies hugely benefited people like Rubin, who made $115 million in cash and even more in stock as a Citigroup executive after leaving public service. Not surprisingly, while at Treasury, Rubin had refused to get behind proposals for greater transparency in options pay. "The whole stock options boom caused so many incentives for bad behavior of all kinds, and for making each [corporation] look better than it was. It's all directly responsible for what I'd term 'creative accounting,' which has had such a devastating effect on our economy," says Stiglitz. It was also fuel on the fire of the growing wealth gap in America. But when Stiglitz raised these issues with people like Rubin, Summers, or then–Federal Reserve chairman Alan Greenspan, they would say, "We shouldn't interfere with the markets."[20]

Such arguments are often used to justify the position that government intervention in markets destroys innovation. Yet quite the opposite appears to be true. Not only has growth in our economy been higher during times with more regulation, namely the 1950s to the 1970s, but *government itself* has funded the underlying resources that have allowed private firms like Apple and others to become as profitable as they are. As academics William Lazonick, Mariana Mazzucato, and Oner Tulum have argued in a paper outlining why more of Apple's cash should go to taxpayers rather than investors, government innovations have been the very fuel of capitalism.

"Apple did not have to invent the integrated circuit," they write. "It did not have to invent the graphical user interface. It did not have to invent the Internet. Moreover, Apple did not have to build universities to educate engineers or roads to allow those graduates engineers to commute to work or the airplanes to carry goods and people around the world. Nor did Apple have to negotiate trade deals with the governments in Japan during the 1980s and in China during the 1990s to ensure access to growth markets for their products."[21] The government did all those things. But it was executives and investors who profited from price hikes in Apple stock. These people are the biggest beneficiaries of the wealth of such corporations, wealth that has been built up by *many* stakeholders over decades.

DOWNSIZE AND DISTRIBUTE

One unfortunate result of this buyback boom and its funneling of corporate earnings away from Main Street investments and toward Wall Street is an erosion of American competitiveness in a global economy. We have to compete, after all, with many nations that have much less market pressure and more focus on long-term investment. Lazonick says that the move from a "retain-and-reinvest" corporate model to a "downsize-and-distribute" one is in large part responsible for a "national economy characterized by income inequity, employment instability, and diminished innovative capability."[22]

A growing body of research confirms this. Over the last thirty years, buybacks have come to represent the main form of corporate "strategy." With the exception of a few periods of intensive, speculative market activity (like the late-1920s stock market run-up or the tech bubble of the late 1990s), corporations haven't been issuing stock to raise money for their own investments for years. Rather, they've been buying back equities in order to push up the value of their own stock prices. S&P 500 companies have spent $4 trillion on buybacks between 2005 and 2015, representing at least 52.5 percent of their net earnings, and another $2.5 trillion on dividends, which amounted to 37.7 percent.[23] In 2014, buybacks and dividends represented 105 percent of net earnings of publicly traded American companies; in 2015, they reached above 115 percent.[24]

Proponents of the buyback trend will cite gurus like Warren Buffett, who has said that he doesn't mind buybacks as a tactic, as long as they are done when a firm has ample cash to take care of the rest of its business needs, and when the firm's stock is selling at a discount. (Apple, for example, would meet the first criteria, but the second is up for grabs depending on your view of the company's future.) Yet statistics show that those conditions are rarely met. In fact, the bulk of buybacks since 2001 were done during market *peaks,* belying the notion that such purchases represent firms' own belief in a rising share price.[25]

Why would executives buy back their firms' stock at such inopportune moments? Many experts believe it's because buybacks are done at the end of a true growth cycle or, in the case of the most recent boom, at the end of a cycle of easy monetary policy—when the good times are about to end, and buybacks are a way of keeping the party going just a little bit longer. But the buybacks do nothing to help make companies more competitive; in fact, they waste corporate cash, given that they are done when the market was high rather than low. Nonetheless, they do enrich executives, who took from 66 percent to 82 percent of their compensation in stock between 2006 and 2012.[26] "It is surely difficult to praise buybacks as being good for shareholders when they are made at such disadvantageous times," says Andrew Smithers, a British economist and financial consultant. (His book *The Road to Recovery* makes a convincing case that buybacks and the bonus culture are responsible for slow growth not just in the United States but in many rich countries, because they encourage executives to pay themselves, rather than investing in things that will actually make their companies more profitable.) "Buying overpriced shares is a way of destroying value and spending more money when the market is most overpriced is particularly egregious."[27]

What this means on a practical level is that the common claim of corporate leaders—that tight credit conditions, a lack of consumer demand, and an uncertain regulatory environment have kept them from investing their cash hoard back into the real economy—is at best a half-truth. Statistics show that the flow of cash from the financial markets to public companies, which represents 80 percent of business investment in America, didn't change at a net level after the financial crisis. Despite the increase in borrowing during the boom days before 2008, and the collapse in borrowing during the recession, corporations invested at exactly the same rate in the five years after the meltdown as they did in the few years preceding it: around 10 cents of each borrowed dollar. The other 90 cents (which varied in dollar amounts depending on credit and growth conditions) primarily went to shareholder payouts.[28]

That means that far from funding the economy that you and I live and work in, stock markets now basically fund payouts to the wealthy. This "shareholder revolution," based on the Chicago School notion that maximizing shareholder value is the purpose of corporate America (as covered in chapter 3), is the single most important reason why high corporate profits and unprecedented cash hoards have failed to translate into jobs, wage growth, and innovation.

All of this raises a profound question: What is a company for? We thought that companies, like banks themselves, were supposed to be entities that generated wealth broadly, by allocating capital to productive purposes—investing in people, factories, new ideas, and businesses. But something in that cycle is broken. Today's companies, like banks, are keeping their wealth in a closed feedback loop where it enriches only a few at the expense of the many. This is a serious dysfunction in our market system, one with multiple growth-destroying effects that we are only just beginning to understand.

PRIVATE IS THE NEW PUBLIC

One pernicious effect of all this pressure from activist investors is that public markets now are a much less attractive place to raise innovation capital than they used to be, given that they push for short-term gains over long-term objectives. Far from being a place where firms go to fund their best new ideas, markets today have become a place where entrepreneurs and their backers go to cash out via an IPO, or where large public firms manipulate their own stock price via buybacks to please investors. Either way, innovation suffers. For example, Stanford University research shows that tech firms scale back innovation by 40 percent after an IPO, since once a firm goes public, it must focus on pleasing shareholders rather than on investing in the future.[29]

When it comes to the financial sector's dampening effect on growth, private and family-owned firms are in many ways the exception that proves the rule. Research shows that privately owned firms invest more than twice as much in the real economy as public firms of similar size operating in the same sector.[30] They have also weathered the 2008 crisis much better than many public firms and are now on the upswing rather than the downswing; even as profit margins have flattened or contracted at most big public firms, a 2015 survey of major privately held companies found that 31 percent have raised their margins, and the majority expected to achieve growth rates double the average for their industries in the coming year.[31]

Former vice chairman of General Motors Bob Lutz, who used to be the CEO of Exide, a large battery maker, cites East Penn Manufacturing, a privately held battery firm, as a key example of the way in which private firms are able to shrug off the concerns of Wall Street and focus on their long-term growth. "I remember [several years back] visiting East Penn," he says. "At the time, all the [public] battery makers were worrying about Korean competition," which prompted outsourcing and cost cutting. Meanwhile, East Penn, which was founded in 1946 and is still family owned, kept plowing money back into the business and is today the world's largest single-site, independent battery maker—proof that the United States actually can lead in manufacturing, even on commoditized products, with the right incentive structure. "The family lived well, but their home wasn't the Taj Mahal," says Lutz. "They said, hey, we've got enough money for a good life, and the rest of it goes back into the business. If they have a couple of quarters where they don't make any money because they are investing so heavily, so what?"[32]

Wall Street, on the other hand, actively *punishes* public firms when they make decisions that seek to enhance their long-term strategic value. There are thousands of examples that one could cite, but here's a particularly telling one: Less than a year after Apple introduced the iPod, the company's stock began to fall steadily.[33] That was because the product that would kick-start the greatest corporate turnaround in history initially disappointed, selling under 400,000 units in its debut year. Thankfully, Steve Jobs didn't give a fig. He stuck with the idea, and today more than 1.9 billion Apple devices have been sold. Whether Tim Cook's Apple will be remembered in the same way is still an open question, since despite the enormous dividends, Cook's strategy has been very much of the downsize-and-distribute kind, in which profits are handed out to investors to allay concerns over the company's lagging stock price. It's no coincidence that under him (at the time of writing) there hasn't been any truly game-changing new technology (the iPhone 6 is an incremental upgrade and the iWatch more a luxury toy than a new technology).

Many other large firms have been under similar pressure to put the needs of Wall Street above those of their customers. And as most CEOs will tell you, it's very hard for companies to push back. Typically, those leaders who do are not professional managers but founders or entrepreneurs who've built their start-ups into extremely successful firms. Apple under Jobs would be an example, as would Starbucks under Howard Schultz. The latter has done its share of buybacks, but it has also made a lot of real-economy investments that Wall Street wasn't so keen about, because Schultz was willing to take risks. For example, Starbucks was one of the first retailers in the country to offer affordable, comprehensive healthcare to full-time and eligible part-time employees and their families. The company has also made big investments in areas like workforce training, hiring and training of returning veterans (Starbucks has pledged to employ 10,000 of them), and helping its workers go to college and repay student debt. In 2015, Starbucks promised to help pay for employees to get bachelor's degrees, a program that will likely cost the firm tens of millions of dollars. Schultz got a lot of pushback from investors on those costs. "It's the same kind of pushback we got twenty years ago when we provided comprehensive healthcare," he says. "Everyone thinks it's dilutive. But it's not dilutive."

Indeed, Schultz is deeply committed to these ideas not just for social reasons, but because they make good long-term business sense. Making the company a preferred employer via such programs helps keep turnover costs lower and service quality higher than the industry average. More important, Schultz is a true maker who believes such investments are vital for the long-term viability of Starbucks. America has become a nation of both latte drinkers and latte purveyors, and Schultz says that if US businesses want to thrive, they must focus on the former—which means serving a broader economic constituency than just shareholders. "I think the private sector simply has to take a larger role [in supporting Main Street economic growth] than they have in the past. Our responsibility goes beyond the P&L and our stock price. We have to take care of people in the communities that we serve. If half the country or at least a third of the country doesn't have the same opportunities as the rest going forward, then the country won't survive. That's not socialism," says Schultz. To him, it's practical reality.[34]

Unfortunately, most corporate leaders are thrown out the minute they do something that doesn't hike up the share price immediately, even if it will garner value for the long haul—one reason why the average tenure of an S&P 500 CEO is under ten years. Sam Palmisano, the former head of IBM, remembers the flak he got from both activists and institutional shareholders in 2004, when he announced the company's move out of the PC business and into services. "There was huge pressure. People were calling for my head," says Palmisano. Even though the firm was in the midst of returning $70 billion worth of cash to shareholders as it was making that shift, people on the Street thought it wasn't enough. "I remember going to some meeting [with an institutional investor who was questioning the number] and saying, 'You know, I thought $70 billion was adequate but I guess not. What do you think is enough?'"[35] Palmisano eventually decided that the only way forward was to stop issuing quarterly earnings guidance, tell investors who weren't happy with IBM's strategy to just sell their shares, and focus on long-term growth. And that's exactly what he did, executing one of the most successful turnarounds in corporate history and doubling the share price of the company in the process. Since then, though, IBM has come under renewed pressure from the markets to "disgorge" its cash. Altogether, it has shelled out some $138 billion on share buybacks and dividend payments from 2000 to 2014, while spending only $59 billion on its own capital expenditures (along with $32 billion on acquisitions).[36]

Basically, IBM, like so many companies in our taker economy, is using a lot more cash to please investors than to discover the New New Thing. There are those who would argue that $59 billion isn't small change. True enough; yet the mercurial nature of the tech business makes it imperative for companies like Apple and IBM, which depend on innovation for growth, to save as much as possible in order to stay ahead of unexpected competitors, rather than disgorging all their free cash to investors. Even a few years ago, who could have predicted the rise of companies like Facebook, Snapchat, or WhatsApp? In the technology industry in particular, as well as in our increasingly digital and information-oriented economy as a whole, new game-changing companies can appear overnight. Business models can change in a nanosecond. Industries can be completely disrupted not just over many years but within months or even weeks. In this new economic milieu, there's every reason in the world for tech firms to pour every penny into blue-sky research and invest in workers at all levels—as well as pay their fair share of taxes to the federal government, whose investments in basic science and technology are arguably what created most of Silicon Valley's growth potential to begin with.

WE'RE ALL ACTIVISTS NOW

One of the cruel ironies of financialization is that the transformation of public markets from a "restaurant" to a "casino" (to quote Buffett) has been accelerated by average Americans. More and more of them are now in the markets themselves, via their pension funds or 401(k) retirement plans. The privatization of retirement in the 1980s (itself a mere accident of the tax code, as I'll explain in chapter 8) and the widespread growth of stock ownership since then mean that most Americans now have some stake in stock prices going up. No matter that they might be going up for the wrong reasons, and that government and corporate focus on maintaining that rise diverts energy from policies that would do more to enrich the average Joe, like housing reform or wage increases.

Indeed, over the last thirty years, big firms that manage our retirement money, like Fidelity and American Funds, have become the largest owners of corporate shares in America. Theoretically, they should be great long-term corporate owners who might advocate for the kinds of changes in the market system that would help Main Street, whose retirement money they are stewarding. But perversely, it's exactly *because* they are the biggest administrators of corporate pension funds that they don't advocate more vigorously for smarter corporate governance. Their clients and their investments are often one and the same, which creates conflicts of interest and blunts their ability to prod companies in a direction that might not please management. "The growth of fund managers and the entire 401(k) system has really pushed short-term thinking within markets, and hindered growth-producing innovation, because the fund firms are caught between their clients and the markets," says Andrew Smithers.[37]

Certainly, the high fees charged by many of these money managers and other mutual fund firms mean that they *need* big stock price increases to create the kind of returns that will justify their existence. It's a perverse cycle that people like John Bogle, the founder of the Vanguard Group and one of the few reform-minded people in the mutual fund business, have decried. Bogle, who testified before the Senate Finance Committee on the topic in 2014, says today's stock market itself is not unlike a Ponzi scheme. In fact, he estimates that our bloated financial system might be sucking up some 60 percent of the returns that ordinary retirement savers could otherwise earn on their money. "Individual investors who rely on the historical stock market returns presented by mutual fund marketers will be shocked at the paltry amounts they've accumulated in their retirement accounts. Corporations too will face the same shock as shortfalls in pension plan accumulations will have profoundly negative implications for their financial statements," says Bogle.[38]

In the wake of such criticism, some of the big state-run pension funds (which are under political pressure to cut benefits) are finally getting involved in this debate, flexing their muscles as large corporate shareholders. But as often as not, their efforts actually compound the problem. That's because pension funds themselves are desperate to goose near-term returns; in boom times many of them promised retirees the sorts of gains that they can no longer guarantee in today's slow-growth climate.[39] As a result, many have turned their money over to the activists. The amount of money managed by activist funds had grown to $130 billion in the first half of 2015, up from $32 billion in 2008, in large part because pension funds, college endowments, and other large institutions are getting behind them.[40] It's no mystery why: their returns have outperformed the market for the past few years. Activist hedge funds made an annualized return of 14 percent in the period from mid-2012 to mid-2015, compared with 7 percent for hedge funds that invest primarily in equities.[41]

Icahn's fund, Icahn Partners, is the granddaddy of them all. Before closing to outside investors in 2011, it had an annualized return of 27 percent. Now anyone with $80 can buy a share of IEP, Icahn's public company, and invest with Carl. "The fact that these funds have done so well over the last few years is creating a chicken-and-egg cycle—more institutional money flows in, activists take more actions, and returns go up," says Donna Dabney, former executive director of the Conference Board Governance Center.

Yet the gains of activists, born of short-term tricks like buybacks and mergers, can be illusory. Very often such stock-boosting strategies aren't so much growing the firms at the grassroots level as they make them seem more attractive to the market. Moreover, plenty of buy-and-hold investors, like Warren Buffett, would say that several years of good returns is nothing, and that companies should be managed not for short-term profits but for shareholders who truly stick around for the long haul (indeed, Buffett has told Tim Cook to ignore activist demands for a bigger buyback). Icahn has taken the long view with a few of his investments—like industrial-cleaning company Philip Services, which he has held since 1998—but not many. And while Icahn himself is a success, what mainly makes activism look so good on paper is a few big-company deals of the sort that he's most well known for—the ones that really push share prices up. "The large average improvements are driven by a relative minority of activist efforts that result in outsized stock price gains," explains a 2013 report by Citi's Financial Strategy and Solutions Group. A slim majority of companies targeted by corporate activists since 2009 were actually underperforming market benchmarks for stock returns within a year of the campaign.[42]

Still, it's enough to entice pension funds desperate to fulfill their commitments. "The economic landscape is clearly helping spur a lot of interest in activism," says Anne Sheehan, the head of corporate governance for CalSTRS, the California state teachers' pension fund that manages more than $180 billion and has gotten more active around proposals to shift corporate strategies to improve earnings. The fact that it will be tough to make even a 6 percent return over the long haul in an economy struggling to grow at 2 percent is the rationale behind much of CalSTRS activism.

In 2013, for example, the pension fund forced the breakup of Timken, a 114-year-old Ohio steel and bearings maker whose founding family held a significant stake and had (according to some investors) disproportionate board representation. CalSTRS's partner on that campaign was activist fund Relational Investors led by Ralph V. Whitworth, who had earned his stripes working for the corporate raider T. Boone Pickens. While Timken had argued that the company was better off staying together, the two institutional investors said that a split would create more value for their fellow shareholders.[43] They were right in the short term; markets like the quick hit of spinoffs, and immediately following the deal, Timken shares soared and Relational made a handsome profit. Yet, as was explained in chapter 3, the share prices of firms themselves are not the best marker of what will drive longer-term economic growth—and in turn generate wealth that's more broadly shared. In the two years following the split, Timken shares fell sharply as the two smaller, less competitive successor firms were seen as ripe for take-over. The fact that the Timken family, which had run things for five generations, had managed to build up such a flush balance sheet, with a well-funded pension plan and plenty of cash on hand, only made the new companies more ripe for the picking. (These assets, after all, are exactly the kinds of resources private equity investors look to extract when they acquire firms.) In fact, in the wake of the split, the new firms have already begun to cut back capital spending and pension contributions as well as increase share buybacks, something that Timken's family-run board had once dismissed as financial engineering.

The Timken family was by no means rife with bleeding-heart liberals. CEO Ward J. "Tim" Timken Jr. is a Republican who got paid almost $25 million in the three years before the company's split—one of the things that attracted CalSTRS, which is eager to curb corporate compensation, to the fight.[44] But the firm was also known for working with local unions, investing in its people, and not outsourcing when it could be avoided. It's part of being rooted in the local community; when your name is on school buildings, it's tougher to make decisions that work only for Wall Street. This kind of "localnomics" may have resulted in an undervalued share price but it certainly boosted the fortunes of hometown Canton, Ohio, as a whole. After all, US government data shows that a dollar of manufacturing growth at a firm like Timken can translate into an additional $1.37 of spending elsewhere in the community.[45]

This striking contrast in behaviors, attitudes, and growth trajectories of public versus privately run companies shows just how much pressure US public firms and leaders are under to maximize short-term gains, from all sides: institutional investors, individual pensioners, activists, and even politicians who look to inflated asset prices to make voters feel that they are becoming wealthier (even as their paychecks are as flat as ever). It's an issue that is strongly undercutting our national competitiveness, given that US firms are increasingly competing against family-owned emerging-market giants that don't have such short-term pressures, not to mention private foreign companies based in places like Germany. And indeed both groups have, not surprisingly, grabbed global market share from American competitors in recent years. "The idea that what is in the interests of shareholders is what's best for local economies is totally wrong," says Smithers. "And I think that there's been a real retreat from discussion about the topic because it is against so many entrenched interests to have that debate."

HOW THE BARBARIANS STOLE OUR STIMULUS

As I describe in chapters 1 and 10, Washington not only resists this debate, but also often actively encourages the development of finance (pushing more consumer debt and credit) as a way to avoid it. Just as the deregulation and financialization that began in the late 1970s were in part a tactic to avoid a "guns versus butter" discussion about allocating national resources, the Fed's $4.5 trillion money dump following the 2008 financial crisis (which threw a wet blanket over the Great Recession) was a way for politicians to avoid a real discussion about a growth model that enriches Wall Street but not Main Street. As long as the markets could be genetically modified by the Fed, the economy would look healthier than it actually was.

Many experts have argued that an environment like what we've seen since 2008, in which borrowing costs are as low as they've ever been, is the perfect time to build bridges, fund new basic science research, or revamp public schools. Yet thanks to congressional gridlock, it didn't happen. The Federal Reserve alone was able to act to support the economy, with lower rates and quantitative easing (which is essentially pumping money into the economy in the hopes of boosting asset prices and consumption). But one of the many fascinating and downright disturbing things about the current boom in shareholder activism is that it was actually *enabled* by monetary policies that were supposed to help the little guy. Following the financial crisis, the Fed cut interest rates to historic lows and carried out a massive bond and mortgage-backed securities buying program. In purchasing these assets en masse, the idea was to push other investors into riskier areas of the market—like stocks and corporate bonds—which would eventually bolster asset prices and make Americans feel wealthier. So far, so good; the value of stocks and mutual funds owned by US households did increase by several trillion dollars following the 2008 crash. In light of this apparent success, the European Central Bank and many others have followed the Fed's lead, buying up assets, lowering interest rates, and goosing stock prices.

The problem is that this money dump has mainly benefited the wealthiest portion of the population, namely the top tenth, which owns nearly 90 percent of all stocks. As discussed earlier in this chapter, this isn't just a social issue but an economic one. The rich keep their money in banks or in the secondary markets, buying stocks and bonds that already exist, rather than, say, starting new businesses or purchasing new things. The money stays in the financial sector, in other words, instead of being invested in the real economy that we live in. The Fed had hoped that rising asset prices would lead to growing consumer confidence, which would spur business investment in the real economy, boost the demand for labor, and eventually get that virtuous cycle of job creation started. But it didn't work that way. While quantitative easing has helped lift the job market somewhat at the lower end of the socioeconomic spectrum (one big reason that companies like Walmart have raised their wages by a dollar or two per hour), it has done almost nothing for the middle class.

There are two reasons why. The first is that, as I've explained above, companies didn't take advantage of low borrowing rates in order to invest in Main Street; they did it to buy back stock and enrich corporate leaders and investors. The other is that middle-class people still keep most of their wealth in housing, rather than in stocks, and the Fed's efforts couldn't do as much to bolster housing wealth as, say, a true housing reform program might have. Meanwhile, 60 percent of the gains in property values over the last few years have accrued to just ten of the nation's top real-estate markets: rich areas like Manhattan and Brooklyn, parts of Los Angeles, San Francisco, Austin, and so forth. The easy money gave the rich more cash to play with but it couldn't fix the underlying economic problems that made it tough for most people to buy houses to begin with. The result is that cash-rich investors, many of them in the shadow banking sector, now dominate the housing market, as I'll explore in chapter 7. People who don't have 30 percent money down to buy a house have a hard time getting a mortgage—a problem compounded by the fact that small-time American savers have lost an estimated $470 billion in foregone interest on their bank deposits between 2008 and 2013 because of very low rates.[46] The policies that were meant to save Main Street ended up bolstering Wall Street instead.

None of this is to say that the Fed deserves blame for trying to do what it could, via monetary policy, to keep the economy from dipping even further than it did. But the truth is that only *real* fiscal stimulus doled out by the government itself (in the form of infrastructure spending, worker retraining, educational improvements, public works programs, and investment in core science research) would have done anything to improve the livelihood of the average American. What we got instead was a Fed-induced stock boost that not only increased inequality by making the rich richer, but also—perversely—encouraged companies to borrow as much money as they can, as fast as they can, and then turn it over to the top tier of our society. It's ironic but true: the solution to a debt crisis has been to encourage more debt, albeit on the part of companies rather than consumers. Corporate debt (not including the debt held by banks) has risen from $5.7 trillion in 2006 to $7.4 trillion today.[47]

The result has been a tripling in the value of the markets accompanied by a decline in real corporate competitiveness. Wall Street advocates will say that stocks have risen because corporate earnings were strong between 2010 and 2014. But as a 2015 report from the Office of Financial Research (OFR, the government body set up to monitor the market in the wake of the 2008 crisis) shows, that fact obscures a more troubling truth. Companies have higher profit margins—and thus higher stock prices—not because the economy is booming and they are selling more stuff, but because they have cut costs, kept salaries flat, and avoided investing in new factories and R&D. Basically, American firms are acting like low-wage companies in a high-wage economy, which gives them a temporary boost but ultimately results in a tragedy of the commons—once everyone runs a low-wage company, no one will make much money at all. As the OFR report puts it, "Although this financial engineering has contributed to higher stock prices in the short run, it detracts from opportunities to invest capital to support longer-term organic growth."[48] Indeed, it's already having that effect. Even as share buybacks peaked in 2015, corporate profits as a whole have begun to flatten, and fall.

The bottom line in all this? The economic "recovery" that we have now isn't a real one; it has been genetically modified by the Fed and enjoyed mainly by the investor class.

BARBARIANS, BUBBLES, AND THE FUTURE OF BUSINESS

So where will the recovery go from here? I suspect that the impetus to goose markets will only increase as corporate earnings and eventually stock prices go down. But the tactics of the activists may change as the Fed slowly begins to tighten interest rates and corporations find it more expensive to borrow money to pay out shareholders and avoid taxes (not to mention the cost of servicing their existing record debt). Indeed, some investors are already fretting about what could happen in the markets, now that the days of easy money are at an end and interest rates would seem to have nowhere to go but up. As Larry Fink, the chief executive of the asset management firm Black-Rock, said in an open letter that he sent to S&P 500 executives in 2014, "Too many companies have cut capital expenditure and even increased debt to boost dividends and increase share buybacks. We certainly believe that returning cash to shareholders should be part of a balanced capital strategy; however, when done for the wrong reasons . . . it can jeopardize a company's ability to generate sustainable long-term returns."[49]

Yet even as buybacks are likely to slow, mergers and acquisitions are at a record high. Global M&A transactions in early 2015 were worth more than $900 billion, the highest level since 2007.[50] Activists love M&A because it always generates quick-hit growth (and bankers love it, too, because it allows them to pocket large fees, both from putting companies together and, later, from breaking them apart if the mergers don't work). But the game has changed since the infamous wheeling and dealing of the barbarians in the 1980s, evolving to encompass more subtle pressures, too. Activists like Icahn, Einhorn, and Ackman are now themselves pursuing board seats that would allow them greater control over corporate strategy (and of course, cash). Activists justify the intrusion by saying that they are, quite simply, smarter than everyone else. "If you could sit in on some of these board meetings, you'd be shocked," says Icahn, who compares CEOs and boards to eating-club presidents and their slightly dumber friends whose job it is to make them look good. Plenty of other activist investors actually believe that their brand of activism is the cure for what ails America, both economically and socially. Icahn, for one, blames "poor corporate governance for a growing disparity in income and slow growth" in the country. "If we don't get better corporate governance, we're going to lose our hegemony," he says.[51]

It's a fascinating inversion of logic. But the truth is that most activists don't develop deep relationships with the firms they invest in; they merely troll through SEC filings looking for indications that a company might be weak or underpriced—and then pounce. That's what Relational Investors did to find Timken, and that's what Icahn does to find many of the firms that he pursues. Icahn, for his part, defends his recent targeting of companies, from Apple to Netflix to Motorola, and says that he plans to push not only for more buy-backs but also for more seats on their corporate boards. Sometimes that goal doesn't even require a push. Several big companies have invited Icahn to add directors to their boards within the last few years, perhaps thinking, as Icahn likes to say, that "peace is better than war." Tim Cook himself has met regularly with Icahn since he began squaring off against Apple, dining in the latter's lavish robber-baron-style duplex in New York overlooking the shining GE sign on top of the 30 Rock Building and conducting late-night phone calls to talk strategy. "A lot of people say Steve Jobs probably wouldn't have talked to me, and maybe that's true," Icahn told me back in 2013, when he first began his campaign. "But I think he [Cook] found our conversation interesting. He said, 'Look, you've accomplished a lot, and we want to listen to you.'"[52]

That may not be a great decision. Research by Columbia University Law School belies some of the data on broader hedge fund returns, showing that companies shaken up by activist investors usually don't outperform over the long haul.[53] Indeed, in the midst of the biggest spate of activism in history, corporate earnings as a whole have been decreasing at faster and faster rates. One Citi report found that 57 percent of the activist campaigns waged against S&P 1500 companies in 2013 targeted firms whose share prices were *already outperforming* those of their peers.[54] Activists aren't interested in culling bad CEOs so much as in getting control of stronger companies and milking them for all they are worth. The big prize in the new era is, of course, the record $2 trillion in cash that American corporations currently have on their books. (Most of it remains off-shore for now, because Congress hasn't yet passed tax reform that would make the corporate rate in the United States more globally competitive while also closing the loopholes that make it possible to stash corporate money abroad in the first place.) And when that much is at stake, you can expect that lots of new players will soon be entering the game.

HOW TO FIX THE SYSTEM

So, until tax and other market and governance reforms happen, look for this type of corporate financial wizardry to continue. As economist Joseph Stiglitz and others have pointed out, fixing things like the buyback dilemma is tough, because it's not a matter of finding a silver bullet. As I have sketched in this chapter, the Kafkaesque financial market dysfunction exemplified by the share buyback boom is the result of more than thirty years of policy decisions and market shifts—from legal changes to financial deregulation to the privatization of retirement to easy-money monetary policy and terrible incentive structures for corporate leaders. There's no one fix that will change the system overnight. But there are several smart things we could do to start moving toward that change.

One solution that has been proposed to create a more equal distribution of corporate wealth is cash profit sharing, an idea put forward by Joseph Blasi, a professor at Rutgers University's School of Management and Labor Relations. A book Blasi coauthored with two colleagues, *The Citizen's Share*, outlines how this policy has worked in companies from Southwest Airlines to Procter & Gamble.[55] The authors suggest, in simple terms, that firms disgorge the cash not just to investors but also to their own workers. It's an idea that has some merit and is being advocated by Hillary Clinton, among others. But as Blasi himself admits, "research shows that profit sharing can increase productivity, improve corporate performance and even pay for itself by growing the pie bigger, but only if it is part of a more participative corporate culture with training for workers."[56]

There is a fairly long history of share-ownership schemes in the

United States, with many millions of workers already participating. But labor advocates give programs of this kind mixed reviews. Some worry that the tax breaks associated with profit sharing can be easily manipulated by management and large shareholders for their own benefit rather than that of labor. Others feel that such schemes are little more than bonus incentive plans. That's a fair point, but research shows that simply giving workers shares in a firm doesn't necessarily give them a seat at the table in terms of decision making[57]—a key factor in changing the way companies actually operate.

There are also many models for more participatory management that might combine profit sharing with a seat at the table for a broader group of corporate stakeholders. Some firms are run as cooperatives; two examples are Ocean Spray (a collective of cranberry farmers) and W. L. Gore (the maker of Gore-Tex fabrics), in which workers own and operate 100 percent of the firm. Many of these companies tend to be quite profitable and have high standards of transparency and corporate governance as well as enviable cultures. (Gore's was famously profiled in Malcolm Gladwell's book *The Tipping Point*. The company's products are made in teams of no more than 150 people, each of whom has operational as well as strategic input.)[58]

Another model is that of co-determination, in which labor representatives sit on the board of major companies, a system practiced quite successfully in many German firms. In fact, many of Germany's big companies have works councils in which management, workers, and even civic leaders collaborate on determining schedules, furloughs, pay, expansion plans, and even the products that a factory might make. The idea is for management and labor to work together on issues before they become problems. This kind of collective problem solving helped BASF, the world's largest chemical producer based in Ludwigshafen, to avoid mass layoffs when demand for its products tanked in 2008. Instead of cutting staff, BASF managers used a government subsidy to reassign idled workers to a recycling operation, preserving critical skills and keeping the company primed to capitalize on the recovery. It's this kind of collaboration that has made Germany into the export powerhouse it is today; as other economies struggled to regain their footing, Germany's unemployment actually *fell* during the crisis, and in 2010, the country accounted for a full 60 percent of the Eurozone's GDP growth.[59]

The historic tensions around management and labor relations in the United States may make these management models an uphill slog. But the tax code is another way that control of firms could be passed to a broader group of stakeholders. Buybacks themselves aren't tax deductible, but related practices, such as taking on debt to make such purchases, offer companies tax advantages (because the interest on this debt is tax deductible), as do stock options awarded to top executives, as laid out above. Shifting to a tax code that doesn't give debt such preferential treatment would be a great way to shift the buyback dynamic, and this is a topic I will cover in much more depth in chapter 9.

Cracking down on overseas tax havens and closing corporate loopholes is another obvious measure that's long overdue. This is especially true given the fact that most other G8 nations are considering similar proposals, which would help offset some of the threat of a corporate race to the bottom, in which corporations offshore to the most attractive tax havens. Similarly, taxing capital gains on a sliding scale, with higher rates for shorter holding periods and lower rates for longer ones, could discourage the seekers of quick gains from distorting the markets. (Bonus pay might also be spread out over time and linked not to share prices but to real business performance, something that a number of firms are beginning to experiment with.)

Some advocates are also calling on the SEC to put a complete end to open-market buybacks, rein in stock-based pay, and allow not only labor but also taxpayers to have representation on corporate boards. It's not as crazy as it might sound. After all, many of the firms that issue the largest numbers of buybacks—Apple, GE, Exxon Mobil, Intel, Merck, and the like—are also those that have depended most heavily on government R&D investment in areas like energy, nanotechnology, and health and medical research. If our uniquely American capitalist mythology allows us to rebrand the barbarians storming the corporate gates as "activists," then it should also allow us to envision a more sustainable economic growth model in which government isn't all bad, labor has a seat at the table, and companies can focus more on real engineering and less on the financial kind. In fact, there are already firms and communities in the United States and abroad that offer successful models of how this might be done, a topic that will be more fully explored in the solutions portion of this book in chapter 11.

Until these things happen, our market system will remain myopic and our nation's richest firms will continue to disgorge their profits mainly to the richest Americans. When Apple began returning cash to investors, the company's share price spiked (it was around $150 in the spring of 2017). "We're not hoarders . . . [of] cash that we don't need," Cook said, justifying his decision to borrow nearly all of the money he turned back over to investors.[60] Icahn tweeted his approval, as well as his next demand: Apple should hand over even more cash, in order to hit a new share price target of $216. What was Icahn's justification for the increase? Amazingly, it was in part his own calculation that Apple was paying far less tax on its earnings than it appeared to be—around 20 percent, versus the 26 percent that most of Wall Street assumed. In other words, Apple's impressive skills in manipulating global tax loopholes had become an advantage that investors like Icahn could trade on.

Ultimately, though, Icahn cut back on Apple, after worries about the company's future in China emerged.[61] The stake fell. And predictably, more buybacks eventually brought it back up. All this says a tremendous amount about how far America's most beloved firm has come from its roots under Steve Jobs, who once summed up his own business philosophy in this simple way: "Manage the top line, which is your business strategy, your people—the talent that you have—and your products. Do all that stuff right, and the bottom line will follow." For Tim Cook, the opposite would seem to be true. That's a pity for all of us.

CHAPTER 5

WE'RE ALL BANKERS NOW

*GE and the Story of How American
Business Came to Emulate Finance*

IN EARLY April 2015, Jeffrey Immelt, the CEO of one of America's largest and most famous conglomerates, General Electric, made a landmark announcement. After spending several decades bolstering its finance arm, which did everything from consumer lending to credit cards to commercial real estate deals, GE was getting out of the banking business—for good. To say that it was the end of an era doesn't do the shift justice. GE, the only American company that has remained in the Dow Jones Industrial Average since the index launched 120 years ago, has always been a bellwether for American business.

The firm founded by Thomas Alva Edison was the country's original innovator for decades, a maker in the largest sense. But while most Americans still think of GE as the company that creates lightbulbs and microwaves, less known is the fact that it redefined the nature of American industrial corporations by dramatically expanding its finance business in the 1980s. In the years leading up to the financial crisis of 2008, GE had become one of the world's largest financial services companies. It was the country's largest nonbank financial firm—a Too Big to Fail entity, but without the level of regulatory scrutiny required for official players like Wall Street banks. And now, Immelt said, its financial division, GE Capital, which had been one of the key participants in the subprime meltdown in 2008, would be spun off entirely. The rest of the company would go back to its industrial roots, dumping all its financial activities and focusing solely on manufacturing. Being so deeply in finance, said Immelt, "doesn't really make sense for us" anymore.[1] He announced his intention to offload GE Capital as quickly as possible, to the highest bidders. It was as radical a strategic shift as has been seen in American business for years.

It was also a 180-degree turn for a company that had, under its previous CEO, Jack Welch, come to represent more than any other nonbank firm the financialization of American business. When Welch, the man whom *Fortune* eventually crowned "Manager of the Century," took over the company in 1981, the vast majority of its sales came from things like jet turbines, nuclear power reactors, mining equipment, complex materials, and electronics. The company was famous for innovations like the X-ray machine, the lightbulb, and unbreakable plastic.[2] GE was both big and fast growing—its earnings tripled over the 1970s—but its mediocre stock price didn't reflect that. It was the beginning of the go-go 1980s, and the Street wanted more than the growth rate of 7 or 8 percent a year typical for big industrial firms—it wanted double digits.

That's exactly what Welch, who became the model CEO of the age, gave them. Over his tenure, the company bought and sold hundreds of businesses to bolster its share price, trading its own divisions the way a portfolio manager trades stock. Finance, in particular the wholesale funding pioneered by former Citibank CEO Walter Wriston, became the mainstay of its operations. Debt became essential for greasing the wheels of daily operations. The portions of the business focused on consumer credit and lending doubled, as manufacturing stagnated. GE Capital became the largest issuer of commercial paper (a kind of short-term IOU) in the world—a borrower of mammoth proportions that in 2008 required $88 billion in loans to conduct its normal business.

Prior to 2008, Wall Street loved firms like GE that got much of their revenues from moving money around rather than from making things. Sure, the company still manufactured everything from lightbulbs to locomotives. But that's not where the big profit growth was. Its capital arm was established in 1932 to help customers, but over time, GE eventually came to act like a bank itself, borrowing money to conduct daily operations, and focusing more on the manipulation of its capital than on the creation of truly innovative products and services.

And it certainly ceased to be a creator of jobs. By the time Lehman Brothers collapsed, GE had gone from being a place where the country's top engineering grads were hired into lifetime employment to being an infamous downsizer. Welch fired 112,000 people[3] in the first five years of his tenure in an effort to bolster the firm's stock price by cost cutting; the efforts earned him his infamous nickname Neutron Jack, after the bomb that eradicates people but leaves buildings standing. Under Welch, GE came to rely on financial wizardry rather than new technological breakthroughs to satisfy investors. GE Capital, a major profit center of the business, was focused not on making but on taking, across every possible area of finance, from equipment leasing to leveraged buyouts and even subprime mortgages.

It was that last category that imploded so spectacularly during the financial crisis of 2008. Indeed, though its role has not been as widely reported as that of, say, Fannie Mae and Freddie Mac, or even Goldman Sachs and Lehman Brothers, America's original innovator played a huge role in the subprime mortgage meltdown. The assets of GE Capital, which had swollen from $371 billion in 2001 to nearly $700 billion at the time of the crisis, crashed and burned in America's real estate collapse. GE had to be bailed out by taxpayers to the tune of $139 billion in guaranteed loans from the FDIC.[4] Things got so bad that Immelt, who had the misfortune to take over from Welch several years earlier, right before September 11, had to go to Omaha, Nebraska, hat in hand, and beg for $3 billion from Warren Buffett, who was of course one of the few private-sector investors who had any money and was willing to invest at that point.

"Fear is contagious, and it paralyzes everybody," says Buffett.

"When GE called us to get the three billion, and they said, we need it and we need it now, well, if they are that afraid, think of the eighteen million people who have mortgage payments that they can't meet and they thought they'd be able to refinance their house to take care of it. You can't have things [in a capitalist system] stop for very long, or a whole other set of terrible things start happening."[5] Buffett, who had in his own businesses always avoided the kind of leverage- and debt-fueled dealings that were part of everyday business for GE, used the moment as a buying opportunity, getting the company's stock on the cheap. As part of the price paid to Buffett for saving GE, Immelt vowed to retool the firm and take it away from complex financial schemes and back toward making things. GE, in other words, would try to do what the United States as a whole needed to do: rebalance its economy and get back to basics. As CFO Jeff Bornstein summed it up to me in late 2014, "we had to decide whether we wanted to be a tech company that solves the world's big problems or a finance company that makes a few things."

FINANCE COMPANIES THAT MAKE A FEW THINGS

In choosing to reinvent itself, GE has become a canary in the coal mine of corporate America. Much of the future of corporate financialization will depend on whether the company's efforts to put its business model back in service to the real economy will succeed. If they do, GE's transition might become an inflection point at which the trajectory of the past four decades, during which companies have been acting more and more like financial institutions, is reversed. While GE Capital represented the largest and most visible example of that trend, it was by no means the only one. Indeed, the turn of American businesses in nearly every sector toward finance is just as much a part of the larger story of financialization as is the growth of the largest banks and asset managers.

Over the last few decades, Sears, GM, Ford, and many other large firms focused on retail and consumer products have created stand-alone lending units. These units "were originally intended to support consumer purchases of their products by offering installment financing but [they] eventually became financial behemoths that overshadowed the manufacturing or retailing activities of the parent firm," says University of Michigan academic Greta Krippner, whose book *Capitalizing on Crisis* provides the best quantitative analysis of the shift.[6] Krippner tallies the extent to which nonfinancial firms derive revenues from financial investments as opposed to more traditional productive activities (read: making stuff) and finds an alarming trend. While the share of revenues from financial activities vis-à-vis everything else was relatively stable in the 1950s and 1960s, it began to climb in 1970s and then increase sharply over the course of the 1980s. By the late 1980s, the ratio peaked at about *five times* the levels of the previous postwar decades. After some brief retreats during periods of market boom and bust, the ratio continued rising by the second half of the 1990s and has never stopped.[7]

Today's firms represent the apex of this trend. Corporate borrowing is at an all-time high, as are share buybacks, dividend payments, outsourcing, and tax optimizing—all factors that increase the share of financial activities in companies' revenues. And of course, firms' investment into jobs, factories, and innovation is near record lows, a decline that has run concurrently to the rise of financial activity within all American businesses.[8]

Proof of the shift is everywhere. Automakers often generate large chunks of their profits by selling consumers loans to purchase cars, rather than by simply selling the vehicles themselves.[9] Energy companies regularly try to boost their profits by speculating in oil futures, a shift that actually *undermines* their own core business models by creating more volatility in the oil markets. And airlines commonly make more money from hedging on oil prices than on selling airfare, although this strategy can also unexpectedly backfire.[10] Indeed, with the 50 percent plunge in oil prices from 2014 to 2015, the airline industry has lost more than $1 billion to bad bets on fuel prices.[11] "If I were on the board of a [large airline] I would not hedge oil," says Warren Buffett, who indeed limited fuel hedging at

Burlington Northern Santa Fe railway when he took over the company in 2009. "It doesn't make any sense to me. If you really think you have an edge in predicting the price of oil futures," just get into that business, he says. Otherwise, buy your fuel on the spot market, know what your costs will be, and be done with it.[12]

Whether or not companies are legitimately hedging their own commodity needs or are trying to make a profit in the markets (or both), they are part of the financialization of commodities that has caused them so much pain. As experts like Ruchir Sharma, head of emerging markets at Morgan Stanley Investment Management, have noted, the sudden plunge in the world oil prices in mid-2014 can't be fully explained by slowing Chinese demand for commodities or the fact that Saudi Arabia kept pumping crude to put pressure on higher-priced rivals like Iran. (Both of these fundamental trends played an important role, Sharma says, but they were longer-term phenomena and so don't explain why the collapse was so abrupt.) What triggered that plunge was the financialization of the oil market, particularly the growing role played by speculators such as hedge funds and large banks.[13] As the Federal Reserve pumped money into the economy after the financial crisis, speculators funneled much of it into commodities. Predictably, the hot money quickly got out of those markets when the Fed decided to pull back from that program, and oil prices began to drop—a sure sign that much of their value has been moving on trading dynamics rather than on basic supply and demand.[14]

And who does much of the trading these days? Oil and other commodities-oriented companies themselves that have nothing to do with banking. That not only gives them an unfair advantage in the market but also encourages the very firms that are supposed to ensure a safe and steady supply of the world's raw materials to potentially distort or exploit the market for their own gain. Three years ago, Cargill, the Minneapolis-based agricultural firm, registered in the United States as a swaps dealer, right alongside banking giants like J.P. Morgan and Goldman Sachs, and expanded its office in Houston to make room for more than 100 traders, supplementing the 1,000 it already employed in Geneva. (Switzerland, which has lax regulation that draws commodities hedging funds from all over the world, is a separate story. Glencore, the commodities trading firm started by financier, fugitive, and Democratic supporter Marc Rich, who was controversially pardoned by Bill Clinton for tax evasion and making illegal oil deals with Iran, is based there.) Koch Supply & Trading, a subsidiary of Koch Industries, the behemoth owned by the right-wing Koch brothers, deals in oil swaps as well. In fact, the company known best for its construction, chemical, and real estate activities traded the world's first oil swap thirty years ago.[15]

But the biggest nonfinancial oil derivatives players of all are the oil companies themselves, some of which now have trading arms that are as much a part of their core business model as energy development is. This is sadly ironic, given that the ups and downs of oil and other commodity prices are a huge reason behind the cyclical woes of energy firms. When oil prices are high, everyone rushes to extract as much as possible, inflating prices for equipment like rigs (the cost of a daily fee for an ultra-deepwater rig rose from $400,000 to $700,000 during the last big price run-up in 2011–2012). Later, when prices collapse, talent and money quickly leave the industry, forcing many players to slash costs and capacity. It's a roller-coaster ride that's only exacerbated by companies' own trading.

All the international oil majors do it, but the biggest by far in this arena is BP, a London-headquartered multinational that does about one-fourth of its business in the United States, via BP America. It's a perfect example not only of the rise of financial activities as a percentage of business, but also of the perverse effect that financialization can have on corporate culture. A focus on trading can lead to excessive risk taking, and an overemphasis on short-term profit can undermine a company's financial future. BP first got into the trading business years ago under Lord John Browne, the erudite CEO who was the first in the industry to acknowledge climate change, creating a Teflon-like veneer around the firm, in contrast to rivals like Exxon. (No matter that green technologies never made up more than a couple of percentage points of BP's business.) Browne, a sophisticate with a taste for fine wine, art, and Savile Row suits, stood in contrast to the tough-talking archetype of an oilman, embodied by rivals like Exxon's Lee Raymond.

Browne was loved by the public and lauded by environmentalists, but he was also known within the industry as a spreadsheet-driven risk taker. When he took over BP in the 1990s, he became the most aggressive cost cutter of the era, leading whistle-blowers to accuse the company of skimping on maintenance and safety and using outdated equipment, even as it encouraged traders in its burgeoning US office to take bigger risks in search of trading-desk profits. The strategy exploded in 2005 and 2006 when BP suffered a number of back-to-back disasters, including a refinery explosion in Texas City, Texas, an oil spill at Prudhoe Bay, Alaska, and accusations of manipulating energy markets via its US trading arm. In a move that echoed the manipulation of the California energy markets a few years earlier, Houston-based traders for BP America had used company resources to purchase a large quantity of propane gas, which they later sold to other market players for inflated prices, costing consumers $53 million in overcharges. BP eventually had to pay back that amount, as well as a criminal penalty of $100 million and another $125 million in civil charges to the CFTC. (The environmental disasters resulting from the explosion and Alaskan leaks cost tens of millions of dollars more in criminal and civil payments.) As Browne told me before the ruling came down, "we're moving . . . to a situation of business as unusual." But insiders said it was just the opposite. "Everyone knew that BP's short-term focus on the bottom line and lack of investment was a safety issue," said one industry veteran who worked as a consultant investigating the Prudhoe Bay spill. "If you were going to be in the foxhole with someone, you didn't want it to be those guys."[16]

Today, in the wake of BP's Deepwater Horizon disaster in the Gulf of Mexico in 2010, which became the largest marine oil spill in global history and has cost the company more than $50 billion in legal fees, penalties, and cleanup charges, his point only seems sharper. Yet far from pulling back and focusing on the core business,

BP has charged full steam ahead into trading, becoming one of the largest nonfinancial players in the field. (Like Cargill, BP is registered with the CFTC as a swaps dealer.)

Warren Buffett's view aside, you can argue that it makes sense for multinational energy companies to do some oil hedging, given that the price of oil is a core part of their business model (just as it's sensible for companies that do business in many territories at once to hedge against the shifts in currency valuations in various countries). But the amount of trading done by these organizations now far exceeds the value of their own real-world investments. To many experts, the disconnect between what's truly at stake in the real economy and the staggering volume of trading that takes place in the markets signifies the point at which trading begins to lose social value and undermine market stability. BP, for example, now gets at least 20 percent of its income from dealing in swaps, futures, and other financial instruments, up from 10 percent in 2005, the last time it disclosed profitability figures for its trading division. BP and other major oil producers trade not only in oil (enough to meet the needs of several major countries per day) but also in gas, electricity, petrochemicals, currencies, and even metals.[17] Volatility in all these markets has, of course, increased as trading levels have gone up. It's a vicious cycle that not only creates business management troubles for the companies, but also makes one of the world's most important natural resources a less stable commodity (more on that in chapter 6).

Technology companies have also suffered for their turn toward finance. Firms like Kodak, Hewlett-Packard, RCA, Microsoft, and Intel all diminished in terms of market share, new innovations, and eventually even share price as they began to focus more on financial engineering rather than the real kind. Indeed, you can often chart the high point of such companies by looking at when the buybacks begin and the growth in R&D investment stalls—two trends that, as we learned in the introduction, often make a perfect X.[18] Financial thinking, especially the use of leverage and hedging to offload risk onto weaker market players, is now a key part of the global technology business. As more and more Wall Street refugees make their way to Silicon Valley, there's growing concern that America's largest tech firms will soon look more like banks, and less like the rare American innovation and job hubs that they've been over the last several decades.

As just one example, Yahoo has faced relentless pressure from shareholder activists to boost its share price by either selling off its stake in the Chinese ecommerce giant Alibaba or spinning off its core advertisement business to do investor payouts. At Google, the new finance chief Ruth Porat, who formerly held the same job at Morgan Stanley, has vowed to crack down on costs and rein in spending on the company's most ambitious "moonshot" projects— exactly the sort of research that could lead to the next major technology breakthrough and that a hugely cash-rich company like Google should be doing.[19] And Apple, the most successful tech firm in history, makes a huge amount of money from its money (via interest income, tax-preferential debt deals, and holding billions of dollars in profits in offshore tax havens) as it struggles to come up with the next big innovation.

SPINNING STRAW INTO GOLD

How and why did all these American corporations decide that finance was the best kind of business to be in? The reasons are myriad. For one, business obsession with finance reflects the broad shift in the US economy from manufacturing to services over the last several decades. But why did that shift really happen? In part it's *because* companies began to focus on higher-profit areas of the economy. Services, with their lower overhead and potentially higher demand, are much easier to make money on than manufacturing. And finance, as we've already discovered, is the easiest place of all in which to turn a profit. You don't need much in the way of investment; you mainly need a few very clever people and a lot of superfast computers.

Of course, you also need a lax regulatory environment in which this shift from safe, real-economy investments to riskier, more volatile financial ones can take place. Unfortunately, in the late 1970s and the 1980s, policy makers in the United States and in much of the rest of the world were more than happy to oblige. Deregulation of interest rates and the politically sanctioned shift toward easy money and increased credit (outlined in chapter 1) did more than make the financial sector bigger. They also made financial sector *profits* larger, since credit booms always increase the volume of financial transactions and inflate asset prices relative to everything else. Then, as now, it's no wonder that firms like GE wanted to shift away from making things and toward doing finance. It was simply where the largest profits lay.

Indeed, the manufacturing sector, that traditional generator of middle-class jobs and sustainable economic growth, turned toward finance faster than any other part of the economy. In fact, manufacturing has led that charge since the 1970s—not only because the profits and stock valuations promised by the switch were so much higher, but also because (ironically) the volatility introduced into the economy by the growth of finance made it more difficult to plan future investment in things like plants and equipment. Of course, the subsequent corporate turn toward financial activities only increased risk within firms, creating a destructive cycle as business tried to smooth out volatility with further balance sheet manipulations. And so, as corporations became increasingly dependent on financial revenues to subsidize their core businesses, they also became increasingly focused on financial assets rather than those underlying businesses.

"The old view is that if you're in the bolt business, you take risks in the bolt business," one investment banker proclaimed in *BusinessWeek* in 1986. "You don't take risks with the cash."[20] The new view was that cash was there to be poured back into the markets, where it would always earn more than you would make by selling more bolts, or so the thinking went. Pretty soon corporations were nothing more than portfolios, bundles of assets to be managed like stocks. Finally free to turn money into more money—to spin straw, as it were, into gold—CFOs would frequently nix investments in real, tangible products in favor of new financial products like money-market mutual funds, "stripped" Treasuries, offshore dollar accounts, foreign currency hedges, and the most high-risk, high-return asset of all: futures contracts and other sorts of derivatives.

The trading culture infected all operations; productive assets became merely commodities to be traded, and quarterly profits were all. One of the most poignant examples of how this kind of thinking tanked once-competitive firms is Kodak, which famously decided to forgo investment into digital film technology. The result speaks for itself. In 1990, Kodak had 145,000 employees and $19 billion in revenue. Today, having come out of bankruptcy in 2013, it employs 8,000 people and makes $2 billion a year.[21]

There are, of course, countless other examples. Westinghouse, a once-great manufacturing company that was a leader of the Pittsburgh economy for decades after its founding in 1886, was, from the 1980s onward, sold off in bits, on the advice of management consultants, to bolster stock valuations. (Service sector businesses typically command higher stock valuations than manufacturing firms.) By 1997 it was a mere media company. Today the only thing left of the original Westinghouse—the firm that once made generators, household appliances, radios, broadcasting equipment, and office furniture—is CBS, a struggling TV and radio network that might itself be sold in the near future.

Sara Lee, another firm that shed jobs and ultimately lost market value after switching from manufacturing to brand management, is another case in point. As its CEO once summed it up, "Wall Street can wipe you out. They are the rule-setters. They do have their fads . . . and they have decided to give premiums to companies that harbor the most profits for the least assets. I can't argue with that."[22]

GE's Jack Welch was, of course, the master of figuring out how to make the most money with the fewest possible assets. "My gut told me that compared to the industrial operations I did know, this business [meaning financial operations like lending and credit] seemed an easy way to make money," he wrote in his autobiography. "You didn't have to invest heavily in R&D, build factories, and bend metal day after day."[23] While previous GE leaders had poured excess profits into their firm and shared them with employees (in the form of raises) or customers (in the form of price cuts), Welch bought wholesale into the Chicago School thinking around creating shareholder value. To him stock owners were king, and soon after taking over the company, he promised to deliver them an unheard-of 15 percent earnings increase per year. Over the course of his tenure, he fulfilled that promise by cutting tens of thousands of jobs, slashing R&D spending as a percentage of sales by half,[24] selling off GE's famous small appliance division (yes, the one that made televisions and toasters), and imposing a single rule for top managers: Be first or second in your products' market, and raise your profits every quarter. At GE, it was up or out.

In another vicious cycle, expectations of those kinds of returns, combined with now common multimillion-dollar executive pay packages (which resembled Wall Street bankers' pay more than the comfortable corporate salaries of the time), all but *necessitated* a move to financial activities. That, after all, was the only way to generate such profits in such a short amount of time. But as GE moved into finance, it began to resemble Wall Street in not just its business model but also its culture, starting with a spate of scandals that began under Welch: improper time card charges on a defense contract; accusations of tax evasion; defrauding the US government on an Israeli Aid Force deal; dumping tons of toxic waste; and a revelation that the firm's investment banking unit booked $350 million in phantom profits from fake trades.[25] The list goes on, including charges of insider trading, fraud, and racketeering.

Then there were the everyday accounting high jinks that were a disconcertingly common way of doing business in the pre-Enron era. To keep up his promise of 15 percent growth in earnings every year, Welch frequently resorted to moving money (not to mention jobs) offshore. He also booked income and expenses in ways that were technically legal but were designed to obscure what was really happening within various divisions, allowing him to "pull profits seemingly out of thin air," as the business-friendly *Economist* magazine once put it.[26] One telling example: Over the last five years of Welch's reign, between 1996 and 2001, GE earnings per share grew at 90.2 percent, an unprecedented figure for a large conglomerate. But without massive under-reserving at its reinsurance unit (meaning, it didn't put aside enough for the possibility that many claims would be called in at once), the company would have shown a gain of only 5.6 percent.[27] Meanwhile, GE Capital regularly allowed GE to manipulate its quarterly statements by engaging in trades right before reporting day, which would artificially push up the company's earnings. Such number games were technically forbidden by corporate governance watchdogs, but it was an open secret that GE played them. The company didn't try particularly hard to hide such maneuvers—after all, Wall Street just wanted its take; it didn't much care how it was generated.[28]

RISKY BUSINESS AND THE BUSINESS OF RISK

Of course, this kind of financial engineering introduces unseen risk into the business, whatever the rising share price might say to the Street and to the public. The focus on accounting tricks, spreadsheets, and shareholder primacy was like laying dynamite in secret places throughout corporations, where it could blow up in unexpected ways. In the effort to achieve efficiency and maximize profits for investors, many firms set the stage for their own reputational demise. It's happening now, with the subprime auto loan problems of the automotive majors. It happened with the telecom and Web companies of the late 1990s, many of which commanded huge valuations on the basis of fictional profits (Enron and WorldCom are prime examples).[29] And of course, it happened at GE, which wasn't regulated by the Federal Reserve until after the financial crisis (and after hard-fought battles over the Dodd-Frank reform legislation). Its creative accounting and triple-A rating had allowed GE to borrow money more cheaply than competitors did, many of them large banks. GE was so leveraged in the run-up to the financial crisis that it couldn't make it through a single day without selling billions of dollars of commercial paper to cover its many loans.

The painful result of such reckless risk taking doesn't only show up on bottom lines and in bailouts; it can often lead to real human tragedy. The spate of disasters at BP is one example, but a more recent and even more devastating event in terms of lives lost was the 2013 disaster at the Rana Plaza garment-making complex in Bangladesh. Of the 3,500 workers who labored there to churn out cheap clothing for brands like Walmart, more than 1,100 died when a poorly constructed factory collapsed on top of them.

As it turned out, the cause wasn't just a lack of adequate safety standards in Bangladesh (though that was part of the story). The complexity that outsourcing introduces into the supply chain was also at play. In the aftermath of the collapse, Walmart claimed that it didn't even know Rana Plaza was used to make girls' jeans it was planning to sell. (After documents surfaced showing that its Canadian supplier had indeed ordered pants from Rana Plaza, that firm blamed a "rogue employee" for filing the order.)[30] The revelations were all the more unsettling given that just eight months prior, Walmart-bound apparel had turned up in another disaster-stricken Bangladeshi factory, after a fire there had killed 120 people. In that instance, too, Walmart's supplier had farmed its work out to even cheaper, black-market subcontractors. Walmart was left holding the bag, paying out millions in compensation while it tries desperately to repair its reputation and ward off lawsuits.

The tragedies underscore the close links between financialization and outsourcing to cheap-labor countries, since the key goal of finance is to move liabilities (like labor costs and factories) off the balance sheet. The last few decades of outsourcing saved American business lots of money and helped push profit margins to record highs, but they also introduced a level of supply chain complexity and risk that companies are only just beginning to grapple with.

In addition to the considerable human toll, such supply chain disasters cost multinational brands billions of dollars, not to mention reputational downgrades. (Think of the repeated scandals over unsafe working conditions at factories used by Apple's suppliers in China.) One survey of global executives, conducted by McKinsey in 2010, found that two-thirds believed that supply chain risk had been on the rise since 2008. Executives in Asian nations were particularly worried; 82 percent believed the risks would continue to grow over the next five years.[31] Now events like those in Bangladesh are encouraging some companies to rethink basing their supply chain structure on production costs alone and to move business closer to home, which can be more expensive in the short run, but might offset risk and even bolster revenue (via improved PR and increased customer satisfaction) in the longer term. As disaster after disaster in overseas supply chains has made clear, even if multinationals are policing their direct suppliers, it's impossible for them to investigate every small-scale operation of their far-flung subcontractors. Risk is simply baked into this kind of complex manufacturing paradigm.

Even when firms do know exactly what's happening and where, the financially driven trend toward outsourcing still creates big problems. Consider the case of Boeing's 787 Dreamliner aircraft, which famously ran into all sorts of delays and cost overruns due to its incredibly complex supply chain, which involved outsourcing 70 percent of the airplane's component parts to myriad countries all over the world. The decisions were taken after Boeing's merger in 1997 with McDonnell Douglas, a much more financially oriented firm that focused not so much on the best engineering but on cost cutting and minimizing financial risk. After the merger, Boeing moved its headquarters from Seattle, where it had been for eighty-five years, to Chicago, farther from its engineering base and closer to financial markets, a decision taken explicitly by the new management. Despite protests from Boeing engineers, the Dreamliner supply chain reflected the pressure to maximize the company's return on net assets (RONA), a measure that Wall Street uses to evaluate what the share price of firms should be.

The McDonnell Douglas newcomers, firmly in charge, didn't

want to make investments in the proven but more expensive team of US engineers and designers, so they turned to a complex web abroad. When the Street heard how much was to be saved on the new designs by outsourcing so many components, Boeing's stock price jumped from $30 to $100 a share. Yet only a few years into the project, problems began to mount. For one, customers began to cancel their orders as the inability of suppliers to communicate with one another, deliver to specs (including safety), and bring designs in on time resulted in massive development delays. More than 25,000 disgruntled employees went on strike in the middle of the project. And there were so many technical problems with one supplier that Boeing had to pay $580 million to buy the firm and integrate it into their existing operations. Ultimately, the Dreamliner became an embarrassing money pit that has so far cost Boeing $28 billion more than it should have, and it probably won't reap the company any profits until at least the 2020s. Sadly, "by doing exactly what Wall Street wanted, they actually increased risk," says Harvard Business School professor Gautam Mukunda (who's trying to help his students understand the downside of financialization).[32] So much for shareholder value.[33]

CULTURE SHOCK

Financialization doesn't just shift how and where companies do business; it changes their very culture, making organizations value risky gambles and quick, easy wins over steady product quality and a consumer-oriented approach. In finance, the trader is at the top of the food chain—he's the alpha man (they are almost entirely men) who brings home the bear he's slaughtered and decides who gets to eat what. This culture encourages the glamorization of the individual trader over the firm as a whole, rewarding leaders for large deals and killer trades, rather than for slow and steady growth. Yet these hunters are not penalized for the risk that such actions bring to the firm.

Consider the rise of the winner-take-all system of corporate compensation that has prevailed on Wall Street and is now becoming more pervasive throughout corporate America. The last several decades have seen the rise of a ridiculously unfair compensation paradigm in American business, in which CEOs are paid more than *three hundred times* the salary of their average workers, and an up-or-out system of talent management that rewards type-A stars rather than encouraging team play. Never mind the mounting evidence, offered by academic research, that it's almost always successful teams, rather than single individuals, that drive a corporation's success.[34]

Meanwhile, some of the most innovative and competitive companies around—from Google to the cranberry farming cooperative Ocean Spray to Arup, a leading architectural engineering firm—have moved away from up-or-out style of management and now focus on team building. Such progressive thinking is still woefully rare in corporate America, however. "Organizations are systems, not subject to silver bullets but responsive to just cultures that touch everyone," says organizational consultant Margaret Heffernan, whose book *Beyond Measure* looks at how a variety of companies are trying to reject corporate hero worship in favor of a more cooperative style of business.[35]

GE's Jack Welch was, of course, the poster boy for the former style, one that unfortunately still dominates corporate America. A *Fortune* magazine story from 1997 lauded the brutal environment that he had created, particularly at GE Capital: "The culture at Capital isn't just entrepreneurial, it's aggressively so. 'You don't work there unless you're very self-confident,' says an executive recruiter. 'They can smell weakness and indecision.' The growth anxiety is pervasive. 'They're all afraid of not making their numbers,' says a consultant who works with Capital. That includes CFO Jim Parke, who oversees more than $1.5 trillion of commercial paper issuance each year, not to mention $100 billion of derivative 'hedging' contracts. What worries him most? 'Growth,' he says simply."[36]

Perhaps not surprisingly, this toxic culture resulted in lots of top engineering talent leaving GE. It got so bad that one manager checked himself into a mental hospital after a particularly brutal encounter with Welch. Despite the countless stories of Welch terrorizing employees, however, many stayed, and if you made it at GE, you were rewarded richly with stock options. Indeed, the company was at the forefront of the huge hike in executive pay from the 1980s onward.

By fomenting constant, ruthless competition within the firm and rewarding those who took big risks for big payoffs, Welch did more than build the sorts of hidden debt bombs that went off so famously during the subprime crisis. He was also instrumental in ending GE's tradition of secure lifetime employment and creating what might be called the "gig economy," in which firms could get rid of anyone, even their top people, at any time. Every employee became, in essence, a temp. This again was a shift in which business had come to mirror finance, where service tenures for employees had always been lower (and paydays bigger, as part of the high-risk, high-reward model that worked for the few but not for the many). Tenures at GE and most of the rest of the Fortune 500 companies decreased dramatically from the 1980s onward, a change that Welch lauded. "No one can guarantee lifetime employment," he once told a class of graduating Harvard Business School students. "The dot-coms have learned it." And, in Welch's view, everyone else should, too.[37] The goal should be not job security but worker adaptability to new situations.

MAKING AMERICA COMPETITIVE AGAIN

Fair enough. Yet the end result of all the financial maneuvering was fewer and fewer jobs for American workers to adapt to. Financially driven outsourcing, worker displacement by cost-saving technology, payouts to investors rather than investments in workers and assets, and short-term thinking in the boardroom and C-suites has undermined American business's competitiveness and the ability of US firms to create secure, decent-paying jobs. By the late 1970s these corrosive effects of financialization had begun to show up in economic data, which pointed to slower growth and lower investment in the real economy as firms jockeyed to make higher margins from speculating with their cash. Even Ronald Reagan, one of the biggest advocates of unfettered capitalism around, knew it. Changes in the regulations governing mergers and acquisitions during the early part of his presidency, in 1982, had opened the way for the proliferation of giant conglomerates prone to financial wheeling and dealing. Between 1980 and 1990, a full 28 percent of the Fortune 500's largest manufacturing firms received tender bids, most of them hostile, from people like T. Boone Pickens, Carl Icahn, and other corporate raiders. Firms would be spliced, diced, and spliced again, their component parts sold off to the highest bidder, who would often promptly bleed the companies dry. By the end of this period, around a third of the largest firms in the United States had ceased to exist as independent companies.[38]

Yet even as their laws were helping to create a climate ripe for financialization, Reagan and his advisers had begun to worry about the results, which included the eroding market share of US manufacturing firms vis-à-vis their Asian and European competitors. One report released by Reagan's Commission on Industrial Competitiveness in 1985 sounds, amazingly enough, like something that could have been written by President Obama's Council on Jobs and Competitiveness today: "In the 1960s, the real rates of return earned by manufacturing assets were substantially above those available on financial assets. Today, the situation is reversed. Passive investment in financial assets has pretax returns higher than the rates of return on manufacturing assets. . . . As a result, the relative attractiveness of investing in our vital manufacturing core has been compromised."[39]

A little-known and truly stupefying fact is that Reagan was so worried about the financialization of the US economy and its impact on competitiveness that he actually launched a secret project to develop a US industrial policy—a term that is still so strongly associated in the public consciousness with Soviet Russia that it has become (wrongly) a third-rail topic even among most American liberals, not to mention conservatives. The idea behind that Reagan administration effort, known as Project Socrates, was to figure out why America's foreign competitors were succeeding in establishing highly efficient, thriving corporations while their US counterparts were withering. The team found that foreign firms based in Japan, France, Germany, and other developed countries enjoyed a wide spectrum of advantages that allowed them to trounce US companies: government assistance, generous subsidies, R&D initiatives, industrial intelligence gathering, and unofficial non-tariff barriers. The project's mission was to then map out a strategy of industrial and technological development that would allow the United States to close the gap.[40] The effort was shut down under the Bush administration, but it's a battle that is in many ways still being fought. It is also one that, ironically, brings together political forces from both sides of the aisle. Not only liberals like Elizabeth Warren, for example, but even some conservatives worry about the transatlantic and transpacific trade deals currently in the works (the so-called TTIP and TPP). One concern is that these deals will undermine the Dodd-Frank legislation designed to curb the financial sector, by allowing backdoor ways around government regulation.

Such legislation has been one of the most powerful reasons for GE's departure from finance. When asked why GE had decided to roll back the finance division that the company had spent so long building, Jack Welch himself summed it up quite nicely: "Two words: Dodd-Frank."[41] Prior to the crisis, GE had been a Too Big to Fail financial firm, but it hadn't been regulated like one. By 2013 the industrial giant had been designated a "systemically important financial institution," which, far from making Wall Street happy, made it worried because the company was now under heightened regulatory scrutiny. Activities that were once a part of daily business could suddenly be illegal. GE's stock valuation was increasingly under pressure as investors began to realize that big banks and institutions that acted like them would be forced to hold more capital on their balance sheets, lowering their profit margins. Indeed, while corporate makers, including big industrial and manufacturing firms, used to trade at a discount relative to banks, which were seen as more global and glamorous, the opposite is increasingly true. Spinning off GE Capital, it turns out, may actually be good not only for business, but also for the market's perception of the firm. The day that Immelt announced that GE would be getting fully and permanently out of finance (with the caveat that it would still help existing manufacturing clients with their funding needs—a portion of the finance operation that actually *did* help Main Street firms), the company's stock price rose more than 10 percent. "It was very clear that we needed to not be a financial firm," says GE CFO Jeff Bornstein. "Nobody really pushed back on that. Dodd-Frank just completely changed the regulatory landscape."[42]

What's more, the corporate debt market itself is changing in a way that would make financial machinations of the kind GE Capital once undertook much more difficult. The short-term money-market lending business in which GE had played prior to the 2008 financial meltdown (the business invented by Citi's Walter Wriston, as outlined in chapter 1) has largely dried up after investors realized the risks involved. The short-term IOUs that GE had issued before the crisis, which essentially involved hocking its own corporate bonds as collateral for cheap loans, had once seemed like an easy way to fund lots of debt spending. The idea that there could suddenly be no one left to buy those bonds in the middle of a market panic had never occurred to anyone—until it happened. The 2008 crisis proved just how dangerous it was for a business to operate as banks did, by counting on its ability to borrow billions of dollars each day just to stay solvent.[43]

With the spin-off of GE's consumer-finance division in late 2014, the share of profits that came from finance fell from about 40 percent to 28 percent.[44] The ongoing shedding of GE Capital promises to get it down to around 10 percent by 2018.[45] Now the challenge for GE will be figuring out how to turn a buck without relying on financial engineering. Ironically, that challenge may be leading GE to a future that looks very much like its past, though this time its main growth markets might lie overseas. Emerging economies are entering a period quite like the post–World War II consumption boom in the United States, during which GE was at its peak as an innovator. Countries such as China, India, Turkey, and South Africa will need new houses, bridges, roads, airports, and all types of consumer goods in unprecedented quantities as their middle classes expand. The McKinsey Global Institute estimates that by 2025, emerging-economy nations will be spending $30 trillion a year in this way.[46] That means future growth for companies like GE may once again center on making things. Indeed, GE has staked its future on that shift, with a new mandate to tackle real-world problems and products. The company will be providing fewer snazzy financial services and more "basic things, the sort of things that when you don't have them, you have trouble—electricity, clean water, jet engines, efficient locomotives," says Bornstein. "We want to be a technology company focused on solving the world's biggest problems."[47] To that end, GE is trying to copy some of Silicon Valley's methods. The company is crowdsourcing all over the world, posting engineering problems online and letting anyone who can solve them propose their solutions. (One recent design for a bracket on a jet engine came from a twenty-two-year-old in Indonesia.)

GE is also partnering with a number of high-tech start-ups to jump-start new ideas. And it's using more local small and midsize suppliers, thanks to new technologies that let start-ups achieve more speed and scale. The once-disparate steps of designing a product, making or buying the parts, and putting everything together are beginning to blend, because of such technologies as additive manufacturing and 3-D printing. As a result, manufacturing operations now want to be physically closer to engineering and design. This dynamic will likely benefit the United States, which still rules those high-end job categories, and allow small and midsize American firms to get back into manufacturing. Add in the ability to include sensors in every part and process and you've got a whole new manufacturing ecosystem that allows companies to accelerate product development and deliver more variety and value more quickly to consumers. Detroit in particular has become a hub for advanced manufacturing partnerships of this kind, as it benefits from what is still the deepest pool of industrial engineers in the world.

For its part, GE has set up a "growth board" that operates like an internal venture capital firm, vetting new ideas presented by employees and then dishing out a bit of capital to explore them. The result is that production cycles for projects like new oil-drilling equipment or LED lighting systems are shortening dramatically. An idea that once took two years to test might go from paper to production in forty-five days. R&D spending is back up from around 2 percent of revenues to more than 5 percent, according to GE's former chief technology officer, Mark Little.[48]

The result of all of this has been a new paradigm in which GE is once again making, in America, products for the rest of the world. Just one example of this renewed ability is a bright red cellphone tower on the outskirts of Nairobi, Kenya, that delivers coverage to thousands of city residents. Inside it, there are high-tech batteries that serve a simple but critical purpose: they provide backup power to keep calls connected when the main electrical grid goes down. The batteries come from a GE plant in Schenectady, New York—a Rust Belt city that was once seen as a relic of an earlier industrial age but that now houses a new GE factory on the site of a former turbine plan, which churns out the batteries twenty-four hours a day. Schenectady, the home of GE's first research facility in 1900, is once again a growing R&D hub for the company.

This has huge implications for the local economy of Schenectady as well as for other such communities around the country. The official figure for US manufacturing employment, 9 percent, belies the true importance of the sector. Manufacturing represents a whopping 69 percent of private-sector R&D spending as well as 30 percent of the country's productivity growth.[49] And, according to US government figures, every $1 of manufacturing activity returns $1.37 to the economy. "The ability to make things is fundamental to the ability to innovate things over the long term," says Willy Shih, a Harvard Business School professor and coauthor of *Producing Prosperity: Why America Needs a Manufacturing Renaissance*. "When you give up making products, you lose a lot of the added value." In other words, what you make makes you, economically anyway.[50] Certainly, all this was on GE executives' minds when they made the decision to move manufacturing back to upstate New York. "In the old days, we spent a lot of time looking for sources [globally] for everything we did, and then we picked the cheapest source," says GE's Little. "Now we've realized that if we can control things and vertically integrate our activities in local markets, then we don't have to give up that margin that we might have once given to a vendor," not to mention the value of any intellectual property created as a result.[51]

It's a smarter way to think about business, and it's certainly better for local economies. The question is just how many good new jobs such operations will actually create in America in the coming years. The Boston Consulting Group's 2014 annual survey of senior manufacturing executives found that the number of respondents bringing production back from China to the United States had risen 20 percent from the previous year. But that won't come close to replacing the 2.3 million manufacturing jobs lost in the recession that followed the 2008 financial crisis.

As soon as you step into GE's Schenectady plant, which is as clean and bright as a medical lab, you begin to see why. The 200,000-square-foot facility requires only 370 full-time employees, a mere 210 of them on the factory floor. The plant manager runs the entire operation—from lights to heat to inventory to purchasing and maintenance—from an iPad, on which he gets a real-time stream of data from wireless sensors embedded in each product rolling off the line. The sensors let the batteries talk to GE via the Internet once they've left the factory. Each part of the product and, indeed, the factory, including the equipment and the workers who run it, will soon communicate with one another over the Internet. Not only does the data allow production to be monitored as it occurs; it can also help predict what might go wrong—graphing, for instance, the average battery life in Bangladeshi heat versus Mongolian cold. Designs will be altered in real time to reflect the knowledge.

But while all this technology in Schenectady has reduced the number of machinists needed to make a battery, it has also fueled the creation of a GE global research center in San Ramon, California. The center now employs more than one thousand software engineers, data scientists, and user-experience designers who are well paid to develop the software for that kind of industrial Internet—otherwise known as the Internet of things. GE plans to hire thousands more such employees within the next half-decade. "We are probably the most competitive, on a global basis, that we've been in the past 30 years," in terms of being able to make things again in the United States, says CEO Jeffrey Immelt. "Will US manufacturing go from 9 percent to 30 percent of all jobs? That's unlikely. But could you see a steady increase in jobs over the next quarters and years? I think that will happen."[52]

Despite Immelt's optimism, the jury is still out on America's manufacturing renaissance and GE's own resurgence. Both will require a retooling of the workforce (many factory jobs now require at least a two-year associate's degree) and a further revamping of corporate business models. The new economics of Made in the USA are built in large part around acquiring cutting-edge technologies ahead of global competitors and then using those new techniques to produce more efficiently on superautomated factory floors. That means companies still need to focus on long-term R&D rather than short-term investor payouts. And while all the technology will translate into higher-end jobs, it may also mean—barring dramatic growth—fewer jobs overall in the short term, especially in the middle. Positions will either be high-end knowledge jobs or lower-paid jobs, since workers will still have to compete with cheaper overseas labor. (Even with wage inflation in China, it will be years before the country is on par with US wages.) Manufacturing is coming back, yes. But these makers are different than those of the past, and industrial companies will continue to be under pressure from Wall Street to keep providing the kinds of big, short-term-return boosts that overseas competitors, many of them family owned, simply don't have to worry about.

To that point, it's telling that the very first thing Immelt did with the money from the GE Capital spin-off was promise a big payday for shareholders. Proceeds from the sale will allow GE to hand out $90 billion through a mix of buybacks and dividend payments over the next few years. As Immelt himself put it, it was a "classic capital allocation move" that would please investors, even as GE shed its designation as a Too Big to Fail institution to avoid the higher capital and regulatory costs that would come if it didn't. Certainly, when he made the decision to hand back cash, Immelt must have considered the fact that he'd already held his CEO position some five years longer than was typical for an S&P 500 leader in recent years, and that investors had begun to tire of his reinvention story. Paying them then was clearly the cost of continuing to move GE to a more sustainable growth model for the future. Wall Street, of course, rallied on the news of the payouts.

Whether Wall Street's cheers remain as loud when GE moves forward and reconnects with its innovative roots will be a telling statement about the public markets' readiness to embrace companies that prioritize real engineering over the financial kind.

CHAPTER 6

FINANCIAL WEAPONS OF MASS DESTRUCTION

*Commodities, Derivatives, and
How Wall Street Created a Food Crisis*

SHORTLY AFTER becoming head of the United Nations' World Food Programme in 2007, Josette Sheeran started carrying a small red cup with her to meetings with world leaders. To make them understand how the rise in global food prices could translate into starvation, she would pull out the standard-issue cup that the WFP used to portion out porridge, one full serving of it a day, to 20 million schoolchildren around the globe. On the bottom of Sheeran's cup was scrawled the name Lily, identifying the little girl who'd once used it. Sheeran would show finance ministers and presidents and billionaires the small object, which held another day of life for each child the WFP fed. Then she would show the 1/2 cup line to demonstrate how a doubling of food prices had driven 140 million more people into abject hunger worldwide.[1]

It's a stark reminder that for most of the world, food is something you eat to stay alive. But on Wall Street, it's also something you trade—and the more it gets traded, the higher prices the rest of the world must pay. In 2008, for the first time in thirty-five years, the world faced a serious and unusually synchronized surge in inflation, the bulk of it due to a precipitous rise in the price of food and energy commodities. Some of that was the result of global growth, which had been going strong prior to the financial crisis of 2008; people in emerging markets were eating better and driving more cars. But as the Great Recession began to sink in, and demand around the world dropped like a stone, it also became clear that something aside from supply and demand was at work in inflating the price of commodities, which had been rising in every category, across every country.[2] That something was financialization.

The real price of food in 2008 reached its highest level since at least 1845, according to *The Economist*.[3] The year 2008 was also the first on record that one billion people worldwide went hungry. In the United States, prices of food, fuel, and other commodities like cotton kept rising for more than a year afterward. We felt the pain at the gas pumps (in the spring of 2009, gas prices increased fifty-four days in a row, the longest streak on record since 1996),[4] in restaurants, and while paying our heating bills. In vast swaths of the developing world, hyperinflation due to rising commodities prices caused much greater pain: widespread hunger and even in some places starvation, riots, and political instability. In Russia, for example, consumers went back to stockpiling food, as they did in the days of chronic shortages under communism, hoarding enough staples like flour, pasta, and oil to last for months—as inflation reached a staggering 15 percent. Meanwhile China faced record power shortages, as soaring coal prices and government-set electricity tariffs forced smaller power plants to shut down.

There were food-related riots in twenty-two countries; a government in Haiti fell after massive rioting because of food and fuel inflation. Even in the United States, price volatility caused serious pain in the agriculture sector. A letter to President Obama in March 2009, signed by 184 human rights and hunger relief organizations urging him to curb commodities speculation, put the problem of price volatility in stark terms. Rapidly rising food prices caused children in developing countries to perish, the letter said. And later, when prices plunged just as fast, they "forced farmers in the developing world and the United States from their farms."[5]

A Morgan Stanley report released in June 2008 summed it up this way: "Much to our own surprise, we find that 50 of the 190 or so countries in the world now have inflation running at double-digit rates," including most emerging markets. In other words, Morgan Stanley was shocked to learn—which is somewhat ironic given Wall Street's role in the spike—that about half the world's population was experiencing double-digit price increases on basic living staples.

Much of this is forgotten now because the $1.3 trillion subprime mortgage mess, which happened at roughly the same time, dwarfed the food crisis in terms of economic impact and also eventually caused prices to fall by throwing much of the world into a recession. But you can't eat stocks. And after the meltdown was over, and the central banks of the world, led by the Federal Reserve, began dumping huge amounts of money into markets to try to stem the effects of the Great Recession, commodity prices began rising once again. Global economic growth was still slow, yet the cost of basic food and energy, costs that make up 60 percent or more of the budgets of most of the people in the world (and around 20 percent of the typical household budget in the United States), started to rise precipitously.

Why? Because investors had more money to play with—and they put it into commodities. As Michael Masters, an American hedge fund titan, pointed out back in 2009, for years there had been something fishy about the fact that commodities didn't seem to be rising and falling on supply-and-demand dynamics alone. In Senate testimony on the issue of market speculation back in 2009, Masters said, "US economic output was dropping during the first six months of 2008. During that time, the worldwide supply of oil was increasing and worldwide demand for oil was decreasing. . . . And yet, despite this glut of unwanted oil, the price has risen an amazing 85 percent per barrel."[6]

The same was true across many more categories of commodities just a couple of years later, starting in 2010, when things like rubber, wheat, corn, and oil began to spike again. In the spring of 2011, the US recovery was only just beginning to take off in earnest. Yet Walmart CEO William Simon warned shoppers to be prepared for what he called "serious" inflation. "We're seeing cost increases starting to come through at a pretty rapid rate," he said.[7] That same year, with many middle- and lower-income Americans suffering the aftermath of the financial crisis, the effects of food inflation began to be more keenly felt. Data from the US Agricultural Department showed that 21 percent of American households with children were now "food insecure," meaning that they worried about not having enough money to buy food, or had to skip meals or eat less for financial reasons.[8]

Meanwhile, the world saw the first bout of the social unrest in Tunisia that would eventually become the Arab Spring, a change that has totally transformed the Middle East. It began, as so many revolutions do, with food riots. "Food is a radically different threat [than other kinds of financial crises], because it affects so many of the world's poor so profoundly," Erwann Michel-Kerjan, managing director of the Risk Management and Decision Processes Center at the Wharton School, told me at the time. Food is also an amplifier of many other kinds of risk, particularly political risk. And today its effects are traveling much more rapidly because of the increasing interconnectedness of the world, as well as the increasing power that Wall Street has over the price of a loaf of bread.[9]

There has been much debate since 2008 about the role that Wall Street has played in commodities markets. The effects have been difficult to tease out, precisely because for the five years leading up to the financial crisis, the world as a whole grew faster than ever before. Yet nearly every economist and many bankers I've spoken to believe that financial speculation is playing a greater and greater role in fueling volatility in commodities, a suspicion that is bolstered by the fact that prices of all kinds have begun rising and falling in sync with one another—a historically unusual trend.

In April 2011, journalist Frederick Kaufman wrote an article for *Foreign Policy* magazine titled "How Goldman Sachs Created the Food Crisis," which put the blame squarely on Wall Street.[10] Kaufman outlined many of the headline statistics about just how financialized food and all sorts of other commodities had become. Since 2000 there has been a fiftyfold increase in dollars invested into commodities-linked index funds. It was a shift that was due to several things: the creation of a commodity index fund by Goldman Sachs in 1991, which allowed raw materials to become securities that could be bought and sold by investors; the deregulation of commodities markets in 2000, which poured gasoline on that process; the financial crisis of 2008, which scared everyone out of stocks and drove investors into "safety" bets like raw materials; and the beginning of the Federal Reserve's quantitative easing program the following year, a $4.5 trillion money dump that was meant to help Main Street but ended up giving Wall Street a lot of easy money to burn. Much of that money ended up in commodities markets, dramatically boosting the prices of those commodities—the raw materials that people depend on to heat their homes, fill up their gas tanks, and feed their families. For many people around the world, this made something as basic as eating literally unaffordable.

THE PRICE OF A LOAF OF BREAD

Commodities markets are tricky in all kinds of ways. For starters, they involve raw materials that are often owned and extracted by state-run firms in difficult places (Russia, the Middle East, West Africa, and so on). Access to these materials—such as corn, wheat, oil, metal ores, uranium, gas, coal, and rare earth minerals—is dependent on many volatile factors, like weather and politics. The commodities aren't just what we all need to survive; they are also the basic building blocks of business. Asset flows between two banks can certainly affect the real world, as we saw in 2008. But flows of commodities are even more important. They are essential to the daily economic operations of the entire planet. Quite simply, we can't live without them.

Commodities are also inexorably tied to one of the most crucial, and yet most problematic, financial markets out there: derivatives. The traders who helped trigger worldwide food riots and drive up gas prices were in some cases buying actual raw materials for their clients (or their own banks), but in most cases they were merely buying *bets* on the future price of those materials. Derivatives are a financial tool that has been used for centuries, even millennia, as an insurance policy on the risk of owning things like rice, or oil, or property. Purchasing a derivative that helps you hedge against a loss or an adverse shift in the markets can be useful. Farmers, for example, need to be able to make such bets to lock in prices for their crops in advance, lest they drop before the crops get harvested. Airlines or trucking companies might need to "hedge" oil so that price increases don't put them out of business.

But by the 1990s, and much more so after 2000, derivatives began to explode and expand in a way that made it clear that at least some of what was being traded had nothing to do with protecting people or companies in the real economy, but was more about speculation—one could call it gambling—with an increasingly complex array of financial instruments, on things like interest rate swaps, credit default swaps, and even bets on what the weather would be like from day to day. Derivatives are best known to most people as the "financial weapons of mass destruction" that Warren Buffett has warned us about, the complex securities that blew up our financial system in 2008. These financial instruments—be they interest rate swaps, foreign exchange bets, or grain futures—have very real, very tangible impacts. Yet to the banks, hedge funds, and the other institutions that trade them, they are simply another part of the economy that can be arbitraged for profit. That kind of trading for its own sake is part of the closed financial loop described in the introduction to this book, a loop that enriches mostly financiers but can endanger both businesses and consumers.

As if Wall Street's ability to buy as many grain or oil futures as it wants—often with our retirement money—and contribute to runaway inflation weren't enough, there's another problematic wrinkle that finance has brought to the commodities markets: Today bankers can both trade commodities *and* buy up the physical goods being traded. Goldman Sachs can technically own farmland, for example, *and* trade the grain grown on it. Although Wall Street has long bought and sold commodities futures and swaps, the combination of purely financial trading and ownership of physical commodities was a trend that began to accelerate around 2000, thanks to deregulation and a torrent of pension money that began to flow into commodities as an asset class. Only financial institutions have this ability to both make the market and be the market—to trade the products they own, hoarding or even manipulating them if they like, to raise or lower prices at will. They are the fox in the henhouse— except they also designed and built the henhouse, and they get to butcher the hens, and sell the eggs if they want. This unique market position does more than enable them to push food prices so high that people go hungry. It also puts them in direct competition with the businesses that actually need such raw materials to make products: car companies, bottle makers, gas station chains, airlines, and such. The financialization of commodities markets means that American business now has to compete with its own bankers. It's a perverse cycle that is wreaking competitive havoc on US industry, as described in the story below.

GOOSING THE MARKETS

Most people think that giant multinational companies like Coca-Cola rule the world. But as a recent scandal in the commodities market illustrates, they are nothing compared to Too Big to Fail financial institutions like Goldman Sachs. This point was brought into sharp relief in the summer of 2011, when executives from Coke began publicly complaining that something dicey was happening in the aluminum market. Prices for the metal had been going up, but demand hadn't changed. What's more, the time it took Coke and other big consumer brands, like the beer company MillerCoors, along with metal fabricators like Novelis, to get the raw materials they needed to make their cans and other aluminum products out of the warehouses in the Midwest (where such metal is traditionally stored) was mysteriously rising as well. The result was that Coke and other product manufacturers, desperate not to run out of supplies, were being forced to pay not only a higher price for the metal but also a premium for delivery.[11] "The situation has been organized artificially to drive premiums up," said Dave Smith, Coke's head of strategic procurement, at an industry conference in June 2011. "It takes two weeks to put aluminum in, and six months to get it out."[12]

Guess who Coke, Coors, and their thirsty consumers were paying that premium to? Goldman Sachs. It's an amazing tale that provides a window into the complex and costly shenanigans that can result when banks move too far out of their traditional purview of simple lending and financial intermediation and into other types of business. While the Goldman aluminum-hoarding scandal has less human significance than the food and fuel bubbles of 2008 and 2010, it has received significant legal attention and documentation. It thus provides a sharp lens through which to understand the confluence of events that created the dysfunctional system in which financial institutions are allowed to both *make* the market and *be* the market.

The problem had been growing behind the scenes for years and had been followed by academics and some trade press, but it sprang onto the public radar in July 20, 2013, when the *New York Times* ran a front-page piece on how Goldman Sachs had taken advantage of a tiny loophole in a 1999 amendment to the 1956 piece of regulation known as the Bank Holding Company Act. The loophole allowed Goldman to buy up thousands of tons of aluminum and hoard it in twenty-seven separate Detroit warehouses to exploit regulations that had been set up by the London Metal Exchange (LME), a global commodities marketplace that sets industry standards for metals trading. In a complex arbitrage of cross-border laws and decades-old legislative rulings that could be interpreted in myriad ways, Goldman was essentially able to do something banks traditionally hadn't been able to do—control and release the supply of aluminum as and when it wanted. The result: the price of the metal went up, meaning that Coke, Coors, and many other companies had to pay more, a lot more, to package their products.[13] Industry experts say that higher aluminum prices cost American shoppers somewhere between $3.5

billion[14] to $5 billion[15] between 2010 and 2013, since the companies passed on their costs in the form of higher consumer prices.

What was in it for Goldman? Plenty. For starters, the bank made money on aluminum storage fees via a wholly owned company called Metro International Trade Services, which charged about 40 cents per metric ton per day to store the metal, yielding around $100 million in revenue each year.[16] Metro created incentives for customers to cancel and reestablish contracts for aluminum; the cancellation of a contract allowed Metro to move the metal, thus getting around LME stipulations that a certain amount of metal had to be moved out of a particular storage area by a particular time (regulations that were meant to *prevent hoarding*). Because Metro didn't actually have to sell the metal to end users, the merry-go-round could keep going, and money could continue to be made on aluminum storage. Without breaking any LME regulations, Metro was actually moving at least 3,000 tons of aluminum a day into other warehouses, sometimes just a few feet away. This, of course, created a backlog for customers who actually wanted to buy and use the aluminum, higher premiums for the metal, and more rent revenue for Metro.

A few numbers give a sense of the magnitude of the scheme. When Goldman bought Metro in 2010, it took around 40 days to get aluminum out of the warehouse. By 2014, the wait time was 674 days.[17] The amount of aluminum stored at Metro, meanwhile, grew from 50,000 tons in 2008 to 850,000 tons in 2010 to 1.5 million tons in 2013.[18] That year more than a quarter of the supply of aluminum available on the market sat in Metro's warehouses.[19] The rent for storing aluminum grew from 41 cents a ton per day in 2011 to 45 cents a ton per day in 2012, to 48 cents a ton per day in 2013.[20] All this translated into hundreds of millions of dollars in profits for Goldman, as Metro's earnings grew from $67 million in 2009 to $211 million in 2012 and wait times began to lengthen.[21]

As strange as the market run-up was, Metro's regulator, the London Metal Exchange, had reasons not to look at the issue too closely, since the LME itself earned 1 percent of all the rental revenue from warehouses it regulated. This relationship gets at a major systemic problem in the financial markets, which is that people within the system are very often incentivized to do exactly what's *not* good for the economy as a whole. The LME's warehousing board was made up of executives from the warehouses it regulated. As amazing as this might seem, it's quite a common situation in financial markets, which often leaves companies, in essence or even in practice, to self-regulate. There was another troubling wrinkle in the story, too: As one of the world's top derivatives traders, Goldman Sachs may well have made a large chunk of money trading commodities-linked derivatives based on the *privileged information* that owning the raw materials would have provided.

The Goldman aluminum-hoarding tale underscores many elements of the dysfunctional market ecosystem in which businesses are forced to operate. First, it shows in a particularly concrete way how the commodities market can be controlled by speculators. Second, it shows that much of what the speculators do may actually be legal, thanks to changes in the laws governing the boundaries between commerce and finance, changes that were made in large part because of heavy lobbying by the financial industry and support from finance-friendly politicians. It is truly amazing that investment banks (Goldman wasn't the only one) were allowed to hoard a basic natural resource in such a way that they managed to rip off one of the world's biggest companies, Coca-Cola, not to mention the soda-buying public, and that it may have actually been legal because of a loophole in a law that was bought and paid for by the financial industry. But in many ways, it is even more amazing that after years of investigation into the incident by the Commodity Futures Trading Commission, the Federal Reserve, the US Senate's Permanent Subcommittee on Investigations, and the Justice Department, the experts still don't have a full and definitive picture of who did what, or when, or how. The sheer complexity of the situation, as well as many others like it, and the fact that no single regulatory body can get a handle on it, is a huge problem. But the core issue, that of banks using their superior assets and information to become sharp competitors to industries they are supposed to support, results in a market distortion that is taking an untallied but undoubtedly large toll on business and our economy.

"I'm sure that Goldman used the information they had about aluminum to influence the market between 2010 and 2013," says Cornell law professor Saule Omarova. (Her paper on the problems inherent in banks both owning and trading commodities, "The Merchants of Wall Street: Banking, Commerce, and Commodities," first sparked serious media interest in the topic.) "But can I prove it? No. Can the CFTC? I doubt it. And if that's the case, should Goldman be doing any of this? Absolutely not."[22]

Part of the complexity of the commodities-linked derivatives markets, like derivatives trading markets as a whole, is that until quite recently they weren't subject to very much federal oversight. According to former CFTC head Gary Gensler, also a former Goldman Sachs derivatives expert (and now CFO of Hillary Clinton's presidential campaign), prior to the 2008 crisis around 90 percent of the entire derivatives market was in an unregulated space, not subject to oversight or central clearing on public exchanges.[23] Gensler, who made it his business while at the CFTC to try to change that, has special insight into just how damaging that opacity can be. In 1998, while working in the Clinton administration for then–Treasury secretary Robert Rubin, he was assigned the task of trying to sort out the potential financial implications of the implosion of the hedge fund Long-Term Capital Management (LTCM). The culprit: a $1.25 trillion swaps portfolio gone bad. Gensler remembers going out to LTCM's headquarters in Greenwich, Connecticut, on a Sunday to investigate. "It quickly became clear to me that we had no idea what the ramifications would be in our financial system, and where, because these trades were booked in the Cayman Islands," he says. "It was a terrible feeling."[24]

Derivatives—be they interest rate swaps, foreign exchange bets, or energy futures—have real-world impacts, as we've already seen. Yet to the banks, hedge funds, and the other institutions that trade them, they are simply another moneymaking vehicle, something to be bought and sold. What's more, most of us play a part in the cycle that drives up commodity prices and disproportionately enriches the financial sector, via our retirement savings. After the bursting of the tech bubble, in the wake of the market downturn, institutional investors like pension funds and endowments, along with big asset managers like Fidelity, began looking for a new place to make money. Commodities markets had always been attractive to certain risk-taking speculators, but they weren't typically a place where institutional investors would put their funds.[25] Yet around 2004, as China's energy needs were heating up and commodity prices were rising, a couple of Yale academics put out a paper heralding the virtues of commodities investing as a way to balance big portfolios, arguing that historically, commodities typically didn't rise and fall in the same cycles as other assets such as stocks and bonds. It was a catalyst for many big asset managers to start getting into the commodities space. Amazingly, nobody thought too much about the fact that those academics had been funded to do their research by AIG Financial Products, which was looking to expand the portion of its business that allowed investors to buy index-linked bundles of commodities.[26] Of course, by 2008, AIG, which helped bring down the US and global economy with its enormous credit default swap bets, was in the news for bigger and more alarming reasons. Academics pushing paid-for research that made a potentially risky market segment look safe were a minor thing by comparison.

In any case, the financialization of commodities had already begun to take off. Institutional investors poured into the market for natural resources; between 2004 and 2007, the number of commodities futures contracts outstanding in the world nearly doubled. Because commodities futures prices are the benchmark for the prices of actual physical commodities that people use on a daily basis, when speculators drive futures prices higher, it affects the real economy immediately. (Indeed, it was during that time that food and fuel price inflation began to rise globally.) In 2003, big investors were putting $13 billion into commodity index trading strategies. By March 2008, they were pouring in $260 billion.[27] During that time, the prices of 25 commodities, from cotton to cocoa, cattle to heating oil, aluminum to copper, rose by a whopping 183 percent. "Are institutional investors contributing to food and energy price inflation? My unequivocal answer is, YES!" said hedge fund portfolio manager Michael Masters in testimony on the topic before the US Senate Committee on Homeland Security and Governmental Affairs in May 2008. "What we are experiencing is a demand shock coming from a new category of participant in the commodities futures markets ... corporate and government pension funds, sovereign wealth funds, university endowments, and other institutional investors. Collectively, these investors now account on average for a larger share of outstanding commodities futures contracts than any other market participant."[28]

It's a trend that has only strengthened since then, as a good chunk of the $4.5 trillion that the Federal Reserve dumped into the markets to try to buoy the economy following the financial crisis ended up either in commodities or in emerging market economies that were essentially plays on the commodity markets.[29] The fact that these markets have since collapsed, as hot money fled in the wake of the Fed's pullback from quantitative easing, only shows just how financialized they've become. Indeed, a 2015 report from the Bank for International Settlements concluded that the scale and volatility of the price collapse meant that oil, long seen as an essential fuel, was starting to behave like a "financial asset."[30]

FOXES IN THE HENHOUSE

Many of the biggest institutional investors who are now in the market for oil and other commodities have gotten there via banks like Goldman Sachs and Morgan Stanley, who run dedicated commodities trading desks that specialize in betting on the future prices of natural resources. Both Goldman and Morgan, unfettered until 2008 by the prudential banking regulation imposed on commercial banking institutions, had since the 1980s been serious players in commodities trading. As investment banks, they could pretty much do what they liked in the area. Goldman, which started its namesake Commodity Index in 1991 (one of the key steps that allowed for the huge influx of pension money into commodities)[31] already ran a large over-the-counter (OTC) derivatives trading business. These types of trades were historically unregulated since they were done off exchanges.[32]

Goldman also owned *physical commodities*—so many of them, in fact, that in 1994 the bank actually got a complaint from airport officials in the Netherlands regarding the large masses of aluminum it was storing around Rotterdam. The piles had gotten so big that they were starting to reflect the sun in ways that were confusing local air traffic controllers. Airport officials asked if Goldman could please throw a tarp over its metal stash to make the skies a bit safer.[33]

Morgan Stanley was an even bigger player in the physical ownership and movement of commodities. Between 2002 and 2012, its commodities unit generated an estimated $17 billion in revenue, trading both financial contracts and physical commodities.[34] In the early 1990s, its chief oil trader, Olav Refvik, struck so many deals to buy and deliver oil to large commercial users around the world that he was known as the King of New York Harbor.[35] The company had its own oil tank operation, a fuel distributor, electricity plants, fertilizers, asphalt, chemicals, and pipelines, all of which gave it special insight into the trading markets for these things.

What was already a hot business heated up further after the repeal of Glass-Steagall regulations in 1999. Banks like Goldman Sachs and Morgan Stanley were suddenly facing competition from much bigger publicly traded and publicly backed institutions. They needed to come up with more revenue fast, and trading was the easiest and most profitable way to do it. Speculation in commodities got an even bigger boost from the passage of the Commodity Futures Modernization Act (CFMA) in 2000.[36] Not only did that law, in one fell swoop, exempt financial derivatives traded over the counter or off regulated exchanges from CFTC or SEC oversight; it also turned back centuries of common law that said it was fine to trade such instruments, but the government wouldn't necessarily enforce the contracts unless the parties involved could prove that they were used for real hedging of real assets. Now the CFMA made OTC derivatives speculation legally enforceable *even if traders couldn't prove it was being done for anything but pure speculation.*[37] There was no longer any reason not to engage in as much speculation as possible, which helps explain why the OTC derivatives market has grown exponentially between then and now. "Basically, that law made pure bets, for the first time in Anglo-Saxon legal history, enforceable in court," says Cornell law professor and securities expert Lynn Stout, who has written extensively about the issue. "I always joke that if Congress decided to legalize murder, they'd call the legislation the Homicide Modernization Act."[38]

Commodities quickly became a key growth area for banks like Goldman and Morgan. They took a page from firms like Enron, who had pioneered "innovative" (read: speculative) markets for the trading of things like energy and utilities, leveraging both ownership and trading. (No matter that they went up in flames; the financial industry was still eager to copy many aspects of the high-profit model.) Between 2006 and 2008, Goldman alone made $3 to $4 billion per year on both ownership of raw materials and trading of commodities-linked derivatives.[39] As commodities trading volumes shot up, so did price volatility, meaning that real-world businesses like airlines and manufacturers, for which raw materials were a major cost, suffered disproportionately. Some, like Delta Air Lines, got further into the commodities trading business themselves as a way to try to make money beyond just hedging their own bets (a common practice, as described in chapter 5). But in general, the percentage of business done by real "physical hedgers," meaning airlines, trucking companies, etc., began to decline relative to those who were trading commodities that they didn't actually *need* for their business. In 2000, physical hedgers accounted for 63 percent of the oil futures market; speculators accounted for the rest. By April 2008, those percentages had shifted to 29 percent and 71 percent respectively.[40] Speculators now controlled the market.

THE HOUSE ALWAYS WINS

As financial institutions expanded their commodities wheeling and dealing, they moved beyond the trading done on behalf of bank clients, and began doing more and more trading for "the house," meaning for the bank itself.[41] While these operations were often quite small, they were very profitable—at Goldman, for example, commodities trading for the house historically represented as much as 20 percent of the entire commodity trading unit's revenue.[42] One telling anecdote based on Bloomberg research in 2010 showed that while the bank was consistently losing clients' money during a particularly tricky quarter, it made trading profits for itself every single day of that same quarter, an indication not only of the informational advantage large banks have, but of where emphasis within such firms lies—namely, with the bank's own interests above all.[43]

Meanwhile, some of the commodities being traded by financial institutions were no longer linked to one specific risk or product. Instead, they were now linked to many risks, spliced and diced in such a way that it became impossible even for the buyers and sellers themselves to know exactly what was at stake. Because derivatives trading has historically been quite opaque, with a large chunk of it being done off the public trading exchanges, it has always been difficult to pinpoint how much of what's being done involves the real economy, and how much is just virtual. But here's a telling statistic on the credit default swaps, those risky securities that blew up the housing market: Back in 2008, their notional value was $67 trillion, while the market value of all the outstanding bonds issued by US companies underlying that market was only $15 trillion. When the value of what's being traded is more than four times the underlying asset that actually exists in the real world, it's safe to say that a good chunk of what's happening in the market is purely speculative.[44]

While some portions of the derivatives markets, including credit default swaps, have contracted sharply since the 2008 crisis, the overall market remains enormous. Globally, the value of all outstanding derivatives contracts (including credit default swaps, interest rate derivatives, foreign exchange rate derivatives, commodities-linked derivatives, and so on) was $630 trillion at the beginning of 2015, while the gross market value of those contracts was $21 trillion.[45]

One big problem with derivatives is that it's often difficult to tell apart speculation and healthy hedging of real risks, especially when large, complex institutions are doing it. The commodities market, in which various players may both own raw assets and trade them, is especially tricky. There are essentially four ways that commodities can be traded. One is pure hedging—these are single bets on the future prices of raw materials that are actually owned by the individual or company doing the hedging (such as a farmer or, to the extent that it's hedging a product in the amount that it's actually planning to use, an airline). When your actions are a matter of simply insuring what you already own, it's all aboveboard.

There's also hedging on behalf of customers or clients. Banks do this, but so do big firms like BP or Cargill, as we learned in chapter 5. Then there's market making and pure trading—that's what Goldman Sachs or Glencore, the Swiss-based trading firm founded by Marc Rich, might do—though, again, industrial companies like BP can also do it in their capacity as swaps dealers. Lines start to get blurry here between what's socially useful and what's not, especially when you get into a fifth category, proprietary trading, or "prop" trading as it's known in the industry. That's when financial intermediaries and other big market makers are simply trading for their own profit, rather than to hedge any underlying assets. Activities of this kind are now illegal under the Volcker Rule, but as former CFTC chairman Gary Gensler says, "it's very tough to prove what is permitted prop trading, what is legitimate market making, and what is pure speculation." As he explains, "the lines can get very blurry," and companies can "start off doing one thing, and then move into other areas, because they are at that center of the market's information hourglass" that allows them to do so.[46]

Indeed, that's exactly what some academics and regulators believe was happening with the Goldman Sachs aluminum case—lines blurred between the interests of the bank and its clients, and what may have started as a legitimate business could have ended up as market-distorting speculation. After Goldman purchased Metro in 2010 and increased its holdings of aluminum, it also started increasing its aluminum trades. This raised concern that there may have been collusion between Metro and Goldman's trading desk, which were supposed to be strictly separated. By 2013, the Justice Department, the CFTC, and the Senate's Permanent Subcommittee on Investigations, led by Senator Carl Levin, began looking into the issue. The Senate report, issued in 2014, found that almost fifty Goldman executives, including two of the most senior members of the commodities trading team, had access to confidential and "commercially valuable" Metro information through internal memos and emails.[47] There were also emails from Metro employees expressing concerns about possible collusion.

And that wasn't all. During the Senate hearings, testimonies pointed to many other potentially troublesome scenarios unfolding not just within Goldman, but also at other banks. It emerged, for example, that Goldman played a big role in the uranium trading business via a subsidiary that employed Goldman staff, and that a now sidelined Morgan Stanley natural gas project was essentially a shell company set up by executives from Morgan Stanley's commodities arm. The list of problematic commodities deals goes on. In two others, J.P. Morgan was accused of manipulating copper and electricity markets; it paid $410 million in penalties to settle the latter case.[48] All of this led Senator Levin to conclude, "We've got to get banks out of this kind of business because of the risk to the economy and the possibility of manipulation."[49]

Goldman Sachs, for its part, denied all wrongdoing in the aluminum case and claimed in Senate hearings and public comments that it was always acting on customer orders and needs, and was willing to sell and deliver supplies to customers at any time. In the end, the Senate investigations couldn't prove collusion. This result underscored a bitter truth about the commodity markets: even though they are arguably more important to the real economy than, say, the stock markets, it's much harder to prove market manipulation and insider trading in commodities. That's because big owners of raw materials, too, are legally able to be big traders. Indeed, to become a true player in the trading of physical commodities, you *have* to be willing to take delivery of some of the raw materials, since such knowledge about what's going on at the ground level is crucial to understanding the trading market.

Gaining that informational edge is exactly why large banks pushed for additional tweaks in the Gramm-Leach-Bliley Act of 1999, the famous legislation that repealed Glass-Steagall and lowered the barriers that financial institutions faced in getting into real businesses like mining, oil delivery, and the owning and storage of physical commodities. The law did more than create loopholes allowing banking conglomerates to increase their trading operations by conducting activities that were "financial in nature" (like securities dealing and insurance underwriting). It also introduced important new provisions allowing banks to engage in purely commercial types of business, ones that they had historically been banned from, as long as they were perceived as being "complementary" to their normal financial activities. In their lobbying at the time, the banks pointed to innocuous areas of commerce like publishing or travel that might be of interest to them, and potentially "complementary" to their core businesses.

"Financial firms . . . engage in activities that arguably might be considered non-financial, but which enhance their ability to sell financial products," said Michael Patterson, the vice chair of J. P. Morgan at the time, during congressional testimony in 1999.[50] "One example is American Express, which publishes magazines of interest to its cardholders—*Food & Wine* and *Travel & Leisure. Travel & Leisure* magazine is complementary to the travel business . . . in that it gives customers travel ideas which the company hopes will lead to ticket purchases and other travel arrangements through American Express Travel Services." Such plain-vanilla examples helped make legislators comfortable with the idea of granting exemptions for commercial activities.

But the truth is that banks didn't want to be in the magazine publishing business—they wanted to be in hot Silicon Valley start-ups and, later, in the oil, gas, electricity, and minerals business. And indeed, between 2000 and 2012, *all but one* of the "complementary" activities that firms would seek to engage in via the loophole in the law had to do with commodities ownership and trading.[51] Referring to Goldman's purchase of metal warehouse space, Nick Madden, chief supply chain officer for the giant aluminum maker Novelis, says, "It had all the appearance of being part of an engineered market squeeze. I mean—why would you buy a warehouse? Why not an ice cream parlor? If not to have a lever to move the market, then . . . for what reason?"[52]

The word *complementary* was a loophole big enough to drive millions of tons of aluminum through, and it provided a legal way around one of the core principles of another decades-old piece of legislation, the Bank Holding Company Act of 1956, which separated banking and commerce. The idea behind that law was that banks were supposed to *lend* to businesses, not compete with them. It's a fundamental assumption at the heart of most banking regulation.[53] But financial institutions managed to jump over that hurdle and make their way into lucrative commodities businesses by arguing that this move was in the interests of their clients. Banks needed to be able to do a variety of things aside from simple lending, they said, including underwriting securities, trading complex swaps and futures, even owning pipelines or oil wells—because being in such businesses made things easier, cheaper, or more efficient for their corporate customers, and sometimes even consumers.

Yet the truth is that when banks start doing business in areas that involve real, tangible products that people rely on to live, their meddling invariably benefits just one party: the financial institutions themselves. Indeed, the more complex the business, the more likely it is to benefit the banks vis-à-vis anyone else, given their ability to leverage their superior assets and informational advantages.

It's important, perhaps, to pause here and point out that this isn't really about individual bankers trying to be venal (not to say that doesn't happen). All too often, banker bashing actually misses the point and distracts from a more nuanced and important conversation about the problems in our overall market system. It's easy to understand the populist rage that makes people call for, say, Jamie Dimon or Lloyd Blankfein's head on a platter, and individuals should certainly be held responsible for any wrongdoing. But the truth is that financiers are usually just trying to make as much money as the law allows them to. It's the particular rules of our market *system* that are more often the problem, because they are set up in such a way that the largest financial institutions are able to exploit huge advantages in pretty much every industry, often with federal subsidies that other players don't enjoy and with little, if any, responsibility for the collateral damage to the underlying economy. "Investment banks are at the center of the marketplace of money and risk," says Gary Gensler. "At the center of all that information, it's possible to profit from it. It's sometimes said on Wall Street that 'volatility is our friend.' That is not something you'd generally hear at an airline, or at General Mills, or probably at a community bank."[54]

But for the Too Big to Fail institutions like Goldman, volatility most certainly is an advantage. It enables them to employ their potent combination of massive amounts of capital, up-to-the-minute knowledge of developments in the financial markets, and ownership and information about raw materials, to make money at the expense of other players, be they consumers or big firms like Coke or Coors (who then pass the cost on to consumers in the form of higher prices). As Saule Omarova points out, a great irony of the commodities trading scandals is that the very arguments banks employ to defend their right to own and trade physical commodities are also those that clearly demonstrate the unfair advantages from all the insider information that such ownership brings.

"Financial institutions will say, 'we need to know physical oil to trade oil derivatives more efficiently and serve our clients better,'" says Omarova. That's considered complementary under Gramm-Leach-Bliley, and so it's okay. "And yet, when the CFTC inquires whether these institutions might have improperly benefited in their derivatives trading, from, say, bottlenecks that they created in the warehouses they control, the standard response is, 'oh, there's a strict informational wall between those units—they don't talk.' But if it's the *access to information* that's the basis for finding physical trading complementary to derivatives trading, why wouldn't this information be shared among the firm's units? Isn't the whole point of dealing in various raw materials to get valuable market information, such as the expected delivery backlog at major metals warehouses, for example—and use it to price derivatives trades? Somehow, this fundamental inconsistency in the banks' arguments often gets lost on the regulators. And it leaves big banks always on the winning side."[55]

It's worth noting that arguments of this exact type were employed by bankers and public officials who lobbied for the repeal of Glass-Steagall and the creation of the Too Big to Fail banks themselves. Economist Joseph Stiglitz, who was the head of President Clinton's Council of Economic Advisers in the run-up to the repeal, remembers arguing with Treasury officials on this very point. "People wanted the law overturned to create 'synergies' between different divisions of the banks. And I said, 'what are we going to do about conflicts of interest?' And they said, 'don't worry, we have Chinese walls.' And I said, 'well if you've really constructed Chinese walls, then where are the synergies?'"[56]

Interestingly, the crisis of 2008, which turned Goldman Sachs and Morgan Stanley into Fed-regulated Too Big to Fail bank holding companies as a condition of getting government bailouts, also legitimized their meddling in the aluminum markets. That's because of a fine-print clause grandfathered into the Gramm-Leach-Bliley Act that Stiglitz and others had opposed, which allowed any entity that became a bank holding company following the act's passing to conduct physical commodities activities. The only prerequisite was that this entity had entered the commodities business before 1997.

And so, in the aftermath of the 2008 crisis, both Goldman and Morgan went from being stand-alone investment banks to bank-owning financial holding companies regulated by the Fed.[57] By becoming federally backed banking entities, these institutions got both the freedom to control as many aspects of the market as possible and precious direct access to government subsidies and federal underwriting. J.P. Morgan, already a bank holding company, ended up benefiting too; it got to acquire the large commodities assets of Bear Stearns and RBS Sempra (the energy trading business previously co-owned by the Royal Bank of Scotland) at rock-bottom prices. Just as J.P. Morgan emerged as a bigger and more systemically important bank after 2008, so it became the five-hundred-pound gorilla of the commodities trading markets, boasting a physical commodity inventory valued at over $17 billion.[58] It even bought a stake in the LME, which it purchased from the bankrupt futures firm MF Global, becoming the exchange's largest shareholder.[59]

All this happened despite the fact that the original regulatory exemptions that allowed J.P. Morgan to do physical commodities trading in the first place didn't specially allow it to generate, store, transport, or process physical commodities. The bank had to rely on the good graces of regulators to not look too hard at the fine print—a job made easier by the fact that there are multiple regulators (including the Fed, the CFTC, the SEC, and the Federal Energy Regulatory Commission). Each has its individual areas of responsibility, but none is big enough to examine complex and problematic deals in their entirety. The fact that they are wildly underresourced doesn't help. The CFTC, for example, has around 650 people on the payroll, which may seem like a lot of regulators, but it's just 8 percent more than the agency's staff size in the 1990s, when the futures market was worth a fifth of today's $40 trillion. And that's not even counting the $400 trillion swaps market, which the agency didn't have to cope with then.[60]

There are, of course, huge risks inherent in all this trading, especially when it's done by Goldman Sachs, Morgan Stanley, J.P. Morgan, and the like, since we all pick up the bill when things go bad, thanks to the implicit taxpayer backing of these Too Big to Fail institutions. Sure, the Dodd-Frank regulation promises that taxpayers would never again have to foot the bill, but in practice, it's unclear how the government would avoid future bailouts, particularly given that these banks are bigger and more important now than they were before 2008. What's more, a loophole pushed into the 2015 federal spending bill by the financial lobby means that these banks don't have to separate out that risky trading into new entities that *wouldn't* be taxpayer backed. All this allows such institutions to retain huge market advantages not enjoyed by any other players. In the commodities markets and any other market where they can leverage the word *complementary*, they get the privilege of being in a nonbanking business, with access to information held only by large banks, and with subsidies enjoyed only by Too Big to Fail institutions. It's an unfair advantage over other businesses, as well as a risk to our economic health and safety as a nation. That doesn't please many people, even the creators of the original 1999 loophole that made the whole thing possible. As the ex-congressman Jim Leach, one of the authors of Gramm-Leach-Bliley, said in 2013, around the time of the Senate subcommittee hearings on commodities manipulation, "I assume no one at the time [of the act's writing] would have thought it would apply to commodities brokering of a nature that has recently been reported."[61]

SIMPLIFY, SIMPLIFY, SIMPLIFY

If, at this point, you are feeling overwhelmed by the sheer size and complexity of the problems, that's the idea. The purpose of this chapter is to show that behind price inflation and volatility in any commodity, be it aluminum or wheat, stands an entire dysfunctional market ecosystem that must be understood and addressed. One of the common reactions to financial scandals like the one surrounding Goldman and aluminum is for the media, the public, and even the regulators to zero in on a tiny part of what is a very large problem. But the whole point of this story is that aluminum hoarding in Detroit warehouses happened because of a long history of legislative decisions, legal tweaks, corporate changes, and vested interests both in Washington and on Wall Street. This history, combined with a corrosive incentive structure, has created a situation in which a bank with absolutely no need to own a natural resource is not only allowed to do so but is enabled to stockpile it in a way that ensures the companies that *do* need it can't get it. This drives up the prices and creates market volatility, which in the end means that customers have to pay more.

Jim Collura is vice president of government affairs at the New England Fuel Institute and one of the founders of the Commodity Markets Oversight Coalition, a group of mostly small and midsize businesses, such as heating oil distributors and gas stations, that was set up in 2007 in response to growing volatility in the commodities markets. He remembers how disturbing it was to come to grips with just how complex the system was, and with all the ways in which businesses were beholden to the very banks that competed with them. "The same financial institutions that were making the commodities markets more volatile were also the ones that were providing risk management services to our companies, or investing their pension plans, or owning the pipelines that our assets ran through," Collura says. It was a situation that was at best distorted and at worst ripe for manipulation.

This is not what markets were set up to do. Most people can agree on that. So why haven't legislators and regulators been able to fix the problem? In part because they're focusing too much on small details: What's the precise ratio of equity banks should hold to offset risks if they own 5 percent of a pipeline versus 15 percent? Does each individual institution have enough insurance to offset its own risks? Important though they are, these separate pieces of the puzzle can make us lose sight of the big questions that we should be asking instead, those that would galvanize real change in the system: Is it healthy to have a system in which banks compete directly with their customers, using superior information and resources to best the very businesses they were set up to serve? Is that really what we want our financial system to do?

The answers are obviously no. But getting to a better place requires an understanding that complexity is, as is so often the case, the enemy of the public good. Complexity is ripe for arbitrage, which is what finance does best. To put finance back into the service of the real economy, you have to simplify, simplify, simplify. To do that, you have to increase transparency about what's happening in the first place. In the commodities arena, former CFTC chairman Gary Gensler fought the good fight for stricter regulation of derivatives, bringing a large chunk of the swaps market out of the shadowy darkness and into central clearinghouses where it can be more easily regulated. In the United States most commodities-linked OTC derivatives are now subject to central clearing. The CFTC has also made big progress on real-time reporting and registration of brokers, so that people actually know who's doing the trading.

But achieving even this level of regulation has been a long, hard slog. Thanks to its relentless lobbying of Congress, the administration, and regulators both in the United States and overseas, Wall Street has succeeded in carving out important loopholes in the Dodd-Frank derivatives rules. The loopholes make it possible, for example, for banks and hedge funds to continue their opaque, risky trading of foreign-exchange derivatives in international markets (something former Treasury secretary Timothy Geithner personally signed off on). Is it any wonder, then, that this was the very area in which the next global financial scandal would pop up? In 2015, six global banks, including JPMorgan Chase and Citigroup, were fined a cumulative $5.6 billion to settle charges that they rigged foreign exchange markets.[62] The news followed only a few years on the heels of another similar price-fixing scandal in the Libor, or interbank lending, market. These developments left Gensler and others calling into question whether the banks had really learned anything from any of the previous scandals (or gave a hoot about the large fines they had to pay, which for top banks may still not make much of a dent in yearly profits).

The CFTC has certainly done its best to make it harder for US financial institutions to hang their dirty laundry in the Caribbean. But their jurisdiction is very limited. Roughly 70 percent of the overall OTC futures and swaps market remains opaque, leaving plenty of room for financiers to game the system.[63] And the antiregulatory lobbying continues; in 2014 the financial industry succeeded in pushing back Dodd-Frank rules that would have forced them to put risky credit default swaps in affiliate companies that weren't federally insured—yet another example of how the problems of 2008 are still with us.

So how do we solve these problems? The Federal Reserve, which is the top oversight body for Too Big to Fail Institutions, could do more to limit the banks' virtually unfettered freedom to manipulate commodities markets, particularly since it has the jurisdiction to decide which of the banks' activities are indeed "complementary" to their financial activities and which aren't. The Fed also has the ability to decide if such activities are simply too risky—either for the banks, or for the financial system as a whole.

Even the threat of reform could have an impact. In the wake of the Goldman aluminum scandal, Fed chair Janet Yellen said that the central bank would consider new guidelines that could limit some activities of banks in the commodities arena. Almost immediately, Goldman, J.P. Morgan, and Morgan Stanley began scaling back some of their biggest operations. Goldman dumped Metro. Morgan Stanley sold TransMontaigne, a Denver-based oil transportation and storage company that owned and operated a vast network of pipelines and terminals across the country. They did so, presumably, to take some Fed scrutiny off their backs, because sales reduce the amount of capital used by the commodities business. (This also makes one wonder how many nefarious activities banks were previously hiding on their books.) But big banks aren't out of the commodities game just yet, although new rules being proposed by the Fed may force them to hold more capital against possible risks should they decide to stay in.[64] As just one case in point, the head of Morgan Stanley's trading division recently promised to continue to "service the supply and risk-management needs of our clients across the oil, power and gas, and metals sectors."[65]

It actually wasn't a bad time for the banks to make their sales; commodity prices have been decreasing recently, in part because the Fed has slowed the flow of easy money into the markets, which fueled so much speculation to begin with. That's why experts like Saule Omarova say that the banks' divestments don't represent a triumph for the real economy so much as they do good trading bets for the banks themselves. The banks are getting out of the market at the right time, just as they got in at the right time. Without tougher, clearer rules, they could jump back in at any time as well.

Are such rules coming anytime soon? And even if they do, will they definitively separate banking from commerce in risky areas like commodities? Certainly those proposed so far don't. Many reform advocates are skeptical that they ever will. "I'm not expecting any giant news on this front," says Lisa Donner, executive director of Americans for Financial Reform, a coalition advocating for tighter regulation of Wall Street.[66] Part of the problem, she says, is that no regulators, including the Fed, seem to be asking the profound questions: Why do we have a system that allows finance to be a hindrance to commerce rather than a lubricant to it? How is it that banks could create a bottleneck in raw materials and then profit from it at the expense of their customers? How might we reshape things in a systemic way so that can't happen? Instead, regulators have so far focused on tweaking the administrative aspects of existing laws while maintaining the silos that make the system so hard to police. They might have good intentions, but they are failing at fixing the problem.

"In my view, the Fed has both the legal mandate and the regulatory capacity to address these issues in a more comprehensive way, which is necessary in order to bring the financial markets back in service to the real economy," says Omarova, who wonders if it will take an even bigger crisis to fundamentally change the laws governing how banks engage in commerce. It's a point that was brought into sharp focus by Senator John McCain during the release of the 2014 Senate report on the banking sector's influence in the commodities markets. "Imagine if BP had been a bank," he said, referring to the Deepwater Horizon oil spill, which cost that company billions of dollars in damages. "It could have led to its failure and another round of bailouts."[67]

Unfortunately, says Omarova, "regulators are taking on these relatively low-stakes technical questions about additional capital and insurance, but they aren't asking the big questions—is it a good policy to allow big banks to accumulate so much power, not only over finances, but also over our food, fuel, and other raw materials? What kind of a society will we have if a handful of banking giants end up controlling the country's energy, metals, and agricultural supply chains?" It's quite telling that the law gives the Federal Reserve the power to determine what a "complementary" activity is, and whether conducting it would pose "a substantial risk to the safety or soundness of depository institutions of the financial system generally." But it doesn't say anything about what impact such activities might have on businesses, consumers, and American families.

It's a legal issue that goes far beyond even the crucial commodities markets. Remember, the Bank Holding Company Act of 1956 (the legislation that was so unfortunately tweaked by Gramm-Leach-Bliley) was really about power—and specifically, about ensuring that banks don't have too much of it relative to the rest of the economy and to society. If there's anything that the aluminum fiasco showed, it was that surely the balance isn't yet right. One telling detail is how many companies affected by the aluminum scandal have been reluctant to speak out about the issue. In response to my interview requests for this book, SABMiller, the parent company of MillerCoors, responded with a one-line email: "On this occasion we will decline the interview opportunity but thank you for getting in touch and asking us." There was no response to further emails asking why the company declined to speak about the incident.

The Coca-Cola Company has been somewhat more vocal, with executives blogging about how they are still concerned that the London Metal Exchange hasn't done enough to stop the hoarding of aluminum. (According to a rather sarcastic Coke blog post from June 2015, the waiting time for metal shipments has fallen from a peak of

650 days to "only" 400 days.) Yet interestingly, none of the public comments about the matter mentions Goldman or any other banks, and public relations representatives at the companies declined to comment for this book about the banks' involvement in the issue. No wonder. Coke has been a longtime investment banking client of Goldman Sachs, and at the time of the LME complaint, it had recently hired the bank to advise it on a $12 billion acquisition.[68] "If I were Coca-Cola's general counsel, I wouldn't want my company to start a big fight with Goldman Sachs, either," says Omarova. "What if we need to raise debt on the public markets tomorrow and need an underwriter? What if we plan a merger and need transaction advice? What might Goldman research analysts do to our share price if they wanted to? Coke needs Goldman. They are everywhere."

You could argue, of course, that Coke and other American businesses can simply fight fire with fire and lobby for their own causes in Washington, just as the banks have done. Like it or not, that's the way in which our political system allows various interest groups to counter one another so that no single entity can become too powerful. Yet the aluminum scandal also shows how hard it is for any entity, even one of the largest companies in the world, to escape the orbit of the most powerful financial institutions. They make the markets. They are the markets. They trade the products in the markets, and, as this story shows, they can also own the things that are being traded in those markets. If that's not an oligopoly, I'm not sure what is. It's also one of the best arguments I've heard for reinstating a modern version of the Glass-Steagall Act and for closing the loopholes that allow banks to engage in commerce. American industries simply shouldn't have to compete in their core businesses with their own bankers.

And what of the world's poorest people, the one billion who still don't have enough to eat each day, in part because of Wall Street speculation? They've gotten a break over the last couple of years as commodities prices went down—not because of traders' goodwill, but because emerging market growth has slowed and the era of central-bank-fueled easy money came to an end. That will change at some point in the future, and when it does, there will be nothing to stop Wall Street from brewing up another food bubble, unless our policy makers (or, less likely, the banks themselves) take action to rein in financial speculation in the commerce markets.

Before moving on from her post at the World Food Programme, Josette Sheeran gave a moving TED Talk on the problem of global hunger. "If we look at the economic imperative here, this isn't just about compassion," she said. "The fact is studies show that the cost of malnutrition and hunger—the cost to society, the burden it has to bear—is on average six percent, and in some countries up to 11 percent, of GDP a year. And if you look at the 36 countries with the highest burden of malnutrition, that's 260 billion lost from a productive economy every year. Well, the World Bank estimates it would take about 10.3 billion dollars to address malnutrition in those countries. You look at the cost-benefit analysis, and my dream is to take this issue, not just from the compassion argument, but to the finance ministers of the world, and say we cannot afford to not invest in the access to adequate, affordable nutrition for all of humanity."[69]

It's a laudable goal. However, tackling it will first require not only compassion from world leaders, but real change in Wall Street's business model.

CHAPTER 7

WHEN WALL STREET OWNS MAIN STREET

*Private Equity, Shadow Banking, and How Finance
Reaped the Benefits of the Housing Recovery*

IN THE MIDST of the housing crisis and Great Recession a few years back, I spent a lot of time traveling through the Inland Empire, a large metropolitan area in the middle of Southern California. It stretches an hour or two east of Los Angeles and Orange County, but is about as far away from the tony "OC" lifestyle as you can imagine. Made up primarily of San Bernardino and Riverside counties, the Inland Empire was at the heart of the subprime mortgage crisis and has yet to fully recover.

In the early 2000s, predatory lenders flocked to the area, offering dicey deals to the largely minority and lower-middle-class white populations who, unable to afford housing on the coast, still craved the American Dream of homeownership. It ended, as it did in so many neighborhoods and cities across America, in tears and massive foreclosures, turning entire cities into ghost towns of derelict properties.

As recently as 2012, when I visited the Del Rosa neighborhood of San Bernardino, one of the hardest-hit cities in the housing crisis, remaining homeowners' efforts to keep their properties up were being thwarted left and right. Groups of young men and school-age kids with pit bulls in tow hung out in front of corner bodegas at midday. For every well-kept bungalow with freshly cut grass and potted plants on the porch, there was an abandoned building spray-painted with gang graffiti or strewn with dirty mattresses and empty liquor bottles. Highway billboards featured mainly ads for credit counseling, megachurches, and mobile home dealers.[1]

There's a housing recovery on, but you wouldn't know it in places like San Bernardino—and finance is one big reason why, not just because of its role in the crisis, but also because of its role in the recovery, as this chapter will explore. Such communities are slowly healing, but many still struggle with residual blight from the housing boom and bust. Unemployment rates remain above the national average, mortgage credit is still tight, and few who've managed to hang on to their homes can hope to get anywhere near the prices they paid for them pre-crisis.

But rents, oddly, are rising. In fact, in many parts of the Inland Empire, they are higher than the national average, despite the poor economic statistics of the area. One 2014 survey of a select group of renters conducted in Riverside, a city right next to San Bernardino, found that 63 percent of tenants were paying at least 30 percent of their monthly income in rent, a level that the US Department of Housing and Urban Development considers unaffordable (a full 33 percent were paying more than half of their income to landlords). This strange paradigm, of working-class people in a not particularly desirable economic area paying more than they should for rent, becomes a bit more understandable when you know who their landlord is—Invitation Homes, the property subsidiary of Blackstone Group, the world's largest private equity firm, and of late the nation's largest purchaser of single-family homes.[2] Thanks to its bucketloads of cash, economies of scale, and creative accounting, it's managed to price many individual buyers out of the housing market over the last few years, cashing in on the recovery in housing, even as it made money before and after the crash.

Private equity funds like Blackstone are giant financial institutions that operate largely outside the scrutiny of governmental regulation, since they are officially designated "nonbanks" or "shadow banks"—never mind that many of them are bigger than the better-known institutions that are subject to regulation. Most people rightly associate private equity with offshore bank accounts (remember Mitt Romney and Bain Capital?), big corporate buyouts in which formerly healthy firms are loaded up with debt and stripped of their assets, mass layoffs, and an utter lack of transparency in their financial dealings. But these days, the big news about private equity is that it is at the heart of the country's housing rebound.

Private equity investors have become the single largest group of buyers in the residential housing market, purchasing $20 billion worth of steeply discounted properties between 2012 and 2014 alone[3] and reaping huge rewards as housing prices have slowly risen from their troughs. Blackstone, the biggest of the big private equity firms, with more than $330 billion in assets under management,[4] has become the largest investor landlord in the country, with a portfolio of 46,000 homes and other properties that generated $1.9 billion worth of income in 2014, making real estate the largest profit center for the firm. Blackstone's CEO, the infamous Wall Street titan Stephen Schwarzman, has called the firm's move into the rental business in places like the Inland Empire a "bet on America."[5]

To be more precise, it's a bet on the fact that fewer Americans can afford, in the wake of the financial crisis, to own a home. Thus an increasing number will be forced to rent from a Wall Street investor like Blackstone. Indeed, private equity's rush into real estate goes some way toward answering one of the most perplexing economic questions of late: If housing is back, then why is the percentage of people who own homes in our country at a twenty-year low? Home values began rebounding from their post-financial-crisis trough in the beginning of 2012, and by July 2015, home sales had increased to their highest pace in eight and a half years.[6] But the percentage of Americans who can call themselves homeowners is still declining from its peak in 2004, and many experts expect it to fall further as credit continues to be tight, young people struggle with higher-than-average levels of unemployment, and baby boomers begin moving into retirement housing.[7]

Fixing this housing crisis, as Warren Buffett once told me, is a fundamental prerequisite for fixing our economy. And yet, nearly eight years after the crisis of 2008, we aren't there yet. The national housing market is in recovery, but like the larger economic recovery, it is incredibly bifurcated. Sections of Washington, D.C., and Los Angeles are booming, while Detroit, Atlanta, and California's Inland Empire are still coping with foreclosures and mortgages that are underwater. One study of the housing markets in cities and towns across America found that the top 10 percent richest markets, ranked by the aggregate value of owner-occupied homes, held 52 percent of total housing wealth, equivalent to nearly $4.4 trillion. The bottom 40 percent, by contrast, held only 8 percent. It's a stark statement about who has profited, and who hasn't, from the housing recovery.[8] The federal government is still underwriting most new mortgages in one way or another, via a multitude of state-sponsored programs and federally backed bonds. If a healthy housing market is one that is stable, affordable, inclusive, and not primarily dependent on government life support, then "we're a long way from there," says Yale professor and housing expert Robert Shiller.

How to create a truly healthy housing market is a question that matters to everyone, not just those of us who can't afford homes. American consumers spend $2 trillion a year on housing, which triggers billions of dollars of additional spending in related industries like consumer goods, telecommunications and technology, automotives, construction, retail banking, etc. Research shows that rising housing wealth is much more likely to spur consumer spending than rising stock wealth is. Even after the crisis, people simply feel more economically secure when they own a home. And getting people to feel secure, and thus to spend more, is crucial to a sustainable recovery in an economy like America's, where consumer spending accounts for 70 percent of GDP.[9]

Some economists have called on Americans to reconsider the model of home ownership as the cultural norm, arguing that it would make more economic sense for people to rent rather than own, since the former increases labor mobility and helps diversify investment risk. That may be true for some groups and in certain parts of the country—one thing we learned from the 2008 crisis was that heavy mortgage debts aren't for everyone. But the American Dream of home ownership is deeply entrenched. Like it or not, a home, not stocks or savings, remains the chief financial asset for most Americans. And that's likely to continue to be the case over the next several years, since returns from stocks are unlikely to match those of the recent past, for reasons covered in the previous chapters. Moreover, there's ample proof that home ownership creates more economic and social stability in communities, since owners tend to be more civically engaged than renters and have a greater stake in the quality of local schools, parks, and playgrounds.[10]

Unfortunately, the economic climate and policy decisions taken since the 2008 crisis have resulted in a small group of rich investors— not American families—driving the real estate market and reaping most of the gains. Among them are private equity titans like Blackstone and high-wealth individuals who can pay cash upfront for a property. "Investors remain the dominant force behind the house-price bounce back," property economist Paul Diggle told me a couple years back. They've driven up prices beyond the reach of many individual investors, something that has caught the attention of ratings agencies like Fitch, which reported in 2013 that "the recent home price gains recorded in several residential markets are outpacing improvement in [economic] fundamentals."[11] Discussing these findings, one Fitch analyst said that "the growth is being propelled by institutional money" rather than the growing wealth of households.[12]

That's reflected not only in the lower rate of home ownership but also in the swelling ranks of renters; an increasing number of people simply can't afford to own, which has in turn dramatically tightened the rental market. Not since 1986 have fewer rental properties been empty in the United States, and rents are rising sharply in many cities as a result. According to Harvard's Joint Center for Housing Studies, the share of moderately to severely cost-burdened renters (meaning those who pay at least 30 percent of their income in rent) grew to represent half of all American renters in 2013, up from 38 percent in 2000.[13] "We get lots of people coming to us saying, we wanted to own, but all the affordable properties have been bought up, so now, we're renting from Blackstone for more than the price of a mortgage," says Atlanta-based Tony Romano, the organizing director for the nonprofit Right to the City alliance, which has produced a number of studies on the consequences of private equity moving into the housing market.[14]

THE NEW POTTERSVILLES

One worry in the aftermath of the subprime crisis is that this dynamic, in which those without lots of cash and stellar credit (which is most people) have been left unable to buy homes, while Wall Street is able to continue to shape the housing market in ways that aren't necessarily to the public benefit, will result in a spate of new Pottersvilles—soulless communities owned by investors who couldn't care less what happens in them, as long as they get paid. Most ordinary Americans need mortgages to buy real estate; at current housing prices and incomes, it would take a typical family more than twenty years to save even a 10 percent down payment for a home plus closing costs.[15] But they can't get the loans, because in our post-crisis world, banks are still keeping credit tighter than usual. (The banks would argue it's because of regulation, but many experts believe it's because individual lending is simply less profitable and more risky than other types of businesses.) Besides, many individuals simply don't have the secure employment, nest egg, and increasingly high credit scores needed to obtain a mortgage these days. Cash down of 20–30 percent and credit scores of 700 and up are now the norm for individual mortgages, despite the fact that almost two-thirds of Americans have ratings below 750.

That, of course, goes to the root of the problem, which is that to truly create a viable housing market for individuals, we need not only more reasonable mortgage lending practices, but also a more sustainable recovery and a greater number of good middle-class jobs so that consumers can build up the financial security necessary to buy into the market. "There's no quick fix. You need higher employment and wages [to support housing consumption] and looser credit," says Jonathan Miller, CEO of the New York City–based real estate appraisal company Miller Samuel.

But to get to those things, you also need policies that favor homeowners over investors, and those have been in very short supply since 2008. Many, myself included, would argue that government officials like former Treasury secretary Timothy Geithner should have done much more to bail out homeowners rather than banks after the subprime crisis, and sooner. If they had, Main Street would likely be further along in the economic healing process, since housing represents such a sizable share of the economy (15 percent in direct terms, and much more indirectly).[16] Instead we ended up with bailouts for banks that came with no provisions for lending to individual homeowners, which resulted in—surprise!—much tighter access to mortgages across the board. (The notable exception is for jumbo mortgages, loans of $417,000 or more for single-family homes. Access to those has gotten easier since lenders now want to deal mainly with the top economic tier of society.)[17]

In her 2014 memoir, *A Fighting Chance*, Senator Elizabeth Warren recounts a particularly telling conversation with Geithner on the topic. Warren had asked him, in the fall of 2009, as foreclosures were increasing, why he wasn't doing more for homeowners. His answer? The banks could only handle so many foreclosures at a time, and so Treasury's plan had been calibrated to offer just enough foreclosure relief to "foam the runway" for the banks themselves, so they weren't overwhelmed. As Warren puts it, "Millions of people were getting tossed out on the street, but the secretary of the Treasury believed that government's most important job was to provide a soft landing for the tender fannies of the banks."[18] It's a take that certainly mirrors all the conversations on the topic that I ever had with Secretary Geithner.

Into this dysfunctional fray stepped private equity, ready to make a profit on the very crisis that the financial industry itself caused. It's something that the Obama administration actually welcomed, in the hopes that private investors would help stabilize the housing market.[19] In a sense, it worked. Economists like Moody's Mark Zandi and Adam Kamins note that private equity buyers did set a floor under prices in some beleaguered neighborhoods following the crash. "Purchasing homes in this dark economic time was not for the faint of heart," they write, and some sellers may not have wanted to wait for individual buyers to line up the necessary financing.[20]

Yet private equity brings its own very significant risks to the housing market, as well as a business model that is the very epitome of financialization—one where the only motive is profit for its own sake, not wealth creation in the broader economy. Private equity operates very much like the most leveraged parts of the banking industry, but on steroids. Since their birth four decades ago, private equity firms have perfected a business model that is designed to extract as much wealth from every target company with as little capital or risk to themselves as possible. The current business model "emerged out of the shareholder-value revolution and the leveraged buyout (LBO) movement of the 1970s and 1980s," say Eileen Appelbaum, a senior economist at the Center for Economic and Policy Research (CEPR) in Washington, and Cornell University professor Rosemary Batt in their influential book, *Private Equity at Work*.[21] This mirrors what we've already learned in chapters 3 to 5; as Appelbaum and Batt put it, the rise of private equity represents "a fundamental shift in the concept of the American corporation—from a view of it as a productive enterprise and stable institution serving the needs of a broad spectrum of stakeholders to a view of it as a bundle of assets to be bought and sold with an exclusive goal of maximizing shareholder value."

If the markets are an ocean, private equity firms like Blackstone are the great white sharks that have perfected the use of debt, leverage, asset stripping, tax avoidance, and legal machinations to maximize profits for themselves at the expense of almost everyone else—their investors, their limited partners, their portfolio companies and the workers in them, and certainly society at large.[22] During the 2012 presidential race, Mitt Romney's candidacy spurred a vigorous debate over whether private equity firms create or destroy jobs on a net basis. The research can be spun in many ways, but the upshot is that employment generally declines in companies that spend too much time in private equity's hands. Job destruction is particularly bad in the retail sector, although the other end of the spectrum has some firms in which private equity's overall effect on jobs is modest at best.[23] But what's clear is that the private equity model, even more so than most Wall Street practices, enriches a few investors at great cost to others. Let's not forget that while private equity firms may operate as owners (though they often aren't regulated or taxed as such), they are essentially financial intermediaries; they make money not necessarily by growing the pie, but by taking an ever-larger slice of it.

DANCING WITH THE WOLVES OF WALL STREET

While most people have no idea how the private equity model works, there's a good chance that you or someone you know works for private equity. According to some recent surveys, about 1 in 14 American workers is employed by a firm that's owned at least in part by a private equity company.[24] Even more amazing, many of us are funding these very same firms, via our pension and mutual funds. Private equity has in recent years raised most of its money from institutional investors like pension funds (which supply 44 percent of their capital) as well as mutual funds, sovereign wealth funds, and wealthy individuals, and then invested that money in a group of portfolio companies. It's an incredible system when you think about it. Our nest eggs fund the very firms that are quite likely to cut our jobs, which of course makes it impossible to buy a home. Meanwhile, private equity capitalizes on that fact by making huge profits in a market that many average consumers don't have the financial capacity to engage in. Talk about a closed loop of financialization.

Why would such large institutional investors give their money to the wolves of Wall Street? Because they are under increasing pressure to meet their own return obligations. Pensioners need to be paid, universities need to be funded, governments in repressive countries need to grow their sovereign wealth funds so they can keep offering their people economic subsidies rather than political freedom, and so on. In many cases, the promises that such investors have made to their stakeholders were unrealistic in the first place. Many pension funds, for example, promise 8 percent annual returns, a number that seems unbelievable in the current economic climate. To try to meet these targets, investors turn to private equity titans, who have a reputation for being able to turn big profits quickly, often by down-sizing firms and selling off assets, but also by accessing areas of the private market that are closed to those who aren't financial insiders.

One of those areas is the technology industry. Silicon Valley com-panies, which are the fastest-growing in the country as a group, are opting more and more not to go public unless they absolutely have to. Think of firms like Uber or Airbnb, which have resisted IPOs even though they have raised billions of dollars in private money, the sort of funding that used to require a public listing. This means that if you want to get in on the wealth creation of these firms, you have to team up with a hedge fund or a private equity fund that's investing in such markets.

This area of so-called "growth investing" is relatively new for pri-vate equity firms and is in many ways a reaction to the fact that the old model—buying up companies, loading them up with debt, and selling them off to the highest bidder—is largely tapped out; with corporate valuations as high as they are now, it's clear that in the future private equity funds probably won't be able to get the high re-turns they once did with this model. As an alternative, they've moved to taking minority positions in hot start-ups.[25] This new inversion of the typical start-up funding cycle comes with many disturbing implications—from increasingly unequal access to the wealth cre-ated by America's most innovative firms to less transparency in the finances of such companies as they stay private longer.

Even with the new strategies, the idea that investments in private equity funds pay off over the longer haul is very much open to question. One 2009 study found that investors in private equity buyout funds received a lower-than-average yield, relative to what the S&P 500 would deliver, after the funds' large fees were deducted (we'll come back to that topic a bit later in the chapter).[26] Indeed, the IMF recently issued a warning that pension funds themselves were becoming a Too-Big-to-Fail-type risk in the financial system through their investments in private equity and other risky "alternative" investment classes. Echoing its comments was the OECD, which said last year that pension funds in bed with private equity could end up "seriously compromising" their solvency in periods of market turbulence.[27]

Even some of the most sophisticated and largest pension funds, like CalPERS (the California-based group that manages retirement accounts of teachers, firefighters, police, and other state officials), have had trouble getting full disclosure from private equity firms about exactly how their money is being used, and what they are being charged for. Amazingly, California state treasurer John Chiang complained in 2015 that neither he nor CalPERS officials had any idea how much they've paid their private equity managers for running the fund's assets for twenty-five years. The answer was simply impossible to ferret out in the byzantine and opaque documentation the managers provided to them. The only thing that's certain is that these fees are huge. "CalPERS' total bill is likely to be astronomical," said Professor Ludovic Phalippou, a private equity expert at Oxford University's Saïd Business School. "People will choke when they see the true number."[28] No wonder CalPERS recently made the decision to wind down its $4 billion portfolio of hedge fund holdings, saying that high costs and complexity made the products too risky.

Many people expected this to be a turning point, hoping that other pension funds would follow suit. But surprisingly, the investments in complex, high-fee products has continued.[29] Private equity barons are some of the richest of Wall Street moneymen, and their operations have a certain aura that inspires confidence in less sophisticated financial players. Think of their beautifully appointed offices with panoramic views of Manhattan, palatial Hamptons spreads that showcase world-class art collections, and birthday parties that feature performances by pop stars. The leaders of the shadow banking industry are brilliant, charismatic, convincing—and ruthless. One of the more memorable bits of office décor I've seen in my two decades as a business reporter was an exquisitely polished antique ejector chair from a World War II fighter plane that sat in the conference room of billionaire activist investor Bill Ackman, the man behind the failed revamp of JCPenney and the campaign to drive Herbalife out of business.

The institutional investors and wealthy individuals who give them their money are considered "limited partners" in these firms, but they have few rights. The general partners, people like Schwarzman at Blackstone, use the cash as they like, typically looking for companies that will most quickly generate profits for the private equity firm itself. That might involve buying out public corporations, taking them private and reselling them (often after breaking them up, to increase sale value), buying family-owned businesses from founders, purchasing divisions of big companies that want to offload assets (think Blackstone's acquisition of GE's commercial real estate business), or by acquiring other private equity firms and buying into private firms. The companies in a private equity portfolio often have little to do with one another, since they are purchased not to enhance one another's growth, but to make money for the fund. In this sense, they are simply bundles of assets that could be bought or sold as needed, not entities that should be tended and grown in their own right, as well as organized to support one another.

Structurally, this setup allows private equity firms to act as holding companies for portfolio firms, which enables them to reduce legal liabilities. Consider the bungled 2006 deal involving investors Tishman Speyer and BlackRock, which raised a private equity fund to purchase the famous Manhattan rent-controlled apartment buildings of Stuyvesant Town and Peter Cooper Village. The $5.4 billion deal was done with 20 percent equity and 80 percent debt (maximizing its tax advantages, since our tax code favors debt over equity, as we'll learn in the next chapter). The partners wanted to kick out tenants and turn the rent-controlled apartments into condos, but when that plan was foiled by numerous protests and a court ruling, they defaulted on the mortgage. Their investors—including the Church of England, the government of Singapore, CalPERS, and two other public pension funds based in California and Florida—lost a of total of $850 million as a result. But Tishman Speyer and BlackRock, which had pushed responsibility off their books and onto the equity firm they had formed for this purpose, lost nothing but their initial investments of $112 million each. They also weren't held liable for $215 million in refunds owed to tenants for whom they'd illegally hiked rents—those costs were absorbed by the property's new owners. The whole debacle barely made a dent in Tishman's annual returns.[30]

BRICKS AND MORTAR

One of the reasons why private equity loves deals involving real estate is that they offer hard assets that can be milked for rent, or stripped and sold to the highest bidder. Indeed, that's why the industry has so often gone after restaurants and retail firms with brick-and-mortar shops. Mitt Romney and Bain Capital were among the first to use this tactic on restaurant chains like Domino's Pizza, acquiring them and using the steady cash flow to pay large dividends to the private equity firm. More recently, clothiers like Juicy Couture have been takeover targets, as has the department store chain Mervyn's, which provides a telling example of how portfolio companies can be quickly bled dry.

In 2004, when Mervyn's was purchased from Target by a private equity consortium including Cerberus Capital Management, Sun Capital Partners, Lubert-Adler Management, and Klaff Realty, it was a profitable, if neglected, middle-market retailer with 257 stores. The private equity partners immediately split off the real estate assets from the rest of the firm and used them as collateral to borrow $800 million from Bank of America, which they used to pay Target for the chain. (Mervyn's got nothing from the deal.) The bank spliced and diced that loan and resold it; meanwhile, Mervyn's had to lease its own stores back at rates that were higher than when it actually owned them. To meet these costs without cutting into margins, private equity owners demanded worker layoffs. Remaining employees were forced to work 14- to 15-hour days, and not surprisingly, service and sales suffered. By 2007, a department store chain that had been making $160 million a year in profit before its takeover faced a $64 million loss (though, as Appelbaum and Batt note in their book, that amount was less than the $80 million in additional lease payments Mervyn's was losing thanks to the dicey real estate deals its private equity owners had foisted on it). Predictably, vendors grew worried about Mervyn's ability to pay for their merchandise, and stock began to suffer. The situation reached a fever pitch when the store wasn't able to secure the clothing and goods needed for the all-important back-to-school season in 2008. By July, Mervyn's was in bankruptcy, with its vendors clamoring to get $102 million in outstanding payments. The private equity firm still made money, of course, since profits on the real estate side exceeded losses.

It's a typical private equity tragedy, except for one thing. In September 2008, encouraged by its vendors, Mervyn's sued Target, the equity firms, and other players involved in the deal, alleging that they had engaged in a fraudulent transaction by knowingly putting the company's credit at risk when they sold off its real estate. The court found in favor of the department store, and the private equity owners were forced to pay $166 million to the vendors, making this settlement one of the biggest ever reached against a private equity firm.[31]

Past performance, as they say on Wall Street, is no indication of future results. But the history of private equity and its dealings with American business provides plenty of reasons to fret about the future of the US housing sector, now that the buyout kings have poured $20 billion into the single-family-home market, becoming the major player in a number of key metropolitan areas.[32] The housing industry favors these investors because of the large amounts of cash they carry with them. Private equity firms have been able to outbid not only individual homebuyers, but also nonprofits and community groups, many of which had hoped to buy distressed properties at foreclosure and offer owners the right to rent until they got back on their feet—or to sell these properties to new buyers in a way that would preserve the diversity and social inclusiveness of neighborhoods.[33] "Our goal is community control of stable, affordable, high-quality housing," says Right to the City's Romano. "Private equity firms have one goal: to make money."

Worse yet, because these firms, as part of the shadow banking sector, get much less regulation than many other players in the housing market, they can deploy debt and leverage with less oversight—a worrisome fact given the major role those two ingredients played in the previous crisis. Such firms are also subject to far less scrutiny of their business model, which remains very opaque. "These guys aren't used to reporting in the same way that the banks are," says Sarah Edelman, the head of housing policy for the Center for American Progress and author of a detailed report on private equity's move into housing. "We don't have a lot of information about the way they operate."[34]

Even in low-income neighborhoods, private equity firms have few, if any, incentives to create affordable housing. They can outbid local players for properties, put minimum effort into fixing them up (too much, and public officials can assess higher taxes), and then put homes back onto the market at higher-than-average rental rates, driving out the original tenants and changing the character of neighborhoods. In a recent survey of community-based nonprofits in California, most described their experience with private equity's arrival to their neighborhoods in these exact terms.[35]

And then there's the fact that these corporate owners often make for terrible landlords. One survey of tenants in Blackstone-owned Invitation Homes properties found high levels of property neglect, overcharging, and unfair evictions. Three-quarters of Invitation Homes' tenants surveyed by the Right to the City alliance had never met their landlords in person, and many had access only to online communications. No wonder 39 percent had problems with roaches or insects, 18 percent had roof leaks, and a number were charged deposit amounts that were actually illegal by state laws.[36] "People will call us up and say, 'I'm getting kicked out of my apartment by my landlord but I have no idea who my landlord is,'" says Romano. "The further control is away from the community, the harder it is to get accountability and the more the drive for profit will dictate everything."

It's a trend that the government itself is fueling. As the housing market began to tighten and cheap properties became harder to find, private equity firms and hedge funds have started buying up distressed loan portfolios from public lenders like Fannie Mae and Freddie Mac via the federal Department of Housing and Urban Development (HUD), which has only recently begun to prioritize community-based buyers, long after the bulk of quality cheap properties have been purchased.[37] What's more, Blackstone and others are now *securitizing* rental property portfolios—meaning they're issuing the same kinds of real estate–backed securities that caused the 2008 crisis, only this time they are securitizing rental revenue streams from the homes that they've bought up. These are the same sort of innovations that scuttled the housing market the first time around.

Since private equity firms began buying into the single-family-home market in 2012, investment banks like JPMorgan Chase and Deutsche Bank have provided billions of dollars in credit to boost their property acquisitions. Players like Blackstone, Colony Capital, and American Homes 4 Rent have taken these loans for properties and bundled them together, and then resold them to other players, like mutual funds. In many booming markets, smaller players, in particular new rental companies, are rushing into the game. Large private equity firms have begun providing these real-estate investors with blanket mortgages, which can also be spliced, diced, bundled, and sold again and again until it's difficult to know who's holding the next exploding bag of housing risk. And as interest rates go up, and loans of this kind get harder for cash-hungry rental companies to secure, some companies have begun raising money for fresh buying sprees by going public.[38]

All of it has huge implications for real-world wealth and financial risk. Consider that not only is private equity using rental income to raise huge amounts of debt financing to buy up more properties, but that if the buyers of such bonds ever needed to sell those securities quickly in the case of a market crash, millions of people could end up being evicted from properties that have to be sold. That means, just as was the case before 2008, that we still have a housing market in which the poorest Americans are also the most vulnerable.

Many experts feel there's a good chance that these new rental securities themselves will go bust, given that we are talking about *renters* rather than owners; renters tend to be younger, poorer, and more vulnerable to unemployment and healthcare emergencies than the average American. "Securities backed by rental income are the most unstable revenue stream imaginable," says CEPR's Appelbaum. "I mean, think of the young people you know, who are underemployed and renting and might lose their jobs at any time. Think of yourself when you were younger! These renters are people who could very well end up in their parents' cellars, but if they default on their rents, private equity firms won't be left holding the bag—the people they sold those securities to will be. Really, I don't know why anyone would buy these instruments."[39] And yet billions of them have been sold already, and real estate experts estimate they may well turn into a $1.5 trillion market in the next few years.[40]

It's a truly Kafkaesque response to the housing crisis of 2008, creating another dangerous bubble with many of the same elements as the previous one—massive amounts of debt and leverage, opacity, weak regulation, and little community oversight of lending or accountability—which could end up devastating Main Street, even as it enriches Wall Street. "How do we know this isn't going to end up as subprime times ten?" asks Edelman. "The answer is, we don't. These are shadow banking entities developing an entirely new market. We don't know a lot about the kind of underwriting they are doing. We don't know how they'll fare as property managers. We're at the beginning of a very new kind of paradigm in housing, and we don't yet know where it is going to go."[41]

One thing that we do know, though, is that the growth of the modern financial system has closely tracked shifts in the housing sector. A study done by the Federal Reserve Bank of San Francisco and the University of Bonn found that in the industrialized world, housing finance rose from the equivalent of 20 percent of annual economic activity early in the twentieth century to 69 percent in 2010.[42] Housing is where American consumers spend the biggest chunk of their income, and so, where housing goes, the economy goes. That's a trend that many economists believe will only accelerate. As Adair Turner points out in his book *Between Debt and the Devil*, the largest chunk of financial lending against existing assets (meaning, not stuff that is being built from scratch) already goes to real estate, both in the United States and other developed countries. As people get richer, they want to live in more desirable housing, which pushes up the price of existing property assets, especially in prime cities like New York, London, and Hong Kong. There isn't a lot of new real estate development in such places, but there's a lot of buying and selling of existing property, which creates rising asset values but doesn't add too many jobs. Real estate buying and selling is thus particularly vulnerable to financialization cycles, because we're basically talking about money staying within that closed loop.[43] That's one of the reasons that real estate regulation needs to be crafted much more carefully, as I will explore in chapter 11.

As we saw earlier in the book, many of the major pushes for financial deregulation on the part of the banking industry in recent times have been done with an eye to increasing the amount of business that finance can do in the housing sector. As academics Charles Calomiris and Stephen Haber meticulously outline in their book, *Fragile by Design: The Political Origins of Banking Crises & Scarce Credit*, the subprime crisis itself was "the outcome of a series of spectacular political deals that distorted the incentives of both bankers and debtors."[44] Unfortunately, nothing about this paradigm has changed—indeed, things have arguably gotten worse. Given that some of the largest players in the game now are outside the formal banking sector, you have a particularly dangerous tethering of the country's most important industry, housing, with the fastest-growing and least transparent part of the financial sector, shadow banking. This time around, though, financial institutions aren't just trading risky securities. They actually own and operate real properties—meaning, they have an even more direct impact on the lives of average Americans. Private equity firms already control many people's jobs; now they control the roofs over people's heads, too.

SHADOW LANDLORDS

For housing activists, the biggest task of the last several years has been putting a face to these shadowy new corporate landlords. The task is particularly difficult since in the thirty years leading up to the passage of the Dodd-Frank financial reform act in 2010, nobody in Washington paid much attention to such firms. As part of the shadow banking sector, they were presumed to operate in a sphere that wouldn't touch the average consumer's finances too much, which turned out to be untrue. Just think of the demise of the hedge fund Long-Term Capital Management and the global market ripples it created; the government's intervention to offset the impact of the fund's failure belies the notion that shadow banking entities don't enjoy federal backstopping of the Too Big to Fail kind, albeit implicitly rather than explicitly.

Since the financial crisis of 2008, it's the shadow banking sector rather than the federally guaranteed banks that has grown like kudzu, as risk migrates to the darkest parts of the system. While the share of formal bank assets has declined as a percentage of the total global financial system, shadow banks (which include not only private equity but also hedge funds, money market funds, structured finance vehicles, real estate investment trusts, and other exotic, acronym-wielding creatures) grew by 10 percent in 2014 alone, reaching $36 trillion, or more than twice the size of the U.S. economy.[45] It's telling that as regulators have tried with varying degrees of success to shine a light on the formal banking sector, money, talent, and risk have quickly fled to the informal sector. Private equity is the top area where they headed—it's now the single most popular destination for young financial workers—a clear indicator of where both the risk and the reward are in our financial system today.[46]

While private equity investors used to represent only 1–2 percent of the housing market in cities like Atlanta, Las Vegas, Phoenix, the Inland Empire towns, Miami, and other parts of Florida, they now own up to 10 percent in some neighborhoods, which gives them a lot more clout in shaping the market. There's little question that private equity has raised rents and the price of property, but the particular effects of their buying spree vary from community to community. In Atlanta, for example, some experts say that private equity buyers have helped stabilize certain middle-class neighborhoods, for example in Gwinnett County, where schools are good and residents are mainly middle class, by putting a floor on prices with their mass foreclosure buyouts. (Blackstone alone bought 1,380 Atlanta homes in a single day in April 2013.)[47] "Absent the influx of that capital, there were homes that really needed rehab that weren't going to get purchased," says John O'Callaghan, the CEO of the Atlanta Neighborhood Development Partnership, a twenty-five-year-old nonprofit that is working on housing issues in the city. "I do think they helped get some of that extra vacancy off the market, and that helped us slow foreclosures." That echoes the defense that private equity firms themselves use, which is that they are creating much-needed "liquidity" and stabilizing neighborhoods. Although Invitation Homes officials declined an interview for this book, they did point me to the work of Moody's chief economist Mark Zandi and others who make that point. Still, as even Zandi acknowledges in a recent Moody's memo he coauthored, many of the concerns about institutional investors being bad landlords or raising rents too quickly or not taking care of properties are "reasonable," although they are complaints that are sometimes levied against mom-and-pop shops, too.[48]

But, says O'Callaghan, one fly in the ointment that's quite particular to private equity owners is that they aren't looking to sell the improved properties back to individuals—they are selling mainly to one another or creating real estate investment trusts (REITs) to maximize tax benefits. That has the side effect of eroding the city tax base, because tax collectors can only assess new value and collect taxes on that appreciation when permits are pulled for individual sales. Private equity firms get all the tax benefits of buying and selling distressed properties en masse, but local homeowners, who need higher "comp" sales to raise the value of their own properties, are bypassed. The wealth flows to Wall Street, rather than Main Street. "The firms and individuals buying distressed properties . . . are typically not located in the communities where they invest, so when investors eventually resell these properties, it is likely that they will take their wealth with them," says Sarah Edelman of the Center for American Progress.[49]

WATER INTO WINE

To be fair, not all private equity owners are created equal. Many housing advocates feel that the more local the owner, the better for the community. O'Callaghan's group has run pilot programs with Atlanta-based private equity firms like Key Properties, in an attempt to leverage the investors' scale and cost of capital. (Private equity firms pay about a third of what nonprofits like the Atlanta Neighborhood Development Partnership would to borrow money.) The aim is to advance a more social mission—making sure investors don't take only the cream of the crop in properties and so encouraging a better mix of rental homes versus houses for individual sale (which creates a more stable growth model for neighborhoods), or giving first dibs to specific groups in need, such as veterans. "There are neighborhoods that are always going to be harder to rehab than others, but the whole private equity model just works better if it's local," says O'Callaghan. Most housing experts would agree. In Congress, legislators like California representative Mark Takano (whose constituency includes much of the Inland Empire) and Massachusetts representative Michael Capuano have begun pressuring HUD to give preferential sale treatment to community groups rather than selling distressed loan packages en masse to private equity just because it's quicker to get them off the books that way.

"We've been selling these houses in batches to the richest people in the world," said Capuano in a 2015 congressional hearing on the topic in front of HUD secretary Julian Castro. "I thought part of HUD's mission was to actually create strong, sustainable, inclusive communities and quality, affordable homes for all. . . . I'm just wondering, do you really think that someone in a nice, beautiful building in Agoura Hills [in California] knows better what to do with 42 foreclosed properties in San Antonio than, say, maybe the mayor of San Antonio?"[50] Strong anecdotal evidence shows that local ownership is a better bet in terms of housing stability, anyway. In Boston's Roxbury section, which belongs to Capuano's congressional district, the Dudley Street neighborhood was one of the only places in Boston not to suffer during the subprime crisis, despite being populated mainly by lower-middle-class families. The reason? The majority of homes are owned, or rented, through a community land trust that provides safe and reasonable credit, offers rent-to-own opportunities, and keeps predatory lending at bay.

The prospects for communities in which investors are the main landlords may well be dimmer. Should private equity's real estate bets go belly-up, many experts worry that remote ownership will increase the chance that properties will be flipped, housing prices will be more volatile, and tenants and individual owners alike will be more vulnerable to the whims of a Wall Street landlord. Dan Immergluck, a professor at Georgia Tech who has researched private equity investment in housing, notes that private equity firms have so far tended to buy not only in neighborhoods where property values were low following the crisis, but also in ones where tenant protection laws are weak. "As these groups now represent a sizeable ownership block in many neighborhoods, there's a concern that they could try to exert influence on policy making, pushing back against more tenant rights or fighting for more control over land use," Immergluck says. And true to form, private equity firms have already formed a trade association to lobby at the federal level. "Given that we are moving to more of a rental society, we need to make sure that we're creating a rental market that is stable and safe," he adds.[51]

Doing that will require more monitoring of exactly how private equity is reshaping the property market. To that end, private equity has been under increased scrutiny since the 2010 passage of the Dodd-Frank financial reform act, and many of the largest private equity funds now have to register with the Securities and Exchange Commission. Since this process has begun, a whole host of problems with the private equity business model have come to light, including unfair fee structures and dicey tax maneuvers. In May 2014, former SEC compliance chief Andrew Bowden gave what has become known as his "sunshine speech," in which he announced that *more than half* of the private equity firms examined by the agency had serious legal or compliance violations and were not sharing fee income that rightfully belonged to fund investors. Many funds were not above "charging hidden fees" that they never disclosed, Bowden said—which allowed at least one Manhattan private equity manager to bilk his clients out of $9 million.[52] With a number of enforcement actions creeping up in recent months and rising pressure from the SEC and investors (including major pension funds), many private equity firms have begun paying investors the fee income instead of pocketing it. It's a small step in the right direction, but private equity and the shadow banking industry at large are lobbying hard against the Dodd-Frank rules, trying to roll back reporting standards.[53]

Meanwhile, some private equity firms are getting around the fee issue with a tax scam known as a "management fee waiver," in which they simply relabel the income they receive from their fixed management fees as capital gains, which means it gets taxed at a much lower rate (and doesn't need to be shared with investors). Bain Capital partners made good use of this loophole by waiving more than $1 billion in management fees over ten years. The tactic allowed them to save more than $250 million in federal income taxes on what was, essentially, salary income that should have been taxed at the rate paid by every other working American. This practice is "the tax equivalent of turning water into wine," says CEPR's Appelbaum.[54] The US Treasury Department and the IRS have tried to craft new rules that would hopefully make it crystal clear that such maneuvering is illegal. But in the meantime, private equity firms are under no requirements to share any correspondence from the SEC with their investors. That means that the pension funds and mutual funds that manage our retirement savings may be unknowingly continuing to fund private equity companies that are breaking the law.

And what about the housing market itself? Some private equity firms are beginning to cash out their earnings in real estate, a sign that prices may have peaked and that Wall Street, rather than Main Street, will have taken the bulk of the profits from the country's housing recovery. Neighborhood advocates worry about what might happen if a major corporate buyer decides to sell properties en masse at some point in the future, dumping homes just as quickly as it bought them. Such a situation could lead to price collapses and a further erosion of local tax bases, not to mention any number of negative social consequences (think Pottersville). Housing advocates are up in arms about the fact that investors are being allowed to buy up government-owned distressed properties, reaping the tax benefits from owning such foreclosed homes even as they continue to receive rent from the former homeowners (many of whom end up becoming tenants in their own properties). "It's a complete failure of public policy," says Appelbaum, given that the government itself could have done the exact same thing and kept the tax and revenue benefits in public coffers while also guaranteeing the stability of rental housing in a way that investors aren't obliged to. "There's nothing to stop private equity from kicking people out of their homes and renting them out at higher prices to new tenants," she adds. "We've seen what the private equity business model looks like in the past. Why anyone thought it would be different this time around, I have no idea."

RETHINKING HOUSING

So what might be done to make the housing market healthier? And could existing housing laws be better leveraged to police the market for any private equity abuses? While private equity firms don't fall under the restrictions of the Community Reinvestment Act (CRA), which requires financiers to lend to a diverse group of borrowers, the banks that provide their credit (like JPMorgan Chase, Wells Fargo, and Citigroup) do. The California Reinvestment Coalition has begun lobbying the Federal Reserve to cut banks' rating grades around CRA lending if they give credit to private equity firms buying and renting foreclosed homes or securitizing these properties, as a backdoor way of increasing pressure on such investors.

The Federal Housing Finance Agency, the Federal Housing Administration, and HUD could also study and release more public data on exactly how private equity investors have affected various American neighborhoods thus far, and they could make sure that these new corporate owners are being held accountable if they don't maintain properties or illegally evict tenants. So far, federal agencies have sold tens of thousands of distressed homes and mortgages to investors, but the public has gotten no follow-up data about how such investments have performed, or how owners and tenants have been treated by private sector owners. (According to the Center for American Progress, tenants are sometimes given only a few days to leave properties during evictions and often get little or no notice before rents are increased.)[55]

Beyond this, the United States needs to overhaul the mortgage market to make it work for individuals, who still either keep their nest eggs in their homes or aspire to do so. That requires a number of steps, including fixing Fannie Mae and Freddie Mac, which are still the main supporters of the secondary mortgage market. Mainstream lenders are reluctant to loan if they think they won't be able to sell a mortgage on the secondary market. Yet seven years after the crisis, Fannie and Freddie are still in "conservatorship," a kind of purgatory in which their profits are slowly being bled to reduce the budget deficit, leaving them dangerously low on reserves. (This predicament has prompted another Kafkaesque situation in which hedge funds are suing the US government over its handling of the two housing giants in the very bailouts that have saved the financial industry itself.)[56]

Fixing the housing market will also require rethinking who, exactly, should own a home, which will in turn require tackling the bias that exists in the market right now. We know that minority Americans were hit much harder by the subprime crisis than others. A 2014 study by Duke University and the Center for Global Policy Solutions, a Washington, D.C.–based consultancy, found that the median amount of liquid wealth (assets that can easily be turned into cash) held by African American households was $200. For Latino households it was $340. The median for white households: $23,000.[57] One reason for the difference is that a disproportionate number of nonwhites, along with women and younger workers of all races, have little or no access to formal retirement savings plans. But another key reason is that they suffered greater losses in the mortgage crisis, both because they were more likely to be victimized by predatory lenders, and because relative to whites, they keep even more of their money in housing. In this sense, the government's policy decision to favor lenders over homeowners in the 2008 bailouts favored whites over people of color. But if most Americans, especially lower-income individuals and minorities, keep the bulk of their wealth in housing, we should rethink lending practices to allow for a broader range of credit metrics, which currently tend to be biased toward whites. (Credit ratings agencies should, for example, treat on-time payment of local department store cards, held more frequently by minorities, the same as those of major national cards.)

We should also consider lower down payments for good borrowers. That's a controversial statement, given that some experts believe that minimal down payments fueled the housing crisis by allowing underwater borrowers to walk away from homes more easily (plenty of others disagree). There was a mythology following the subprime crisis that low-income earners who put only a few percentage points down on a mortgage simply should never have been homeowners. But research shows it's not that simple—people who defaulted on their mortgages came from a wide swath of the socioeconomic spectrum, and a number of reports have found that policies aimed at increasing affordable housing had little to do with speculative lending, which would have happened regardless.[58] Moreover, it's often not the sheer amount of cash that people can throw at a mortgage that identifies them as a good credit risk. One ten-year study by the University of North Carolina at Chapel Hill, for example, found that poor buyers putting less than 5 percent down are no different from the average Americans as credit risks go, if they are vetted by metrics other than how much cash they have on hand. That's not to say we should have runaway borrowing as we did in the run-up to 2008, but credit is still constrained relative to historical averages.

As recently as 2014, former Fed chair Ben Bernanke, who isn't exactly hard-up (he reportedly makes at least $200,000 a speech), lamented that he wasn't able to refinance his home because of tight credit conditions. This is yet another reminder that the housing recovery is being driven not by first-time homebuyers or people who want to trade up but by the wealthiest people and investors in the country. If we don't find a way to fix the housing market so that its gains can be more widely shared, we might once again find the larger growth prospects of our country in peril. After all, in a $17 trillion economy, catering to the 1 percent—or the 0.001 percent—can take you only so far.

CHAPTER 8

THE END OF RETIREMENT

How Wall Street Ate Our Nest Eggs

IF YOU WONDER what the future of retirement savings will look like, consider the story of Paula Dromi. She is a seventy-six-year-old social worker who lives in a small three-bedroom house in downtown Los Angeles with one of her two grown sons, who moved back home to save money after a period of unemployment and helps Dromi pay major living expenses. Her Social Security plus the money she makes working as a part-time freelance therapist comes to not much more than what she owes each month for her home insurance, property taxes, and mortgage, with not a lot left over. Both she and her journalist husband (who died in 2000) saved for retirement, but years of copayments on medical bills for his brain illness depleted both his individual retirement account (IRA) and their savings. Dromi was left with just her IRA—which was lower than it might have been because she changed jobs often and, like many other women, took time off to raise children—and her home, which is valued at $442,000. She could always sell the house. But if she did, she'd have to move out of Los Angeles, away from her work and everyone she knows, because of the lack of cheaper housing. Instead she has pieced together a multigenerational home and a freelance work life that she hopes she can maintain indefinitely. "I'll be working another twenty years, assuming I can," says Dromi.

In a way, Dromi is lucky. She has a house that she can share and is healthy enough to work, at least for the time being. But the fact that an educated professional who saved as much as possible can end up scraping just to get by in her golden years underscores how fragile the American retirement system has become. Dromi is by no means alone in her struggle to craft a decent standard of living in retirement. Statistics show that more than half of all Americans haven't saved enough money to maintain their current standard of living after they stop working; indeed, the average total retirement savings of a typical American household ages 55 to 64 is a mere $104,000, a fraction of what it would take to live decently for another couple of decades.[1] It's a looming crisis, something that political leaders like former senator Tom Harkin, a retirement reform advocate, have called a "tsunami."

As with other big, slow-moving crises (climate change, healthcare, the quality of education), it's difficult to create a sense of urgency over retirement security. But in the past few years, the financial meltdown and its aftermath have thrown the problem into sharper relief, as many groups—women and minorities in particular—have lost a large chunk of their asset base and been forced, like Dromi, to come up with patchwork solutions and live with a sense of anxiety about what might lie ahead. "My clothes come from thrift shops. I do a lot of crafts and make whatever I can. I'm very careful, very cautious," she says. "I keep saving. But I feel pretty pessimistic about the future."

One big reason people like Paula Dromi don't have more is that our retirement system has been hijacked by finance. Not only is the privatization of retirement a failed experiment, but, as this chapter will explain, much of the gains in our portfolios are being eaten up by fees that financiers themselves have done little to nothing to earn. It's a problem that has been building for some time. But the urgency around fixing retirement is rapidly growing, since the scenario everyone wants to avoid arrives in 2030. That's when the largest demographic group in US history, the baby boomers, will have nearly depleted the Social Security trust fund. It's also when older Generation Xers will begin moving out of work and into retirement. But these won't be the golden years of leisure that recent generations have known.

Consider a typical 2030 retiree. Like Dromi, she will be an educated woman. Part of the GenX generation, she'll be around sixty-five years old, and will have worked all her life at small and midsize companies, exiting the workforce with no retirement plan. (Although small firms have created most of the new jobs in the economy for the past fifty years, only 14 percent of them sponsor formal retirement plans today.)[2] Our retiree will have put away some savings here and there, but she'll also be part of the middle class, which has taken the biggest wealth hit during the financial crisis of 2008. That, along with the assumption that average real wages will stay virtually flat for the next three decades, even as living costs continue to rise, means that she will have minimal savings, even less than the $42,000 that today's average retiree leaves work with.

More than half her income will come from Social Security. When you factor in healthcare spending, once she stops bringing in a salary she'll be living on only about 41 percent of the average national wage.[3] In all likelihood, she won't actually be retired. Like many of her peers, our GenXer will likely find herself needing a part-time job to maintain even a minimal standard of living. She may take a position bagging groceries at a local supermarket, or cleaning homes, or as a nanny—or pretty much anyplace willing to hire a sixty-five-year-old retiree rather than an energetic twentysomething.

Or she may, like Dromi, share her home and many living expenses with her children: Millennials who aren't doing so well themselves. More members of this generation live with mom and dad at the moment than any generation since the 1960s, according to the Pew Research Center, in part because they came of age in the post-financial-crisis era, when wages were stagnant and unemployment was high. If you enter the workplace during such cycles, your income never catches up. As these Millennials struggle to pay down student loans and save enough money to move out, there's very little left over, which means they are on course for an even less secure retirement than their parents will have.

Boomers scrambling to get by on a minimal income. GenXers who can't afford to stop working. Millennials staring at a bleak financial future. This is the retirement apocalypse that we are only beginning to grapple with.[4]

How did we get here? The conventional wisdom is to blame the culture or individuals themselves for moving away from America's traditional puritan values of savings and thrift. It's true that Americans save less than they did in the 1950s as a percentage of their disposable income. But that has to do with two facts. First, the cost of basic middle-class trappings like education, healthcare, and housing has exponentially increased over the last few decades, and second, consumer debt has ballooned as the financial industry has offered up credit bubbles to support what real economic growth does not. It's a chicken-and-egg cycle, as we've already seen in many chapters of this book. Whenever economic growth slows in such a way that the middle class can no longer support its lifestyle, finance parachutes in to offer up debt as a balm. This dysfunctional stopgap is usually facilitated by politicians, who don't want to tell their constituents that they can't live like they used to (in part because the politicians themselves haven't had the courage to push through truly growth-enhancing economic platforms).

But the retirement crisis isn't just about these meta-trends. It's about the fact that finance itself, and in particular the asset management industry that runs our retirement savings, is taking a disproportionate amount of our nest eggs in fees, while offering less return than what we would get by simply throwing our money in an index fund that tracks the market itself. It's about the failed experiment of the 401(k), an accidental system that has worked well for the top tier of society but not for the majority of Americans. It's also about the end of private company pensions, as well as a broken state pension system that has been exploited by Wall Street, tanking entire cities and economic regions. And it's about the increasing pullback of both government and companies from the business of helping Americans save for their retirement. We've been left on our own to figure out how to swim in this coming tsunami. It's not irresponsible consumers who are the problem—it's our system. Far from being a safety net, our retirement system has become an area of major risk, and one that directly touches the lives of each and every American.

THE TOPPLING OF THE THREE-LEGGED STOOL

Our retirement system, a three-legged stool made up of Social Security, pension funds, and, most important, private savings vehicles like the 401(k), has been toppled, and—not surprisingly—in a way that enriches Wall Street rather than Main Street. John Bogle, the founder of the Vanguard Group and one of the true makers of the financial industry, is the rare insider who's taken on the issue. His book *The Clash of the Cultures: Investment vs. Speculation* lays out the problems in detail.[5] But the short of it is that all three legs of the stool are now faltering. "Our nation's system of retirement security is imperiled, headed for a serious train wreck," says Bogle.[6]

Consider each of the wobbly legs. Social Security, perhaps the most successful government program of all time and the key reason that more older Americans aren't currently in poverty, is underfunded and under attack from forces on the right and even some on the left, who believe that government should get out of the retirement business and leave it to the markets.

Defined-benefit pension plans, the kind of lifetime retirement plans that many companies used to offer, have shrunk dramatically. Corporate CFOs have cut them over the years as a way to bolster corporate profit margins (which, as we've already learned, have stayed mostly in the pockets of the rich, undermining overall economic growth in the process). What pension plans exist are mostly in the public sector—but they are set for a fall, as many state and local governments have been wildly overoptimistic in their promises to pensioners. The majority of public pension plans in the United States are underfunded,[7] a situation that has left pensions and governments themselves ripe for exploitation by Wall Street.

Then there is our private system of IRAs and defined-contribution retirement plans, like corporate-run 401(k)s, which have become structurally unsound. These plans, which most Americans depend on, represent $14.2 trillion in wealth.[8] Yet the system is opaque and expensive, and it serves mostly the upper third of our society—people who work in the kinds of jobs where they can benefit from corporate programs that match their savings. Even those people, however, are being fleeced by the Street, which has for decades tried to push investors out of index funds and into mutual funds that systemically underperform the market as a whole. That record is not only because of manic trading that rarely produces gains, but also because these funds end up pressuring their client corporations themselves (whose shares they own) to focus on the short term over the long term. It's a strategy that tends to yield fruits only by the quarter or, with luck, the year (which is exactly the time period over which fund managers themselves are typically paid).

Worse yet, for such short-term gains, we all get charged massive fees. In one study on the topic, Stanford professor emeritus and Nobel laureate William Sharpe calculated that investing in low- or no-cost funds rather than actively managed funds could result in a 20 percent higher standard of living in retirement, in part due to the fees commanded by the managed funds.[9] Bogle has run his own numbers, including not only the lower returns for active funds but additional hidden fees from portfolio turnover costs, charges for investment advice, and other such expenses. As he put it in 2014 testimony to the Senate Finance Committee, "the high costs of ownership of mutual fund shares, over the long-term, are likely to confiscate *as much as 65 percent or more* of the wealth that retirement plan investors could otherwise easily earn, simply by diverting market returns from fund investors to fund managers." He added, "many of the infirmities of our retirement system are the result of the heavy costs incurred by investors because of our bloated financial system." Popping that finance bubble, the one that takes nearly 25 percent of corporate profits and creates only 4 percent of the jobs, is crucial to getting both retirement and the economy back on track.[10] It's an enormous task, one as big as the fund business itself.

A BUSINESS WITH ELEMENTS OF A PROFESSION

Asset management used to be a safe, staid, boring business. In the years after World War II, the industry was centered not in razzle-dazzle New York but in puritan Boston. Asset managers were mostly old-line stewards of family wealth, people who invested conservatively and for the long haul. A 1949 *Fortune* magazine story on the nascent mutual fund industry, titled "Big Money in Boston," featured a photo of five somber, clean-cut trustees of the Massachusetts Investors Trust, the largest fund at the time, with $277 million in assets. Like most funds, it was operated by individuals with their own capital at risk, working together in a partnership or a closely held corporation. These men and their institutions radiated Yankee thrift. Everyone knew everyone else in the clubby business, and anyone who was perceived as being a risk taker with clients' money would have been shunned as quickly as Hawthorne's Hester Prynne. At that point, the fund industry was, as Bogle puts it, "a profession with elements of a business."[11]

But it was soon to become a business with fewer and fewer elements of a profession. The shift was driven by a wave of new money, as a growing American middle class began pouring savings into stocks and bonds (see chapters 1 and 2). In 1951, US mutual fund assets totaled $2.5 billion. Today they are around $16 trillion. This influx of money encouraged fund companies to grow and expand into new business lines. The increasing competition and product proliferation that followed necessitated riskier management strategies, which could potentially vault the returns of one product above another, at least for a short time.

By the late 1960s, companies were touting "hot" fund managers and treating them like Hollywood stars. Volatility in such funds was increasing dramatically, but the growth of inflation in the 1970s meant that investors were desperate to earn a decent return. Despite the risks, they began moving money from bank deposit accounts to money market funds and mutual funds. This shift, as we have seen, had the domino effect of encouraging the banking industry to push for deregulation that would allow it more access to the consumer market, contributing to debacles like the 2008 subprime crisis. "With the rise of bond funds and money market funds, nearly all of the major fund managers—which for a half-century had primarily operated as professional *investment* managers for one or two equity funds—became *business* managers, offering a smorgasbord of investment options," says Bogle.[12] Suddenly the primary goal of funds wasn't to earn steady returns for clients, but to earn profits for the firm. Fund managers began advertising various bells and whistles of their specific investment strategies, and charging higher fees for them.

Then, as now, there was little data to show that any actively managed fund could regularly outperform the market, particularly when you factored in fees. (Morningstar, the respected purveyor of mutual fund analysis services, basically conceded this point in 2010.)[13] A particularly telling recent piece of research done by law academics at Yale and the University of Virginia found that after considering costs, not only did index funds outperform actively managed portfolios by a significant amount, but 16 percent of the time the impact of high fees would actually *offset the entire tax benefit* of investing in a 401(k) plan for young workers over the course of their careers.[14] Investors then and now were better off simply linking their investments to the market via an index fund, an industry that Bogle and others had begun to develop. But active fund management was much more profitable, and the industry worked hard to convince average Joe investors that they needed to pay for professional guidance through this wild world of investing. "You wouldn't settle for an 'average' brain surgeon," said one index fund critic. "So why would you settle for an 'average' mutual fund?"[15] Another fund management firm papered Wall Street with posters showing an angry Uncle Sam putting a rubber stamp across index funds. "Index funds are un-American!" the ad screamed. "Help stamp out index funds."

Even the prudent Bostonians got into the game. My husband's father, Robert Minturn Sedgwick, happened to be one of those stewards who worked in the Boston asset management industry before and after World War II. During his time as an associate with Scudder, Stevens & Clark, he came to believe (like Bogle and a growing number of others of that generation) that the whole actively managed fund business was basically a scam. The average investor was far better off putting his or her money into what Sedgwick called the "20 largest," a group of big-cap US stocks that he came up with, which essentially mimicked a modern index fund. He published an article about his idea in the *Harvard Business Review* and began raising it within his firm. Not surprisingly, the notion met with a chilly reception amongst Scudder principals, who could see the handwriting on the wall—index funds, and passively managed products in general, might eventually put them out of business. Sedgwick didn't get rich, never made partner, and died a rather frustrated man, upholding his ideas about passive investing to the end.[16] His article about how the "20 largest" had beaten all actively managed funds between 1948 and 1972, published in the *Financial Analysts Journal* in 1973, three years before his death, had the plaintive title "The Record of Conventional Investment Management: Is There Not a Better Way?"[17]

The answer, of course, was yes. But that way wouldn't enrich the financial industry. By the 1970s, the die was basically cast. Fund management firms themselves began to move away from the unlimited liability partnership structure and to go public, creating further conflict between the needs of clients and the incentives for the firm to maximize profits for itself, whatever the risks to investors. This has created a dizzying amount of wheeling and dealing, which may be good for the fund companies but is of questionable interest to investors. Consider Ameriprise Financial, which traces its roots back to the nineteenth century and entered the fund business in the

1940s. American Express acquired it in 1984, under the leadership of the infamous deal maker Sandy Weill, and then spun it off in an IPO in 2005. Ameriprise went on in 2010 to acquire another massive fund company, Columbia Management, creating a $652 billion fund behemoth. When asked why he did the merger, the chief of Ameriprise didn't beat around the bush: "It enhances our scale, broadens our distribution and strengthens and diversifies our [fund] lineup"—steps that "will be instrumental in driving improved asset management returns and [profit] margins [for Ameriprise] over time."[18]

Amazingly, nothing was said about what it would do for the people whose retirement money was being invested with the company. But the numbers told the tale—the lineup included nearly twice as many poorly performing funds as it did top ones, as ranked by Morningstar ratings.[19]

The upshot is that the staid Boston trustee culture has now fully given way to a freewheeling strategy of market speculation. Today managers are rewarded by the year or even the quarter, and if they don't perform, they get tossed out. Desperate to hit their numbers, they trade more and more aggressively (which, scientific studies say, leads to more and more risk taking). In the 1960s, the turnover rate of stocks in actively managed funds was around 30 percent a year; more recently, it has been around 140 percent. But as these desperate financiers strive to meet their targets, fewer and fewer succeed. That's true for everyone, not just fund managers—plenty of research shows that more trading generally means worse trading.[20] In the 1960s, only about 1 percent of mutual funds went under in any given year. By 2012, that rate had soared to 7 percent. Assuming that such a failure rate will persist, around 3,500 of the 5,000 equity funds in existence today won't be around by 2023.[21] So much for the long term.

Meanwhile, fees have soared. Conventional economic wisdom holds that as the industry gets bigger, costs to consumers should get lower. Those are the basic economies of scale that you see in most industries. (Think of Walmart and how it gets its "everyday low prices"—by employing tons of people very cheaply, yes, but also by buying from suppliers in mass quantities to dramatically lower wholesale costs.) But in finance, where a small number of insiders control the flow of information and money through that narrow middle of the hourglass, it works the other way. The assets of all stock and bond mutual funds had risen from $5.2 trillion in 1999 to around $13 trillion in 2014. But despite a more than doubling of the industry's asset base, fees have actually risen, too, by a whopping 81 percent—from $48 billion to $87 billion.[22] "The staggering economies of scale that characterize money management have been largely arrogated by fund managers to themselves, rather than shared with their fund shareholders," concludes Bogle. Or, as the great economist Paul Samuelson put it presciently in 1967, "I decided that there was only one place to make money in the mutual fund business—as there is only one place for a temperate man to be in a saloon, behind the bar and not in front of the bar. And I invested in . . . [a] management company."[23]

In lieu of pouring all your money into Fidelity or BlackRock, there are any number of studies that tell us how much better off we are investing the Vanguard way, in low- or no-fee index funds. The world's smartest investors buy it—Warren Buffett recently told me that upon his death, his wife's inheritance would be invested 90 percent in Vanguard's S&P 500 equity index funds.[24] So why don't we all follow that wisdom? The answer has its roots in behavioral economics, which tells us that the "rational man" is more than capable of making irrational decisions. As *The Economist* put it recently, "everyone knows that if you go to a casino, the odds are rigged in favour of the house. But people still dream of making a killing. The same psychology seems to apply to fund management, where investors flock to high-cost mutual funds even though the odds are against them."[25] Most of us simply don't trust ourselves about investing, and it's in the interests of the industry to make it seem much more confusing than it is. That gives them more business; as we have seen, one of the great tricks of finance is to advance the cult of the expert. By cloaking what is essentially a pretty simple decision (put your money in index funds and forget about it until you are sixty-five) in all sorts of complicated jargon, the industry convinces people that they need someone to explain it to them. No wonder a recent survey found that 7 out of 10 wealthy individuals say their financial adviser, the person who sells them on all those high-fee funds, is as important to them as their doctor.[26]

THE ACCIDENTAL INVESTORS

This perplexing phenomenon—wherein individuals who are unable to make the best market decisions nonetheless get forced into taking more personal responsibility for their retirement future—became more common through the 1980s. That was when the private 401(k) retirement investing system, on which about half of us depend today, really took off. Amazingly, the creation of this entire system was an accident. Like our bloated healthcare system, our modern 401(k) retirement savings arrangement was a fluke that some clever people came up with in an effort to exploit parts of the tax code.

In 1980, a benefits consultant working on a cash bonus plan for bankers had the idea to take advantage of an obscure provision in the tax code passed two years earlier, which allowed employees to set aside money to be matched by employers, which would increase tax deductions that could be taken by the corporation. That moment was the beginning of the 401(k), a savings account that lets employees contribute pretax income from their paycheck (sometimes with employers matching some or all of the amount) but that, unlike the traditional pension, does not promise a specific regular payment upon retirement. Holders of these plans amass a hopefully growing fund from which they can draw money when they retire. But nothing about this system is guaranteed, and participation is usually up to the individual, another big problem with the system.[27]

Research shows that 20 percent of people who are eligible for corporate plans simply don't sign up for them. (Who isn't put off by yet another bit of complicated shadow work involving navigating a complicated benefits website on your own?)[28] Also, a large number of participants under sixty withdraw funds early or borrow against their retirement accounts, taking big tax hits and defying the whole point of saving for the future. "Congress did not intend for [401(k)s] to replace traditional pensions as a primary retirement vehicle, and they are poorly designed for this role," says Monique Morrissey, an economist at the Economic Policy Institute who testified to the Senate on the topic in 2014. "Few people have the math skills, financial sophistication, or time to make sense of often conflicting financial advice and make sound investment decisions." The complexity of the system results in high numbers of people taking money out early, squandering the tax benefits of such programs, or simply making bad choices in terms of asset allocation.

Indeed, anyone who has ever tried to pore over the benefits websites of their employer to try to make the smartest decision (or, God forbid, call the help line "advisers") knows what she means. Even for people who know something about finance it's a confusing maze of options, and as behavioral economics research shows us, more options often result in bad decisions or no decision at all.[29] IRAs, which freelancers and people who don't have access to 401(k)s use to save, are even worse, since they offer fewer investor protections and typically have even higher fees.[30]

Yet bad policy decisions and the desire of both the public and private sector to push retirement responsibilities onto individuals have resulted in a system where such programs are now the norm for most people—or at least most wealthy people. As Social Security was cut in 1983, and companies began to scale back their own pension plans, 401(k)s took off. The result has been a retirement system that is hugely bifurcated along economic and social lines. Research shows that 401(k) plans are mainly utilized by the upper third of the socioeconomic spectrum. But even those people haven't done as well as they might have in previous generations. Statistics show that people retiring today who have invested in 401(k)s rather than traditional defined-benefit pensions are far less well-off than those who came before them, when the model was skewed the opposite way.

What about Americans who don't fall within that lucky group? Just 66 percent of private sector workers have access to any kind of formal retirement plan, and fewer than half sign up for one (again, because of confusion and choice paralysis). And as noted earlier, the number is even worse for small businesses, only 14 percent of which sponsor a retirement savings plan such as a 401(k) or an IRA. What's more, the number of people with access to plans may actually decline in the future, given current labor trends. Many small and mid-size businesses that are creating the majority of new jobs can't afford to offer retirement benefits, and most freelancers as well as part-time workers at companies of all sizes usually don't qualify. Yet those are exactly the groups that are growing in number, as the American workforce becomes a "gig" economy in which more and more people work on contract, and often without benefits. The 401(k) system itself may be flawed, but any vehicle for retirement savings is better than none.

PENSIONERS VERSUS WALL STREET

The failed experiment that is our 401(k) system is just one part of the retirement crisis; the other is the beleaguered defined-benefit pension system (in which individuals retire with a fixed monthly benefit) that serves millions of workers. This system is much less common today than private 401(k)s. But some 75 percent of state and local government workers still rely on defined-benefit programs, and they've grown dramatically over the last couple of decades, tripling in value since 1995 to represent $3.3 trillion worth of retirement assets today.[31]

When public pension plans go awry, they can tank entire cities and regional economic systems—just think of areas like San Bernardino and Stockton, California, where pension troubles have led to bankruptcy and even calls for cities to establish eminent domain to get out from under crushing debt. Yet the stories of firemen who retire with million-dollar pensions are mostly myths that don't capture the reality of the situation. The truth is that in many cases, it isn't the pension load itself that is bankrupting governments and threatening entire regional economies, but the way in which local and state officials were fleeced by Wall Street during times of economic hardship.

Consider the story of Detroit, the biggest municipal bankruptcy in American history, and the high-profile pensions fight at the heart of it. At its peak in 1950, Motown's population was more than double the 700,000 people living in the city today. Detroit's long-term decline was about many things, including civic mismanagement, political corruption, and systemic labor issues. The malaise of American manufacturing from the 1980s onward hit Detroit harder than any other major city. Talent left, property values declined, growth slowed, and by the mid-2000s the tax base had been all but decimated. Detroit was left struggling to pay its bills.

That's when Wall Street came into the picture, selling the city on $1.4 billion of complex and risky securities deals in 2005 and 2006, including a type of pension obligation bonds called certificates of participation. These bonds offered easy cash in exchange for a share of the city's future revenues, albeit with many small-print clauses that put most of the risk for the deal on the city itself, and very little on the bankers. When $800 million of the debt—which had been issued in a way that many experts believed was fraudulent—blew up during the financial crisis, bankers demanded full payment, as was typically their right under the sorts of contracts they negotiated. (Wall Street usually cuts deals that stipulate it gets paid before anyone else.) As a result, Detroit's public employee pensioners—hardworking Main Street Americans who had toiled in often thankless jobs, like bus drivers, clerks, sewage workers, and trash collectors—were asked to take huge cuts in their retirement income to pay hundreds of millions of dollars to bankers.[32] Some creditors were even pushing Detroit to mortgage the priceless art in its hallmark museum—including works by Van Gogh, Whistler, and Degas—to keep cops and ambulances on the street.

Many people who read the coverage of the Detroit crisis have the idea that a rich generation of city workers living in the past simply didn't want to move with the times and take their share of the pain, or that Detroit itself was an irreversibly corrupt city that simply couldn't get its books in order. But that's a false narrative, and a classic case of blaming the victims. Yes, the city had suffered under poor leadership, particularly the administration of Kwame Kilpatrick, who resigned in 2008 after six years in office and is now serving twenty-eight years in jail for corruption. But there were plenty of well-meaning leaders in Detroit, too. And the math shows that the city's fiscal woes were more a revenue problem than a spending problem—Detroit had been in decline for years, and its tax base had simply not kept up with expenses, as sketched above. That's not a surprise, given that municipalities like Detroit depend primarily on real estate, consumption, and income taxes, all of which declined precipitously in the Great Recession. That's exactly what pushed Detroit into a dubious debt deal with Wall Street to begin with.

Detroit's woes weren't about being unwilling to cut budgets—city fathers *did* cut Detroit's operating budget by 38 percent in the wake of the crisis.[33] Yet that still wasn't enough to make up for the decline in revenue. Meanwhile, pensioners who had done nothing wrong were asked to take huge cuts, and Wall Street financial institutions that had gotten the city into a lot of its budgetary trouble were lining up for far more generous deals.

When the bankruptcy of Detroit began in late 2013, the terms of the settlement quickly took center stage and became "a discussion between an emergency manager, from a law firm dedicated to the financial sector, and the financial sector," explained the late Wallace Turbeville, a former Goldman Sachs banker and senior fellow at the nonprofit think tank Demos. "The people [meaning pensioners] tried to get a seat at the table, but the emergency manager had a monopoly on the information [on city finances] and for the first four months of the process his was the only story available."[34] That, says Turbeville, along with what he believes were dubiously calculated numbers (crunched by emergency manager Kevin Orr's team) that overestimated pension liabilities, resulted in a widespread belief that oversize pensions had caused Detroit's demise. In fact, he says, it was the financiers who cut the dubious bond deals with the city in the first place that put Detroit into bankruptcy. That Wall Street debt was "the biggest contributing factor to the increase in Detroit's legacy expenses," explains Turbeville, who wrote an influential report in 2013 outlining the role that finance had played in Detroit's demise.[35] The long and short of it was that the people negotiating the debt settlement on behalf of the city were completely outsmarted and outflanked by financiers, who cut deals for millions of dollars of extremely long-term interest rate swaps that were subject to immediate termination if the city's credit deteriorated, which of course it quickly did. The termination of the contracts required immediate payment of all projected profits that would be earned by the banks had the contract *not* been terminated. That meant that Detroit was suddenly on the hook for a huge lump-sum payment that made its cash flow position completely untenable.

If this contract sounds Kafkaesque, you're right, it is. But this sort of "heads I win, tails you lose" wording is woefully common in municipal finance deals, which pit Wall Street against Main Street in a completely unfair way and tend to include all kinds of tax loopholes that further add to the complexity.

The Detroit story has something of a happy ending. Thankfully, activists and local politicians decided to fight back, and federal judge Steven Rhodes eventually approved the city's bankruptcy plan, threw out the initial settlement of the $800 million derivatives deal, and made financial institutions settle for a fraction of that amount, as part of a larger settlement to rid the city of $7 billion in debt. After sixteen months of legal wrangling, fighting, and soulsearching, a group of private donors, including family foundations with landmark names like Ford and Kellogg, banded together with community development agencies, big businesses, and the state itself. They decided that it was inconceivable that the onetime heart of American economic power—which had already lost much of its tax base, more than half its population, and a devastating portion of its labor pool—should fall further. They came up with the $800 million to offset some of the pension pain and save Detroit's art—a "grand bargain," as it has become known, that gave the city a future. Suddenly the government, its workers, and Detroit's creditors were more willing to come to terms. Residents got creative, and financial institutions took payment in assets that represented a bet on Motown's future, rather than grabbing what cash they could before fleeing. Union reps accepted decreases of 5–10 percent in pension payments, a painful and contentious decision, but much less draconian than what Orr had originally proposed.

In the end, no major stakeholders refused to be part of the almost universally praised settlement, which turned the page on the largest municipal bankruptcy in history. As Michigan's Republican governor, Rick Snyder, told me, "none of this would have been possible without the grand bargain. If people were going to accept this kind of pain, they had to feel that the private sector—and the state—were helping." It was something rare in American civic life these days: compromise. And it was a compromise driven by the original makers of the city, industrialists whose wealth had been forged in the Arsenal of Democracy, as Detroit was once known.[36]

The big lesson from Detroit's bankruptcy is that cities need to manage their finances and dealings with capital markets much more carefully. And Detroit is far from the only American city where the monopoly power of finance and the way in which it takes disproportionate fees for relatively small services are draining public coffers. Los Angeles, for example, pays more in Wall Street fees than it spends on street and sidewalk repairs.[37] And dozens of other cities have been fleeced by bond deals pegged to Libor (the short-term interest rate that banks charge one another for loans), which was famously manipulated by some of the world's most powerful banks. So far, nine financial institutions settled those charges by paying more than $9 billion. Yet the cities victimized by bad deals are still paying. Oakland, California, for instance, has already paid Goldman Sachs more than $50 million in interest on a dicey bond deal. Even after the city passed a resolution to boycott Goldman, it remained legally obliged to keep forking over more cash.[38] In Chicago, risky bonds issued by the public school system are causing serious public finance problems; they'll likely add another $100 million to the school district's already crushing debt burden over the next two decades. And by all indications, issuances of the sort of pension obligation bonds that got Detroit in trouble are set to rise, as a number of states struggle to meet their obligations to retirement savers. (Many state and local pension systems in the country today are underfunded, resulting in a potential shortfall of *$1 trillion* in payouts to pensioners.)[39]

It's a sad fact that the worse a government's finances are, the more likely that it will be sucked in by a risky Wall Street arbitrage play. A study by the Center for Retirement Research at Boston College looked at 270 pension obligation bonds issued since 1992 and found that most of the governments involved had been borrowing in the wake of market run-ups. That led them to overestimate potential gains, investing when their asset returns were high and then taking big losses when the market would, inevitably, correct.[40] Still, the pendulum may be shifting in terms of what the Street can hope to regain should such risky deals go bad. While there's nothing in the Detroit ruling that prevents finance from trying to peddle such risky deals to city governments, it is, in Turbeville's words, "a shot across the bow to show banks that you can't do crazy deals with desperate municipalities and think you'll get away with it."[41] The Detroit resolution shows that with enough determination, makers can fight takers, and win. It also underscores how important it is that cities understand what they are getting into when they deal with Wall Street, and that regulators at a federal level do a better job of enforcing fraud rules. (Paging the SEC and the Fed!)

SAVING RETIREMENT

Clearly, both the public and the private retirement systems need fixing. The good news is that we are now at a major inflection point in that struggle, and for a number of reasons. First, the multiyear bull market that has buoyed stock and bond returns is very likely ending.

Most of the smartest investors I consulted believe that earning even a 4–5 percent annual return is going to be tricky going forward—let alone the 7–9 percent that many Americans have based their retirement calculations on. That is bad news for investors but it provides some concrete impetus to fix the system, now.

Second, public finances at the federal, state, and local levels are under strain. Amazingly, there is more debt in the world today than there was before the 2008 financial crisis—the difference is that now governments have even more debt than the financial sector.[42] That means governments will not easily be able to take up the slack from the markets and provide a retirement safety net for citizens. Indeed, governments not just in the United States but everywhere will increasingly be looking to cut social programs and benefits rather than augment them (just look at what's happening in Europe today). This adds further fuel to the fire of the pension crisis.

Finally, retail and institutional investors are beginning to understand how badly they've been fleeced by the asset management business. The year 2014 was a particularly dismal one for active fund managers—more of them failed to beat the market benchmarks than at any time in the past thirty years. Perhaps out of obliviousness to rising populist anger, or maybe out of an urge to grab the last gains from a gravy train that will surely leave soon, asset managers have been paying themselves more, even as they offer investors less. Their average compensation has doubled over the last decade and could eventually surpass that of investment bankers themselves by some estimates. That raises important questions about whether asset managers can truly be a force for good on issues like corporate pay and governance when it's so clear that they can't even properly govern themselves.[43] The fact that the industry's pay has tracked the amount of assets under management rather than the performance of those assets also makes this particular part of finance look more and more like the healthcare industry—an overgrown monopoly in which prices have become completely disconnected from results, or demand. As a result, consumers are finally beginning to vote with their feet. In 2014 investors took $92 billion out of actively managed funds and put $156 billion into rival, passive index funds.[44] Vanguard in particular has benefited, as its assets under management rose above $3 trillion for the first time in its history.

Given the growing public awareness of the issue, now would be an ideal moment for major root-and-branch reform of the retirement system. How to do this? We should start by committing to maintaining Social Security in its present form, given that it's the only part of the system that's unfailingly effective at keeping most elderly people secure. To protect the solvency of the system, we could increase the maximum income level subject to the payroll tax, change the formula for benefit levels while limiting payouts to wealthy people who don't need them, and raise the retirement age for some Americans. (This last issue needs to be examined carefully to avoid creating hardships for people like manual laborers and others who do physical work that can't be sustained over a certain age.) Public pension plans, for their part, will need to come clean about over-optimistic return projections—they should start basing their forecasts on 5 percent a year, not 8 percent, and be obligated to tell both pensioners and the public whether they can meet them. Getting out in front of shortfalls early will help cities avoid the fate of Detroit.

As for Americans who currently save via 401(k)s or IRAs, there is a much more straightforward solution. They should simply move their savings into programs that are dominated by low- or no-fee index funds (and be auto-enrolled in such programs unless they choose otherwise). For their part, the purveyors of these funds should ensure that fee loads and returns are clearly stated and easily accessible so individuals don't have to hunt for and guess about them. Regulators should also strictly limit early withdrawals or loans against such private savings, which should do what the 401(k) was intended to do in the first place—protect us in our golden years. There's already a model that provides many of these things and could be easily copied: the Thrift Savings Plan used by federal workers, which is large, cheap, and effective. If Congress has a problem replicating its own successful savings model for the broader public, then voters should ask who, exactly, their elected officials are serving—Wall Street or Main Street?

At the state level, the shift has already begun. The California Secure Choice (CSC) Retirement Savings plan, for example, aims to guarantee every Californian working in the private sector a living wage in retirement. CSC was signed into law in 2012 by Governor Jerry Brown. It combines the best of old-style defined-benefit plans (traditional pensions that guarantee workers a certain level of yearly income in retirement) with the flexibility and mobility of a 401(k). This plan will cover workers in California who don't currently have access to formal retirement savings via their work, which is a particularly big number, since California has more immigrants, freelancers, and young people working without benefits than many other states. "I'm a big fan," says the Economic Policy Institute's Monique Morrissey. "It's probably the farthest along of all the retirement reform ideas in terms of practical implementation."

It's likely that CSC will use behavioral nudges to get as many eligible people as possible to participate, for instance by making enrollment automatic unless a worker opts out, rather than requiring a sign-up to opt in.[45] Participants in CSC would sock away at least 3 percent of their income, most likely in a conservative index fund like an S&P 500 fund, where the pooled money is invested in all 500 stocks in that index. Index funds are considered a simple way to ensure that investors see the same return as the overall stock market—and they're cheaper, too, since index funds don't employ stock-picking wizards and charge the related fees.

Advocates say that the government role will be to help recruit more people to save, and that costs of such plans will be kept low through efficiencies of scale derived from all those participants, much as happens at some big public employee plans. But the reforms are being challenged by everyone from small-government conservatives, alarmed by a growing public role, to financial services companies, which fear that government-run plans will put money into simple index funds rather than the managed kinds that generate more lucrative fees for the industry. Unfortunately, the asset management industry lobby is just as aggressive, if not more so, than the Too Big to Fail banking lobby. In just one example of their bullying tactics, Ian Ayres, the Yale academic who coauthored the study on poor returns of actively managed plans I mentioned earlier in the chapter, was bombarded with protests from asset management firms after the study came out. So were his bosses and high-level administrators at the university. The industry has waged a campaign of intimidation against other academics, politicians, and policy makers who speak out on such issues.

Ironically, though, the size of the asset management industry is part of not just the problem but also potentially the *solution* to both the retirement crisis and the overgrowth of finance in America. Asset management firms are the fastest-growing players in the securities industry.[46] The sector, made up of behemoths like Fidelity, BlackRock, and Vanguard as well as numerous other smaller institutions, holds 65 percent of all the stocks in the country. If the people who run these firms can be convinced to focus on long-term growth over short-term gain, we could see a huge benevolent ripple effect throughout our entire economy: finance itself as an industry would shrink, but more of the wealth of corporate America would flow back to investors, and our economy would grow more strongly. "Money management, by definition, extracts value from the returns earned by our business enterprises," says Bogle.[47] Indeed, most mutual fund managers are essentially takers, not makers. But if more of them use their power to buy and hold shares of firms that practice good corporate governance and follow business strategies that support the real economy, then finance could potentially become not an impediment to growth but in fact a true supporter of it.

It's a bold goal, but one that authentic wealth makers like Bogle believe is attainable. Indeed, he believes it's something that the father of modern capitalism, Adam Smith, would have favored. Bogle recalls a conversation he had a few years back with several other big fund managers who'd gotten together to talk about how the industry might encourage better corporate governance within firms.

Bogle felt that asset managers like Vanguard had the potential to play a critical role in fighting off activist investors (like the sort covered in chapter 4) and the high-frequency traders of the world. After all, large asset managers could use the power of their massive stock holdings to support corporate executives who were thinking for the long haul. It made good business sense; retirement money management should be a long-term proposition by definition. Still, this was a sensitive topic—since asset managers are hired to manage the retirement money of the very firms whose corporate governance they might be trying to direct—and Bogle's suggestion got a rather mixed reaction. "I remember one of the guys from some big firm said, 'We all know what you're trying to do, Jack. Why don't you just leave it to the markets? Leave it to Adam Smith's Invisible Hand!' And I said, 'Don't you realize that we *are* Adam Smith's Invisible Hand?'"[48]

It's a profound statement. Finance is in control, yes. But that means that it has the potential to be a force for economic and social good, rather than exploitation. Yet in this case, harnessing that force would require that the asset management industry turn its back on a business model that has been yielding unbelievably easy money for decades.

Of course, asset management is doing everything it can to fight plans that threaten its fat margins. The California Secure Choice program, for example, has gotten heavy resistance from the Securities Industry and Financial Markets Association (SIFMA), a trade group for securities firms and asset managers. In a letter to the California treasurer in 2013 arguing against the CSC plan, SIFMA contended that the program would "directly compete for business with a wide range of California financial services firms" and that state money should be put not into creating universal retirement plans but rather into educating individuals "about the benefits of early and regular saving for retirement." The need for more financial education for consumers has become a clarion call from finance. But it rarely amounts to more than a barrage of marketing information from financial firms, most of which are simply selling the same old products. What's more, the people who need "educating" about finance the most are rarely those whom the industry wants to serve. It is perhaps no surprise that in Paula Dromi's ethnically mixed Los Angeles neighborhood, there isn't a Fidelity office to be found. Most asset managers don't really get interested in serving communities until they are filled with people who have tens of thousands of dollars to invest.

All of this draws out perhaps the most important lesson of the retirement crisis, which is that the financiers in charge of managing our life's savings need to rethink their industry's purpose. David Swensen, the chief investment officer at Yale University, who's run its endowment since 1985 with stellar results, put it succinctly: "The fundamental market failure in the mutual fund industry involves the interaction between sophisticated, profit-seeking providers of financial services and naïve, return-seeking consumers of investment products. The drive for profits by Wall Street and the mutual fund industry overwhelms the concept of fiduciary responsibility, leading to an all too predictable outcome: . . . the powerful financial services industry exploits vulnerable individual investors."[49] Information asymmetry will always work in favor of Wall Street. But asset managers could be forced to take a fiduciary pledge, a kind of Socratic oath for bankers, just like the one medical professionals must take, which would bind them to serving their customers rather than primarily themselves. Those found to be in violation of such an oath could be subject to strict penalties and big fines.

It's something that industry leaders like Bogle have proposed, and that many financiers and corporate leaders (including Warren Buffett and Swensen) have supported. Dodd-Frank already requires that nearly every other group of financial professionals—investment advisers, brokers, and securities dealers—take an oath of this kind (though President Trump has attempted to delay its implementation). Asset managers, the group that interacts more closely than any other with Main Street, is a strange exception to that list. The Department of Labor could help implement a fiduciary oath for these professionals, since it has regulatory power over company retirement plans; indeed, the department has already proposed that money managers responsible for IRAs be added to the list. But the department has been under pressure from the SEC not to institute its own proposals around fiduciary duty until the SEC hears advice from the "retail investment community"—meaning the mutual fund industry itself. This request is part of a long list of questionable judgment calls from the SEC, which has yet to implement even such simple rules as the CEO-to-worker pay ratio from Dodd-Frank. (That rule would require companies to clearly list what the CEO makes in relation to average workers. At this book's writing, this ratio stood at 300-to-1 for top American firms, compared to 20-to-1 in 1965.)[50] The SEC's dithering raises interesting questions about the "cognitive capture" by the financial lobby, a topic to which we'll return in chapter 10. But what you can be sure about is this: As with the crafting of Dodd-Frank itself, once the industry gets involved in rule writing, the process will lengthen and the rules themselves may well end up looking like Swiss cheese.

That would be a huge pity, because asset management has a tremendous opportunity both to redeem itself in the eyes of investors and to help police the market system in a way that neither regulators nor the public can. If every asset manager in the country were forced to use his or her corporate proxy vote (the vote that gives them a say on issues like executive pay, corporate boards, and even some big company decisions) to help enforce better corporate governance, they could help businesses push back against the short-term pressure from Wall Street for quick returns and easy profits that undermine longer-term growth. (Such actions would work only if the entire system were focused on passively managed funds, so that fund managers themselves didn't have incentives to push the quarter over the longer haul.)

To be sure, some fund managers have complained that such forays into corporate governance would be too costly. Yet one large asset manager, TIAA-CREF, has already taken on the challenge. A few years back it started allocating more than $1 million a year to its corporate governance program—an expenditure that amounted to only about three-tenths of a percent of its total invested assets,[51] which would seem to be well worth the cost. Of course, it helped that TIAA-CREF managed not corporate plans, but rather defined-contribution plans for nonprofits in education, medical, and research fields, and so it had no big-name corporate clients to offend. Still, as more and more consumers begin to understand how much of their nest egg is going to finance, it's hard to imagine that the industry itself won't begin to change—and even shrink. Bogle, for one, thinks the crisis in retirement may bring the financial sector down from its present highs to a more manageable 5–6 percent of the economy. Maybe then we'll be more able to have the kind of market system Adam Smith had hoped for, one in which "the interest of the consumer [must be] the ultimate end and object of all industry and commerce."[52]

CHAPTER 9

THE ARTFUL DODGERS

*How Our Tax Code Rewards the
Takers Instead of the Makers*

AS WE LEARNED earlier, Apple, the world's richest company, has employed truly mind-boggling financial maneuvers to stash nearly all of its $200 billion in cash in overseas bank accounts—all in order to avoid tax collectors in the United States. Remarkably, the firm did so while issuing debt on American markets to fund the stock buy-backs and dividend payments that would line the pockets of some of the world's wealthiest people. But that scenario is by no means the weirdest corporate tax contortion out there. In fact, recent years have seen a proliferation of a truly amazing kind of fiscal gymnastics known as tax inversions, which are essentially complicated schemes by which American companies avoid paying their fair share in taxes by buying foreign firms in cheaper overseas tax jurisdictions.

The most famous recent attempts at a tax backflip of this sort have been undertaken by the American pharmaceutical behemoth Pfizer, a troubled firm that had for years seen its revenue slip as it struggled to discover big new drugs. First, in an attempt to generate both quick revenue and tax breaks, it made an unsuccessful bid for the British drug giant AstraZeneca in 2014. Pfizer landed in a big PR mess after that proposed deal; President Obama even declared firms that pursued tax inversions to be corporate "deserters." Yet just a year and a half later, Pfizer went on to make a successful bid for the Dublin-based firm Allergan (itself a US-founded company that had relocated to Ireland to cut its taxes). If the deal goes through, it will save Pfizer $21 billion in taxes—news that has led politicians like Hillary Clinton to ramp up calls for regulatory reform that would put an end to such practices. It was imperative, Clinton said, to prevent companies like Pfizer, which have for decades benefited hugely from government-funded scientific research, from shirking their "fair share" of taxes.[1]

Pfizer's CEO certainly showed no compunction about the deal, which is not surprising given the culture and history of the company. During my reporting for this book, one consultant who worked with the firm joked to me that Pfizer was really a "financial strategy in the form of a company," since it made most of its revenues acquiring other firms that actually knew how to create drugs, rather than investing in its own drug discovery. Another consultant said that Pfizer would be better off taking all the money it spent on R&D and burning it to heat its buildings in winter, given the general level of payoff from the firm's own research efforts.

But the inversion deals were about more than just saving money in R&D expenses. By Pfizer's own admission, the bids were made in part to hoard the cash that would otherwise end up in the US government's coffers. By creating a merged company that could be domiciled abroad, Pfizer could keep the company's non-US profits from being subject to US tax. Pfizer, of course, offered the sort of explanation that one could expect only of a financialized company, saying that such strategies were "in the best interests of the combined company's shareholders."[2]

Of course, to save some face, the company also cited the economies of scale that would be delivered by combining development sites and centralizing R&D, as it had done with a number of previously acquired firms. And in an effort to tamp down the public and political outrage, Pfizer chairman and CEO Ian Read delivered some boilerplate lines. "Through this combination, Pfizer will have greater financial flexibility that will facilitate our continued discovery and development of new innovative medicines for patients," he said, adding that the merger will also "direct return of capital to shareholders, and continued investment in the United States, while also enabling our pursuit of business development opportunities on a more competitive footing within our industry."

Few, even on Wall Street, believed him. The argument simply held little water historically. The company's past attempts at such mergers had forced tens of thousands of people from their jobs, and the big innovations never materialized, which was a key reason that the stock price of Pfizer declined from $46 to $32 between 2000 and 2015, even as the Dow itself rose 55 percent. In the case of the aborted AstraZeneca merger, Pfizer said that its own drugs would be complementary to those being developed by the target firm, an argument that found little traction even with many on the Street. "Does anyone believe pharmaceutical companies can create long-term shareholder value by chasing lower tax venues and cutting research and development spending?" asked Harvard Business School professor Bill George at the time of the AstraZeneca bid, in a *New York Times* opinion piece. A similar question can be asked, of course, about Allergan, and in both cases, the answer is clearly no.

Pfizer's inversion deal, which is bizarrely set up in a way that makes it appear as if Allergan, not Pfizer, is doing the purchasing (in order to avoid any US legal barriers), had terrible political timing. The bid came on the back of a wave of similar tax inversions. At least fifty American corporations have done such deals in recent years, with twenty occurring from 2012 to 2014. The deals have been a boon for banks—Goldman Sachs, J.P. Morgan, Morgan Stanley, and Citigroup have made nearly $1 billion in fees over that time advising firms on executing the maneuvers. But not surprisingly, these gains came at the direct expense of Main Street Americans; according to Congress's Joint Committee on Taxation, tax inversions will keep $19.46 billion out of government coffers in the next decade.[3] The situation has also launched a transatlantic political backlash and raised important questions about what exactly constitutes "innovation" in such firms. Bill George put the salient question succinctly: "Is the role of leading large pharmaceutical companies to discover lifesaving drugs, or to make money for shareholders through financial engineering?"[4]

Sadly, we know the answer, at least when it comes to Pfizer. Although Obama has proposed rules that could make it tougher for companies to relocate abroad specifically for tax reasons, politicians haven't made a dent in the usual offshore financial wizardry practiced by many of the country's largest firms. These tactics are particularly common in sectors like finance, technology, and pharmaceuticals—that is, intellectual-property-driven industries in which the virtual nature of assets (ideas, formulas, patents, algorithms, and the like) makes it especially easy to shift profits to the cheapest possible tax jurisdiction, regardless of where they really came from.

Ever hear of a double Irish? How about a Dutch sandwich? These aren't cocktails or bar snacks but rather complex financial strategies used by many American companies to transfer profits they earn abroad to countries with the lowest tax rates. Despite the goofy nicknames, these techniques have a serious and nefarious purpose: to keep money away from the United States whenever possible so as to avoid paying the higher corporate tax rates in effect at home. Ireland, for instance, taxes corporate earnings at 12.5 percent, compared with the US rate of 35 percent. Similar story with the Netherlands, which has a corporate tax rate of under 25 percent.

With this kind of money at stake it's no shock that big companies have gotten very good at this game of international tax arbitrage. By some estimates, US corporations have $2.1 trillion in foreign earnings stashed under mattresses abroad.[5] Their argument, of course, is that they have to hoard money overseas because tax rates in the United States are simply too high—the statutory US rate is around 39 percent, compared to the OECD average of 29.7 percent.[6] Yet thanks to legions of smart lawyers, the average Fortune 500 company pays a 19.4 percent rate, and many pay less than 10 percent because of all the generous loopholes that Congress has afforded them over the years (more on how that happens in the next chapter). Indeed, this is one of the reasons why US firms are enjoying record profit margins while paying a lower share of the overall US tax burden than they have in decades.

BITING THE HAND THAT FEEDS THEM

The creative ways in which corporations have stashed their money in Ireland, the Netherlands, and the Cayman Islands have enraged the US public for good reason. By engaging in such financial wizardry, corporations are basically announcing that they want the benefits of US talent and markets but not the responsibilities. This strikes many as grossly unfair, particularly given that taxpayer-funded, early-stage investments in areas like the Internet, transportation, and healthcare research are the reason many of the largest US companies got so big and successful to begin with. That's a leg up—call it corporate welfare—that most firms conveniently forget when they start looking for places to hide their profits. As the academic Mariana Mazzucato argues in her excellent book *The Entrepreneurial State*, many of the most lauded corporate innovations, including the particular parts of our smartphones that make them smart (the Internet, GPS, touchscreen display, and voice recognition), came out of state-funded research. Ditto any number of pharmaceutical, biotech, and cybersecurity innovations. "In so many cases, public investments have become business giveaways, making individuals and their companies rich but providing little (direct or indirect) return to the economy or to the State," says Mazzucato.[7]

By this logic, Apple, Facebook, Google, Pfizer, and any other companies whose core innovations have been based on taxpayer-funded R&D should be giving a much larger slice of their profits back to all of us. And while making them do that will be a huge political challenge, it's a conversation that's already happening at the highest levels. President Obama, for example, has at various points met with CEOs of some of the country's biggest and most innovative Internet firms to talk about ways of sharing corporate wealth. According to a source who attended that meeting and spoke to me off the record, one of the radical ideas attendees bounced around envisioned companies writing checks to social media users, based on how much their data streams are monetized by these firms.[8]

But in terms of how to reward makers over takers, tax reform remains the largest and most immediate fight. The US code is ripe for an overhaul, in both the corporate and the consumer sphere. Tax inversions, Dutch sandwiches, and Cayman Islands wizardry that expatriate the gains of American corporations to enrich a tiny managerial caste suggest a whole new genre of selfish capitalism. As this book has attempted to illustrate, globalization and financialization, working hand in hand, allow firms to fly thirty-five thousand feet over the problems of both individual nations and people, who are all too familiar with the reality on the ground: an economy in which wages still aren't rising fast enough, good middle-class jobs remain hard to come by, and public deficits remain large, since the private sector won't spend on real-economy investments to fill the void.

Economics 101 tells us that when one sector saves, another must spend, but that's not how things work today. As a recent Harvard Business School alumni survey summed up the problem, we're stuck in an economy that's "doing only half its job."[9] Says Michael E. Porter, a coauthor of the study: "The United States is competitive to the extent that firms operating here do two things—win in global markets and lift the living standards of the average American." At the moment, we're still succeeding at the first but failing at the second. But "business leaders and policymakers need a strategy to get our country on a path toward broadly shared prosperity," Porter adds. And one of the biggest challenges in that respect will be creating a tax code that stops rewarding taking over making.[10]

PERVERSE INCENTIVES

The US tax code is nearly seventy-five thousand pages long. That fact right there tells you a lot about what's wrong with it, but its perversity can also be summed up in a very simple way: The American tax code rewards debt over equity, at both the corporate and consumer level, a structure that has contributed mightily to the rise of finance and the fall of American business. The US tax code has made it much more advantageous for both companies and consumers to borrow than to save. That has in turn added fuel to the fire of financialization, since banks and other financial institutions are basically in the business of issuing debt—the main way they make their money. It has also contributed to slower growth, as capital is misallocated and mispriced, flowing to all the wrong places for all the wrong reasons.[11]

Consider the way the tax code works today. Corporations can deduct interest payments on debt from their taxes, yet their dividends and retained profits can't be written off and are taxed at the full corporate load. Jason Furman, the head of the National Economic Council, has estimated that these and other similar tax breaks make corporate debt as much as 42 percent cheaper than corporate equity.[12] No wonder Apple finds it so advantageous to borrow money to hand out to investors, rather than repatriate the cash it has stashed abroad and pay taxes on it.

How do Apple and other US firms keep their cash abroad, and do it legally? That's where the crazy loopholes come in. A "double Irish," for example, involves a US corporation setting up an Irish company and reregistering this company again to a low-tax or non-tax country, like the Bahamas. Loopholes in US laws allow the first relocation to happen, and loopholes in Irish laws mean that the Irish company doesn't have to pay Irish taxes because it's "owned" by a non-Irish tax resident (head-spinning, I know). The Irish system can be further exploited if a US firm sets up a second overseas subsidiary in Ireland to manage non-US sales on patents.

American firms do a lot of this, redirecting to the most tax-advantageous country the intellectual property that may have been the work of many people in many countries. Basically, this strategy funnels the profits from the knowledge economy, where the innovation actually occurred, to a different economy that offers the cheapest cash haven. Firms can go further and add a "Dutch sandwich" onto this maneuver. Because there are European Union tax agreements in place that allow money to move freely between EU countries, American firms can set up Dutch subsidiaries and transfer more money from more countries into Irish subsidiaries. The whole thing creates a global race to the bottom, which underscores one of the key problems of tax avoidance: the so-called "tragedy of the commons" where, in the end, everyone loses. This is a key reason that the G8, the OECD, and other international bodies are making global tax reform a big priority. (Ireland in particular, under pressure from other countries like the United States, is now reconsidering some of its dicey exceptions.)[13]

There are plenty of crazy exemptions and rules that enrich the takers by encouraging debt in the consumer sphere, too. The American tax code makes debt cheap and as a result virtually guarantees the growth of the financial sector. Individuals can deduct all sorts of debt: the interest on student loans, home equity, and business-related credit card debt, among other kinds. Most notably, they can deduct their home mortgage interest payments, which represent a huge amount of money—around 14 percent of the entire value of the stock of American homes.[14] Yet these individuals receive proportionately little tax reward for saving. Is it any wonder, then, that the personal savings rate in the United States hovers around 5 percent, less than half of what it was in the 1970s, when both consumer debt and corporate debt really exploded?

As we've already discovered in Chapter 1, the late 1970s was a crucial turning point in the process of financialization; the growth of debt has tracked the growth of the financial sector itself over the last four decades. Banks, eager to find new revenue streams as regulatory changes and inflation threatened their existing business models from the 1970s onward, began selling customers debt products of all kinds. It was a rich business model, not only because it resulted in more and more lucrative interest payments on the part of a growing debtor class, but also because it increased fees from financial transactions, which by 2005 made up nearly half of all revenues for financial companies, up from around 20 percent in the

1980s.[15] Household debt as a share of disposable income has soared from 54 percent in 1970 to 96 percent today.[16] And corporate debt is at a record high.[17] It's quite telling that even after the financial crisis of 2008, there is actually more debt out there today in the world, not less. From 2007 through the second quarter of 2015, global debt and leverage have grown by a whopping $57 trillion, reaching unprecedented levels.[18] The world is more awash in debt now than ever before in history. And who benefits from all this? The financial industry, of course. Today four-fifths of all the stock of global financial assets is in debt or deposits.[19] That's due in large part to the fact that we have a tax code that rewards debt so disproportionately.

Unfortunately, all this has made our economy extremely prone to bubbles, crises, and stagnation. As we have learned throughout this book, the number of financial crises in the modern era has increased in lockstep with rising debt.[20] Indeed, the famous economist John Kenneth Galbraith believed that all financial crises stemmed from too much debt and credit, and there is a wealth of research to back up that notion.[21] One of the biggest myths put forward during the financial meltdown of 2008 was that we had to save banks to save the economy, but in fact, a growing body of academic research has found that just the opposite is true. In their seminal book *House of Debt*, economists Atif Mian of Princeton and Amir Sufi of the University of Chicago make a very strong case that what we need isn't more debt-fueled finance and credit to fix the economy, but much, much less of it.[22] Marshaling a large body of research and data stretching over one hundred years, they present a compelling case that the financial crisis started not with the failure of the banks, but with the collapse of consumer spending, which began well before the fall of Lehman Brothers—as early as two years before in some areas of the country. The fall in consumer spending was most pronounced and happened earliest in communities most heavily saddled with debt. (It was by no means limited to those areas, however. As the authors explain, when consumption in one city or region collapses, it has a knock-on effect of job losses and slower growth throughout the nation.)

Basically, *House of Debt* makes a very convincing argument that recessions occur when finance arrives on the scene and offers middle- and lower-income people more and more debt. That brews up asset bubbles, which eventually burst, hitting the biggest debt holders—which also tend to be the poorest people—hardest. Everyone hunkers down and stops spending, and unemployment grows. The perverse cycle continues, as out-of-work people with even less spending power are buried under mounds of debt (no federally subsidized bailouts for them). Indeed, *House of Debt* paints a fascinating picture of how similar the periods leading up to the Great Depression and the Great Recession were in this regard. From 1920 to 1929 there was "an explosion in both mortgage debt and installment debt for purchasing automobiles and furniture," a consumer spending spree based on easy credit that mirrors the doubling of consumer debt in America between 2000 and 2007 in the run-up to the housing crisis.[23]

Monetary policy of the sort we've had for the last several years—meaning superlow interest rates and big asset purchases by central bankers—can't do much to help, since the people benefiting from it are those who actually own *assets*, not debt. That of course means the wealthy; in 2010, the top 10 percent of the population by net worth owned 74 percent of the assets. These lucky few can only use the gain in their asset values to buy so many new cars or homes or pairs of jeans, and they don't create enough demand to keep the ship afloat at a national level.[24] So inequality gets a boost, which further constrains the economy.

That cycle creates an interesting point of tension for political liberals who over the last few years have supported the Fed's money dump, which many experts believe has already planted the seeds for the *next* debt-induced crisis. "In some ways, the fact that we've had such a long period of easy money is the very best reward for Wall Street," says Ruchir Sharma, head of macroeconomics and emerging markets for Morgan Stanley Investment Management. "I mean, if you give a bunch of financiers zero interest rates, and a lot of money, what are they going to do with it? They'll try to make more money [by taking on more debt]."[25] Certainly, Sharma and many other economists would agree with the *House of Debt* authors when they assert that "economic disasters are almost always preceded by a large increase in household debt. In fact, the correlation is so robust that it is as close to an empirical law as it gets in macroeconomics." To fix it, say Mian and Sufi, "we must fundamentally rethink the financial system." (I will expand on some of their excellent ideas and include a few of my own, as well as those of other experts, in the final chapter.)

One clear fix has to do with tax reform. If debt is so dangerous, why the heck do we have a tax code that encourages nothing but debt? Why does our government actively provide huge subsidies for the very thing that brings down our financial system and our economy again and again? Why does it reward takers over makers so thoroughly? There's no clear or complete answer. Certainly a large part of it is politics. Our entire financial system is based on debt, and, as we know, the financial lobby wields tremendous political power. Financiers have used that power over these many decades to push for a system that rewards the creation of debt, which is the core of their business model. But the truth is that like many large and complex systems (take healthcare, or the retirement system, which I covered in chapter 8), the American tax code's favoring of debt over equity isn't the result of some grand design, but rather "the unintended consequence of an extended series of discrete, reactive, short-term political decisions," in one economic historian's words.[26] Interest groups lobby for this or that loophole, and little by little, rules and regulations that might seem to make sense in a vacuum combine to create a system of perverse incentives that reward exactly the kind of behavior the economy doesn't need.

Consider the mortgage interest deduction, which was first put into effect in 1894, mostly as a way to help farmers keep their family homesteads and make a decent living. Today it has become a boon for the middle and upper classes. Anyone who buys a house (or two houses) can deduct the interest payments on the loan to buy the property as long as it doesn't exceed $1 million. *One million bucks!*

That's a lot of money. No one really *needs* that much house, but quite a few have it anyway. In my Brooklyn neighborhood, for example, $1 million down will get you a $3–4 million townhouse. But if wealthy people weren't able to reduce their house payments via the mortgage interest tax deduction, the homes wouldn't be going for those rates.

This is a crucial point: debt inflates asset prices. That's great for the wealthy, who own a lot of assets, and even better for their banks. But it's not so good for poorer, more highly leveraged people who don't have as much equity skin in the game and can be hit very hard when bubbles burst. (Consider that poorer people with higher debt loads lost about a quarter of their net worth in the housing crash, while the wealthy lost almost nothing on a net basis.)[27] When you stand back and think about it, it really is a crazy kind of cycle—thanks to asset inflation, $1 million will barely buy you a two-bedroom apartment in a good public school district in Brooklyn. If everyone were paying more cash down and not borrowing as much, property prices would be lower and we'd all sleep better at night. But as it is, it makes much more financial sense for the rich to borrow (which they can do more cheaply than most, given their assets and the size of their loans; in the bizarro world of finance you are rewarded for borrowing *more* rather than less) and write the interest off on their taxes—just as it makes more sense for Apple to stash cash abroad and borrow at supercheap interest rates to pay off rich shareholders. It's a system that subsidizes the wealthy. A full 90 percent of the value of the mortgage-interest tax subsidy goes to households making more than $75,000 a year.[28] But even more, it rewards the financial industry itself. Financial institutions are of course the main beneficiaries of massive interest payments on home mortgages, just as they are of Apple's big bond deals.

There are many other such perversions that are encouraged by our tax code. The rich can get second mortgage tax credits on their yachts, for example, provided they stay on them more than fourteen days a year (Congress tried unsuccessfully to close that loophole in 2014).[29] There are tax breaks for the use of personal travel and corporate jets for "security reasons."[30] Our tax dollars help underwrite federal flood insurance in some of the richest waterfront property areas in the country.[31] But the most appalling—and one of the most famous—of all these perverse tax provisions is that people who make money from making money are taxed at lower rates than those of us who actually work for it. Income that you earn by actually doing a job is taxed at a much higher rate than income you earn from your investments.

Warren Buffett famously took on this issue in 2011 in a *New York Times* piece, noting that while the taxes he paid the previous year amounted to 17.4 percent of his income—or $6,938,744 total—the tax burden on other people in his office averaged 36 percent.[32] (For his assistant Debbie Bosanek it was 35.8 percent.)[33] That's because Buffett makes money from things like "carried interest" on investments, capital gains from selling stocks, and so on. Like most billionaires and many millionaires, he declares very little "earned" income but a lot of asset wealth gains. As Buffett says, "these and other blessings are showered upon us [meaning, the rich] much as if we were spotted owls or some other endangered species. It's nice to have friends in high places."[34]

Most of us, however, make money from the pay we get working day jobs, which is taxed at a far higher rate (most middle-class people fall into a 15–25 percent income tax bracket and then pay high payroll taxes to boot). There's a good argument to be made that the wealth made from investments is actually earned income—it's just earned the way the wealthy earn it, via jobs that move money around—and so it should be taxed at the higher rate. Most rich people try to structure their compensation in a way that takes full advantage of this disparity. For example, hedge fund managers make most of their income not from management fees (which get taxed at the earned income rate) but from profits on investments; *New York Times* columnist Nicholas Kristof and others have argued that those profits are the result not of capital but of labor, and so should be taxed as ordinary income, a point with which I agree.[35]

But the idea that profits from capital should be favored over income from labor dies hard. The rationale for this unfair divide is rooted in the misguided premise that the very wealthy are the country's main economic value creators, the "makers" whose entrepreneurial zeal supposedly drives all the growth and supports the "takers." The latter are the 47 percent that the 2012 presidential candidate Mitt Romney famously referred to in a secret speech to campaign donors that was taped and went viral. (These people, he said "pay no income taxes." So the fact that they "are dependent upon government" for healthcare, housing, and food means they can't "take personal responsibility and care for their lives.") But the maker-versus-taker meme itself was the product of his running mate, Paul Ryan. Back in June 2010, Ryan went on *Washington Watch*, a cable show hosted by Representative Walter Jones, to announce that "right now about 60 percent of the American people get more benefits in dollar value from the federal government than they pay back in taxes. So we're going to a majority of takers versus makers."

The absurdity and utter wrongheadedness of Ryan's claim (which he later dialed back in a *Wall Street Journal* op-ed) inspired the title of this book, which I hope will redefine exactly who are the makers and who are the takers in our society. To be sure, many Americans don't pay federal income taxes. But a large portion of them are ultrawealthy—and so they, like Buffett, pay capital gains taxes instead—and most others are the elderly, students, military personnel, or people who are employed but simply don't earn enough to pay income tax.[36] Moreover, as this entire book has shown, it's the supposed "makers" who are doing most of the taking in society: paying the least taxes as a percentage of income, grabbing a disproportionate share of the economic pie, and advancing business models that often run counter to growth. Meanwhile, the supposed "takers" are getting less than ever.

One of the great myths of our capitalist system is that we need to keep taxes on investors low because otherwise they simply won't invest and the economy won't grow. As we've already seen, though, much of investors' money simply stays within the financial system itself, rather than going into new business or job creation. But beyond that, there's the simple fact that this logic has never held.

"You can go back over fifty years to the post–World War II period and look at the tax rates being paid then, which were much higher, and the economy was doing very well. And people at both ends of the socioeconomic spectrum were doing well. Back then, corporate taxes were 4 percent of GDP, and today they are 2 percent. So this idea that we are not competitive today because of our tax code just isn't right," says Buffett, who like many top investors believes that tax rates have little to do with animal spirits and the desire of capitalists to invest in the economy.[37] Indeed, nobody shied away from investing in the United States when the capital gains rate was nearly 40 percent in the late 1970s. And of course, high rates didn't hurt job creation, either—40 million new jobs were created between 1980 and 2000. But when rates came down after that, due in large part to the massive tax cuts in 2001 and 2003 under George W. Bush that benefited mainly the wealthy, both jobs and growth languished. The simple truth is that there isn't a shred of evidence to suggest that lowering taxes on the rich makes them any more or less likely to invest and start businesses. (Likewise, research shows that giving larger mortgage interest deductions to the wealthy doesn't increase the rate of home ownership, but merely inflates prices.)[38]

There is, however, plenty of data to show that tax loopholes that benefit the top tier also increase short-term, growth-punishing decision making by companies. One of the most damning pieces of evidence on this front is a study done by Harvard and New York University academics that found that private companies invest about twice as much in growth-enhancing areas like R&D, factory and technology upgrades, and worker education than comparable public companies do.[39] The reason? As we have already seen in chapters 4 and 5, public companies are pouring their money into stock buybacks and dividend payments that enrich mainly those who are already wealthy, and encourage executives to focus on quarterly returns rather than longer-term growth prospects, given that they are among the chief beneficiaries of those payouts, which are taxed at much lower rates than earned income.

One of the biggest global critics of this trend, British economist and trader Andrew Smithers, lays out a very persuasive data-driven case in his book *The Road to Recovery* that the decline in productivity of corporations is closely linked to a rise in stock option pay to top executives. In the early 1970s, for example, American companies invested fifteen times as much money as they gave back to shareholders; in recent years the ratio has plummeted to below two.[40] This in turn has resulted in slower growth for the economy as a whole, as corporate leaders sacrifice long-term investments for bigger paychecks. "The idea that what is in the interest of shareholders is also in the interest of the economy is totally wrong," says Smithers. "Bonuses paid in stock are simply bad for corporations, and for growth."[41]

Indeed, a 2015 report from the Office of Financial Research, a US government body that monitors financial stability, proves this. The report dug into why the value of US stocks has tripled over the last few years, even as economic recovery and wage growth have remained weak. It found that while the gains in the market have been driven by rising corporate earnings, that fact obscured a more troubling truth beneath—namely, that while earnings are rising, sales growth for most public US companies is not. Corporate stock prices are booming not because of fundamental economic improvements, but because of a toxic combination of flat salaries, lowered investment in the real economy, and stock buybacks. Corporate debt (not including debt held by banks) has risen from $5.7 trillion in 2006 to $7.4 trillion today. Much of that money has been used for buybacks, dividend increases, and mergers and acquisitions. The OFR believes that "although this financial engineering has contributed to higher stock prices in the short run, it detracts from opportunities to invest capital to support longer-term organic growth."[42] As we've already learned, debt is always linked to financial insecurity—which is why many economists now think that corporate debt will be ground zero for the next financial crisis.

Unfortunately, there's little incentive for companies to do anything differently, because the debt-fueled increase in buybacks and stock options payments is so good from a tax-avoidance perspective. While many of the tax cuts that favor the wealthy can be traced to Republican administrations, the legislative changes that fueled the current buyback craze actually happened under Democratic president Bill Clinton, whose economic team was at various points led by finance-friendly people like Robert Rubin and Lawrence Summers. The Clinton team not only cut the capital gains tax rate (which was later cut again under George W. Bush) but, more crucially, passed a 1993 provision on corporate pay, as noted in chapter 4. The measure limited corporate tax deductions for regular salaried income to $1 million but *exempted* "performance-related" pay above and beyond that—pay that was typically awarded in stock options. (Joseph Stiglitz, a former head of Clinton's Council of Economic Advisers, remembers this move as "one of the worst things that the Clinton administration did").[43] At the time, rising CEO salaries sparked numerous public outcries, which prompted the $1 million limit. Yet thanks to support from policy makers like Rubin (who'd soon benefit from the exemption by leaving Treasury to work for Citigroup and earning $126 million in cash and stock over nine years), the performance pay loophole was passed. It certainly negated any good that would have come from the base salary limit on tax deductions and created a tremendous incentive for companies to pay more compensation in options—which fed the cycle of short-termism in our economy, since executives would from then on be focused primarily on boosting stock prices, by any means necessary.

Stiglitz lobbied against the loophole in meetings with Rubin (who declined to be interviewed for this book) and other Clinton officials, but to no avail. "It just opened up this huge span of bonus pay which was not for performance. I had written a lot about this before, that it was largely phony," Stiglitz says. "I argued very strongly during the 1990s that the whole stock option pay trend caused a lot of incentives for nontransparency, and that it was directly responsible for what I call creative accounting. The financial sector used this creative accounting not just to deceive the market but also to avoid paying the taxes that they should have paid." This view is backed by economists like Thomas Piketty and Emmanuel Saez, who've tallied the massive increase in pretax personal income claimed by the top 1 percent since then.[44] That increase, their research shows, is linked to growing inequality (which requires greater government payouts to the poor) and slower economic growth, thanks to flat salaries for the majority of Americans. What's more, says Stiglitz, the performance exception didn't really reward performance as much as any number of other factors, such as monetary policy that boosted stock prices. "If you're really talking about performance, you should not get higher pay when your stock price goes up because the interest rate goes down," he explains. "I mean, maybe Janet Yellen should get higher pay for that, but CEOs certainly shouldn't."[45] He wrote in his searing memoir of the time, *The Roaring Nineties*, that "as the Clinton years came to a close, I wondered: What message had we in the end sent through the changes that had been brought about in our taxes? What were we saying to the country, to our young people, when we lowered capital gains taxes and raised taxes on those who earned their living by working?"[46]

It's a question that has just as much resonance today as it did then. Fixing these perverse incentives will require more than just limiting the number of buybacks that companies can do. It will require soup-to-nuts tax reform to create a tax system that rewards makers rather than takers. "You need a revolution," says Andrew Smithers, "a real change in the paradigm. And it has to happen at the political level. Or you are going to see a slow adjustment in which private firms, rather than public ones, become the growth engines of the economy."[47] That would of course have massive ramifications for all of us who are invested in the public equity markets and depend on them for our wealth and retirement savings.

CLOSING THE LOOPHOLES

So how to bring about such a revolution? Ideally, legislators would craft proposals for a system that would reward savings, rather than debt, and encourage long-term investment over speculation. There are many ways in which this could be done. A 2011 report by the IMF, for example, suggested that companies might be allowed deductions for equity returns, as well as for debt, crafting a system that balances the two more evenly, of the kind that already exists in many parts of Europe.[48] Certainly top marginal rates for the rich should rise, out of basic fairness, and the performance pay loopholes and other exemptions that distort the pay of top earners should be closed. Capital gains tax deductions should be calculated on a sliding scale, so that people who hold a stock for, say, a year don't benefit as much as those who hold it for many decades. And, as much as people like me benefit from it, it's only fair that the mortgage interest tax deduction should be reformed (meaning, lowered or even abolished in some cases). This step would probably hurt consumption in the short term, since homeowners wouldn't feel as rich, but in the longer term it would very likely help deflate housing asset bubbles and financially empower Millennials and older people who have trouble paying for housing in today's market.

We might also consider enacting a financial transaction tax, which would reflect the fact that the current system rewards the financial industry most of all, and that each debt-driven transaction that is made in the economy today generates profit that tends to stay in the hands of people who are the least likely to use it for economically productive purposes. And we should of course continue to draw attention to corporate "deserters" like Pfizer that eschew responsibility to the nation that made them rich.

The pressure for these changes has been building for some time. Witness Apple CEO Tim Cook's 2013 testimony on Capitol Hill, where senators praised their favorite iGadgets while also accusing the world's most valuable company of being one of its biggest tax avoiders, laying out how Apple jumped through loopholes to save some $44 billion of otherwise taxable income. As Senator Carl Levin, then chair of the Investigations Subcommittee, put it, Apple "sought the holy grail" of tax avoidance by funneling vast earnings to overseas subsidiaries. (Cook responded that Apple paid $6 billion in US corporate taxes the previous year.) Bottom line: when you have a lot of cash and can move much of it abroad easily, as the biggest tech companies do, everyone will start watching you more closely. As Steve Jobs once said, "It's better to be a pirate than to join the navy." But when you are the world's most valuable company, it's harder to play the rebel. The truth is that Big Tech is as corporate as it comes, and since Big Tech is also where most of the new growth and income creation in the United States lies right now, there's little doubt that it will draw more and more attention from regulators, tax collectors, and social activists.

The investigation into Apple's finances was clearly a warning shot to other US multinationals. Thankfully, tax reform is not only a huge issue in the 2016 US presidential election, but also a growing policy drumbeat in all developed countries. The silver lining of large government debts and shrinking public budgets is that all rich nations will be looking more closely at corporate tax avoidance. A few years back, British prime minister David Cameron remarked at the World Economic Forum at Davos that multinational tax avoiders should "wake up and smell the coffee." It was a pointed reference to Starbucks, which had recently volunteered to pay more tax in the United Kingdom in response to public outrage and threats of a boycott. In 2012, the company ran into PR trouble in Britain from revelations that it had paid only minimal corporate taxes on many hundreds of millions of dollars in sales. The company had been domiciling in the Netherlands (legally, of course) to avoid them. Starbucks has since voluntarily paid more, and it has moved its European headquarters to the United Kingdom, proof that it is quite possible for corporations to both be wildly profitable and pay their fare share of taxes.[49]

Limiting corporate tax avoidance is, of course, just the beginning of what's needed to fix the tax code and ensure that it rewards makers over takers. The moment for the United States to move away from a debt-driven tax code is now; as interest rates go up, the cost of debt does, too. As that happens, economic fragility will grow. With global debt at record highs, and the public sector in particular carrying an unprecedented debt load, it's unlikely that we'll see the kind of bailouts we saw in 2008 the next time around. In an economically bifurcated world, where companies are flush but workers are not, and where the historical relationship between corporate profits and local economic growth is broken, big companies will be under a lot more pressure to do more for the countries in which they operate. Fixing our tax code is a good way to start, and it may be the best way to avoid another Great Recession, or something much worse.

CHAPTER 10

THE REVOLVING DOOR

How Washington Favors Wall Street over Main Street

WHEN TALLYING the influence that Wall Street has in Washington, it's hard to know where to start; it's a bit like shooting fish in a barrel. But the last-minute rider that was pushed into the federal spending bill in 2014, a loophole that rolled back an important chunk of Dodd-Frank financial reform, is as good a place as any to begin. The bit of legislation in question took up just 85 lines of the 1,600-page spending bill. The problem was that about 70 of those lines seemed to be written by Citigroup lobbyists, who, like the rest of the financial industry, were eager to overturn legislation that would have forced the bank to move its riskiest and most profitable activities—things like default swaps, commodities, and derivatives—to new entities outside the parent firm that *wouldn't* be guaranteed by taxpayer money.

This rule was one of the key provisions in Dodd-Frank, something that would have gone a long way toward ending the Too Big to Fail problem, or at least the part of it involving the socialization of risk and the privatization of profits. That's exactly why the financial lobby had spent millions of dollars trying to make sure that they could sneak an amendment into the spending bill that would revoke the provision. Reform advocates like Massachusetts senator Elizabeth Warren fought these tactics vigorously with barn-burning speeches on the Senate floor. Some Democrats, like House minority leader Nancy Pelosi, even pledged to vote against the federal spending bill itself—never mind that it was backed by their own president—if it meant that the last six years of financial reform efforts would be watered down. "What I am saying is: the taxpayer should not assume the risk," said Pelosi at the time, citing the fact that the provision would take America back to the same old formula in which when banks succeed, profits go in their pockets, and when they fail, "the taxpayer pays the bill. It's just not right."[1]

And yet the provision was so important to the financial industry that Jamie Dimon, the head of JPMorgan Chase, personally called various lawmakers to encourage them to keep it in and vote the bill through, cleverly flipping the debate to focus on the fact that if Congress didn't pass the spending bill, the United States could be in for another government shutdown, creating the sort of gridlock that had shaved points off economic growth and undermined trust in democracy itself back in October 2013.

In the end, Dimon and the banks won. It was masterful PR jujitsu. Dimon had managed to convince lawmakers that they, not the financial industry, risked undermining trust in the entire system of democratic capitalism if they didn't do as he urged. Not like that argument was tough to make, given public disenchantment with Washington, after years of ugly partisan politics and gross mishandling of the post-crisis cleanup of the financial system, as well as the government's role in decades of deregulation, easy money monetary policy, and poorly enforced financial standards leading up to the meltdown. Still, Dimon's feat certainly reflected who was still in charge of Beltway money politics—the financial industry itself. "I thought that, when Dodd-Frank started, the banks would not succeed in influencing it," said Stanley Fischer, the vice chairman of the Fed, the day after the bill cleared the House of Representatives. "Boy, was I wrong."[2]

That's a fairly stunning statement coming from an experienced central banker like Fischer. But it reflects a key truth of the postcrisis era, which is that from the minute lawmakers in Washington started trying to reform the financial industry, Wall Street has been waging a land, sea, and air campaign against regulation. Its concerted resistance is the reason that, nearly eight years after the fall of Lehman Brothers, only a handful of the deep financial reforms that we were promised following the 2008 crisis have been implemented. It's a story that reflects the unprecedented power of finance not only in Washington, but also in our country as a whole.

There has literally been no theater of our economy or society left untouched over the last several years by the financial industry's efforts to avoid being put in check in the wake of the subprime disaster and the Great Recession. Financial institutions have fought the regulators on Washington, D.C.'s lobbying mecca, K Street; on Wall Street; and on Main Street, never giving up. They have thrown some $1.4 billion[3] into the effort to fight myriad efforts around reform in nearly every part of the industry during the 2013–14 election cycle alone, according to Americans for Financial Reform (the key consumer advocacy group, which, by contrast, had a $1 million yearly budget).[4] And it's a fight that has been extremely strategic and targeted. Consider that on the Citi-influenced spending bill alone, a post-vote analysis showed that the PACs of financial institutions such as Bank of America, Citigroup, Goldman Sachs, and J.P. Morgan, which control more than 90 percent of the swaps market, gave on average 2.6 times more money to members of Congress who voted "yes" than to those who voted "no."[5] Indeed, these four institutions spent a combined $30.7 million lobbying Congress in the run-up to the bill's passing.[6] Key lawmakers like Representative Sean Patrick Maloney, a New York Democrat who cosponsored the bill, got Wall Street–backed fundraisers (in Maloney's case, at $200 to $2,500 a seat) in advance of its passing.

But that was just the tip of the iceberg. In 2014 finance outspent even the mighty healthcare industry in terms of lobbying (spending $498 million total, $10 million more than Big Health).[7] In the 2013–14 election cycle, finance shelled out more than twice as much as any other single industry on contributions to federal candidates for office.[8] In some ways, the tidal wave of money reflects just how much public support there has been *for* financial reform. In a survey conducted in late 2014 by the University of Chicago's Booth School of Business and Northwestern University's Kellogg School of Management, about 1,000 American households were asked whether they thought the US financial system was benefiting, or hurting, the US economy. Only 36 percent thought finance was an economic benefit, while 50 percent saw it as actively hindering Main Street.[9] As Luigi Zingales, a professor at the University of Chicago's Booth School of Business, points out, "without public support, financiers need . . . political protection to operate."[10]

The result is a perfect storm whereby as the takers ramp up their lobbying, a perception (or reality) of oligopoly develops, which increases public distrust and political backlash, which results in even more lobbying, and so and so on . . . until we brew up exactly the kind of dysfunctional, clubby relationship between Wall Street and Washington that we currently have (not to mention populist rage about it on both sides of the aisle). Outrage against our unfair financial system, the vested interests behind it, and the egregious amount of wealth it extracts from all of us is where the Tea Party and Occupy Wall Street movements intersect. And unless we understand and fix the political environment that enables all this, we'll eventually end up looking a lot more like a crony capitalist emerging market (think China, Russia, Brazil, Nigeria), with all the economic and social instability that entails, than a liberal democracy. In this sense, the stakes of reforming our financial system could not be higher.

THE POWER OF THE FINANCIAL LOBBY

Lobbying budgets reflect only a small part of finance's influence over government—the one that we can actually see in public filings. But the industry's influence goes much deeper and broader than that. Professional lobbyists are people who officially spend more than 20 percent of their time trying to get lawmakers to see things from their point of view. But as the examples above indicate, formal lobbying is only one facet of Wall Street power in Washington. Jamie Dimon isn't a lobbyist. Nor is Goldman Sachs chief Lloyd Blankfein, nor are any of the other top financiers who regularly consort with the people who regulate them. Yet these and other top bankers, along with their trade groups and lawyers, were among those who were constantly taking meetings with the federal agencies and regulators that were crafting the Dodd-Frank reform rules. As just one example of many, in the year after Dodd-Frank's passing, Goldman Sachs (the most active among financial institutions) paid eighty-three visits to regulators to discuss topics like derivatives reform.[11]

In 2013, Duke University academic Kimberly Krawiec published a startling research paper analyzing more than eight thousand public comment letters received by the Financial Stability Oversight Council as it prepared to study the ways of implementing the Volcker Rule, a particularly contentious piece of the Dodd-Frank reform that aimed to reinstate some of the spirit of the Glass-Steagall legislation by separating risky proprietary trading from federally insured commercial banking. Krawiec analyzed the meeting logs of the Treasury Department, Federal Reserve, Commodity Futures Trading Commission, Securities and Exchange Commission, and Federal Deposit Insurance Corporation. The bottom line? "Financial institutions, financial industry trade groups, and law firms representing such institutions and trade groups collectively accounted for roughly 93% of all federal agency contacts on the Volcker Rule," between July 2010 and October 2011. "In contrast, public interest, labor, advocacy, and research groups, and other persons and organizations accounted for only about 7%. Moreover, the quality of federal agency contacts with financial industry representatives exceeds that of other contacts on several measures. Finally, the meeting logs, particularly when combined with the comment letters, reveal a level of industry cohesion that would not be predicted based on either press reports or the legislative history."[12]

Is it any wonder, then, that the Volcker Rule was watered down in myriad ways? In December 2014, the Fed and other regulators gave big banks an extension on the Volcker Rule that bans them from holding on to billions of dollars in private equity and hedge fund investments from 2016 to 2017. Former Fed chair Paul Volcker himself blasted the decision, saying, "It is striking, that the world's leading investment bankers, noted for their cleverness and agility in advising clients on how to restructure companies and even industries, however complicated, apparently can't manage the orderly reorganization of their own activities in more than five years." He added, "or, do I understand that lobbying is eternal, and by 2017 or beyond, the expectation can be fostered that the law itself can be changed?"[13]

Indeed, the Volcker Rule *was* changed, thanks to the financial lobby, to allow for what's called "portfolio hedging," meaning that banks can still do risky trades, as long as they are in the interest of protecting their existing assets rather than making new money. The problem is how to tell the difference. Even the heads of the banks often can't. Remember the 2012 "London Whale" trading debacle, in which J.P. Morgan suffered a $6 billion loss when synthetic derivatives trades went awry? The write-down represented a major loss of face for Jamie Dimon, who had been nicknamed "the Teflon banker" for his reputation for managing risk and had lobbied hard against reregulation after 2008, particularly against the Volcker Rule. (J.P. Morgan executives and representatives met with federal regulators twenty-seven times on the issue between July 2010 and October 2011.)[14] Famous for his command of banking detail, Dimon was forced to eat a huge helping of humble pie following the incident, which he had at first dismissed as no big deal, admitting only later that the offending trade had been "flawed, complex, poorly reviewed, poorly executed and poorly monitored." It's hard to believe that J.P. Morgan's chief investment office, which made the trades, wasn't designed to be a profit center, given that its head, who was let go from the bank following the London Whale event, earned $15 million a year. But even if you buy that claim, the case underscores that any kind of portfolio hedging carries what's known as basis risk. In the case of a huge bank like JPMorgan Chase, which is several times as big as the world's largest hedge funds, its very size is bound to create a market-moving event when it takes a position large enough to protect itself. "If you are the market," one risk expert told me, "you can't hedge it."[15]

A MERRY-GO-ROUND FOR THE 1 PERCENT

The power of the financial industry within our political system isn't exerted only through direct and indirect lobbying on the part of bankers and those they employ, but also via regulators and administration officials themselves, many of whom go through the revolving door between Wall Street and Washington multiple times throughout their careers. The Treasury Department in particular tends to be Wall Street–friendly as a result of this back-and-forth. Of the 35 individuals to hold the post of Treasury secretary since 1900, at least 13 had prior banking careers, and 17 went into finance following their tenure.[16] The most notable such officials in recent memory are Robert Rubin and Hank Paulson, both of whom worked at Goldman Sachs, an institution that has always exerted a special influence in the nation's capital. Top regulators are as often as not from the Street. (SEC head Mary Jo White, who worked previously at a white-shoe Wall Street law firm, and former CFTC chair Gary Gensler, who'd been a Goldman Sachs partner, are two recent examples.)

This isn't to say that former financiers can't be good public servants. Gensler, for example, was a true reformer and watchdog for the public, someone who used his financial expertise and considerable knowledge about the riskiest areas of the industry to put unprecedented pressure on banks in regard to derivatives trading. But many other officials who have worked on the Street before or after their tenure in government have tended toward a worldview that is favorable to finance—one that can obscure the reality of how the industry has thrived at the expense of everyone and everything else. It's an attitude that is rife on both sides of the aisle, of course; witness all the Republican members of Congress who helped make sure finance wasn't reregulated in the wake of 2008. "I am amazed [today] when I sit in Banking Committee hearings, and pro–Wall Street people and many Republicans and conservative think tank people have this sort of purposeful obliviousness to the fact that there was ever any kind of a problem—that we even *had* a financial crisis," says Senator Sherrod Brown, the ranking member of the Senate Banking Committee who's been a strong advocate for financial reform over the past few years. "The banks really haven't lost a step in the power that they wield, and it kind of amazes me that the media bought it, and that many people are fairly indifferent to it."[17]

This situation reflects what academics call "cognitive capture." In essence, Wall Street's implicit and explicit power has ensured that its finance-centric view of the world has become the status quo and is rarely questioned in a deep way. This has come ever more to front and center during the Trump administration, but is sadly true on both sides of the political spectrum. As journalist Noam Scheiber notes in his book *The Escape Artists*, which examines how the Obama administration fumbled the handling of the financial crisis and its aftermath, nearly everyone advising the president or working on the bailouts and reregulation of banking either had come from the Street or had been heavily influenced by it—something that can be seen in many of the policy decisions taken after the meltdown. "Most had worked for former Clinton Treasury secretary Robert Rubin at one point or another and largely echoed his views,"[18] meaning that they were inclined to see the financial industry as the center of the economic universe. "When the president took office, I think he felt he needed to put some of the old sort of Wall Street types in place, to reassure people that, one, he knew what he was doing, and also because some of the old hands knew a lot of things," says Brown. "Of course, at the same time, it was the old hands that got us into the stew, obviously."[19]

The stage was set for the financial crisis in part by Clinton-era deregulation orchestrated by financially captured officials like former Treasury secretaries Rubin and Summers, shifts including the repeal of Glass-Steagall (covered in chapter 1), and the tax code changes favoring performance pay (covered in the previous chapter), which enriched such officials themselves, as well as many of their acolytes and former and future colleagues on the Street and in the Beltway. It didn't help that derivatives regulation was blocked in the late 1990s by people like Rubin and Summers, who took down former CFTC regulator Brooksley Born when she dared to complain about it, as well as former Democratic congressman Phil Gramm, one of the coauthors of the Gramm-Leach-Bliley Act. (Gramm's wife, Wendy, another former CFTC chair, went off to Enron and got rich on derivatives before the implosion of that company.)[20]

It's hard to get around the fact that Washington helped create the rules that allowed banks to manipulate commodities in a way that has hurt some of America's most important businesses, not to mention consumers, while often enriching policy makers themselves. Almost directly after the CFTC granted many companies, including Enron, exemptions from public scrutiny of derivatives trading, there was a spate of swaps-fueled disasters: Orange County's bankruptcy in 1994, the crisis at Barings Bank in 1995, and the fall of the hedge fund Long-Term Capital Management in 1998. None of that hurt the Gramms, though—Wendy Gramm took a seat on the Enron board after leaving the CFTC, and by 2001 her husband was the company's second-largest recipient in Congress of the firm's political contributions. No wonder Gramm was all for breaking down walls between business and commerce in his namesake 1999 legislation. And little surprise, too, that he was one of the biggest allies of Rubin and former Fed chief Alan Greenspan in the fight to keep derivatives unregulated.

Of course, we must also lay a fair share of blame for our dysfunctional financial system at the feet of the Reagan administration, which really started the deregulation wheels turning. Some Reagan-era legislative changes, such as the legalization of large amounts of share buybacks (which had previously been considered market manipulation) under John Shad, a former financier who was chairman of the SEC from 1981 to 1987, have been covered in chapter 4 of this book. But financialization in the Reagan years wasn't just about legislative shifts that favored finance explicitly. It was also about things like the relaxing of antitrust enforcement, which not only made it much easier for corporations to amass the monopoly power that could squelch innovation, but also fueled massive growth within the financial industry itself. When big companies merge, it's good for the bankers—but not so good for the rest of us. M&A activity has always been linked to periods of financialization, and we are currently in a new golden age of mergers and acquisitions, whose number rose sharply in 2014 and, at the time of writing, already reached pre-financial-crisis levels.

Will these deals bring consumers anything good? Since the early 1980s, antitrust regulators like the Department of Justice and the Federal Trade Commission have tried to answer that question by asking another: will a given merger bring down prices and improve services for consumers? If answering "yes" was even remotely possible, then the merger—no matter how big—was likely to go through. But voices on all sides of the antitrust debate are beginning to question whether that rationale is actually still working. Nobody would argue that the megamergers that have taken place over the past thirty years in pharmaceuticals, for example, have brought down drug prices. Or that the tie-ups between big airlines have made flying more enjoyable. Or that conglomerate banks have made our financial system more robust (or prices cheaper—as we've already seen, efficiency has gone down and fees in the financial industry have actually gone *up* as banking has become more concentrated).[21]

As with deregulation, the political capture that has created such a system isn't limited to one side of the aisle. The bigger-is-better ethos of the 1980s and '90s grew not only out of conservative, markets-know-best thinking. It was also fueled by a belief on the left that antitrust enforcement was wasteful and that regulating big companies was preferable to trying to stop them from becoming too big in the first place. Neither side got it right. Big companies aren't always concerned primarily with the welfare of their customers— nor are they particularly easy to regulate. But the idea of letting companies do whatever they want as long as they can prove that they are decreasing prices may be far too simplistic a logic to serve the public—or even the corporate—good.

THE FINANCIALIZATION OF THE FED

If there is one entity that should *not* be part of the revolving door between Washington and Wall Street it's the Federal Reserve Bank. But it has been under increasing pressure over the last few years to become so. Like administration officials, Fed officials can—and do—rotate between being central bankers and regulators and being financiers on Wall Street. In particular, the New York Fed, which is a bank regulator as well as a lender of last resort, has become uncomfortably beholden to financiers. Anyone who doubts this should take a listen to the forty-six hours of secret audiotapes recorded by then–New York Fed bank examiner Carmen Segarra in 2012. The tapes, made with a spy recorder, were made public in a joint report by ProPublica and This American Life in 2014.[22] They tell in painful, crackling detail how the Fed's financial cops slipped on their velvet gloves to deal with banks such as Goldman Sachs, and how Segarra, one of a group of examiners brought in after the financial crisis to keep a closer watch on the till, was fired, perhaps for doing her job a little too well.

Consider one of the shady deals discussed on the tapes: a 2012 Goldman transaction with Banco Santander initiated in the midst of the European debt crisis, which ensured that the Spanish bank would look better on paper than it did in reality. Santander paid Goldman a $40 million fee to hold shares in a Brazilian subsidiary so that it could meet European Banking Authority rules. The Fed employees, who work inside the banks they examine (yes, it's literally an inside job), knew the deal was dodgy. One even compared it to Goldman's "getting paid to watch a briefcase." But it was technically legal, and nobody wanted to make a fuss, so the transaction went through.[23] When Segarra asked too many questions, she was quietly let go from her job. In some ways, the most shocking thing about the tapes is that they are no shock at all. Did anyone ever doubt that the New York Fed bank examiners—the regulators tasked with monitoring the risks banks take—might fear alienating the powerful financiers on whom they might depend for information or future jobs?

Another instance of how the New York Fed favors finance, an example that perhaps hasn't gotten enough attention, is the way in which it set a new precedent for the socialization of risk and privatization of reward with the bailout of AIG, the giant insurer that was blown up in the subprime crisis. That event was managed by then–New York Fed chief Timothy Geithner. There was no question that AIG had to be bailed out. The question was who would pick up the tab—the banks that had created the subprime problems to begin with, or the public. As a June 2010 report by the Congressional Oversight Panel of the Troubled Asset Relief Program (TARP) lays out, there were certain precedents to handling a destabilizing situation of this kind, like the blowup of the hedge fund Long-Term Capital Management in 1998.[24] Back then, LTCM's mismanaged trades likewise threatened financial panic. But in that crisis, the New York Fed (led by William McDonough, an old-school financier who, like many effective regulators, had come of age at a time when Wall Street was much less dominant) was able to press private banks that had been involved with LTCM to take the first hit. Private money, not public resources, was used to bail out the hedge fund. The Fed simply made it clear that if the banks didn't play ball, it had any number of ways in which it could make their lives miserable, and it would use them all.[25]

Not so in the AIG deal that Geithner orchestrated. This time, as the TARP report puts it, "the Federal Reserve and Treasury broke new ground. They put US taxpayers on the line for the full cost and the full risk of rescuing a failing company."[26] There were, of course, many differences in the two scenarios—back in 1998, nobody seriously thought that the domino effect from the fall of one or a few financial giants would bring down the global financial system, while quite a few people were worried about that outcome in

2008. But another key difference was the size of Wall Street, which grew exponentially in the time between the two crises, along with its power relative to Washington's. Put in that context, the AIG deal signaled a broader tectonic shift. "The issue in AIG was that AIG was a key player in the derivatives system, and that solvent mega-institutions like Chase and Goldman couldn't afford the systemic effect of an AIG collapse," says Damon Silvers, policy director for the AFL-CIO, who was one of the Democratic appointees to the TARP oversight commission." The Fed knew this and asked Chase and Goldman to take first dollar risk in the bailout, and then took 'no' for an answer. I think that the AIG bailout was a moment in which public confidence in the government's decisions in the crisis being in the public interest started to collapse. Later on, some called this dynamic 'crony capitalism.' "

To be fair, Geithner was probably doing his best in a tough situation, one that had been unfolding for quite a while, rather than exploding in a short burst like LTCM. But it's interesting to note, as the TARP investigation report does, that he backed down rather quickly when bank leaders like J.P. Morgan's Dimon and Goldman's Blankfein refused to pony up their own institutions' cash to save AIG. Geithner declined to be interviewed on the topic for this book. But my sense from conversations on and off the record that I've had with him over the years is that he (like Rubin and Summers, who were his mentors) simply holds that same finance-centric view of the economy, in which banks are the dog, not the tail. One detail I find quite telling is a key argument Geithner offers in his memoir, *Stress Test*, to defend the AIG rescue and the TARP bailouts as a whole: "the markets loved it."[27] Perhaps predictably, he has now joined the ranks of many other former Treasury secretaries who headed to Wall Street, taking up a position as president of the private equity firm Warburg Pincus.

FOUNDING FATHERS AND FINANCIALIZATION

The dysfunctional relationship between Washington and Wall Street is in some ways nothing new. Finance has always influenced politics, and vice versa—all the way back to the founding of our republic. As academics Charles W. Calomiris and Stephen H. Haber describe in their excellent book, *Fragile by Design: The Political Origins of Banking Crises & Scarce Credit,* the political economy of our nation's banking system was somewhat flawed from the get-go, thanks to a fight between Alexander Hamilton, who favored large national banks, and Thomas Jefferson, who represented rural interests suspicious of concentrations of power in urban areas like New York.[28] The result was thousands of small banks operating in regional markets, all subject to different regulations. This system eventually spawned megabanks that cared little about lending to the real economy, along with regional banks that wanted to but couldn't spread risk as efficiently as they might have—thanks to the lack of a cohesive national system of branch banking.

That was one reason for the severity of the crash of 1929 and the subsequent depression, as chapter 1 explained. The decades between the 1933 Glass-Steagall regulation and the late 1970s were exceptionally healthy ones, a time during which banks were seen as facilitators of the real economy, not the main event. By and large, government decisions around finance taken during that period reflected that (plus there simply weren't as many financial crises to deal with, given that the industry was smaller and more constrained). But thanks to the "guns versus butter" pressure around how to allocate resources in an economy that began to grow more slowly from the 1970s onward, new dysfunctional alliances between Washington and Wall Street emerged. As outlined in chapter 1, banks and activists both pushed the government to deregulate interest rates. Politicians tried to pass the buck on financial decision making back to Wall Street rather than make difficult choices about resource allocation in society. The rise of the money culture in the 1980s and the deregulation policies of that era led to a credit boom, wrapping more and more of the American middle class in a cloak of debt that made it increasingly hard for politicians to stand up to the banking industry. Is it any wonder then that debt, deregulation, finance, and money politics have grown hand in hand?[29] In this sense, the subprime crisis of 2008–9 and the ways in which it was aided and abetted by Washington—as well as Washington's failure to properly clean up the system afterward—is only the latest sequence in a dysfunctional dance between finance and politics that has been going on for hundreds of years.

FINANCE AND THE LEGAL SYSTEM

Beyond the cognitive capture of public officials and the historically flawed structure of the financial system, there is also the way in which our legal system has enabled financialization. Key changes in the legal structure of banks and corporations as a whole have been an important factor in creating excess risk in financial markets, by allowing individual bankers off the hook for bad deals. Andrew Haldane, the chief economist of the Bank of England and an outspoken advocate of banking reform, believes that the legal shift from a partnership structure to limited-liability corporate structure, in which individuals are no longer personally accountable for losing money or taking on too much risk, is a key reason for the Too Big to Fail problem we have today.[30]

Up until the mid-nineteenth century, laws that made bank owners personally liable for the reckless deals of their institutions helped keep risk in check. Indeed, it wasn't just their personal capital that was at stake; medieval bankers could even get executed in front of their failed banks for going bust.[31] Such a system was harsh, no doubt. But, as Haldane points out, unlimited liability (at least in terms of personal capital at risk) meant that "the interests of shareholders, bank managers, and the larger society were roughly in line."[32] In the United States and Great Britain alike, early banking was a fragmented, low-leverage, high-liquidity business. Financial sector assets represented fractions of national GDP, as opposed to far above 100 percent today. Banks typically held more than a quarter of their assets in cash and stored the resources needed to cover at least half of their liabilities at any given time. By contrast, the big banks of today would be lucky to be able to cover 10 percent.

That's a direct result of the shift to limited liability banking, which began in the nineteenth century and continued well into the twentieth. Rich countries, hungry for capital to finance investment in railways, factories, and homes, decided to unleash the banking sector, by lifting regulation and allowing firms to operate not just as partnerships or joint stock companies in which each owner held ultimate responsibility for risk, but as limited liability entities in which no individual owner had to take responsibility if things went south. Instead, that duty fell to the government—and, ultimately, the taxpayers.

At first banks themselves were skeptical about limited liability status. They thought of unlimited liability as a badge of honor, proof that they were secure institutions. But the collapse of the City of Glasgow bank in 1878, caused by speculative lending and flawed accounting practices, ended that. Eighty percent of the bank's shareholders, many of whom were widows and spinsters who'd bought the shares as a pension bet, were made destitute. In the years leading up to the collapse, people like influential British journalist and businessman Walter Bagehot, then editor in chief of *The Economist*, argued that the benefits of unlimited liability were illusory because investors on the hook for everything they had simply wouldn't invest what was required for the rapidly expanding British economy. The opinions of bankers and the public alike turned. The British began a swift transition to a limited liability system, and by 1889 only two unlimited-liability British banks remained. In the United States, a comparable major shift happened after the Great Depression.

Limited liability certainly unleashed more capital. Banks got bigger—and riskier; limited liability meant that bankers, undeterred by personal responsibility for losses, took on more debt. Leverage ratios (the amount of debt versus safe assets that a bank uses to conduct business) grew from 3–4 times in mid-nineteenth century to about 5–6 times in the beginning of the twentieth. (Today, leverage is around 20–30 times assets at most big banks.) Returns, bolstered by these higher bets, rose—but so did the number of financial crises. A boom-and-bust cycle, which would reach its climax in the United States in 1929 with devastating global results, had begun.

But in 1920s America, none of this was well documented or understood yet. The systemic failure of small local and regional banks (which were undercapitalized compared to the small number of national banks) during the ensuing Great Depression was taken as evidence that unlimited liability didn't help stem panic. Despite protests from President Franklin Delano Roosevelt, who believed that small banks had behaved better in the run-up to the crisis than larger ones, legislators decided to move to limited liability. They envisioned a more concentrated national banking system underwritten by a new system of deposit insurance and a central bank—the Federal Reserve—that would play the role of the national lender of last resort. It was a structure that made sense at the time. Yet it was also in some ways the beginning of the moral hazard problem that we all know so well today.

All these legal changes fed into the Too Big to Fail financial industry we have now, one in which gains are privatized but losses are socialized.[33] Indeed, the incorporation of many American investment banks in the 1980s and '90s allowed them to grow the kinds of huge balance sheets that were a prerequisite to becoming serious players in new domains such as the derivatives market. As Haldane, who was formerly executive director of the Bank of England's financial stability committee, summed it up in a damning speech on the topic in 2011, this century-long evolution has resulted in a situation in which bankers' own interests are "out of line with the interests of other bank stakeholders, much less society. This fault-line lies at the heart of the imbalance between privatized returns and socialized risks. Only in banking do control rights and incentive wrongs combine so uncomfortably."[34]

You can certainly see the effects at Goldman Sachs, which gave up its traditional partnership structure to go public in 1999. It would be naïve to say that the bank wasn't changing even before this—trading had already replaced relationship banking as the principal source of profits, and compensation structures were evolving to put more pressure on individuals to take risk—but the firm's IPO certainly accelerated and deepened those changes.[35] How could it not? Before then, partners had to make cash investments into the bank large enough to be material to their own net wealth. They weren't allowed to withdraw any capital until retirement, and even then only a small amount over a long period of time. Most important, all partners had personal liability for the exposure of the institution to any bad bets—that meant their homes, their cars, everything.[36] After the IPO, risk was farmed out more widely, to shareholders themselves. Given this, and particularly after Goldman qualified for federal backing in 2008, is it any wonder that the bank that was once Wall Street's most respected broker has turned into a place so famously described by a frustrated former employee, Greg Smith, in 2012? Smith published his searing resignation letter in the *New York Times*, portraying Goldman as an institution in which there were only three ways to become a leader. One was "persuading your clients to invest in the stocks or other products that we are trying to get rid of because they are not seen as having a lot of potential profit." The second was to get clients "to trade whatever will bring the biggest profit to Goldman." Or, third, you could find your way to "a seat where your job is to trade any illiquid, opaque product with a three-letter acronym."

Beyond this massive issue of who holds liability when, there are any number of ways in which our legal system favors large companies and financial institutions over smaller players. Some of these shifts were part of the shareholder revolution of the 1980s, an ideological turn that produced not only new ideas about the meaning of corporations and who they should be run for, but also profound changes in the tax code and consumer protection and bankruptcy structures. These changes tend to favor corporate interests over those of individuals, an issue that Senator Elizabeth Warren has written much about. Consider for example the Bankruptcy Abuse Prevention and Consumer Protection Act of 2005, a typically Kafkaesque name for a piece of legislation that effectively removed bankruptcy protections on things like student loan debt yet appeased finance by cementing the protection of derivatives (yes, those financial weapons of mass destruction) within bankruptcy law. It's a truly incredible legislative decision; people who are going into debt because they are desperately trying to get a leg up in society—and whose opportunities have been constrained by the growth of finance—are penalized, while the industry itself is protected.[37] Would such a "reform" law have been passed if so many politicians weren't captured, monetarily and cognitively, by the financial industry? I doubt it.

TOO BIG TO JAIL

Part of the legal system, of course, is the justice system—and that's another area in which finance has gotten off easy since 2008. The culture of finance hasn't really changed, as continuing scandals and fines within the industry show. In order to reboot this culture, you need for people to believe they might actually go to jail for doing bad things. "If we had been able to put some people in prison, many fewer would have wanted to join in the bad behavior the next time around," says economist Joseph Stiglitz.[38] Yet far fewer people went to jail during the 2008 financial crisis and its aftermath than did after such recent events as the 1980s savings and loan (S&L) crisis, when more than 1,000 bankers were jailed for making bad loans. Sadly, one reason for that contrast is that some of the things that happened in the latest meltdown, despicable though they might be, were actually legal. But that's not true in all cases. People like Stiglitz and many others believe that existing laws (under bits of legislation like the 2002 Sarbanes-Oxley Act, which was enacted after the Enron debacle to hold corporate leaders more accountable for their actions) could have been better leveraged to prosecute finance executives responsible for the crisis.

But that didn't happen. Why not? In an essay for the *New York Review of Books* in 2014, Jed Rakoff, US district judge for the Southern District of New York, made a persuasive case that the dysfunctional relationship between Washington and Wall Street was at the heart of this failure of justice. While it is true that federal prosecutors are often overworked, underpaid, and have too much on their plates, Rakoff argued that it was also "the government's own involvement in the underlying circumstances that led to the financial crisis," via weak oversight, deregulation, and buck passing through monetary policy that made officials willfully blind to the problems. As cover, officials sometimes even cited worries that prosecutions could negatively impact the financial system and thus the global economy, as then–US attorney general Eric Holder himself argued in front of the Senate Judiciary Committee in 2013.[39] "To a federal judge who takes an oath to apply the law equally to rich and to poor," writes Rakoff, "this excuse—sometimes labeled the 'too big to jail' excuse—is disturbing, frankly, in what it says about the department's apparent disregard for equality under the law."[40]

Of course, some would argue that the industry has taken its pain in fines—$139 billion of them from 2012 through 2014[41]—for everything from money laundering to collusion, lack of disclosure to foreclosure abuses, and interest rate fixing to insider trading (I could go on, but you get the idea). Yet the industry is so flush that fines, even mammoth ones, simply don't have the same effect as jail time. What's more, these are penalties that are shared at an institutional level, with the pain spread far and wide to people who had little or nothing to do with the problems, rather than punishments that target the individuals who were really at fault. No wonder that when Senator Warren confronted Jamie Dimon a few years ago about fines his institution might face under Dodd-Frank, he said, "So hit me with a fine. We can afford it."[42] Indeed, when you consider not only the quarterly profits of the major banks (which often run into the multibillions) but the variety of explicit and implicit subsidies given to them by taxpayers and the government, the fines really don't amount to much. During the financial crisis, bank stock prices reflected implicit bailout expectations equivalent to around $100 billion, which dramatically reduced the pain of subprime-related losses.[43]

There is another and perhaps even more troubling part to the fine issue, though. While some of the fines that have been levied on the industry have been clear and well deserved, there are other cases in which they've been levied retroactively and with a certain amount of opacity that actually undermines trust in the law. For example, in March 2009, even though the legality of the move was hazy, the House overwhelmingly approved a retroactive tax of 90 percent on bonuses that bailed-out banks had given to their employees that year. You can see why—there was a huge sense of public outrage about the bailouts and the fact that the public was paying to save bankers who'd been given absolutely no real punishment or put much skin in the game. Yet as University of Chicago professor Luigi Zingales points out, when mob rule takes the place of clear penalties for crimes within a well-enforced system, public faith in democracy itself can suffer, as indeed it often does in emerging-market countries where arbitrary penalties for ill-defined violations are common. "Even in the United States public resentment against finance can undermine the expectation that the rule of law will be respected in the future," writes Zingales. "Without this expectation, the competitive, democratic, and inclusive finance will quickly become unsustainable."[44] It would have been far better for independent prosecutors to jail individuals who had broken well-enforced laws than for angry policy makers to levy billions of dollars in somewhat nebulous fines—which ultimately did nothing to change the behavior of the financial industry.

TO BAIL, OR NOT TO BAIL?

I do think it was necessary for the government to bail out the financial system following the crisis. There is a Hayekian argument, made by some conservatives and libertarians, that letting the system go under would have produced a true and complete cleanup of finance, unlike the piecemeal, watered-down regulation that we got with Dodd-Frank. But few would agree that it would have been worth more pain and suffering in the real economy to accomplish that. My misgivings have more to do with the fact that financially captured public officials simply didn't use all the levers they had available to put pressure on the financial community during those bailouts. And they certainly didn't do as much as they should have to ensure that finance was reconnected to the real economy in the wake of the crisis. (The list of what might have been done is long, starting with bonus prohibitions for Too Big To Fail banks that were bailed out until they got their capital structures in order.)

All the different ways in which the handling of the crisis favored the financial industry over any other group of stakeholders—homeowners, small businesses, consumers, or community banks—is one sharp example of this. "I don't think we ever collectively, in this country, got to the point of saying, yes, it's more important to bail out banks than to bail out homeowners or families in general, or people who've lost their jobs, or seen their 401(k) savings decimated," says Senator Warren. "But the economic leadership [of the country] had its own theory of the case and decided based on that. . . . There was just never the democratic notion that you were going to have to persuade people that this was the right approach, to have some public policy debate—you know, the kinds of debates that we have for better and for worse about whether or not to go to war, or build an Interstate Highway System, or figure out what we might do about the environment. None of that. It just didn't work that way."[45]

The way in which the Obama administration tried to declare victory against Wall Street at the first sign of economic green shoots, and then quickly move on from any deeper soul-searching about the structure and purpose of our financial system, is another reminder of our missed opportunity to put finance back in service to the real economy. As I explained in a *Time* cover story on the fifth anniversary of the financial crisis, "the truth is, Washington did a great job saving the banking system in '08 and '09 with swift bailouts that averted even worse damage to the economy. But . . . it has done a terrible job of reregulating the financial industry and reconnecting it to the real economy."[46]

I got quite a bit of blowback from the Treasury for that article. A high-level official called my boss to complain about the piece, and the then–deputy assistant secretary of the Treasury, Anthony Coley, issued a formal rebuttal, saying, "The notion that these reforms are somehow a 'myth,' as Rana Foroohar suggests in her September 23, 2013 story, is wrong. It is an undeniable fact that the financial system we have today—the system that Americans rely on to take out a mortgage, save for college, open a small business, even write a check—is safer, stronger and more resilient than it was five years ago."[47] (I posted my own rebuttal blog, responding to each point of criticism.)[48]

Sorry, guys, but as I hope this book has shown, the system is not in better shape. Although it's true that some banks may individually be stronger than they were before the crisis, our system as a whole is not. Banking has not been re-moored in the real economy. The creation of institutions like the Consumer Financial Protection Bureau was a great step forward, but it hasn't changed the underlying business model of many of the largest banks, which still make the majority of their profits from trading rather than plain-vanilla lending. Nor has it hindered the ability of Wall Street to continue to take opaque risks that compromise the integrity of our financial sector as a whole. Many of these risks are due to loopholes in Dodd-Frank as a result of vigorous banking industry lobbying. While Dodd-Frank has created something of a road map to wind down banks, most experts believe that it's still unclear how the rules would work in practical terms, especially given that the biggest banks are now larger—not smaller—than they were before the crisis.

The majority of reform-minded economists believe that breaking up banks to make them both smaller and simpler is the best way to reduce risk in the financial system. Interestingly, it's something that the markets themselves would probably also reward; industry analysts calculate that companies like JPMorgan Chase and Citigroup would actually be valued higher in market capitalization terms if they were broken up, a reflection of the investor view on the risks that such Too Big to Fail entities pose not only to the system, but to shareholders.[49]

One of the points that Obama administration officials like to cite when responding to criticism of their handling of the financial crisis, and of the trend toward financialization in general, is that the banking sector as a percentage of GDP is smaller in the United States compared to other countries or regions, like Europe and Japan. But while that's true about banks, it's absolutely not true if you count the US financial sector as a whole (including insurance, real estate, money market funds, mutual funds, real estate trusts, and so on).[50] As I've tried to illustrate in this book, it's not just big banks that matter when we think about the power of financial markets, but the entire dysfunctional ecosystem of finance and the way in which it strangles the real economy. What's more, the unregulated portion of the industry has gotten bigger since the crisis. The size of the informal lending sector, which includes shadow banking, has actually grown by $13 trillion since before the meltdown, reaching a dizzying $80 trillion in 2014, according to the Bank for International Settlements.[51]

When defending their handling of the crisis, officials will also argue that most of the largest banks have since offloaded risky assets and increased the level of risk-absorbing capital. But it's important to consider context. Raising "Tier 1" capital (which means cash, or cash equivalents, held by banks to offset risk) by, say, 70 percent may sound impressive, but not when you consider that it has been raised from a base of almost nothing relative to risk—which means that this accomplishment still leaves much work to be done. As FDIC vice chairman and financial reform proponent Thomas Hoenig argued in an April 2013 speech, many of the complicated rules that officials evoke to show how much they've done to make banks safer are pretty much just "well-intended illusions." Hoenig outlined just how easy it is for banks to game the risk assessments and stress tests that officials concoct for them. To think that there is a perfect metric that can capture the health of a financial institution, Hoenig says, is "a fallacy that puts the entire economic system at risk."[52] As I demonstrated through a different lens in chapter 2, putting complex metrics above common sense is very often a recipe for disaster.

INSIDERS AND OUTSIDERS

Unfortunately, a tremendous part of the debate in the post-crisis era about how to make the financial system safer has centered on complex financial risk calculations. Yet one reason it has been so difficult to have a clear and sensible debate in Washington, D.C., or anywhere else about the role of finance in our society is the obsessive attention given to such numbers, and the complex language and "cult of the expert" that go along with them. When financiers and financially captured officials are faced with critical questions posed in plain English, they all too frequently beat them back by denouncing them as too simplistic or populist, or claim that the questioners simply aren't sophisticated enough to "get it."[53] If you tell them they should be putting more of their own skin in the game, or that you don't understand why asking them to hold more capital should make it any harder for them to lend, they will uncork lots of complex financial terms—"Tier 1 capital," "liquidity ratios," "risk-weighted off-balance-sheet credit exposures"—that tend to suffocate useful (aka comprehensible) debate. As Elizabeth Warren put it to me, "You'd turn on the TV [during the financial crisis] and hear these guys using all this complicated language and effectively saying, 'Don't worry about it. We're the experts. We know what should happen here. We're in charge and we will take care of this.' Which, by the way, is how we ended up in the whole situation—[by assuming] that the experts would take care of it."[54]

It's important to see these smoke screens for what they are. Finance and its supporters, like any tribe, can use insider jargon to intimidate and obfuscate. Yet when we are thinking about how to re-moor banking in the real economy, complexity is the enemy. The right questions are the simplest ones. Are financial institutions doing things that provide a clear, measurable benefit to the real economy? As we have seen, the answer is all too often no.

The media, for its part, has not done a good enough job at expressing this to the public in clear terms. Part of the reason is a shortage of reporters with good financial chops (a problem that has always existed during the twenty-five years I've been in the business but one that has recently gotten worse, as resources at news organizations have dwindled). But another part of it, in my experience, is subtle intimidation. Meetings between Washington economic officials and the media are often taken in groups, which allows them to be better controlled by officials and also lends them a high-school lunchroom quality. There's a pecking order, with certain reporters in the club and others clearly out. Those who ask for slower or clearer answers to difficult questions or admit to not understanding something (usually some decision that reflects badly on the administration when explained more clearly) are liable to get an eye roll, an impatient drumming of fingers, or even an end to invitations to future meetings of this kind. It's a subtle but effective way of keeping control of the narrative, especially among financial beat reporters who will have to return to the same source well again and again, and who can't risk losing their contacts.

Squelching dissent by trying to make people feel stupid, or by creating a special clique, is a manipulation tactic that isn't limited to the press. In her book *A Fighting Chance*, Warren tells an amazing story about a dinner she had with Lawrence Summers, then director of the National Economic Council, in which he made it clear that Warren had a choice. "I could be an insider or I could be an outsider," she writes. "Outsiders can say whatever they want. But people on the inside don't listen to them. Insiders, however, get lots of access and a chance to push their ideas. People—powerful people—listen to what they have to say. But insiders also understand one unbreakable rule: *They don't criticize other insiders.* I had been warned."[55]

Senator Sherrod Brown, ranking member of the Senate Banking Committee and another well-known advocate of financial reform, laments that Washington is replete with lobbyists and officials who use this cult of the insider, subtle intimidation, and complex language to obfuscate the facts. "The people that lobby on medical issues talk in a different language, as do the people who lobby on banking issues. And a lot of congressmen or senators don't want to appear stupid and so perhaps they don't ask as many questions as they might," says Brown. "I kind of woke up to that, and I thought, Okay, I don't care if I ask questions that sound stupid because eventually I'm going to learn things. That freed me up to put aside insecurities and start asking tougher questions."[56]

MAKERS VERSUS TAKERS

All this is a threat not just to the financial system and to the economy, but to democracy itself. As Thomas Piketty has argued, capital "is always in part a social and political construct: it reflects each society's notion of property and depends on the many policies and institutions that regulate relations among different social groups, and especially between those who own capital and those who do not."[57]

But today the size and power of the financial sector, and the way in which it has perverted our society and our democracy, have brought us to a tipping point in this cycle. In a broad sense, we have become what academic Gerald Davis calls "a portfolio society," one in which "entire categories of social life have been securitized, turned into a kind of capital."[58] In this world, nearly everything becomes transactional: human relationships are "social capital," people themselves become "human capital," and opportunities of any kind must be "monetized." "It's finance as a *practice* that is in charge, even more than financial *institutions* themselves," says Davis. "It's the 'markets rule' approach that is the issue—the markets have come to dominate any and all other institutions within our society."[59]

As he and others, such as Mike Konczal and Nell Abernathy at the Roosevelt Institute, have written, this seismic change, in which the model of finance has become the model for the economy and for society as a whole, has any number of disturbing effects—starting with the shifting of responsibility away from corporations and government and onto the individual. Consider our failing retirement system and the way in which public services have been privatized, or the way in which our tax system rewards takers over makers. As Konczal and Abernathy put it, "privatization replaces the discussion of what the government should do with the allocation of what it does."[60] Financialization has always been an easy way for the government to avoid the big and contentious questions of who gets what in our society—an unsettling tendency I discussed in chapter 1. By letting the financial sector offer up credit and balm slower growth with more debt, politicians could put off giving voters any bad news. And yet, by increasing inequality and undermining economic growth over the last several decades, financialization has actually only made those questions more pressing. "We've indulged in this fiction that we can build a vibrant economy by deregulating the financial sector, and cutting taxes, and putting off investments in things like infrastructure and education and our kids," says Senator Warren. "But we can't any more. And now we have to ask the question about what really went wrong. Because without the right story about what went wrong, we won't fix what really needs to be fixed."[61]

This is a moment to truly ask, and answer, that question in a deep and authentic way. The mishandling of the financial crisis by politicians and regulators marked what many believe is a deep and broad loss of faith in Washington's ability to tame Wall Street. This loss that has set off a cascade of destructive effects on our country, from a rising populist sentiment, to an unsettling and growing sense that the American Dream is fundamentally broken, to a belief that we are heading towards an entirely new, postcapitalist society.

What that might look like is anyone's guess. Some, like British economic journalist Paul Mason, are relatively optimistic. His book *Postcapitalism* argues that financialization is at the heart of wage stagnation and has been for decades. His focus on the links between debt and economic malaise and his analysis of how finance (which is mostly short term) has broken the link between saving and real economy investment (which are nearly always long term) are particularly persuasive. Mason believes that we are at a tipping point in the process of financialization, which has allowed capitalism to grow, like a virus, beyond its useful life span. He thinks that the technology-driven "sharing economy" in which information is freer and capital is less important will empower workers to fight financial capitalists in a new and more powerful way.[62] But I'm less optimistic. In my own reporting experience, I've found Silicon Valley titans at the heart of the technology revolution to be just as rapacious and arguably even more tribal than many financiers. And as I discussed in chapter 4, the technology industry itself is becoming increasingly financialized.

Indeed, I tend to think that the rather pessimistic French economist Thomas Piketty is, in lieu of any big vector changes, broadly correct about our economic future. "The one percent in America right now is still a bit lower than the one percent in prerevolutionary France but is getting closer," says Piketty. The idea that the United States today could be on the same economic trajectory as late-eighteenth-century France, a society in which many of the 1 percent eventually had their heads lopped off, is, as Piketty writes in his book, "terrifying." Yet he believes it is likely the natural order of things. "It's quite possible that inequality will keep getting worse for many more years," he says.[63] His book shows that historically, the only time inequality actually decreases is during a war—when the rich tend to lose a bundle—or when government jump-starts growth through direct intervention, as the United States did both with the New Deal in the 1930s and with the Marshall Plan in the late 1940s and early 1950s.

Since the rate of return on capital is, according to Piketty, naturally greater than the rate of growth in the economy as a whole, in the absence of such redistributive world events, people who get most of their wealth from investments inevitably grow richer compared to those who get their money from salaries. Economic, political, and social bifurcation increases. In other words, thanks to financialization, the golden age of the average American may have been a brief historical anomaly rather than a permanent phenomenon. That notion will certainly strike a chord with anyone who has watched the stock market reach record highs over the past few years even as real wages have stagnated. "Nothing becomes resonant unless it relates to our experience," says Robert Johnson, president of the Institute for New Economic Thinking, a George Soros–backed nonprofit that funded some of Piketty's research. "The trend described by Piketty and the trend of financialization are absolutely resonant with the experience of most Americans over the last few decades."[64]

It doesn't have to be this way. Much of this book has focused on explaining the myriad ways in which the destructive trend of financialization plays out in our businesses, our communities, our jobs, and our economy at large. But things could be very different. History has shown us that the takers don't always trump the makers. The next chapter will focus on the top five things we can do to put our financial system back in service to the real, tangible economy that most of us have the fortune to inhabit.

CHAPTER 11

HOW TO PUT FINANCE BACK IN SERVICE TO BUSINESS AND SOCIETY

OUR SYSTEM of market capitalism wasn't handed down to us in perfect form from the heavens. It's merely a set of rules that we ourselves have crafted over decades. We made those rules. And we can remake them as we see fit, to better serve our shared prosperity and economic growth. Much time has been spent and much ink spilled on the particulars of how to regulate finance, fix corporate governance, and rejigger our tax system. Rather than focus on the details of those and other points of reform, which should be hashed out by a broad group of stakeholders over time, I propose five big ideas for how we might move toward a financial system that is a help, rather than a hindrance, to business and society. Into these buckets I have placed a number of action points that should be considered as we work to reintegrate finance into the real economy.

END COMPLEXITY, CUT LEVERAGE

We need to make our financial system a lot simpler and a lot more transparent. We've heard plenty about banks that are Too Big to Fail, but in some ways, the more crucial issue is that most financial institutions are just Too Complex to Manage. As we've seen, even the smartest global risk managers at the most reputable institutions don't know everything that's going on inside their firms because, as former CFTC chair Gary Gensler pointed out, "it's not possible to know."[1] How could anyone fully police the millions of transactions happening daily in a US financial system worth $81.7 trillion?[2]

In that sense, there is reason to worry about how much the Dodd-Frank Act of 2010 (assuming it isn't dismantled) will actually do to make our financial system safer, because the law itself is incredibly complicated. Dodd-Frank is 2,319 pages long, as compared to the 1933 Glass-Steagall Act that separated investment banking from commercial banking in just 37 pages. The length of Dodd-Frank reflects the efforts of lobbyists outlined in chapter 10. It also creates ample new loopholes for clever lawyers to jump through.

Critics who argue that reinstating Glass-Steagall wouldn't be a silver bullet to avoiding financial crises are correct. Bad things can certainly happen in stand-alone commercial banks (remember the S&L crisis?). There would be costs as well as benefits to redrawing the red line between lending and trading, and legislation would also need to be retooled for the modern era. That's a process that should happen based on forensic study not only of the crisis of 2008 but also of the many that preceded it, with consideration of where future risks might lie. (They are almost never where you think they'll be, but better forensics on past crises could help us get smarter about this.) It's telling that following the 2008 meltdown, the public was very much in favor of such a law, because it would decree in an easily understandable way that financiers shouldn't gamble with government-insured money. That kind of simplicity is not a bad place to start with regulation. As Luigi Zingales points out in *A Capitalism for the People*, "the United States was born on the principle of no taxation without representation. It should add no regulation without representation. But if regulation is too complex, people have no way to understand it and thus cannot participate properly in democracy. Simplifying regulation, therefore, is essential to building a capitalism for the people."[3]

There are many other parts of the financial system beyond bank structure and practice that must be demystified. Regulators and politicians should continue to fight to move *all* derivatives trading onto regulated exchanges where any market player can see what's being sold, when, and for how much. There's simply no excuse not to. After all, equal access to markets and information was one of Adam Smith's prerequisites for a healthy capitalist system. We also need to better regulate the shadow banking sector, end offshore banking, and close tax and corporate filing loopholes that enable the kind of creative accounting that hides not only what's on corporate balance sheets but also how much CEOs and other executives are being paid in options. This measure would go a long way toward creating more transparency in finance and curtailing the issues of short-termism that were discussed in chapter 4. A financial transaction tax—akin to a proposed Tobin tax—could likewise help in this respect, by forcing banks to pay a small fee for each trade in bonds, stocks, and derivatives that they do, many of which (as this book has explored) have little to no benefit to the real economy anyway.[4]

Beyond this, we need to end the cult of "experts" in finance and open the conversation about how and for whom the financial system should work to a much broader group of people—far beyond the small priesthood of financiers, politicians, and regulators who tend to share the same finance-centric view of the economy. "We need to stop treating banking as if it's a business unlike any other," says Stanford professor Anat Admati, whose book *The Bankers' New Clothes*, coauthored with Martin Hellwig, suggests a number of smart ways to reform and simplify the sector, including requiring banks to use a lot more equity against risk.[5] Indeed, if anything, banking should be thought of as a subsidiary to business, a catalyst that should be held to even higher standards. Banks complain about new rules from the FDIC and the Federal Reserve that require them to use a mere 5 percent of their own money on risky deals, when most of the rest of corporate America wouldn't dream of borrowing even 50 percent relative to assets, never mind 95 percent. Says Admati, "Banks have managed to convince us that they deserve special treatment," often by invoking complicated arguments and using insider lingo. Keep in mind that what bankers refer to as "cash" is very often debt: the deposits they hold for other people.

Admati would like to see regulators require that banks fund 20–30 percent of their investment with equity. "If banks want to trade," she says, "they should be forced to gamble with their own money." Many other reform-minded financial experts agree, especially given how leverage (meaning, the debt that financial institutions use to try to bolster their returns) can multiply the negative effects on the economy when bank trades go bad. "It's crazily irresponsible not to do more to limit leverage," says Princeton professor and former Federal Reserve vice chairman Alan Blinder, whose book *After the Music Stopped* looks at the causes of the crisis and the risks that remain. FDIC vice chairman and bank reform advocate Thomas Hoenig is for that, too, and he says the common Wall Street argument that limiting leverage will keep banks from lending more to real businesses is bunk. If higher leverage boosts lending, he wrote in a *Financial Times* op-ed, then "it does so at the taxpayer's expense, by making large banks—and the real economy—more vulnerable to shocks."[6] Indeed, there's evidence that banks with more capital are better able to maintain lending through cycles of boom and bust.

At the same time as we strive to mitigate risk, we need to accept that no single metric, no magic calculation, will prevent financial crises from happening. As we saw in chapter 2, financialization thrives on the idea that particular metrics hold absolute truth. "We need to stop sifting through the data for answers that please the powerful," says Robert Johnson, the head of the Institute for New Economic Thinking. "We should stop pretending that finance is a hard science and embrace the chaos. Otherwise we are pretending we are in a planned economy." In other words, despite what the high priests of finance would have us believe, finance isn't mechanical like Newtonian physics. It's much more like the messy science of biology: unpredictable and full of human error and emotion. We should expect and be prepared for crises, not only by asking banks to conduct their business more safely and simply, but also by demanding that financiers and the financial system itself take their fair share of pain when crises do happen.

LESS DEBT, MORE EQUITY

As we have discovered, debt is the lifeblood of finance. Issuing debt and moving it around the financial system is where banks and other financial institutions make much of their money. Yet debt holds great risk for our economy as a whole. The conventional wisdom has always been that more credit is good for growth. As we have seen, though, a large body of new research challenges that—by showing that there is a limit to how much credit a healthy economy should have, and how big a financial sector should be. Economists have found that when credit to the private sector rises too quickly, financial crises and slower growth are the result.[7] Other studies show that a larger financial sector means a less stable economy.[8] Debt is always a precursor to financial crises,[9] and yet we subsidize the creation of debt through our tax system, as I explored in chapter 9.

It's no surprise why—encouraging debt and credit issuance can be a way for government to avoid difficult conversations about the fact that real economic growth has slowed by historic standards. Goosing the economy in this new environment would require bigger and more challenging political steps: reforming education, coming up with a cohesive national growth strategy, revamping our tax system, and bolstering the social safety net, among others. Addressing that buck-passing problem involves a deep conversation about how our political economy works (or, more frequently, doesn't work)— one that goes far beyond the structure of our financial system.

But on a practical basis, there are many discrete steps that could be taken to encourage savings and the building of equity rather than debt. One of those, increasing the amount of self-funding done by banks, is laid out above. There are many others. In his book *Between Debt and the Devil*, Adair Turner discusses using regulation and tax credits to encourage banks to lend to more socially useful causes rather than conducting mainly risky, short-term transactions.[10] Nobel laureate Robert Shiller has suggested making all financial contracts, and debt contracts in particular, more flexible. One of the big problems with debt is that it penalizes borrowers much more than lenders for any change in the risk environment. Shiller suggests a number of ways to spread that burden more evenly between lenders and borrowers. Government debt service contracts, for example, might allow payments to fall temporarily if GDP declined (which would encourage lenders to countries like Greece to be more careful). Likewise, individuals could take out mortgage rates that would adjust depending on their economic circumstances or on the fundamentals of house prices in a certain region.[11] As *House of Debt* authors Mian and Sufi have pointed out, this would help mitigate the collapse in consumption (and thus growth) that happens when a debt bubble bursts.[12]

RETHINK WHO COMPANIES ARE FOR

The notion that companies should be run solely for the benefit of shareholders is due for a reexamination. As we know, shareholders, particularly the short-term-focused, quarterly-results-driven activists who are currently shaping the markets, are much less interested in the long-term viability of a firm than in jacking up its share price and cashing out as quickly as possible. This fuels the cycle described in the introductory chapter, in which businesses eschew investment, growth slows, and financial institutions focus on offering up consumer debt products rather than more socially useful investment. The end result is the creation of risky financial bubbles that explode on a regular basis, taking us all down with them. There are any number of immediate steps that could be taken to mitigate this effect, from limiting the amount and size of share buybacks to raising capital gains taxes, to using a sliding scale that accounts for how long an asset is held, to limiting the amount of corporate pay that can be awarded in stock options.

But there is a bigger conversation to be had about who exactly should be benefiting from the riches of corporate America. I'd argue it's all of us—meaning, the workers whose talents and efforts enrich corporations and the taxpayers whose dollars fuel the government funding that has enabled so many US firms to become so rich in the first place. If corporations are people, as Mitt Romney so famously put it, then surely the people who work in them should be receiving a larger share of the pie. Our shareholder value–obsessed culture is the exception to the rule globally. Many other countries, including most European ones, have a broader definition of corporate stakeholders, which include not only investors but also labor (whose representatives typically sit on the board in highly productive and globally competitive countries like Germany) and even civic leaders and nonprofit groups.[13] Many private, family-owned companies in the United States work this way, too—which may be one reason that they tend to invest twice as much in the US economy as public companies of similar size do, creating more sustainable, broadly shared growth.[14]

BUILD A NEW GROWTH MODEL

This contrast between America's private and public firms underscores a key point, which is that financialization is both a cause and a symptom of slower growth and a corporate sector that spends its seed corn in the markets rather than investing it on Main Street. Too much finance hinders growth, as we've already seen. But slower growth can also encourage policy makers to turn to finance for a quick fix to deep structural problems within the system. In many ways, the recent crash of the Chinese economy and the global market reverberations from it are just the most recent echo of the dysfunctional cycle of financialization that began decades ago. "The rise of the rest," as journalist Fareed Zakaria calls the economic growth of the emerging markets, put pressure on US growth.[15] But it also created huge amounts of new wealth for these developing nations to invest; most of it flowed into our financial markets. As we saw in chapter 1, that cash glut gave bankers plenty of extra funds to play with and helped create new debt bubbles in the United States that papered over slower longer-term growth and rising inequality, at least temporarily. The bubble, aided by deregulation and easy monetary policy from the 1980s onward, finally burst in 2008, as both American companies and American consumers stopped spending.

But debt, like energy, doesn't just disappear. It merely takes on a new shape. When we stopped spending, other countries, like China, had to take up the slack. Over the past six years, the Chinese have brewed up their own unprecedented debt bubble, one that is now popping and affecting global markets just as the US subprime crisis did, albeit to a lesser extent—at least, so far. The US subprime crisis and China's debt crisis are different in many ways, but in one crucial aspect they are quite similar: They both underscore how countries try to use debt and financial markets as a way to artificially buoy growth, in lieu of a strong economic growth model that would bolster the real economy.[16] Sooner or later, it ends in tears.

How to move on from this dysfunctional cycle? Each of the major regions of the global economy—the United States, Europe, Japan, and the emerging markets led by China—must play a part. America needs a new moonshot goal for economic growth, something that will galvanize the country and create the kinds of productivity gains and innovations that the short-term high of finance never will. (Those who say such a plan is antithetical to a free-market society should look to countries like the United Kingdom, Germany, France, and Denmark, all of which have successfully supported national growth plans linking the public and private sector at various points in their history.) Many smart people have suggested ideas along these lines. Academics across the political spectrum, for example, have proposed variations on a national green stimulus program that would encourage innovations like sustainable energy technologies, thus addressing both the issue of growth and the challenge of sustainability on a more crowded planet. But it would require political will on both sides of the aisle. Putting aside the Trump administration, which I hope will be a political aberration, that's something that I am actually becoming more optimistic about, given the growing realization on both the far left and some parts of the right that financialized, market-driven "growth" that rewards mainly the top tier of society isn't the road to shared prosperity. Indeed, the Trump administration's efforts to bolster growth with one last round of "trickle-down" economics, which will inevitably fail, may provide more proof of this.

Europe, for its part, needs to become a true union—a "United States of Europe," with a shared fiscal policy and wealth transfers from rich to poor countries.[17] Not every country can, or should, be Germany (indeed, one of the reasons Germany itself is so rich is that most of its neighbors are consumers of its goods, rather than competitors). If Europeans can find the political will to create the sort of true federalist system that the United States enjoys, they'll have a leg up in terms of creating sustainable growth. That's because many of their existing structures of corporate governance—codetermination, more sensible levels of executive pay, and so forth—as well as their social democratic commitments to the broader public well-being already serve the average citizen quite well.

China may be the toughest part of the economic mix in terms of reform. It is attempting to make a transition from being a place that manufactures cheap shoes and light fixtures to being a sophisticated service-driven economy. That's a transition that only four other Asian markers have made: Japan, South Korea, Singapore, and Taiwan. All of those countries had much smaller populations and much less complex political systems than China, where the Communist Party still runs a command-and-control system that funnels money into unproductive state-owned banks and enterprises and starves the more productive private sector. It's a system that, like the United States, is both highly unequal and highly financialized, albeit in its own way. Compounding the problem is China's enormous debt burden (its total debt, including that of the financial sector, is at a jaw-dropping 282 percent of GDP), complete with a real estate crisis and volatile stock markets.[18] Chinese leader Xi Jinping is trying to consolidate power, supposedly to enact the reforms necessary to change China's model, which will require upsetting the vested interests that have grown rich from the current system. But in the process, thousands of people have been jailed or executed and many Western businesspeople have been kicked out of the country. The jury is still out on whether autocracy and advanced capitalism can coexist forever, even in China. And given that China has represented the biggest chunk of global growth since the financial crisis, that puts the world pretty much back where it was before the last few years of financial crises and recession: looking for a better and more sustainable way to stimulate growth.

CHANGE THE NARRATIVE—EMPOWER THE MAKERS

That will have to come from us. Despite all our problems, America is still the prettiest house on the ugly block that is the global economy. Our modern financial system made the world what it is today. And if we can build a healthier market system, it could help put the entire global economy on a better path.

That will, however, require crafting a new narrative about our financial system and its place in our economy and society. As the crisis of 2008 and its continuing aftermath have surely shown, we are at the end of what financialization can do for growth. We need a new model, one that enriches the many rather than the few, in a more sustainable way. We need markets that are structured fairly, with the kind of equal access that Adam Smith described in *The Wealth of Nations*. We need a political economy that isn't captured by moneyed interests. And we need a financial sector that understands that it should be a helpmeet to business, not an end in and of itself. Even if we don't understand the particulars of Wall Street, we all know on some gut level that the current system isn't working. How could it be when 1 percent of the population takes most of the world's wealth, and a single industry that creates only 4 percent of jobs takes nearly 25 percent of our country's corporate profits?

There are many things that need to change in order for us to reach a better place. Some are major: How do we reform campaign finance so that the banking lobby (or any other industry) doesn't undo the best efforts of legislators and regulators? How do we move on from the contentious and unproductive system of labor relations we currently have? Other challenges are technocratic, such as deciding on the details of bank reform, the structure of incentive pay, and the specific tax loopholes that should be targeted first. Still others are philosophical: How should our system of market capitalism best be structured and policed? How should our business leaders be educated? What is the best way to allocate capital and wealth in our society?

I don't believe that there is one right answer to any of these questions, but I think that we need to develop a new and more accurate story about the role finance plays in our economy to answer them properly. As Senator Warren says, "we never really reached consensus as a nation about what happened to our financial system and our economy in 2008." Doing so will require a detailed analysis of the facts by people who don't have vested interests and aren't captured by the system.

To that effect, we might take a page from airline safety. As air travel became ubiquitous several decades ago, and crashes subsequently increased, there was a need to clearly understand the mounting problems. At first the government allowed regulators and the industry to do the forensic job of examining what had happened and making suggestions about how to fix things. This arrangement was similar to the model that exists in finance today. But it resulted in a distorted view of who was at fault, since neither airline companies nor regulators were keen to admit any failings on their part. Eventually, this forensic analysis job was separated out from the Federal Aviation Administration, the regulatory body that oversees the airline industry. Professionals tasked with this work were given independence under the newly created National Transportation Safety Board, and the agency's role has since significantly reduced the number of plane crashes around the world. Experts like MIT's Andrew Lo have proposed that something similar be done for finance.

And in fact, there already exists a government agency—the Office of Financial Research, which sits within the Department of the Treasury—that could play such a function well. The OFR, which was created after the 2008 crisis to examine where risks might lurk in the financial system, has already done great work, although it is currently at risk of being quickly starved of funding by the Trump administration. If given further independence and put outside the jurisdiction of the Treasury, it might go further in exploring the hows and whys of financial crises in a way that would make our system safer. Given how many people are affected by crises in the financial system (obviously many more than are affected by airplane crashes), it's a goal that should be put front and center.

Studying the history of crises in a nonbiased way is one route to change. Rebooting the culture of finance for the future is another. We should start this process by creating a kind of Hippocratic Oath for the financial industry. As the Nobel laureate Joseph Stiglitz once pointed out to me, "We talk a lot about what finance does wrong. But a strong, well-functioning financial system is a prerequisite for a well-functioning economy, not to mention a healthy democracy." That's why, along with debating what Wall Street has done wrong, we should all be asking new questions: What can finance do right? How can bankers help business and society? And how can the markets start working for all of us? In this book, I've sketched stories not only of takers, but also of makers, some of them in the financial sector itself, who are doing well and doing good at the same time. There are many more of them out there, and more still to be created as we change the rules of our system to better serve our economy and society.

As in medicine, so in finance—first, do no harm. We must understand, as I've tried to illustrate in this book, what happens when finance grows at the expense of business. And then we should try to imagine what might happen if it could be put back in service to the economy—to all of us, the people who created the system to begin with. I think we'd have a much brighter future, one in which the makers, rather than the takers, would be ascendant.

ACKNOWLEDGMENTS

MAKERS AND TAKERS has been influenced by dozens of people I've known in my two-plus decades as a journalist. During that time, I've been incredibly lucky to work for and with some of the best people in the business, including Fareed Zakaria, my former boss at *Newsweek* and colleague at *Time* (and now CNN), who first encouraged me to write this book and also introduced me to my amazing literary agent Tina Bennett at WME, who was instrumental in helping to shape my thinking on the topic as well as the structure of the end product. Thank you to my new boss, *Financial Times* editor Lionel Barber, as well as *Financial Times* U.S. editor Gillian Tett, who have been so supportive of this work. I'm also particularly grateful to my former bosses and colleagues at *Time*, especially managing editor Nancy Gibbs and deputy managing editor Michael Duffy, for encouraging much of the reporting that supported this book, giving me the time and space to write it during my tenure there. Thank you to CNN president Jeff Zucker as well, for giving me the opportunity to share my thoughts with a new audience as the network's global economic analyst, and to WNYC executive VP Dean Cappello, VP for news Jim Schachter, and business editor Charlie Herman for allowing me to sound off as a contributor.

Makers and Takers was very much a team effort; I'm particularly grateful for the fact-checking and research support provided by Anna Kordunsky, Barbara Maddux, and Lisa Du, without whom I couldn't have completed the manuscript on time, as well as Svetlana Katz at WME, who provided administrative support. And of course, a huge thanks to the entire Crown staff that was involved in the project—particularly executive editor Dominick Anfuso, who believed in me enough to acquire it; senior editor Talia Krohn, who did an amazing job as line editor; indefatigable publisher Tina Constable; and her amazing sales and marketing staff. They are really the best team in publishing.

The reporting and writing of this book was a huge intellectual and emotional task in which I received much support. On that score, I owe a tremendous debt to Robert Johnson, the president of the Institute for New Economic Thinking. He is a godfather to many in liberal economic policy circles, and from the very beginning of this project, he helped me sharpen my ideas, put me in touch with major sources, and read and critiqued many chapters of the book, all of which are much better for his input (any flaws are mine alone). Also crucial to the success of this project were Columbia professor and Nobel laureate Joseph E. Stiglitz, whose work has been an enormous inspiration to me and so many others; and his wife Anya Schiffrin, who was a hugely supportive reader, connector, and cheerleader.

I must also thank the many other important people who gave their valuable time to sit for interviews and share their thoughts—among them are Senator Elizabeth Warren, Senator Sherrod Brown, Gary Gensler, Damon Silvers, Warren Buffett, Jack Bogle, Andy Haldane, Lord Adair Turner, Richard Trumka, William Lazonick, Mike Konczal, Nell Abernathy, Felicia Wong, Anat Admati, Gerald Davis, Stephen Cecchetti, James Galbraith, Edmund Phelps, Wallace Turbeville, Thomas Hoenig, Charles Morris, Joe Nocera, Charles Ferguson, Bob Lutz, Lisa Donner, Rebecca Henderson, Margaret Heffernan, Andrew Lo, Dominic Barton, Nitin Nohria, Rakesh Khurana, Emanuel Derman, Mark Bertolini, Andrew Smithers, Lynn Stout, Sam Palmisano, Greg Smith, Joseph Blasi, David Rothkopf, Ken Miller,

Marc Fasteau, Robert R. Locke, Ruchir Sharma, Gautam Mukunda, Saule Omarova, Eileen Appelbaum, and Sherle Schwenninger.

Thanks also to the many academics and policy thinkers whose research I relied heavily on, including but not limited to: Greta Krippner, Moritz Schularick, Alan M. Taylor, Robin Greenwood, David Scharfstein, Raghuram G. Rajan, Carmen Reinhart, Ken Rogoff, Thomas Philippon, Robert Atkinson, J. W. Mason, Luigi Zingales, Thomas Piketty, Emmanuel Saez, Gabriel Zucman, Jeff Madrick, George Akerlof, Robert Shiller, John Coates, Karen Ho, Enisse Kharroubi, Claudia Goldin, Lawrence Katz, David Graeber, Charles Calomiris, Stephen H. Haber, Allan H. Meltzer, Robert Reich, Alan Blinder, John Asker, Joan Farre-Mensa, Alexander Ljungqvist, Kimberly Krawiec, Thomas Ferguson, Gerald Epstein, Michael Spence, Sarah Edelman, Monique Morrissey, Mariana Mazzucato, Atif Mian, and Amir Sufi.

Finally, the biggest thanks of all to my husband, John Sedgwick, the author of fifteen books himself, who talked me down from the ledge numerous times during the three years it took to complete this project. Thanks to my parents, Ann and Aygen Dogar, both of whom worked incredibly hard to make sure I had the education and opportunities that enabled me to write for a living. Thanks to my stepdaughters, Josie and Sara, for politely listening to numerous wonky dinner conversations about finance. And to my children, Darya and Alex, thank you for putting up with my constant multitasking, and the many weekend afternoons I spent at the computer rather than in the park. It may not always seem like it, but you two are the reason for everything I do.

NOTES

AUTHOR'S NOTE

1. Thomas Piketty, Emmanuel Saez, and Gabriel Zucman, National Bureau of Economic Research, "Striking It Richer: The Evolution of Top Incomes in the United States," June 30, 2016.

INTRODUCTION

1. David Einhorn, Greenlight Capital, "Vote Against Proposal 2 at the February 27 Annual Meeting to Protect Your Investment in Apple," February 7, 2013, http://investor.apple.com/secfiling.cfm?filingid=1011438 -13-69&cik=320193.

2. The figure is for companies that appeared in the S&P 500 index in February 2015 and that had been publicly listed between 2005 and 2014. See William Lazonick, "Cash Distributions to Shareholders (2005–2014) & Corporate Executive Pay (2006–2014), Research Update #2," Academic-Industry Research Network, August 2015.

3. Ted Berg, Office of Financial Research, "Quicksilver Markets," March 2015.

4. Labor force participation rate hovered at 62.4 percent in September 2015, below the 1978 level of 62.8 percent. See US Department of Labor, "Economic News Release: Employment Situation Summary," October 2, 2015; US Department of Labor, "Labor Force Participation Rate," Statistics from Population Surveys, BLS Data Viewer, online at http://beta.bls .gov/dataQuery. See also Irene Tung, Paul K. Sonn, and Yannet Lathrop, National Employment Law Project, "The Growing Movement for $15," November 4, 2015.

5. Carl C. Icahn, "Sale: Apple Shares at Half Price" (an open letter to Tim Cook), carlicahn.com, October 9, 2014; William Lazonick, Mariana Mazzucato, and Oner Tulum, "Apple's Changing Business Model: What Should the World's Richest Company Do with All Those Profits?" *Accounting Forum* 37, no. 4 (2013): 261; author interviews and reporting for *Time* magazine.

6. Nabila Ahmed and Mary Childs, "Apple Is the New Pimco, and Tim Cook Is the New King of Bonds," Bloomberg, June 4, 2015.

7. Interview with OFR economists and analysts for this book.

8. Greta Krippner, *Capitalizing on Crisis: The Political Origins of the Rise of Finance* (Cambridge, MA: Harvard University Press, 2011), 35.

9. Mike Konczal and Nell Abernathy, "Defining Financialization," Roosevelt Institute, July 27, 2015. The term *portfolio society* is derived from the work of the University of Michigan academic Gerald F. Davis, author of *Managed by the Markets: How Finance Reshaped America* (Oxford: Oxford University Press, 2009).

10. The key piece of research here is Moritz Schularick and Alan M. Taylor, "Credit Booms Gone Bust: Monetary Policy, Leverage Cycles, and Financial Crises, 1870–2008," Working Paper no. 15512, National Bureau of Economic Research, November 2009. It analyzes 140 years of data, in fourteen advanced economies including the United States, and finds that the function of the financial system in these countries is no longer to funnel money to *new* investments, but to funnel it through *existing* assets, such as housing, often via complex securitization.

11. Adair Turner, *Between Debt and the Devil: Money, Credit, and Fixing Global Finance* (Princeton, NJ: Princeton University Press, 2015).

12. Òscar Jordà, Alan Taylor, and Moritz Schularick, VOX, Center for Economic Policy Research, "The Great Mortgaging," October 12, 2014.

13. Bureau of Economic Analysis data ("Table 6.16: Corporate Profits by Industry," "Table 6.4: Full-Time and Part-Time Employees by Industry," and "Industry Data: Value Added by Industry"), online at http://www.bea.gov/iTable, accessed November 2015.

14. Valerie Bogard, "High-Frequency Trading: An Important Conversation," Tabb Forum, March 24, 2014.

15. New York Stock Exchange data ("NYSE Group Turnover"), online at http://www.nyxdata.com, accessed November 2015.

16. Robin Greenwood and David Scharfstein, "The Growth of Finance," *Journal of Economic Perspectives* 27, no. 2 (2013): 7 and 19–20.

17. Schularick and Taylor, "Credit Booms Gone Bust."

18. Greenwood and Scharfstein, "The Growth of Finance," 1.

19. Turner, *Between Debt and the Devil*. See also Atif Mian and Amir Sufi, *House of Debt: How They (and You) Caused the Great Recession and How*

We Can Prevent It from Happening Again (Chicago: University of Chicago Press, 2014).

20. Raghuram G. Rajan, *Fault Lines: How Hidden Fractures Still Threaten the World Economy* (Princeton, NJ: Princeton University Press, 2010), 21.

21. Carmen M. Reinhart and Kenneth Rogoff, *This Time Is Different: Eight Centuries of Financial Folly* (Princeton, NJ: Princeton University Press, 2009).

22. McKinsey Global Institute, "Debt and (Not Much) Deleveraging," February 2015, 98–99.

23. Greenwood and Scharfstein, "The Growth of Finance," 21.

24. Financial efficiency is defined here as the amount of money and engagement that finance provides to Main Street, rather than to the capital markets themselves.

25. Thomas Philippon, "Has the U.S. Finance Industry Become Less Efficient? On the Theory and Measurement of Financial Intermediation," *American Economic Review* 105, no. 4 (2015): 1408–38.

26. Robert D. Atkinson and Stephen J. Ezell, *Innovation Economics: The Race for Global Advantage* (New Haven, CT: Yale University Press, 2012), 21.

27. Victoria Williams, US Small Business Administration, Office of Advocacy, "Small Business Lending in the United States 2013," December 2014.

28. John Haltiwanger, Ron Jarmin, and Javier Miranda, "Business Dynamics Statistics Briefing: Where Have All the Young Firms Gone?" Kauffman Foundation, May 2012, 3–4.

29. They include Nobel laureates Joseph Stiglitz and Edmund Phelps, economist James Galbraith, sociologists Gerald Davis and Greta Krippner, investors Warren Buffett and John Bogle, and numerous other academics and businesspeople quoted throughout this book.

30. J. W. Mason, "Disgorge the Cash: The Disconnect Between Corporate Borrowing and Investment," Roosevelt Institute, February 2015.

31. Ibid.

32. William Lazonick, "The Financialization of the U.S. Corporation: What Has Been Lost, and How It Can Be Regained," *Seattle University Law Review* 36, no. 2 (March 2013): 894–95.

33. Hannah Kuchler, "Activist Investor Warns Yahoo over Seeking Large Deals," *Financial Times*, January 8, 2015.

34. Conference Board and SharkRepellent.net.

35. Bank for International Settlements, "Incentive Structures in Institutional Asset Management and Their Implications for Financial Markets," March 2003.

36. Shai Bernstein, "Does Going Public Affect Innovation?" *Journal of Finance* 70, no. 4 (2015): 1365–1403.

37. Berg, "Quicksilver Markets."

38. McKinsey Global Institute statistics.

39. Ibid.

40. For a good summary of this conventional wisdom, see Ross Levine, "Finance and Growth: Theory and Evidence," in *Handbook of Economic Growth*, ed. Philippe Aghion and Steven N. Durlauf, vol. 1 (New York: Elsevier, 2005).

41. Boris Cournède and Oliver Denk, "Finance and Economic Growth in OECD and G20 Countries," Working Paper No. 1223, OECD Economics Department, 2015.

42. Stephen G. Cecchetti and Enisse Kharroubi, "Why Does Financial Sector Growth Crowd Out Real Economic Growth?" Working Paper No. 490, Bank for International Settlements, Monetary and Economic Department, February 2015.

43. Stephen G. Cecchetti and Enisse Kharroubi, "Reassessing the Impact of Finance on Growth," Working Paper No. 381, Bank for International Settlements, July 2012.

44. Cournède and Denk, "Finance and Economic Growth in OECD and G20 Countries."

45. Jean-Louis Arcand, Enrico Berkes, and Ugo Panizza, "Too Much Finance?" Working Paper 12/161, International Monetary Fund, June 2012; Ratna Sahay et al., "Rethinking Financial Deepening: Stability and Growth in Emerging Markets," Staff Discussion Note 15/08, International Monetary Fund, May 2015.

46. SNL Financial, "Largest 100 Banks in the World," August 3, 2015; Federal Reserve, "Assets and Liabilities of Commercial Banks in the United States," online at http://www.federalreserve.gov/releases/h8/Current/ (accessed November 2015).

47. OpenSecrets.com, "Lobbying, Sector Profile, 2014: Finance, Insurance & Real Estate."

48. Luigi Zingales, *A Capitalism for the People: Recapturing the Lost Genius of American Prosperity* (New York: Basic Books, 2012).

49. Wallace Turbeville, "Financialization & Equal Opportunity," White Paper, Demos, February 10, 2015.

50. Thomas Philippon and Ariell Reshef, "Wages and Human Capital in the U.S. Finance Industry, 1909–2006," *Quarterly Journal of Economics* 127, no. 4 (2012): 1551–1609.

51. Jon Bakija, Adam Cole, and Bradley T. Heim, "Jobs and Income Growth of Top Earners and the Causes of Changing Income Inequality: Evidence from U.S. Tax Return Data," Williams College, April 2012.

52. Emmanuel Saez and Gabriel Zucman, "Wealth Inequality in the United States Since 1913: Evidence from Capitalized Income Tax Data," Working Paper No. 20625, National Bureau of Economic Research, October 2014, 56.

53. Thomas Piketty, *Capital in the Twenty-First Century*, trans. Arthur Goldhammer (Cambridge, MA: Belknap Press of Harvard University Press, 2014), 209.

54. Lauren Carroll, "Hillary Clinton: Top Hedge Fund Managers Make More than All Kindergarten Teachers Combined," PolitiFact, June 15, 2015.

55. William Lazonick, "Profits Without Prosperity," *Harvard Business Review* 92, no. 2 (September 2014).

56. James K. Galbraith and Travis Hale, "Income Distribution and the Information Technology Bubble," Working Paper No. 27, University of Texas Inequality Project, January 2004.

57. Robert Frank, *The High-Beta Rich: How the Manic Wealthy Will Take Us to the Next Boom, Bubble, and Bust* (New York: Crown Business, 2011), 54.

58. Richard Wilkinson and Kate Pickett, *The Spirit Level: Why Equality Is Better for Everyone* (London: Penguin Books, 2009).

59. Rana Foroohar, "Thomas Piketty: Marx 2.0," *Time*, May 19, 2014.

60. Federal Reserve Flow of Funds; Congressional Research Service, "Rebuilding Household Wealth: Implications for Economic Recovery," by Craig K. Elwell, September 13, 2013.

61. Reinhart and Rogoff, *This Time Is Different*, 156.

62. Charles P. Kindleberger and Robert Z. Aliber, *Manias, Panics, and Crashes: A History of Financial Crises* (Hoboken, NJ: Wiley, 2005), 6.

63. Greta R. Krippner, *Capitalizing on Crisis: The Political Origins of the Rise of Finance* (Cambridge, MA: Harvard University Press, 2011).

64. Jeff Madrick, *Age of Greed: The Triumph of Finance and the Decline of America, 1970 to Present* (New York: Knopf, 2011).

65. Weill issued his mea culpa on CNBC in July 2012. See "Wall Street Legend Sandy Weill: Break Up the Big Banks," CNBC, July 25, 2012.

66. FDIC and Federal Reserve statistics on capital ratios.

67. Financial Stability Board, "Global Shadow Banking Monitoring Report 2015," November 12, 2015.

68. Exact numbers are up for some debate because of the complexity of derivatives themselves; expert estimates range from 30 percent to 70 percent.

69. CFTC data as of June 2015.

70. Ann Tenbrunsel and Jordan Thomas, "The Street, the Bull and the Crisis: A Survey of the US & UK Financial Services Industry," University of Notre Dame and Labaton Sucharow LLP, May 2015.

71. Adam Levy, "Brain Scans Show Link Between Lust for Sex and Money (Update 1)," Bloomberg, February 1, 2006; John Coates, *The Hour Between Dog and Wolf: Risk-taking, Gut Feelings, and the Biology of Boom and Bust* (New York: Penguin Press, 2012).

72. Gerald F. Davis, *Managed by the Markets: How Finance Reshaped America* (Oxford: Oxford University Press, 2009).

73. Scott A. Christofferson, Robert S. McNish, and Diane L. Sias, "Where Mergers Go Wrong," *McKinsey Quarterly*, May 2004.

74. Karen Ho, *Liquidated: An Ethnography of Wall Street* (Durham, NC: Duke University Press, 2009).

75. Quoted in Barbara Kiviat, "An Anthropologist on What's Wrong with Wall Street," *Time*, July 22, 2009.

76. Philippon and Reshef, "Wages and Human Capital in the U.S. Finance Industry, 1909–2006."

77. Karl Marx, *Capital: A Critique of Political Economy*, trans. Ben Fowkes (New York: Penguin, 1992).

78. Some, like the British journalist and thinker Paul Mason, believe this change is coming soon. His book *Postcapitalism: A Guide to Our Future* (New York: Farrar, Straus & Giroux, 2016) is a smart sketch of how financialization has undermined capitalism and liberal democracy, and what might come next.

79. Paul M. Sweezy, "Why Stagnation?" *Monthly Review* 34, no. 2 (June 1982).

80. Pew Research Center, "Most See Inequality Growing, but Partisans Differ over Solutions," January 23, 2004.

CHAPTER 1: THE RISE OF FINANCE

1. Sandy Weill, with Judah S. Kraushaar, *The Real Deal: My Life in Business and Philanthropy* (New York: Hachette Book Group, 2006), 300 and 316.

2. "Wall Street Legend Weill: Breaking Up Big Banks," CNBC, July 25, 2012.

3. Estimate by Princeton economist Alan Blinder and Moody's Analytics economist Mark Zandi in "How the Great Recession Was Brought to an End," July 27, 2010, www.economy.com.

4. Rana Foroohar, "A New Age of Global Capitalism Starts Now," *Newsweek*, October 3, 2008.

5. Author interviews with William Lazonick; Mason, "Disgorge the Cash."

6. The Bank for International Settlements reports that the global derivatives market was about $586 trillion in December 2007 and about $710 trillion in December 2013. See BIS Statistics Explorer, "Table D5.1: Global OTC derivatives market" (the values are for "notional amounts outstanding").

7. Financial Stability Board, global shadow banking monitoring reports for respective years and a statistical annex published in 2012 ("Global Shadow Banking Monitoring Report 2012," Exhibits 2-1, 2-2, and 2-3, November 18, 2012).

8. Turbeville, "Financialization & Equal Opportunity."

9. Hyman P. Minsky, "Hyman P. Minsky (1919–1996)," autobiographical article originally written in 1992, in Philip Arestis and Malcolm Sawyer, eds., *A Biographical Dictionary of Dissenting Economists* (Northampton, MA: Edward Elgar, 2000), 416, quoted in John Bellamy Foster and Fred Magdoff, *The Great Financial Crisis: Causes and Consequences* (New York: Monthly Review Press, 2009), 17.

10. The concept of a "symbiotic embrace," a phrase that initially appeared in a *BusinessWeek* editorial in 1985, is discussed in Harry Magdoff and Paul M. Sweezy, *Stagnation and the Financial Explosion* (New York: Monthly Review Press, 1987). For a comparison of American economic recoveries since the 1960s, see Drew Desilver, "Five Years in, Recovery Still Underwhelms Compared with Previous Ones," Pew Research Center, June 23, 2014.

11. Cecchetti and Kharroubi, "Why Does Financial Sector Growth Crowd Out Real Economic Growth?"

12. International Monetary Fund, "Housing Finance and Real-Estate Booms: A Cross-Country Perspective," by Eugenio Cerutti, Jihad Dagher, and Giovanni Dell'Ariccia, Staff Discussion Note 15/12, June 2015.

13. Mason, "Disgorge the Cash," 32.

14. Paul Tucker, "A Perspective on Recent Monetary and Financial System Developments," speech at the Bank of England, April 26, 2007.

15. Author interview with Gensler for this book.

16. Philippon, "Has the U.S. Finance Industry Become Less Efficient?"

17. Claudia Goldin and Lawrence Katz, "Transitions: Career and Family Life Cycles of the Educational Elite," *American Economic Review* 98, no. 2 (2008): 367.

18. Most economists agree with this assessment. For example, Princeton economist and former Fed vice chair Alan Blinder has estimated, in a study he coauthored with Moody's Analytics chief economist Mark Zandi, that without the bailouts, American GDP would have plunged 12 percent rather than 4 percent. See Alan S. Blinder and Mark Zandi, "Stimulus Worked," *Finance & Development* 47, no. 4 (December 2010).

19. David Graeber, *The Utopia of Rules: On Technology, Stupidity, and the Secret Joys of Bureaucracy* (Brooklyn, NY: Melville House, 2015).

20. Mason, "Disgorge the Cash," 32.

21. William Lazonick, "Profits Without Prosperity," *Harvard Business Review*, September 2014; Drew Desilver, Pew Research Center, "For Most Workers, Real Wages Have Barely Budged for Decades," October 9, 2014.

22. Vincent P. Carosso, *Investment Banking in America: A History* (Cambridge, MA: Harvard University Press, 1970).

23. Charles W. Calomiris and Stephen H. Haber, "Why Banking Systems Succeed—and Fail," *Foreign Affairs*, November/December, 2013.

24. Carosso, *Investment Banking in America*, 29–30.

25. Charles W. Calomiris and Stephen H. Haber, *Fragile by Design: The Political Origins of Banking Crises & Scarce Credit* (Princeton, NJ: Princeton University Press, 2014), 176.

26. Carosso, *Investment Banking in America*, 14–27.

27. Ibid., 22, 32, and 46.

28. Ralph W. Hidy and Muriel E. Hidy, *Pioneering in Big Business 1882–1911: The History of the Standard Oil Company of New Jersey (New Jersey)* (New York: Harper, 1955), 607, quoted in Carosso, *Investment Banking in America*.

29. Carosso, *Investment Banking in America*, 45.

30. Ibid., 145–55 and 170–77.

31. Ibid., 238–39, referencing Edwin F. Gay, "The Great Depression," *Foreign Affairs* (July 1932).

32. Author interview with Federal Reserve historian Allan H. Meltzer.

33. Nomi Prins, *All the Presidents' Bankers: The Hidden Alliances That Drive American Power* (New York: Nation, 2014), 93.

34. "Business: Damnation of Mitchell," *Time*, March 6, 1933.

35. Prins, *All the Presidents' Bankers*, 127.

36. Phillip L. Zweig, *Wriston: Walter Wriston, Citibank, and the Rise and Fall of American Financial Supremacy* (New York: Crown, 1995), 45–46.

37. Author interview with Piketty.

38. Madrick, *Age of Greed*, 10.

39. Amey Stone and Mike Brewster, *King of Capital: Sandy Weill and the Making of Citigroup* (New York: John Wiley & Sons, 2002), 110–111.

40. Madrick, *Age of Greed*, 14–15.

41. Zweig, *Wriston*, 66.

42. Ibid., 113.

43. Madrick, *Age of Greed*, 18.

44. Wriston reached that milestone in 1982. See Madrick, *Age of Greed*, 16; and Zweig, *Wriston*, 228.

45. Krippner, *Capitalizing on Crisis*, 69–70.

46. Zweig, *Wriston*, 182, 340–44, 352.

47. Ibid., 343.

48. Krippner, *Capitalizing on Crisis*, 62–63, quoting from a letter to Congressman Wright Patman.

49. Ibid., 70–73.

50. Madrick, *Age of Greed*, 104.

51. Ibid., 102–7.

52. Krippner, *Capitalizing on Crisis*, 76–80.

53. Zweig, *Wriston*, 735–37.

54. Krippner, *Capitalizing on Crisis*, 88.

55. Robert Reich, *Supercapitalism: The Transformation of Business, Democracy, and Everyday Life* (New York: Knopf, 2007).

56. Krippner, *Capitalizing on Crisis*, 97.

57. James Tobin, "On the Efficiency of the Financial System" (a revised version of the Fred Hirsch Memorial Lecture given in New York on May 15, 1984), *Lloyds Bank Review*, July 1984.

58. Author interview with Sharma for this book.

59. Madrick, *Age of Greed*, 396.

60. Krippner, *Capitalizing on Crisis*, 104.

61. Madrick, *Age of Greed*, 241.

62. Board of Governors of the Federal Reserve System, "Report on the Economic Well-Being of U.S. Households in 2013," July 2014, 27.

63. Davis, *Managed by the Markets*, 3.

64. Madrick, *Age of Greed*, 24.

65. Ibid., 107.

66. "A Monster Merger," editorial, *New York Times*, April 8, 1998.

67. Barnaby J. Feder, "Rubin's Pay Is $15 Million, Says Citigroup Proxy Filing," *New York Times*, March 7, 2000.

68. Joseph Stiglitz, *The Roaring Nineties: A New History of the World's Most Prosperous Decade* (New York: Norton, 2004), 164–66, 242–45, 261.

69. Ibid., 164–66.

70. Charles Gasparino, "Inquiry into Salomon Widens to Include Possible Weill Role," *Wall Street Journal*, August 23, 2002.

71. Gretchen Morgenson and Patrick McGeehan, "Wall St. and the Nursery School: A New York Story," *New York Times*, November 14, 2002.

72. Gillian Tett, *Fool's Gold: The Inside Story of J.P. Morgan and How Wall Street Greed Corrupted Its Bold Dream and Created a Financial Catastrophe* (New York: Free Press, 2010), 97.

73. My favorites include Alan Blinder, *After the Music Stopped: The Financial Crisis, the Response, and the Work Ahead* (New York: Penguin Press, 2013); and Martin Wolf, *The Shifts and the Shocks: What We've Learned—and Have Still to Learn—from the Financial Crisis* (New York: Penguin Press, 2014). For specifics on the complex securitization leading up to the crisis, see Charles R. Morris, *The Two Trillion Dollar Meltdown: Easy Money, High Rollers, and the Great Credit Crash* (New York: PublicAffairs, 2009); and Tett, *Fool's Gold*.

74. Author interview with Warren for this book.

75. Luigi Zingales, "Does Finance Benefit Society?" Working Paper 20894, National Bureau of Economic Research, January 2015, 42.

CHAPTER 2: THE FALL OF BUSINESS

1. Rana Foroohar, "Mary Barra's Bumpy Ride at the Wheel of GM," *Time*, September 25, 2014; author interviews with Barra.

2. Patricia Hurtado and David Welch, "GM to Pay $900 Million to End U.S. Switch-Defect Probe," *Bloomberg Business*, September 17, 2015.

3. Anton R. Valukas, Jenner & Block, "Report to Board of Directors of General Motors Company Regarding Ignition Switch Recalls," May 29, 2014 (hereinafter, "Valukas report"), 255.

4. Figures from GM's 2003 and 2007 annual reports, cited in the Valukas report, 22.

5. Ibid., 250.

6. Ibid., 22.

7. Gillian Tett, *The Silo Effect: The Peril of Expertise and the Promise of Breaking Down Barriers* (New York: Simon & Schuster, 2015).

8. Bob Lutz, *Car Guys vs. Bean Counters: The Battle for the Soul of American Business* (New York: Portfolio/Penguin, 2011), x and 130.

9. Jonathan Weisman, "Biggest Automaker Needs Big Changes," *Washington Post*, June 11, 2005.

10. Justin Hyde, "First Pontiac Aztek's Sale Highlights the Long Half-Life of Ugly," Motoramic, *Yahoo Autos*, August 1, 2013.

11. Lutz, *Car Guys vs. Bean Counters*, 73.

12. Robert D. Atkinson and Stephen J. Ezell, *Innovation Economics: The Race for Global Advantage* (New Haven, CT: Yale University Press, 2012), 22.

13. Gary Rivlin and John Markoff, "Tossing Out a Chief Executive," *New York Times*, February 14, 2005.

14. Kimberly D. Elsbach, Ileana Stigliani, and Amy Stroud, "The Building of Employee Distrust: A Case Study of Hewlett-Packard from 1995 to 2010," *Organizational Dynamics* 41, no. 3 (2012): 254–63.

15. Alfred Sloan, *My Years with General Motors*, reissue ed. (New York: Doubleday, 1990), 62 (emphasis added).

16. *Dodge v. Ford Motor Co.*, 170 N.W. 668 (1919).

17. Standard & Poor's Ratings Services calculated that American nonfinancial companies held $1.82 trillion in cash at the end of 2014. See Vipal Monga, "Record Cash Hoard Concentrated Among Few Companies," *Wall Street Journal*, June 11, 2015.

18. Frederick Winslow Taylor, *The Principles of Scientific Management* (New York: Harper, 1913), 59.

19. Frederick Winslow Taylor, *Shop Management* (New York: Harper, 1912), 99 and 104.

20. Robert R. Locke and J. C. Spender, *Confronting Managerialism: How the Business Elite and Their Schools Threw Our Lives out of Balance* (London: Zed Books, 2011).

21. Ibid., 5.

22. Taylor, *The Principles of Scientific Management*, 7.

23. David Halberstam, *The Best and the Brightest*, 20th anniversary ed. (New York: Ballantine Books, 2008).

24. Peter F. Drucker, *Concept of the Corporation* (New York: John Day, 1946).

25. Andrea Gabor, *The Capitalist Philosophers: The Geniuses of Modern Business—Their Lives, Times, and Ideas* (New York: Times Business, 2000), 135.

26. John A. Byrne, *The Whiz Kids: The Founding Fathers of American Business—and the Legacy They Left Us* (New York: Doubleday, 1993), 36.

27. Ibid., 50; Abraham Zaleznik, "The Education of Robert S. McNamara, Secretary of Defense, 1961–1968," *Revue Française de Gestion* 6, no. 159 (2005).

28. David R. Jardini, "Out of the Blue Yonder: The RAND Corporation's Diversification into Social Welfare Research, 1946–1968" (PhD diss., Carnegie Mellon University, 1996); Gabor, *The Capitalist Philosophers*, 136.

29. E. J. Barlow, "Preliminary Proposal for Air Defense Study," RAND Archives D(L)-816-2, October 1950, quoted in Jardini, "Out of the Blue Yonder," 67.

30. Halberstam, *The Best and the Brightest*, 229–30.

31. Byrne, *The Whiz Kids*, 175.

32. David Halberstam, *The Reckoning* (New York: William Morrow, 1986), 207.

33. Deborah Shapley, *Promise and Power: The Life and Times of Robert McNamara* (Boston: Little, Brown, 1993), 66.

34. Byrne, *The Whiz Kids*, 367.

35. Shapley, *Promise and Power*, 48.

36. Byrne, *The Whiz Kids*, 217.

37. Halberstam, *The Reckoning*, 224.

38. Ibid., 226–27.

39. John Asker, Joan Farre-Mensa, and Alexander Ljungqvist, "Comparing the Investment Behavior of Public and Private Firms," Working Paper No. 17394, National Bureau of Economic Research, September 2011.

40. Susan Helper and Rebecca Henderson, "Management Practices, Relational Contracts and the Decline of General Motors," Working Paper No. 14-062, Harvard Business School, January 28, 2014, 17.

41. Halberstam, *The Reckoning*, 245.

42. Byrne, *The Whiz Kids*, 337.

43. Halberstam, *The Reckoning*, 245.

44. Byrne, *The Whiz Kids*, 363.

45. Gabor, *The Capitalist Philosophers*, 140.

46. Halberstam, *The Best and the Brightest*, 214.

47. Robert H. Hayes and William J. Abernathy, "Managing Our Way to Economic Decline: Modern Management Principles May Cause Rather than Cure Sluggish Economic Performance," *Harvard Business Review* 58, no. 4 (1980): 67–77.

48. Byrne, *The Whiz Kids*, 432.

49. Gabor, *The Capitalist Philosophers*, 150.

50. Byrne, *The Whiz Kids*, 432–34.

51. Margaret Heffernan, *A Bigger Prize: How We Can Do Better than the Competition* (New York: PublicAffairs, 2014).

CHAPTER 3: WHAT AN MBA WON'T TEACH YOU

1. Author interviews with Lo for this book.

2. Per second quarter of fiscal year 2015.

3. Rana Foroohar, "Why Hillary Clinton Is Right About Pfizer," *Time*, November 24, 2015.

4. Morgan Stanley Research Europe, "Pharmaceuticals: Exit Research and Create Value," January 20, 2010.

5. Gretchen Morgenson, "Valeant's Fantastic(al) Numbers," *New York Times*, November 1, 2015.

6. Andrew Lo, presentation at the Future of Finance Conference, Yale School of Management, September 2015.

7. Although corporate R&D as a share of GDP grew by 3 percent between 1999 and 2006, this growth was far outpaced by the progress achieved by countries such as Germany (11 percent), Japan (27 percent), Finland (28 percent), and China (187 percent). As a result, the American share of global R&D investments declined from 39 to 34 percent in 1999–2011. See Robert D. Atkinson and Stephen J. Ezell, *Innovation Economics: The Race for Global Advantage* (New Haven, CT: Yale University Press, 2012), 22.

8. In 2008–12, new businesses in the United States accounted for 8.3 percent of the total, declining from 12.4 percent in the 1980s. See Dane Stangler, Ewing Marion Kauffman Foundation, "You Can't Scale What You Don't Start," October 17, 2014.

9. In 2004–14, labor productivity grew by an average of 1.4 percent a year, according to the Bureau of Labor Statistics—which represents half the

growth rate of the previous decade. See Scott Andes and Jessica A. Lee, "Why Is Labor Productivity So Low? Consider Investments in Skills," Brookings, May 8, 2015.

10. Gallup polls show Americans' trust in big business falling from over 30 percent of respondents (those who had a "great deal" or "quite a lot" of confidence in it) in the late 1970s to about 20 percent today. See Gallup, "Confidence in Institutions: Big Business," online at http://www.gallup.com/poll/1597/confidence-institutions.aspx (accessed November 2015).

11. Dominic Barton, "Capitalism for the Long Term," *Harvard Business Review* 89, no. 3 (March 2011).

12. Author interview with Nohria for this book.

13. Author interviews with various business school deans and professors.

14. Rana Foroohar, "The $2 Billion Boo-Boo," *Time*, May 28, 2012.

15. Author interview with Johnson for this book.

16. Norman S. Wright and Hadyn Bennett, "Business Ethics, CSR, Sustainability and the MBA," *Journal of Management & Organization* 17, no. 5 (September 2011): 646.

17. Robert G. Eccles, Ioannis Ioannou, and George Serafeim, "The Impact of Corporate Sustainability on Organizational Processes and Performance," Working Paper, Harvard Business School, November 14, 2011.

18. National Center on Education Statistics, "Table 318.30: Bachelor's, master's, and doctor's degrees conferred by postsecondary institutions, by sex of student and discipline division: 2011–12."

19. Off-the-record interview with Columbia University student for this book.

20. Author interview with Lutz for this book.

21. Robert S. Kaplan, "The Topic of Quality in Business School Education and Research," *Selections* (Autumn 1991): 13–22; Howard Rheingold, *Virtual Reality* (New York: Summit Books, 2001).

22. John R. Graham, Campbell R. Harvey, and Shivaram Rajgopal, "Value Destruction and Financial Reporting Decisions," *Financial Analysts Journal* 62, no. 6 (December 2006): 8.

23. Anthony J. Mayo, Nitin Nohria, and Laura G. Singleton, *Paths to Power: How Insiders and Outsiders Shaped American Business Leadership* (Boston: Harvard Business School Press, 2006).

24. Rakesh Khurana, *From Higher Aims to Hired Hands: The Social Transformation of American Business Schools and the Unfulfilled Promise of Management as a Profession* (Princeton, NJ: Princeton University Press, 2007), 88.

25. "Schools of Finance and Economy," *Engineering and Mining Journal* 49, no. 27 (May 24, 1890): 582.

26. Ibid., 23.

27. Locke and Spender, *Confronting Managerialism*.

28. Donald K. David, "Business Leadership and the War of Ideas," Paper presented at the Magazine Forum, April 27, 1948, quoted in Khurana, *From Higher Aims to Hired Hands*, 202.

29. "Can You Teach Management?" *BusinessWeek*, April 19, 1952, 126.

30. Sheldon Zalaznick, "The M.B.A., the Man, the Myth, and the Method," *Fortune*, May 1968.

31. John W. Boyer, "Academic Freedom and the Modern University: The Experience of the University of Chicago," Occasional Papers on Higher Education X, the College of the University of Chicago, October 2002; "Guide to the Charles R. Walgreen Foundation Records 1938-1956: Abstract," Special Collections Research Center, University of Chicago Library.

32. Marion Fourcade and Rakesh Khurana, "From Social Control to Financial Economics: The Linked Ecologies of Economics and Business in Twentieth Century America," Working paper 09-037 (Harvard Business School: 2013), 26.

33. Milton Friedman, "The Social Responsibility of Business Is to Increase Its Profits," *New York Times Magazine*, September 13, 1970.

34. The third winner of the Nobel Prize of economics that year was the University of Chicago economist Lars Peter Hansen.

35. Author interview with Shiller for this book.

36. Author interview with Lo for this book.

37. Khurana, *From Higher Aims to Hired Hands*, 298.

38. T. Boone Pickens, "Shareholders: The Forgotten People," *Journal of Business Strategy* 6, no. 1 (1985): 4.

39. Rana Foroohar, "The Original Wolf of Wall Street," *Time*, December 16, 2013.

40. Barton, "Capitalism for the Long Term."

41. Author interview with Johnson for this book.

42. Author interview with Barton for this book.

43. Business Roundtable 1990, "Corporate Governance and American Competitiveness," *Directors & Boards* 22, no. 2 (Winter 1998): 26; Business Roundtable 1997, "Statement on Corporate Governance," *Directors & Boards* 22, no. 2 (Winter 1998): 25.

44. The average tenure of a CEO in the S&P 500 ranged between 7.2 and 9.7 years in the past decade. See Conference Board, "Departing CEO tenure (2000–2013)," Chart of the Week No. 056, June 2014.

45. Aspen Institute, "Where Will They Lead? MBA Student Attitudes About Business & Society," Initiative for Social Innovation through Business, 2002.

46. Helen J. Muller, James L. Porter, and Robert R. Rehder, "Have the Business Schools Let Down U.S. Corporations?" *Management Review* 77, no. 10 (October 1988): 25–26.

47. Author interview with Nohria for this book.

48. Khurana, *From Higher Aims to Hired Hands*, 331–32.

49. Author interview with Khurana for this book.

50. Jessica Carrick-Hagenbarth and Gerald A. Epstein, "Dangerous Interconnectedness: Economists' Conflicts of Interest, Ideology, and Financial Crisis," *Cambridge Journal of Economics* 36, no. 1 (January 2012): 43–63.

51. Charles Ferguson, director, *Inside Job*, Sony Pictures Classics, 2010.

52. Charles Ferguson, "Romney's Other Credibility Problem: Glenn Hubbard," *Huffington Post*, October 27, 2012.

53. Goldman Sachs Global Markets Institute, "How Capital Markets Enhance Economic Performance and Facilitate Job Creation," by William C. Dudley and R. Glenn Hubbard, November 2004.

54. Khurana, *From Higher Aims to Hired Hands*, 346.

55. Jesse Eisinger, "Challenging the Long-Held Belief in 'Shareholder Value,'" *New York Times*, June 27, 2012. Also see LPL Financial Research, "Weekly Market Commentary," by Jeffrey Kleintop, CFA, August 6, 2012.

56. Emanuel Derman, "Apologia Pro Vita Sua," *Journal of Derivatives* 20, no. 1 (2012).

57. Author interview with Nitin Nohria, dean of Harvard Business School, for this book.

58. "MIT Facts 2016: MIT Students After Graduation," Massachusetts Institute of Technology, online at http://web.mit.edu/facts/alum.html.

59. Author interview with Smith for this book.

60. Henry Sanderson and Neil Hume, "China Funds Bring Chaos to Metals Markets," *Financial Times*, January 15, 2015; Gregory Meyer, "Bunge Says China Lenders Distorting Soybean Trade," *Financial Times*, February 12, 2015; author interview with Derman for this book, 2015.

61. Author interview with Bertolini for this book.

62. Author interview with Lo for this book.

CHAPTER 4: BARBARIANS AT THE GATE

1. Author interviews with Icahn; Rana Foroohar, "The Original Wolf of Wall Street," *Time*, December 16, 2013.

2. Securities and Exchange Commission, Definitive Proxy Statement, Schedule 14A, Apple Inc., January 9, 2015.

3. Matt Levine, "Apple Bonds and Endless Mortgage Suits," *Bloomberg View*, June 5, 2015; Ahmed and Childs, "Apple Is the New PIMCO and Tim Cook Is the New King of Bonds."

4. Interview with OFR economists and analysts for this book.

5. William Lazonick, Mariana Mazzucato, and Oner Tulum, "Apple's Changing Business Model: What Should the World's Richest Company Do with All Those Profits?" *Accounting Forum* 37, no. 4 (2013): 249–67.

6. Edward N. Wolff, "Household Wealth Trends in the United States, 1962–2013: What Happened Over the Great Recession?" National Bureau of Economic Research, Working Paper No. 20733 (December 2014), 56; Apple, Inc., "Apple Expands Capital Return Program to $200 Billion," press release, April 27, 2015.

7. Lazonick, Mazzucato, and Tulum, "Apple's Changing Business Model."

8. Data compiled by Mustafa Erdem Sakinç of the Academic-Industry Research Network; author interview with William Lazonick for this book.

9. Author interview with Stiglitz for this book.

10. Hillary Clinton, "Moving Beyond Quarterly Capitalism," lecture, New York University, July 24, 2015 (also published online on Medium.com).

11. Andrew Smithers, *The Road to Recovery: How and Why Economic Policy Must Change* (Chichester, England: Wiley, 2013).

12. Michael Spence and Sandile Hlatshwayo, "The Evolving Structure of the American Economy and the Employment Challenge," Working Paper, Council on Foreign Relations, March 2011, 13.

13. Mason, "Disgorge the Cash," 32.

14. Author interview with Haldane for this book.

15. Mason, "Disgorge the Cash."

16. William Lazonick, "Labor in the Twenty-First Century: The Top 0.1% and the Disappearing Middle-Class," Working Paper No. 4, Institute for New Economic Thinking, February 2015.

17. Bryan Burrough and John Helyar, *Barbarians at the Gate: The Fall of RJR Nabisco* (New York: Harper & Row, 1990).

18. Jia Lynn Yang, "Maximizing Shareholder Value: The Goal That Changed Corporate America," *Washington Post*, August 26, 2013; author interviews with Cornell Law School professor Lynn Stout.

19. Stiglitz, *The Roaring Nineties*, 115–17.

20. Author interview with Stiglitz for this book.

21. Lazonick, Mazzucato, and Tulum, "Apple's Changing Business Model," 30.

22. William Lazonick, "Stock Buybacks: From Retain-and-Reinvest to Downsize-and-Distribute," Brookings, April 2015.

23. This data is for 458 companies; it appeared in the S&P 500 index in February 2015 and had been publicly listed between 2005 and 2014.

See William Lazonick, "Cash Distributions to Shareholders (2005–2014) & Corporate Executive Pay (2006–2014)," Research Update #2, Academic-Industry Research Network, August 2015. See also Maxwell Murphy, "Record Year for S&P 500 Dividends, Buybacks Combined," *The Wall Street Journal*, March 23, 2015.

24. Karen Brettell, David Gaffens, and David Rohde, "The Cannibalized Company: How the Cult of Shareholder Value Has Reshaped Corporate America," Reuters, November 16, 2015.

25. Research by Andrew Smithers, 2014.

26. Matt Hopkins and William Lazonick, "Who Invests in the High Tech Knowledge Base?" Working Paper No. 14-09/01, Academic-Industry Research Network, October 2014.

27. Andrew Smithers, "Buybacks and the Parallel Universe of Bankers," *Financial Times*, November 5, 2014; author interview with Smithers for this book.

28. Mason, "Disgorge the Cash," 25.

29. Shai Bernstein, "Does Going Public Affect Innovation?" *Journal of Finance* 70, no. 4 (2015): 1365–1403.

30. John Asker, Joan Farre-Mensa, and Alexander Ljungqvist, "Comparing the Investment Behavior of Public and Private Firms," Working Paper No. 17394, the National Bureau of Economic Research, September 2011.

31. PricewaterhouseCoopers, "Trendsetter Barometer: Business Outlook 1Q 2015," April 2015, 4–5.

32. Author interview with Lutz, 2014.

33. Benny Evangelista, "Apple's Quarterly Profits Sliced in Half," *San Francisco Chronicle*, July 17, 2002; Dominic Barton, "Capitalism for the Long Term," *Harvard Business Review* (March 2011).

34. Author interviews with Schultz, 2015; Rana Foroohar, "Starbucks for America," *Time*, February 5, 2015.

35. Author interview with Palmisano for this book, 2014.

36. Andrew Ross Sorkin, "The Truth Hidden by IBM's Buybacks," *New York Times*, October 20, 2014.

37. Author interview with Smithers for this book.

38. John C. Bogle, "Wall St's Illusion on Historical Performance," *Financial Times*, March 30, 2011.

39. According to the State Budget Crisis Task Force, cochaired by former Fed chairman Paul Volcker, about 25 percent of the actuarial liabilities of the country's major state and local pension plans are unfunded—meaning that the plans won't be able to meet one-quarter of their obligations to pensioners based on current market returns. See State Budget Crisis Task Force, "Full Report," July 31, 2012, 35–36.

40. Hedge Fund Research data, as quoted in J.P. Morgan, "The 2015 U.S. Proxy Season Through the Activist Lens," August 2015.

41. Hedge Fund Research data, as quoted in Inyoung Hwang, "Activists Now Cross the Pond to Jolt Europe's Stuffy Boardrooms," *Bloomberg Business*, May 12, 2015.

42. Ajay Khorana et al, Citi, "Rising Tide of Global Shareholder Activism," October 2013, 14.

43. Michael J. de la Merced, "Timken Agrees to Split in Two After Pressure from Activist Investors," *New York Times*, September 5, 2013.

44. Data based on annual statements of the Timken Company for 2010–12 filed with the Securities and Exchange Commission.

45. U.S. Economic Development Administration, "U.S. Commerce Department to Celebrate American Manufacturing," Press release, September 30, 2015.

46. This estimate was calculated by Swiss Re, a global reinsurance company. See Swiss Re, "Annual Report 2014," March 2015, 30.

47. Ted Berg, Office of Financial Research, "Quicksilver Markets," March 2015, 7.

48. Ibid.

49. Quoted in "BlackRock CEO Warns Top U.S. Firms: Don't Overdo Dividends, Buybacks," Reuters, March 26, 2014.

50. Dealogic, "Global M&A Review: First Quarter 2015," April 2015.

51. Foroohar, "The Original Wolf of Wall Street."

52. Author interviews; Foroohar, "The Original Wolf of Wall Street."

53. John C. Coffee and Darius Palia, "The Impact of Hedge Fund Activism: Evidence and Implications," Columbia Law School Working Paper no. 489, September 15, 2014.

54. Khorana et al., Citi, "Rising Tide of Global Shareholder Activism," 7.

55. Joseph R. Blasi, Richard B. Freeman, and Douglas L. Kruse, *The Citizen's Share: Putting Ownership Back into Democracy* (New Haven, CT: Yale University Press, 2013).

56. Joseph Blasi, "Profit Sharing: Labor's New Opportunity," *Huffington Post Business*, September 6, 2015; author interviews with Blasi for this book.

57. Patrick Michael Rooney, "Worker Participation in Employee Owned Firms," *Journal of Economic Issues* 22, no. 2 (June 1988): 451–58.

58. Malcolm Gladwell, *The Tipping Point: How Little Things Can Make a Big Difference* (Boston: Little, Brown, 2000).

59. Michael Schuman, "How Germany Became the China of Europe," *Time*, February 24, 2011.

60. Cook made the remark during his address at the 2015 Goldman Sachs Technology and Internet Conference in San Francisco. See Tim Higgins, "Apple CEO Cook Says Company Doesn't Want to Hoard Cash," *Bloomberg Business*, February 10, 2015.

61. Liz Moyer, *New York Times*, "Carl Icahn Says He Has Sold Stake in Apple Over China Concerns," April 28, 2016.

CHAPTER 5: WE'RE ALL BANKERS NOW

1. General Electric, "GE at Electrical Products Group Conference," edited transcript, May 20, 2015. Online at https://www.ge.com/sites/default/files/ge_webcast_transcript_05202015_0.pdf.

2. John Cassidy, "Gut Punch: How Great Was Jack Welch?" *New Yorker*, October 1, 2001.

3. Robert Slater, *Jack Welch and the GE Way: Management Insights and Leadership Secrets of the Legendary CEO* (New York: McGraw-Hill, 1999), 112.

4. Rachel Layne and Rebecca Christie, "GE Wins FDIC Insurance for Up to $139 Billion in Debt (Update 3)," Bloomberg, November 12, 2008.

5. Author interview with Buffett for this book.

6. Krippner, *Capitalizing on Crisis*, 28–29.

7. Ibid., 34–41.

8. Data from ibid., chapter 1. See also Ozgur Orhangazi, "Financialisation and Capital Accumulation in the Non-financial Corporate Sector: A Theoretical and Empirical Investigation on the US Economy: 1973–2003," *Cambridge Journal of Economics* 38, no. 6 (November 2008); Office of Financial Research; and Mason, "Disgorge the Cash."

9. Krippner, *Capitalizing on Crisis*, 3–4, citing Julie Froud et al., *Financialization and Strategy: Narrative and Numbers* (London: Routledge, 2006).

10. "How Money Got Weird," *Planet Money* podcast, NPR, September 30, 2011. See also Satyajit Das, *Extreme Money: Masters of the Universe and the Cult of Risk* (Upper Saddle River, NJ: FT Press, 2011).

11. Catherine Ngai and Jeffrey Dastin, "U.S. Airlines Confront Cheap Oil's Flip Side: Costly Hedges," Reuters, December 23, 2014.

12. Author interview with Buffett for this book.

13. Author interview with Sharma for this book.

14. Dietrich Domanski, Jonathan Kearns, Marco Jacopo Lombardi, and Hyun Song Shin, "Oil and Debt," *BIS Quarterly Review*, Bank for International Settlements, March 2015.

15. Jonathan Leff, "Insight: Wall Street's Energy Rivals—Big Oil, a French Utility, the Koch Brothers," Reuters, December 15, 2013.

16. Rana Foroohar, "Big Oil's Big Problem," *Newsweek*, October 29, 2006; additional author reporting.

17. Javier Blas, "How Big Oil Is Profiting from the Slump," *Bloomberg Business*, March 11, 2015.

18. J. W. Mason, "Disgorge the Cash."

19. Richard Waters, "New Google CFO Promises More Discipline," *Financial Times*, July 16, 2015.

20. Christopher Farrell and Jeffrey M. Laderman, "Wringing More Profits from Idle Corporate Cash," *BusinessWeek*, May 12, 1986, 86; cited in Krippner, *Capitalizing on Crisis*, 55.

21. Quentin Hardy, "At Kodak, Clinging to a Future Beyond Film," *New York Times*, March 20, 2015.

22. "Remember When Companies Actually Created Products?" *Wall Street Journal*, September 18, 1997, cited in Davis, *Managed by the Markets*, 86.

23. Jack Welch, *Jack: Straight from the Gut*, with John A. Byrne (New York: Warner Books, 2003).

24. James Surowiecki, "Back to Basics," *New Yorker*, May 4, 2015.

25. Matt Murray, "Why Jack Welch's Brand of Leadership Matters," *Wall Street Journal*, September 5, 2001; Thomas J. Lueck, "Why Jack Welch Is Changing GE," *New York Times*, May 5, 1985.

26. "A Hard Act to Follow," *Economist*, June 28, 2014.

27. Jonathan Laing, "Jack's Magic," *Barron's*, December 26, 2005.

28. Madrick, *Age of Greed*, 199.

29. For an in-depth account of those cases, see Stiglitz, *The Roaring Nineties*, chapters 5 and 10.

30. Matthew Mosk, "Wal-Mart Fires Supplier After Bangladesh Revelation," ABC News, May 15, 2013; Steven Greenhouse, "As Firms Line Up on Factories, Wal-Mart Plans Solo Effort," *New York Times*, May 14, 2013.

31. Trish Gyorey, Matt Jochim, and Sabina Norton, "The challenges ahead for supply chains: McKinsey Global Survey results," McKinsey & Company, November 2010.

32. Author interview with Mukunda; Gautam Mukunda, "The Price of Wall Street's Power," *Harvard Business Review* 92, no. 6 (June 2014).

33. Martha C. White, "Is the Dreamliner Becoming a Financial Nightmare for Boeing?" *Time*, January 17, 2013; Christopher M. Muellerleile, "Financialization Takes Off at Boeing," *Journal of Economic Geography* (2009): 663–77; Kyle Peterson, "A Wing and a Prayer: Outsourcing at Boeing," Reuters, special report, January 2011; Christopher Tang and Joshua Zimmerman, "Managing New Product Development and Supply Chain Risks: The Boeing 787 Case," *Supply Chain Forum* 10, no. 2 (2009).

34. Margaret Heffernan's book, *Beyond Measure: The Big Impact of Small Changes* (New York: TED Books, 2015), gives a good summary of this

research and recounts several anecdotes about firms that actually support teams over individuals.

35. Heffernan, *Beyond Measure*, 96

36. John Curran, "GE Capital: Jack Welch's Secret Weapon," *Fortune*, November 10, 1997.

37. Martha Lagace, "Jack Welch to HBS Grads: 'Don't Be a Jerk,'" *Working Knowledge*, June 11, 2001.

38. Davis, *Managed by the Markets*, 84–85.

39. The President's Commission on Industrial Competitiveness, "Global Competition: The New Reality," Washington DC, January 1985, vol. 1, 12.

40. Author interview with Michael Sekora, former head of Project Socrates; Ronald E. Yates, "For Some Executives, 'Trade Wars' Taking on a Literal Meaning," *Chicago Tribune*, July 5, 1992.

41. "Jack and Suzy Welch: Why Strong Leadership Is about Truth and Trust," Knowledge@Wharton podcast, May 8, 2015.

42. Author interview with Bornstein for this book, 2014.

43. Randall W. Forsyth, "Immelt Unlearns Lessons from Citi's Wriston as GE Exits Finance," *Barron's*, April 14, 2015.

44. Michael J. de la Merced and Andrew Ross Sorkin, "G.E. to Retreat from Finance in Post-Crisis Reorganization," *New York Times*, April 10, 2015.

45. Steve Lohr, "General Electric Reports Rise in Industrial Profit," *New York Times*, July 17, 2015.

46. Yuval Atsmon et al., "Winning the $30 Trillion Decathlon: Going for Gold in Emerging Markets," *McKinsey Quarterly*, August 2012.

47. Author interview with Bornstein for this book, 2014.

48. Author interview with Little for this book.

49. National Science Foundation, "Business Research and Development and Innovation: 2012," statistical tables (updated October 29, 2015).

50. Rana Foroohar and Bill Saporito, "Made in the U.S.A.," *Time*, April 22, 2013.

51. Author interview with Little for this book.

52. Foroohar and Saporito, "Made in the U.S.A."

CHAPTER 6: FINANCIAL WEAPONS OF MASS DESTRUCTION

1. Author interviews; see also World Food Programme, "Frequently Asked Questions about Fill the Cup," February 7, 2008.

2. Rana Foroohar, "Half the World Lives with Double Digit Inflation," *Newsweek*, August 1, 2008.

3. The year 1845 was when the magazine began keeping count. See "The End of Cheap Food," *Economist*, December 6, 2007.

4. Testimony of Senator Bernard Sanders before the Commodity Futures Trading Commission on Energy Positions Limits and Hedge Exemptions, July 28, 2009.

5. "Letter to President Obama on the Global Food Crisis," March 24, 2009. Online at http://namanet.org/files/documents/food%20Crisis%20 letter%2003-24-08.pdf.

6. Michael Masters, testimony before the US Senate Committee on Agriculture, Nutrition, and Forestry, US Senate, June 4, 2009.

7. Jayne O'Donnell, "Wal-Mart CEO Bill Simon Expects Inflation," *USA Today*, April 1, 2011.

8. US Department of Agriculture, "Food Insecurity in Households with Children: Prevalence, Severity, and Household Characteristics, 2010-11," Economic Information Bulletin No. 113, May 2013.

9. Rana Foroohar, "Hunger: The Biggest Crisis of All," *Newsweek*, May 10, 2008.

10. Frederick Kaufman, "How Goldman Sachs Created the Food Crisis," *Foreign Policy*, April 27, 2011.

11. Saule Omarova, "The Merchants of Wall Street: Banking, Commerce, and Commodities," *Minnesota Law Review* 98, no. 1 (2013): 265–355.

12. Quoted in Kate Kelly, *The Secret Club That Runs the World: Inside the Fraternity of Commodities Traders* (New York: Portfolio/Penguin, 2014).

13. Omarova, "The Merchants of Wall Street."

14. Karen McBeth, "U.S. Senators, Goldman Officials Debate if Aluminum Warehouse Deals Hiked Premium," *Platts Metals Daily*, November 20, 2014.

15. David Kocieniewski, "A Shuffle of Aluminum, but to Banks, Pure Gold," *New York Times*, July 20, 2013.

16. Kelly, *The Secret Club That Runs the World*, 151.

17. J. C. Reindl, "Goldman Sachs Sells Its Network of Detroit Warehouses," *Detroit Free Press*, January 18, 2015.

18. Kocieniewski, "A Shuffle of Aluminum."

19. Ibid.

20. Pratima Desai, Clare Baldwin, Susan Thomas, and Melanie Burton, "Heavy Metals; Goldman Sachs Turns Aluminum and Warehouses into Money Machines," Reuters, July 29, 2011; Kocieniewski, "A Shuffle of Aluminum."

21. Ryan Tracy and Christian Berthelsen, "Banks Face Senate Grilling on Commodity Deals," *Wall Street Journal*, November 20, 2014.

22. Author interview with Omarova for this book.

23. Author interview with Gensler for this book.

24. Rana Foroohar, "The Myth of Financial Reform," *Time*, September 23, 2012.

25. Michael Masters, testimony before the Committee on Homeland Security and Governmental Affairs, US Senate, May 20, 2008.

26. Gregory Meyer and John Authers, "Revaluing Commodities," *Financial Times,* June 3, 2015.

27. Michael Masters, testimony before the Committee on Homeland Security and Governmental Affairs, US Senate, May 20, 2008.

28. Ibid.

29. BIS data as well as author interviews with Ruchir Sharma, head of emerging markets at Morgan Stanley Investment Management.

30. Dietrich Domanski, Jonathan Kearns, Marco Jacopo Lombardi, and Hyun Song Shin, "Oil and Debt," *BIS Quarterly Review,* Bank for International Settlements, March 2015.

31. Frederick Kaufman, "The Food Bubble: How Wall Street Starved Millions and Got Away With It," *Harper's,* July 2010.

32. According to BIS statistical releases, as of December 2014, the share of OTC derivatives trades cleared through central counterparties was 29 percent.

33. Kelly, *The Secret Club That Runs the World,* 149–50.

34. "Morgan Stanley May Sell Part of Commods Unit: CNBC," Reuters, June 6, 2012.

35. Omarova, "The Merchants of Wall Street," 314.

36. Norbert Haring and Niall Douglas, *Economists and the Powerful: Convenient Theories, Distorted Facts, Ample Rewards* (New York: Anthem Press, 2012), 89–95.

37. Lynn Stout, "Regulate OTC Derivatives by Deregulating Them," *Regulation* 32, no. 3 (Fall 2009).

38. Author interview with Stout for this book, 2015.

39. Omarova, "The Merchants of Wall Street," 318–19.

40. Representative Bart Stupak, testimony during the Commodity Futures Trading Commission hearing on energy position limits and hedge exceptions, July 28, 2009.

41. Author interview with Charles Morris, former banker, derivatives expert, and author of *The Two Trillion Dollar Meltdown.*

42. Kelly, *The Secret Club That Runs the World,* 153.

43. Ye Xie, "Goldman Sachs Hands Clients Losses in 'Top Trades,'" Bloomberg, May 19, 2010.

44. Stout, "Regulate OTC Derivatives by Deregulating Them."

45. Bank for International Settlements, "OTC Derivatives Statistics at end-December 2014," April 2015.

46. Author interview with Gensler for this book.

47. United States Senate Permanent Subcommittee on Investigations, "Wall Street Bank Involvement with Physical Commodities: Majority and Minority Staff Report," November 2014, 220.

48. Nathaniel Popper and Peter Eavis, "Senate Report Finds Banks Can Influence Commodities," *New York Times,* November 20, 2014; Tracy and Berthelsen, "Banks Face Senate Grilling on Commodity Deals"; Brian Wingfield and Dawn Kopecki, "JPMorgan to Pay $410 Million in US FERC Settlement," *Bloomberg Business,* July 30, 2013.

49. Popper and Eavis, "Senate Report Finds Banks Can Influence Commodities."

50. Michael Patterson, prepared testimony before the Senate Banking Committee, Hearing on Financial Services Modernization, February 25, 1999.

51. Omarova, "The Merchants of Wall Street," 288.

52. Author interview with Madden for this book.

53. Saule Omarova, "Financial Holding Companies' Activities in Physical Commodity Markets: Key Issues from the Perspective of US Banking Law and Policy," written testimony before the US Senate Committee on Homeland Security and Governmental Affairs, Permanent Subcommittee on Investigations, November 21, 2014.

54. Author interview with Gensler for this book.

55. Author interview with Omarova for this book, 2015.

56. Author interview with Stiglitz for this book.

57. "Metal Bashing," *Economist,* August 17, 2013; Matt Taibbi, "The Vampire Squid Strikes Again: The Mega Banks' Most Devious Scam Yet," *Rolling Stone,* February, 12, 2014.

58. United States Senate Permanent Subcommittee on Investigations, "Wall Street Bank Involvement with Physical Commodities: Majority and Minority Staff Report," November 2014, 378.

59. Omarova, "The Merchants of Wall Street," 324–33.

60. CFTC staff size hovered around 600 in 1997–2000. (See "CFTC Says Low Salaries, Retirements to Take Toll," *Wall Street Journal,* September 17, 1997.) The sizes of the US futures market and swaps market are based on CFTC estimates as of June 2015.

61. Taibbi, "The Vampire Squid Strikes Again."

62. Gina Chon, Caroline Binham, and Laura Noonan, "Six Banks Fined Total of $5.6 Billion over Rigging of Forex Markets," *Financial Times,* May 21, 2015.

63. Bank for International Settlements statistics, April 2014.

64. Barney Jopson and Gregory Meyer, "Banks Face Capital Call for Commodity Disaster Costs," *Financial Times,* November 4, 2015.

65. Michael J. Moore, "Morgan Stanley Agrees to Sell TransMontaigne Stake to NGL," *Bloomberg Business,* June 9, 2014.

66. Author interview with Donner for this book.

67. Popper and Eavis, "Senate Report Finds Banks Can Influence Commodities."

68. Kelly, *The Secret Club That Runs the World*, 151.

69. Josette Sheeran, "Ending Hunger Now," TED Talk, July 2011.

CHAPTER 7: WHEN WALL STREET OWNS MAIN STREET

1. Rana Foroohar, "A Tale of Two California Cities," *Time*, October 2, 2012.

2. Right to the City Alliance, "Renting from Wall Street," a report of the Homes for All Campaign, July 2014.

3. John Gittelsohn and Heather Perlberg, "Blackstone's Home Buying Binge Ends as Prices Surge," *Bloomberg Business*, March 14, 2014.

4. Blackstone, "Third Quarter 2015 Earnings Call," October 15, 2015.

5. Matt Scully, "New Uncertainty in Housing as Investors Seek Maximum Profits," *American Banker*, March 2, 2015; Eliot Brown, "Blackstone's Real Estate Muscle on Display in GE Deal: Private-Equity Company's Scale in the Property Market Is 'Unmatched,'" *Wall Street Journal*, April 12, 2015.

6. National Association of Realtors, "Existing-Home Sales Maintain Solid Growth in July," August 20, 2015.

7. U.S. Census Bureau, "Residential Vacancies and Homeownership in the Third Quarter 2015," October 27, 2015; "Housing in a Changing and Aging US: A Primer on the US Housing Stock," Bank of America/Merrill Lynch, June 23, 2015.

8. Louise Keely and Kathy Bostjancic, "A Tale of 2000 Cities: How the Sharp Contrast Between Successful and Struggling Communities Is Reshaping America," Demand Institute, February 2014.

9. Rana Foroohar, "The Housing Mirage," *Time*, May 20, 2013.

10. Sarah Edelman, "Cash for Homes: Policy Implications of an Investor-Led Housing Recovery," Center for American Progress, September 5, 2013.

11. Fitch Ratings, "US Residential Recovery Too Fast in Some Local Economies," Fitch Wire, May 28, 2013.

12. Nathaniel Popper, "Behind the Rise in House Prices, Wall Street Buyers," *New York Times*, June 3, 2013.

13. Joint Center for Housing Studies, Harvard University, "State of the Nation's Housing: 2015" and "Projecting Trends in Severely Cost-Burdened Renters: 2015–2025."

14. Author interview with Romano for this book.

15. Center for Responsible Lending, "The State of Lending in America & Its Impact on U.S. Households," June 16, 2015.

16. National Association of Home Builders, "Healthy Housing Industry Spurs Job Growth," May 7, 2014.

17. Rana Foroohar, "Banking Is for the 1%," *Time*, August 21, 2014.

18. Elizabeth Warren, *A Fighting Chance* (New York: Picador, 2015), 118.

19. Author interview with Eileen Appelbaum, senior economist at the Center for Economic and Policy Research (CEPR), for this book.

20. Mark Zandi and Adam Kamins, "Single-Family Rental—Out of the Ashes," Moody's Analytics, June 2015.

21. Eileen Appelbaum and Rosemary Batt, *Private Equity at Work: When Wall Street Manages Main Street* (New York: Russell Sage Foundation, 2014), 15.

22. For a hilarious and disturbing lesson in the private equity business model and how it works, watch the lecture that Ludovic Phalippou (a professor at Oxford University's Saïd Business School) gave to his MBA students in 2014. The rap explanation of high finance alone is worth the effort. See Ludovic Phalippou, "Money for Nothing? The Wonderful World of Private Equity," lecture at Oxford University, October 2014, online at https://www.youtube.com/watch?v=m1paFqPIj6Q.

23. Steven J. Davis, John Haltiwanger, Ron Jarmin, Josh Lerner, and Javier Miranda, "Private Equity and Employment," Paper No. CES 08-07R, US Census Bureau Center for Economic Studies, October 2011.

24. Private Equity Growth Capital Council estimates that private-equity-backed companies employed 11.3 million people in 2015, which is roughly 7 percent of the total U.S. labor force of 157 million. See Private Equity Growth Capital Council, "PE by the Numbers," updated August 2015 Also see Jason Kelly, *The New Tycoons: Inside the Trillion Dollar Private Equity Industry That Owns Everything* (Hoboken, NJ: Bloomberg Press, 2012), 123.

25. Author interview with Eileen Appelbaum for this book.

26. Ludovic Phalippou, "Beware of Venturing into Private Equity," *Journal of Economic Perspectives* 23, no. 1 (Winter 2009): 147–66.

27. International Monetary Fund, "United States Financial System Stability Assessment," IMF Country Report No. 15/170, July 2015; OECD, *OECD Business and Finance Outlook 2015* (Paris: OECD Publishing, June 2015), 120.

28. Chris Flood and Chris Newlands, "Calpers' Private Equity Problems Pile Up," *Financial Times*, July 12, 2015.

29. Gretchen Morgenson, "A Sales Pitch Casts a Spell on Pensions," *New York Times*, November 6, 2015.

30. Charles V. Bagli and Christine Haughney, "Wide Fallout in Failed Deal for Stuyvesant Town," *New York Times*, January 25, 2010; Appelbaum and Batt, *Private Equity at Work*, 44–45.

31. Ibid., 86–89.

32. "The Rise of the Corporate Landlord: The Institutionalization of the Single-Family Rental Market and Potential Impacts on Renters," Homes for All Campaign of the Right to the City Alliance, July 2014, 13.

33. California Reinvestment Coalition, "There Goes the Neighborhood: Real Estate Investors, Wall Street, Big Banks, and Neighborhood Displacement," June 2015, 22.

34. Author interview with Edelman for this book; Edelman, "Cash for Homes."

35. California Reinvestment Coalition, "There Goes the Neighborhood."

36. The Right to the City Alliance, "Renting from Wall Street."

37. Author interview with Appelbaum and executives from the California Reinvestment Coalition for this book.

38. Jade Rahmani, Bose George, and Ryab Tomasello, "Securitization of Single-Family Rentals," *Mortgage Banking* 74, no. 5 (February 2014): 82; Matthew Goldstein, "Equity Firms Are Lending to Landlords, Signaling a Shift," *New York Times*, March 3, 2015.

39. Author interview with Appelbaum for this book.

40. Rahmani, George, and Tomasello, "Securitization of Single-Family Rentals," 81.

41. Author interview with Edelman for this book.

42. Oscar Jorda, Moritz Schularick, and Alan M. Taylor, Federal Reserve Bank of San Francisco, "The Great Mortgaging: Housing Finance, Crises, and Business Cycles," Working Paper no. 2014-23 (September 2014), 10.

43. Turner, *Between Debt and the Devil*, chapter 4.

44. Calomiris and Haber, *Fragile by Design*, 19 and chapters 6 and 7.

45. Financial Stability Board, "Global Shadow Banking Monitoring Report 2015," November 12, 2005.

46. William Alden, "Private Equity Is Top Choice of Young Wall Street Bankers," *New York Times,* December 4, 2014.

47. Kayla Tausche, "Blackstone's Housing Bet Swells to $4.5 Billion," CNBC, May 2, 2013.

48. Zandi and Kamins, "Single Family Rental—Out of the Ashes."

49. Edelman, "Cash for Homes," 8.

50. Michael Capuano addressing the Housing and Urban Development Department Oversight, June 12, 2015, online at: https://archive.org/details/CSPAN3_20150612_210000_Politics__Public_Policy_Today.

51. Author interview with Immergluck for this book.

52. Andrew Bowden (Director, Office of Compliance Inspections and Examinations), U.S. Securities and Exchange Commission, "Spreading Sunshine in Private Equity," May 6, 2014.

53. Eileen Appelbaum, "Private Equity and the SEC After Dodd-Frank," Center for Economic Policy Research, January 2015.

54. Eileen Appelbaum, "IRS Should Crack Down on Private Equity's Abusive Tax Alchemy," *Huffington Post*, April 15, 2015.

55. Edelman, "Cash for Homes"; Sarah Edelman and Julia Gordon, "5 Ways America's Newest Landlords Can Win the Public's Trust," Center for American Progress, December 18, 2014.

56. Bethany McLean, *Shaky Ground: The Strange Saga of the US Mortgage Giants* (New York: Columbia Global Reports, 2015), 118–125.

57. Rebecca Tippell et al., the Center for Global Policy Solutions and Duke University, "Beyond Broke: Why Closing the Racial Wealth Gap Is a Priority for National Economic Security," May 2014, 3.

58. Ruben Hernandez-Murillo, Andra C. Ghent, and Michael T. Owyang, "Did Affordable Housing Legislation Contribute to the Subprime Securities Boom?" Federal Reserve Bank of St. Louis, Working Paper No. 2012-005D, March 2012; Robert B. Avery and Kenneth P. Brevoort, Federal Reserve Board, "The Subprime Crisis: Is Government Housing Policy to Blame?" Division of Research and Statistics, Board of Governors of the Federal Reserve System, Working Paper No. 2011-36, August 3, 2011.

CHAPTER 8: THE END OF RETIREMENT

1. United States Government Accountability Office, "Retirement Security: Most Households Approaching Retirement Have Low Savings," GAO report no. 15-419, May 2015, 12.

2. United States Government Accountability Office, "Better Agency Coordination Could Help Small Employers Address Challenges to Plan Sponsorship," report to Congressional requesters no. GAO-12-326, March 2012.

3. Barbara A. Butrica and Mikki D. Waid, "What Are the Retirement Prospects of Middle-Class Americans?" AARP Public Policy Institute, January 2013; data from the Center for Retirement Research at Boston College.

4. Foroohar, "2030: The Year Retirement Ends," *Time*, June 19, 2014.

5. John C. Bogle, *The Clash of the Cultures: Investment vs. Speculation* (Hoboken, NJ: Wiley, 2012).

6. Ibid., 215.

7. State Budget Crisis Task Force, "Final Report," January 2014, 16.

8. Investment Company Institute, 2015 *Investment Company Fact Book* (Washington DC, 2015), 137.

9. William Sharpe, "The Arithmetic of Investment Expenses," *Financial Analysts Journal* 69, no. 2 (March/April 2013): 34–41.

10. John C. Bogle, founder of the Vanguard Group, testimony before the Finance Committee of the United States Senate (written statement), September 16, 2014.

11. John C. Bogle, "Big Money in Boston: The Commercialization of the Mutual Fund Industry," *Journal of Portfolio Management* 40, no. 4 (2013): 135.

12. Knut A. Rostad, ed., *The Man in the Arena: Vanguard Founder John C. Bogle and His Lifelong Battle to Serve Investors First* (Hoboken, NJ: Wiley, 2013), 124–25.

13. Bogle, *The Clash of the Cultures*, 111.

14. Ian Ayres and Quinn Curtis, "Beyond Diversification: The Pervasive Problem of Excessive Fees and 'Dominated Funds' in 401(k) Plans," *Yale Law Journal* 124, no. 5 (March 2015): 1501.

15. Bogle, "Big Money in Boston," 142.

16. Author interview with John Shaw Sedgwick, the son of R. Minturn Sedgwick, for this book.

17. R. Minturn Sedgwick, "The Record of Conventional Investment Management: Is There Not a Better Way?" *Financial Analysts Journal* 29, no. 4 (July–August 1973): 41–44.

18. Ameriprise Financial, "Ameriprise Financial Completes Columbia Management Acquisition," news release, May 3, 2010.

19. Bogle, *The Clash of the Cultures*, 117–18.

20. Rana Foroohar, "Why Some Men Are Big Losers," *Time*, June 10, 2013.

21. Bogle, "Big Money in Boston," 138.

22. Bogle Senate testimony, September 16, 2014.

23. Paul Samuelson, Institute Professor, Massachusetts Institute of Technology, statement before the hearing on Mutual Fund Legislation of 1967 by US Senate Committee on Banking and Currency, August 2, 1967.

24. Author interview with Buffett for this book.

25. "Against the Odds: The Costs of Actively Managed Funds Are Higher than Most Investors Realise," *Economist*, February 20, 2014.

26. Wells Fargo, "2015 Affluent Investor Survey," conducted by Harris Poll, July 2015.

27. Rana Foroohar, "2030: The Year Retirement Ends."

28. Bogle Senate testimony, September 16, 2014.

29. Sheena S. Iyengar and Mark R. Lepper, "When Choice Is Demotivating: Can One Desire Too Much of a Good Thing?" *Journal of Personality and Social Psychology* 79, no. 6 (2000): 995–1006.

30. "Prepared Statement of Monique Morrissey," in *The State of US Retirement Security: Can the Middle Class Afford to Retire?* Hearing before the US Senate Subcommittee on Economic Policy of the Committee on Banking, Housing, and Urban Affairs, March 12, 2014.

31. Federal Reserve Statistical Release, "Table L.119: Federal Government Employee Retirement Funds," Financial Accounts of the United States, online at http://www.federalreserve.gov/releases (Accessed November 2015); U.S. Bureau of Labor, "Table 2: Retirement Benefits: Access, Participation, and Take-up Rates, State and Local Government Workers," National Compensation Survey, March 2015.

32. Chris Christof, "Detroit Pension Cuts from Bankruptcy Prompt Cries of Betrayal," Bloomberg, February 5, 2015.

33. Wallace C. Turbeville, "The Detroit Bankruptcy," Demos, November 2013.

34. Wallace C. Turbeville, "Detroit Moves to the Next Phase," Demos, November 7, 2014.

35. Turbeville, "The Detroit Bankruptcy."

36. Rana Foroohar, "Detroit Turns Up," *Time*, November 13, 2014; author interviews with Turbeville; Turbeville, "The Detroit Bankruptcy."

37. Fix LA Coalition, "No Small Fees: LA Spends More on Wall Street than Our Streets," March 25, 2014.

38. "The Looting of Oakland: How Wall Street's Predatory Practices Are Costing Oakland Communities Millions and What We Can Do About It," ReFund and ReBuild Oakland Coalition, June 2013.

39. State Budget Crisis Task Force, "Final Report," 16.

40. Alicia H. Munnell, Jean-Pierre Aubry, and Mark Cafarelli, Center for Retirement Research at Boston College, "An Update on Pension Obligation Bonds," November 4, 2014.

41. Author interview with Turbeville for this book.

42. McKinsey Global Institute, "Debt and (Not Much) Deleveraging."

43. "Fund Managers Face the Spotlight of Higher Pay," editorial, *Financial Times*, February 17, 2015.

44. John Authers, "Loser's Game," *Financial Times*, December 22, 2014.

45. Foroohar, "2030: The Year Retirement Ends"; additional author reporting.

46. Robin Greenwood and David Scharfstein, "The Growth of Finance," *Journal of Economic Perspectives* 27, no. 2 (2013): 3–28.

47. Bogle, *The Clash of the Cultures*, 225.

48. Author interview with Bogle for this book.

49. Bogle Senate testimony, September 16, 2014, 9.

50. Alyssa Davis and Lawrence Mishel, "CEO Pay Continues to Rise as Typical Workers Are Paid Less," Economic Policy Institute, June 12, 2014.

51. Dunstan Prial, "Fund Managers Pressured to Be 'Better Corporate Citizens,'" Associated Press, March 9, 2000; Willard T. Carleton, James M. Nelson, and Michael Weisbach, "The Influence of Institutions on

Corporate Governance Through Private Negotiations: Evidence from TIAA-CREF," *Journal of Finance* 53, no. 4 (1998): 1335–62.

52. Adam Smith, *An Inquiry into the Nature and Causes of The Wealth of Nations*, vol. 2, edited by Edwin Cannan (London: Methuen & Co., 1904), 159.

CHAPTER 9: THE ARTFUL DODGERS

1. Vanessa Houlder and Vicent Boland, "Corporate Tax: The $240bn Black Hole," *Financial Times*, November 25, 2015.

2. Carla Mozée, "What an AstraZeneca Deal Could Do for Pfizer's 'War Chest,' Taxes," *MarketWatch*, April 28, 2014.

3. "Tracking Tax Runaways," Bloomberg, Visual Data (Updated April 13, 2015); Andrew Ross Sorkin, "Banks Cash In on Inversion Deals Intended to Elude Taxes," *New York Times*, July 28, 2014.

4. Bill George, "A Case for Rejecting Pfizer's Bid for AstraZeneca," *New York Times*, May 8, 2014.

5. Richard Rubin, "U.S. Companies Are Stashing $2.1 Trillion Overseas to Avoid Taxes," *Bloomberg Business*, March 4, 2015; Foroohar, "The $2 Billion Boo-Boo."

6. Jason Furman, chairman of the Council of Economic Advisers, "Business Tax Reform and Economic Growth," speech, New York University School of Law, September 22, 2014.

7. Mariana Mazzucato, *The Entrepreneurial State: Debunking Public Vs. Private Sector Myths* (London and New York: Anthem, 2013), 12.

8. Author reporting with an off-the-record source.

9. Michael E. Porter and Jan W. Rivkin, "An Economy Doing Half Its Job: Findings of Harvard Business School's 2013–14 Survey on U.S. Competitiveness," Harvard Business School, September 2014.

10. Rana Foroohar, "The Artful Dodgers," *Time*, September 11, 2014.

11. Ruud A. de Mooij, "Tax Biases to Debt Finance: Assessing the Problem, Finding Solutions," International Monetary Fund, IMF Staff Discussion Note No. SDN/11/11, May 3, 2011.

12. Jason Furman, "The Concept of Neutrality in Tax Policy," testimony before the U.S. Senate Committee on Finance Hearing titled "Tax: Fundamentals in Advance of Reform," April 15, 2008.

13. Author reporting; Sam Schechner, "Ireland to Close 'Double Irish' Tax Loophole," *Wall Street Journal*, October 14, 2014.

14. "A Senseless Subsidy: Ending the Debt Addiction," *Economist*, May 16, 2015.

15. David Henry, "Corporate America's New Achilles' Heel," *Newsweek*, March 27, 2005; Foster and Magdoff, *The Great Financial Crisis*, 55.

16. Ivan Vidangos, Federal Reserve Board, "Deleveraging and Recent Trends in Household Debt," April 2015.

17. Theo Francis, "5 Reasons Corporate Debt Is at a Record High," *Wall Street Journal*, August 1, 2014.

18. McKinsey Global Institute, "Debt and (Not Much) Deleveraging."

19. "A Senseless Subsidy," *Economist*.

20. Luc Laeven and Fabián Valencia, International Monetary Fund, "Systemic Banking Crises Database: An Update," Working Paper No. 12/163, June 2012.

21. A particularly compelling study was done by the economists Moritz Schularick and Alan Taylor, who looked at 140 years of data and found that "credit growth is a powerful predictor of financial crises, suggesting that such crises are 'credit booms gone wrong.'" See Moritz Schularick and Alan M. Taylor, "Credit Booms Gone Bust: Monetary Policy, Leverage Cycles, and Financial Crises, 1870–2008," National Bureau of Economic Research, Working Paper No. 15512, 2009.

22. Mian and Sufi, *House of Debt*.

23. Ibid., 4.

24. Ibid., 24.

25. Author interview with Sharma for this book.

26. Camden Hutchison, "The Historical Origins of the Debt-Equity Distinction," *Florida Tax Review*, January 2, 2015.

27. Mian and Sufi, *House of Debt*, 36.

28. "A Senseless Subsidy," *Economist*.

29. John McCormick, "Yacht Owners Seek to Salvage Deductions for Second Homes," Bloomberg, January 24, 2014.

30. Steven Davidoff Solomon, "For Some Corporate Chiefs, Private Security Is a Tax Break," *New York Times*, April 10, 2012.

31. Gillian Tett, "America Likes Living on the Edge," *Financial Times*, July 19, 2013.

32. Warren E. Buffett, "Stop Coddling the Super-Rich," *New York Times*, August 14, 2011.

33. "Warren Buffett and His Secretary on Their Tax Rates," ABC News, January 25, 2012.

34. Buffett, "Stop Coddling the Super-Rich."

35. Nicholas Kristof, "Taxes and Billionaires," *New York Times*, July 6, 2011.

36. In 2013, the Urban Institute published a short entertaining video that broke down the group that paid no federal income taxes (that year, they made up 43 percent of Americans), showing that only 1 percent could be suspected of free-riding. See Urban Institute, "Debunking Myths About

Who Pays No Federal Income Tax," video, August 29, 2013, https://www.youtube.com/watch?v=nM7orhQIzKM.

37. Author interview with Buffett for this book.

38. James Surowiecki, "The Debt Economy," *New Yorker*, November 23, 2009.

39. Asker, Farre-Mensa, and Ljungqvist, "Comparing the Investment Behavior of Public and Private Firms."

40. Smithers, *The Road to Recovery*, 15; "The Profits Prophet," *Economist*, October 5, 2013.

41. Author interview with Smithers for this book.

42. Office of Financial Research, "Quicksilver Markets," 7.

43. Author interview with Stiglitz for this book.

44. According to a 2014 study co-authored by Saez, the share of pretax personal income claimed by the top 1 percent of tax filers stood at 42 percent in 2012. Moreover, the share claimed by 0.1 percent rose from 7 percent in 1979 to 22 percent in 2012. See Saez and Zucman, "Wealth Inequality in the United States Since 1913."

45. Author interview with Stiglitz for this book.

46. Stiglitz, *The Roaring Nineties*, 178.

47. Author interview with Smithers for this book.

48. International Monetary Fund, "Tax Biases to Debt Finance."

49. Rana Foroohar, "Starbucks for America."

CHAPTER 10: THE REVOLVING DOOR

1. Steve Mufson and Tom Hamberger, "Jamie Dimon Himself Called to Urge Support for the Derivatives Rules in the Spending Bill," *Washington Post*, December 11, 2014.

2. Peter Eavis, "Wall St. Wins a Round in a Dodd-Frank Fight," *New York Times*, December 12, 2014; Mufson and Hamberger, "Jamie Dimon Himself Called."

3. Americans for Financial Reform, "Wall Street Money in Washington: Update on 2013–2014 Campaign and Lobby Spending by the Financial Sector," March 18, 2015.

4. Americans for Financial Reform data.

5. Daniel Stevens, "Wall Street Banks Contribute More than Twice as Much to Members Voting Yes on Dodd-Frank Rollback," Maplight.org, December 17, 2014.

6. Ibid.

7. OpenSecrets.org, "Lobbying, Sector Profile, 2014: Finance, Insurance & Real Estate" and "Lobbying, Sector Profile, 2014: Health" (accessed November 2015).

8. Americans for Financial Reform, "Wall Street Money in Washington: Update on 2013–2014 Campaign and Lobby Spending by the Financial Sector."

9. Chicago Booth/Kellogg School Financial Trust Index, "Financial Trust Index Reveals Public's Slipping Confidence in Banks, Government: Wave 23 Results," June 2015.

10. Luigi Zingales, "Does Finance Benefit Society?" National Bureau of Economic Research, Working Paper 20894, January 2015, 3.

11. Ben Protess, "Wall Street Continues to Spend Big on Lobbying," *New York Times*, August 1, 2011; Nancy Watzman, "Goldman Sachs, Financial Firms Flood Agencies to Influence Financial Law, New Dodd-Frank Tracker Shows," Sunlight Foundation, July 18, 2011.

12. Kimberly D. Krawiec, "Don't 'Screw Joe the Plummer [*sic*]': The Sausage-Making of Financial Reform," *Arizona Law Review* 55, no. 1 (2013): 59.

13. Tom Braithwaite and Richard Blackden, "Volcker Lambasts Wall Street Lobbying," *Financial Times*, December 19, 2014.

14. Krawiec, "Don't 'Screw Joe the Plummer,'" 79.

15. Foroohar, "The $2 Billion Boo-Boo."

16. Author tally and research from public records.

17. Author interview with Brown for this book.

18. Noam Scheiber, *The Escape Artists: How Obama's Team Fumbled the Recovery* (New York: Simon & Schuster, 2012), 3.

19. Author interview with Brown for this book.

20. Thomas Ferguson, "Legislators Never Bowl Alone: Big Money, Mass Media and the Polarization of Congress," INET Conference, Bretton Woods, New Hampshire, April 2011, 20.

21. Philippon, "Has the U.S. Finance Industry Become Less Efficient?"; Greenwood and Scharfstein, "The Growth of Finance."

22. Jake Bernstein, "Inside the New York Fed: Secret Recordings and a Culture Clash," ProPublica, September 26, 2014, published in conjunction with *This American Life*.

23. Rana Foroohar, "Our Dysfunctional Financial System," *Time*, October 2, 2014.

24. "The AIG Rescue, Its Impact on Markets, and the Government's Exit Strategy," June Oversight Report, Congressional Oversight Panel, June 10, 2010.

25. Author interview with an off-the-record source.

26. "The AIG Rescue, Its Impact on Markets, and the Government's Exit Strategy."

27. Timothy F. Geithner, *Stress Test: Reflections on Financial Crises* (New York: Crown, 2014), 334.

28. Calomiris and Haber, *Fragile by Design*, 161.

29. Ferguson, "Legislators Never Bowl Alone."

30. Andrew Haldane, "Control Rights (and Wrongs)," Wincott Annual Memorial Lecture, Westminster, London, October 24, 2011.

31. This happened, for example, to one banker in Catalonia in 1360. See Andrew G. Haldane, "Banking on the State," paper based on a presentation delivered to the Federal Reserve Bank of Chicago, 12th annual International Banking Conference, "The International Financial Crisis: Have the Rules of Finance Changed?" Chicago, September 25, 2009.

32. Author interview with Haldane for this book.

33. Author interview with Haldane; John D. Turner, *Banking in Crisis: The Rise and Fall of British Banking Stability, 1800 to the Present* (Cambridge: Cambridge University Press, 2014).

34. Haldane, "Control Rights (and Wrongs)."

35. Steven Mandis, *What Happened to Goldman Sachs? An Insider's Story of Organizational Drift and Its Unintended Consequences* (Boston: Harvard Business Review Press, 2013).

36. Peter Weinberg, "Wall Street Needs More Skin in the Game," *Wall Street Journal*, September 30, 2009.

37. Mike Konczal and Nell Abernathy, "Defining Financialization," Roosevelt Institute, July 27, 2015.

38. Rana Foroohar, "The Myth of Financial Reform," *Time*, September 23, 2013.

39. "Transcript: Attorney General Eric Holder on 'Too Big to Jail,'" *American Banker*, March 6, 2013.

40. Jed S. Rakoff, "The Financial Crisis: Why Have No High-Level Executives Been Prosecuted?" *New York Review of Books*, January 9, 2014.

41. Zingales, "Does Finance Benefit Society?" 41–42.

42. Warren, *A Fighting Chance*, 284.

43. Bryan T. Kelly, Hanno N. Lustig, and Stijn Van Nieuwerburgh, "Too-Systemic-to-Fail: What Option Markets Imply About Sector-Wide Government Guarantees," Working Paper no. 9023 (Center for Economic Policy Research: March 21, 2012), 3 and 37.

44. Zingales, "Does Finance Benefit Society?" 7.

45. Author interview with Warren for this book.

46. Foroohar, "The Myth of Financial Reform."

47. Anthony Coley, "Response to *TIME* Magazine Article on Financial Reform," US Department of the Treasury, September 13, 2013.

48. Rana Foroohar, "*Time*'s Foroohar Responds to Treasury: Our Financial System Is Not Stronger," *Time*, September 13, 2013.

49. Maureen Farrell, "Goldman Says J.P. Morgan Could Be Worth More Broken Up," *Wall Street Journal,* January 5, 2015.

50. McKinsey Global Institute data. See also Neil Irwin, "Wall Street Is Back, Almost as Big as Ever," *New York Times,* May 18, 2015; and Ratna Sahay et al., "Rethinking Financial Deepening: Stability and Growth in Emerging Markets," Staff Discussion Note no. 15/08, International Monetary Fund, May 2015.

51. Financial Stability Board, "Global Shadow Banking Monitoring Report 2015."

52. "Basel III Capital: A Well-Intended Illusion," remarks by FDIC Vice Chairman Thomas M. Hoenig to the International Association of Deposit Insurers 2013 Research Conference in Basel, Switzerland, April 9, 2013.

53. Warren, *A Fighting Chance,* 124.

54. Author interview with Warren for this book.

55. Warren, *A Fighting Chance,* 106.

56. Author interview with Brown for this book.

57. Piketty, *Capital in the Twenty-First Century,* 188.

58. Davis, *Managed by the Markets,* 235–36.

59. Author interview with Davis for this book.

60. Konczal and Abernathy, "Defining Financialization," 31.

61. Author interview with Warren for this book.

62. Paul Mason, *Postcapitalism: A Guide to Our Future* (New York: Farrar, Straus & Giroux, 2016).

63. Foroohar, "Thomas Piketty: Marx 2.0."

64. Author interview with Johnson for this book.

CHAPTER 11: HOW TO PUT FINANCE BACK IN SERVICE TO BUSINESS AND SOCIETY

1. Author interview with Gensler for this book.

2. McKinsey Global Institute data.

3. Zingales, *A Capitalism for the People,* 205.

4. More on these and other banking reform ideas can be found in the Roosevelt Institute's report by Joseph Stiglitz, "Rewriting the Rules of the American Economy: An Agenda for Growth and Shared Prosperity," May 2015.

5. Author interview with Admati for this book; Anat Admati and Martin Hellwig, *The Bankers' New Clothes: What's Wrong with Banking and What to Do About It* (Princeton, NJ: Princeton University Press, 2013); Foroohar, "The Myth of Financial Reform."

6. Thomas Hoenig, "Safe Banks Need Not Mean Slow Economic Growth," *Financial Times*, August 19, 2013.

7. Jean-Louis Arcand, Enrico Berkes, and Ugo Panizza, International Monetary Fund, "Too Much Finance?" Working Paper 12/161, June 2012.

8. Stephen G. Cecchetti and Enisse Kharroubi, "Reassessing the Impact of Finance on Growth," Working Paper No. 381, Bank for International Settlements, July 2012.

9. Mian and Sufi, *House of Debt*.

10. Turner, *Between Debt and the Devil*.

11. Robert J. Shiller, *Finance and the Good Society* (Princeton, NJ: Princeton University Press, 2012).

12. Mian and Sufi, *House of Debt*.

13. For an interesting discussion of alternative models, see chapter 16 of Richard Wilkinson and Kate Pickett, *The Spirit Level: Why Equality Is Better for Everyone* (New York: Penguin Books, 2009).

14. Asker, Farre-Mensa, and Ljungqvist, "Comparing the Investment Behavior of Public and Private Firms."

15. Fareed Zakaria, *The Post-American World* (New York: Norton, 2012).

16. Rana Foroohar, "What Hasn't Been Fixed Since the Last Market Crash?" *Time*, August 27, 2015. See also Ken Miller, "The China Bubble," *Time*, October 31, 2011.

17. Rana Foroohar, "The End of Europe," *Time*, August 22, 2011; Rana Foroohar, "Your Global Economic Mess Is Now Being Served," *Time*, June 18, 2012; Rana Foroohar, "Europe's Economic Band-Aid Won't Cure What Really Ails It," *Time*, January 22, 2015.

18. McKinsey Global Institute, "Debt and (Not Much) Deleveraging."

BIBLIOGRAPHY

Acemoglu, Daron, and James A. Robinson. *Why Nations Fail: The Origins of Power, Prosperity, and Poverty.* New York: Crown Publishers, 2012.

Admati, Anat, and Martin Hellwig. *The Bankers' New Clothes: What's Wrong with Banking and What to Do About It.* Princeton: Princeton University Press, 2013.

Akerlof, George A., and Robert J. Shiller. *Phishing for Phools: The Economics of Manipulation and Deception.* Princeton, NJ: Princeton University Press, 2015.

Anderson, Chris. *Makers: The New Industrial Revolution.* New York: Crown Business, 2012.

Appelbaum, Eileen, and Rosemary Batt. *Private Equity at Work: When Wall Street Manages Main Street.* New York: Russell Sage Foundation, 2014.

Atkinson, Anthony B. *Inequality: What Can Be Done?* Cambridge, MA: Harvard University Press, 2015.

Atkinson, Robert D., and Stephen J. Ezell. *Innovation Economics: The Race for Global Advantage.* New Haven, CT: Yale University Press, 2012.

Bair, Sheila. *Bull by the Horns: Fighting to Save Main Street from Wall Street and Wall Street from Itself.* New York: Free Press, 2012.

Balkin, Jeremy K. *Investing with Impact: Why Finance Is a Force for Good.* Brookline, MA: Bibliomotion, 2015.

Banerjee, Abhijit V., and Esther Duflo. *Poor Economics: A Radical Rethinking of the Way to Fight Global Poverty.* New York: PublicAffairs, 2011.

Barofsky, Neil M. *Bailout: How Washington Abandoned Main Street While Rescuing Wall Street.* New York: Free Press, 2013.

Bernanke, Ben. *The Federal Reserve and the Financial Crisis: Lectures by Ben S. Bernanke.* Princeton, NJ: Princeton University Press, 2013.

Blasi, Joseph R., Richard B. Freeman, and Douglas L. Kruse. *The Citizen's Share: Putting Ownership Back into Democracy.* New Haven, CT: Yale University Press, 2013.

Blight, James G., and Janet M. Lang. *The Fog of War: Lessons from the Life of Robert S. McNamara.* Lanham, MD: Rowman & Littlefield Publishers, 2005.

Blinder, Alan S. *After the Music Stopped: The Financial Crisis, the Response, and the Work Ahead.* New York: Penguin Press, 2013.

Blyth, Mark. *Austerity: The History of a Dangerous Idea.* Oxford: Oxford University Press, 2015.

Bogle, John C. *The Clash of the Cultures: Investment vs. Speculation.* Hoboken, NJ: John Wiley & Sons, 2012.

Brynjolfsson, Erik, and Andrew McAfee. *The Second Machine Age: Work, Progress, and Prosperity in a Time of Brilliant Technologies.* New York: W. W. Norton & Company, 2014.

Bughin, Jacques, and James Manyika. *Internet Matters: The Rise of the Digital Economy, Essays on Digital Transformation,* Vol. 4. N.p.: McKinsey & Company, 2013.

Burlingham, Bo. *Small Giants: Companies That Choose to Be Great Instead of Big.* New York: Portfolio, 2007.

Byrne, John A. *The Whiz Kids: The Founding Fathers of American Business—and the Legacy They Left Us.* New York: Doubleday, 1993.

Calomiris, Charles W., and Stephen H. Haber. *Fragile by Design: The Political Origins of Banking Crises and Scarce Credit.* Princeton, NJ: Princeton University Press, 2014.

Canderle, Sebastien. *Private Equity's Public Distress: The Rise and Fall of Candover and the Buyout Industry Crash.* Lexington, KY: n.p., 2011.

Carosso, Vincent P. *Investment Banking in America: A History.* Cambridge, MA: Harvard University Press, 1970.

Casey, Michael J. *The Unfair Trade: How Our Broken Global Financial System Destroys the Middle Class.* New York: Crown Business, 2012.

Clark, Gregory. *The Son Also Rises: Surnames and the History of Social Mobility.* Princeton, NJ: Princeton University Press, 2014.

Clinton, Hillary Rodham. *Hard Choices.* New York: Simon & Schuster, 2014.

Coates, John. *The Hour between Dog and Wolf: Risk-taking, Gut Feelings and the Biology of Boom and Bust.* New York: Penguin Press, 2012.

Cowen, Tyler. *Average Is Over: Powering America Beyond the Age of the Great Stagnation.* New York: DUTTON / The Penguin Group, 2013.

Das, Satyajit. *Extreme Money: Masters of the Universe and the Cult of Risk.* Upper Saddle River, NJ: FT Press, 2011.

Davis, Gerald F. *Managed by the Markets: How Finance Reshaped America.* Oxford: Oxford University Press, 2009.

Dobbs, Richard, James Manyika, and Jonathan Woetzel. *No Ordinary Disruption: The Four Global Forces Breaking All the Trends.* New York: PublicAffairs, 2015.

Ellis, Charles D., Alicia H. Munnell, and Andrew D. Eschtruth. *Falling Short: The Coming Retirement Crisis and What to Do About It.* Oxford: Oxford University Press, 2014.

Fallows, James. *China Airborne.* New York: Pantheon Books, 2012.

Faux, Jeff. *The Global Class War: How America's Bipartisan Elite Lost Our Future—and What It Will Take to Win It Back.* Hoboken, NJ: John Wiley & Sons, 2006.

Ferguson, Niall. *The House of Rothschild: Money's Prophets 1798–1848.* London: Penguin Books, 2000.

Fletcher, Ian. *Free Trade Doesn't Work: What Should Replace It and Why.* 2011 ed. Sheffield, MA: Coalition for a Prosperous America, 2011.

Ford, Martin. *Rise of the Robots: Technology and the Threat of a Jobless Future.* New York: Basic Books, 2015.

Foster, John Bellamy, and Fred Magdoff. *The Great Financial Crisis: Causes and Consequences.* New York: Monthly Review Press, 2009.

Frank, Robert H., and Philip J. Cook. *The Winner-take-all Society: Why the Few at the Top Get so Much More than the Rest of Us.* New York: Penguin Books, 1996.

Friedman, Thomas L. *The World Is Flat: A Brief History of the Twenty-first Century.* New York: Farrar, Straus and Giroux, 2005.

Gabor, Andrea. *The Capitalist Philosophers: The Geniuses of Modern Business—Their Lives, Times, and Ideas.* New York: Times Business, 2000.

Geisst, Charles R. *Wall Street: A History.* Updated ed. Oxford: Oxford University Press, 2012.

Geithner, Timothy F. *Stress Test: Reflections on Financial Crises.* New York: Crown Publishers, 2014.

Ghemawat, Pankaj. *World 3.0: Global Prosperity and How to Achieve It.* Boston: Harvard Business Review Press, 2011.

Gleeson-White, Jane. *Double Entry: How the Merchants of Venice Created Modern Finance.* New York: W. W. Norton & Company, 2012.

Gordon, John Steele. *The Great Game: The Emergence of Wall Street as a World Power, 1653–2000.* New York: Scribner, 1999.

Graeber, David. *Debt: The First 5,000 Years.* Brooklyn, NY: Melville House, 2011.

———. *The Utopia of Rules: On Technology, Stupidity and the Secret Joys of Bureaucracy.* Brooklyn: Melville House, 2015.

Greenberg, Stanley B. *America Ascendant: A Revolutionary Nation's Path to Addressing Its Deepest Problems and Leading the 21st Century.* New York: Thomas Dunne Books, 2015.

Greenspan, Alan. *The Map and the Territory: Risk, Human Nature, and the Future of Forecasting.* New York: The Penguin Press, 2013.

Hacker, Jacob S., and Paul Pierson. *Winner-take-all Politics: How Washington Made the Rich Richer—and Turned Its Back on the Middle Class.* New York: Simon & Schuster, 2010.

Halberstam, David. *The Reckoning.* New York: William Morrow and Company, 1986.

———. *The Best and the Brightest.* 20th Anniversary ed. New York: Ballantine Books, 2008.

Hammond, Bray. *Banks and Politics in America: From the Revolution to the Civil War.* Princeton, NJ: Princeton University Press, 1991.

Haring, Norbert, and Niall Douglas. *Economists and the Powerful: Convenient Theories, Distorted Facts, Ample Rewards.* New York: Anthem Press, 2012.

Hayes, Christopher. *Twilight of the Elites: America After Meritocracy.* New York: Crown Publishers, 2012.

Heffernan, Margaret. *Willful Blindness: Why We Ignore the Obvious at Our Peril.* New York: Walker & Company, 2011.

———. *Beyond Measure: The Big Impact of Small Changes.* New York: TED Books, Simon & Schuster, 2015.

Hirsh, Michael. *Capital Offense: How Washington's Wise Men Turned America's Future over to Wall Street.* Hoboken, NJ: John Wiley & Sons, 2010.

Hochschild, Arlie Russell. *The Outsourced Self: What Happens When We Pay Others to Live Our Lives for Us.* New York: Metropolitan Books, 2012.

Irwin, Neil. *The Alchemists: Three Central Bankers and a World on Fire.* New York: The Penguin Press, 2013.

Janeway, William H. *Doing Capitalism in the Innovation Economy: Markets, Speculation and the State.* Cambridge: Cambridge University Press, 2012.

Johnson, Simon, and James Kwak. *White House Burning: The Founding Fathers, the National Debt, and Why It Matters to You.* New York: Pantheon Books, 2012.

Kahneman, Daniel. *Thinking, Fast and Slow.* New York: Farrar, Straus and Giroux, 2013.

Kay, John. *Other People's Money: The Real Business of Finance.* New York: PublicAffairs, 2015.

Kelly, Jason. *The New Tycoons: Inside the Trillion Dollar Private Equity Industry That Owns Everything.* Hoboken, NJ: Bloomberg Press, 2012.

Kelly, Kate. *The Secret Club That Runs the World: Inside the Fraternity of Commodities Traders.* New York: Portfolio/Penguin, 2014.

Kelly, Marjorie. *The Divine Right of Capital: Dethroning the Corporate Aristocracy.* San Francisco: Berrett-Koehler Publishers, 2001.

Khurana, Rakesh. *From Higher Aims to Hired Hands: The Social Transformation of American Business Schools and the Unfulfilled Promise of Management as a Profession*. Princeton, NJ: Princeton University Press, 2007.

Kindleberger, Charles P., and Robert Z. Aliber. *Maniacs, Panics, and Crashes: A History of Financial Crises*. Hoboken, NJ: John Wiley & Sons, 2005.

Klaus, Ian. *Forging Capitalism: Rogues, Swindlers, Frauds, and the Rise of Modern Finance*. New Haven, CT: Yale University Press, 2014.

Krippner, Greta R. *Capitalizing on Crisis: The Political Origins of the Rise of Finance*. Cambridge, MA: Harvard University Press, 2011.

Krugman, Paul. *End This Depression Now!* New York: W. W. Norton & Company, 2012.

Lack, Simon. *The Hedge Fund Mirage: The Illusion of Big Money and Why It's Too Good to Be True*. Hoboken, NJ: John Wiley & Sons, 2012.

Lazonick, William. *Sustainable Prosperity in the New Economy? Business Organization and High-Tech Employment in the United States*. Kalamazoo, MI: W. E. Upjohn Institute for Employment Research, 2009.

Lewis, Michael. *Boomerang: Travels in the New Third World*. New York: W. W. Norton & Company, 2011.

———. *Liar's Poker: Rising Through the Wreckage on Wall Street*. 25th anniversary ed. New York: W. W. Norton & Company, 2014.

———. *Flash Boys: A Wall Street Revolt*. New York: W. W. Norton & Company, 2015.

Litan, Robert E. *Trillion Dollar Economists: How Economists and Their Ideas Have Transformed Business*. Hoboken, NJ: John Wiley & Sons, 2014.

Locke, Robert R., and J.-C. Spender. *Confronting Managerialism: How the Business Elite and Their Schools Threw Our Lives out of Balance*. London: Zed Books, 2011.

Lowenstein, Roger. *When Genius Failed: The Rise and Fall of Long-Term Capital Management*. New York: Random House Trade Paperbacks, 2011.

Lutz, Bob. *Car Guys vs. Bean Counters: The Battle for the Soul of American Business*. New York: Portfolio/Penguin, 2011.

———. *Icons and Idiots: Straight Talk on Leadership*. New York: Portfolio/Penguin, 2013.

Madrick, Jeff. *Age of Greed: The Triumph of Finance and the Decline of America, 1970 to the Present*. New York: Alfred A. Knopf, 2011.

Malkiel, Burton G. *A Random Walk Down Wall Street: The Time-Tested Strategy for Successful Investing*. 10th ed. New York: W. W. Norton & Company, 2012.

Malleson, Tom. *After Occupy: Economic Democracy for the 21st Century*. Oxford: Oxford University Press, 2009.

Mandis, Steven G. *What Happened to Goldman Sachs? An Insider's Story of Organizational Drift and Its Unintended Consequences*. Boston: Harvard Business Review Press, 2013.

Markham, Jerry W. *A Financial History of the United States: From the Subprime Crisis to the Great Recession (2006–2009).* Armonk, NY: M. E. Sharpe, 2011.

Martin, Felix. *Money: The Unauthorised Biography.* New York: Alfred A. Knopf, 2014.

Marx, Karl, and Friedrich Engels. *The Communist Manifesto.* New York: Penguin Books, 2011.

Mason, Paul. *Postcapitalism: A Guide to Our Future.* New York: Farrar, Straus and Giroux, 2016.

Mayo, Mike. *Exile on Wall Street: One Analyst's Fight to Save the Big Banks from Themselves.* Hoboken, NJ: John Wiley & Sons, 2011.

McKinsey Global Institute. "Financial Globalization: Retreat or Reset?" March, 2013.

———. "Global Flows in a Digital Age: How Trade, Finance, People, and Data Connect the World Economy." April 2014.

———. "Global Growth: Can Productivity Save the Day in an Aging World?" January 2015.

———. "Debt and (Not Much) Deleveraging." February 2015.

McLean, Bethany. *Shaky Ground: The Strange Saga of the U.S. Mortgage Giants.* New York: Columbia Global Reports, 2015.

McNamara, Robert S., and Brian VanDeMark. *In Retrospect: The Tragedy and Lessons of Vietnam.* New York: Vintage Books, 1996.

Mian, Atif, and Amir Sufi. *House of Debt: How They (and You) Caused the Great Recession, and How We Can Prevent It from Happening Again.* Chicago: University of Chicago Press, 2014.

Micklethwait, John, and Adrian Wooldridge. *The Fourth Revolution: The Global Race to Reinvent the State.* New York: Penguin Books, 2015.

Morris, Charles R. *Money, Greed, and Risk: Why Financial Crises and Crashes Happen.* New York: Times Business, 1999.

———. *The Two Trillion Dollar Meltdown: Easy Money, High Rollers, and the Great Credit Crash.* New York: PublicAffairs, 2009.

Mullainathan, Sendhil, and Eldar Shafir. *Scarcity: Why Having Too Little Means So Much.* New York: Times Books, 2013.

Nocera, Joe. *A Piece of the Action: How the Middle Class Joined the Money Class.* New York: Simon & Schuster Paperbacks, 2013.

Partnoy, Frank. *Wait: The Art and Science of Delay.* New York: PublicAffairs, 2012.

Pasquale, Frank. *The Black Box Society: The Secret Algorithms That Control Money and Information.* Cambridge, MA: Harvard University Press, 2015.

Phelps, Edmund. *Mass Flourishing: How Grassroots Innovation Created Jobs, Challenge, and Change.* Princeton, NJ: Princeton University Press, 2013.

Piketty, Thomas. *Capital in the Twenty-First Century*. Translated by Arthur Goldhammer. Cambridge, MA: Belknap Press of Harvard University Press, 2014.

———. *The Economics of Inequality*. Translated by Arthur Goldhammer. Cambridge, MA: Belknap Press of Harvard University Press, 2015.

Prins, Nomi. *All the Presidents' Bankers: The Hidden Alliances That Drive American Power*. New York: Nation Books, 2014.

Putnam, Robert D. *Our Kids: The American Dream in Crisis*. New York: Simon & Schuster, 2015.

Rajan, Raghuram G. *Fault Lines: How Hidden Fractures Still Threaten the World Economy*. Princeton, NJ: Princeton University Press, 2010.

Reich, Robert B. *Supercapitalism: The Transformation of Business, Democracy, and Everyday Life*. New York: Alfred A. Knopf, 2007.

Reinhart, Carmen M., and Kenneth S. Rogoff. *This Time Is Different: Eight Centuries of Financial Folly*. Princeton, NJ: Princeton University Press, 2009.

Roth, Alvin E. *Who Gets What—and Why: The New Economics of Matchmaking and Market Design*. Boston: Houghton Mifflin Harcourt, 2015.

Rothkopf, David. *Power, Inc.: The Epic Rivalry Between Big Business and Government—and the Reckoning That Lies Ahead*. New York: Farrar, Straus and Giroux, 2012.

Saval, Nikil. *Cubed: The Secret History of the Workplace*. New York: Doubleday, 2014.

Scheiber, Noam. *The Escape Artists: How Obama's Team Fumbled the Recovery*. New York: Simon & Schuster, 2012.

Schmidt, Eric, and Jared Cohen. *The New Digital Age: Transforming Nations, Businesses, and Our Lives*. New York: Vintage Books, 2014.

Schroeder, Alice. *The Snowball: Warren Buffett and the Business of Life*. Updated and condensed ed. New York: Bantam Books, 2009.

Schwed Jr., Fred. *Where Are the Customers' Yachts? Or A Good Hard Look at Wall Street*. Hoboken, NJ: John Wiley & Sons, 2006.

Sehgal, Kabir. *Coined: The Rich Life of Money and How Its History Has Shaped Us*. New York: Grand Central Publishing, 2015.

Shapley, Deborah. *Promise and Power: The Life and Times of Robert McNamara*. Boston: Little, Brown & Company, 1993.

Shiller, Robert J. *The Subprime Solution: How Today's Global Financial Crisis Happened, and What to Do about It*. Princeton, NJ: Princeton University Press, 2008.

———. *Finance and the Good Society*. Princeton, NJ: Princeton University Press, 2012.

———. *Irrational Exuberance*. Revised and expanded 3rd ed. Princeton, NJ: Princeton University Press, 2015.

Skidelsky, Robert, and Edward Skidelsky. *How Much Is Enough? Money and the Good Life*. New York: Other Press, 2012.

Smithers, Andrew. *The Road to Recovery: How and Why Economic Policy Must Change*. N.p.: Wiley, 2013.

Spence, Michael. *The Next Convergence: The Future of Economic Growth in a Multispeed World*. New York: Farrar, Straus and Giroux, 2011.

Stiglitz, Joseph E. *The Roaring Nineties: A New History of the World's Most Prosperous Decade*. New York: W. W. Norton & Company, 2004.

———. *The Price of Inequality: How Today's Divided Society Endangers Our Future*. New York: W. W. Norton & Company, 2013.

———. *The Great Divide: Unequal Societies and What We Can Do About Them*. New York: W. W. Norton & Company, 2015.

Stone, Amey, and Mike Brewster. *King of Capital: Sandy Weill and the Making of Citigroup*. New York: John Wiley & Sons, 2002.

Stout, Lynn. *The Shareholder Value Myth: How Putting Shareholders First Harms Investors, Corporations, and the Public*. San Francisco: Berrett-Koehler Publishers, 2012.

Taylor, Paul, and the Pew Research Center. *The Next America: Boomers, Millennials, and the Looming Generational Showdown*. New York: PublicAffairs, 2014.

Tett, Gillian. *Fool's Gold: The Inside Story of J.P. Morgan and How Wall St. Greed Corrupted Its Bold Dream and Created a Financial Catastrophe*. New York: Free Press, 2010.

———. *The Silo Effect: The Peril of Expertise and the Promise of Breaking Down Barriers*. New York: Simon & Schuster, 2015.

Thaler, Richard H. *Misbehaving: The Making of Behavioral Economics*. New York: W. W. Norton & Company, 2015.

Thorndike Jr., William N. *The Outsiders: Eight Unconventional CEOs and Their Radically Rational Blueprint for Success*. Boston: Harvard Business Review Press, 2012.

Tobe, Chris, with Ken Tobe. *Kentucky Fried Pensions: Worse Than Detroit Edition*. 2nd ed. Middleton, DE: CreateSpace, 2013.

Tse, Edward. *China's Disruptors: How Alibaba, Xiaomi, Tencent, and Other Companies Are Changing the Rules of Business*. New York: Portfolio/Penguin, 2015.

Turner, Adair. *Between Debt and the Devil: Money, Credit, and Fixing Global Finance*. Princeton, NJ: Princeton University Press, 2015.

Turner, John D. *Banking in Crisis: The Rise and Fall of British Banking Stability, 1800 to the Present*. Cambridge: Cambridge University Press, 2014.

USB, "The New Global Context: Could Economic Transformations Threaten Stability?" USB White Paper for the World Economic Forum. January, 2015.

Warren, Elizabeth. *A Fighting Chance.* New York: Picador, 2015.

Weill, Sandy, and Judah S. Kraushaar. *The Real Deal: My Life in Business and Philanthropy.* New York: Warner Business Books, 2006.

Whitney, Meredith. *Fate of the States: The New Geography of American Prosperity.* New York: Penguin Press, 2013.

Wilkinson, Richard, and Kate Pickett. *The Spirit Level: Why Equality Is Better for Everyone.* London: Penguin Books, 2009.

Wolf, Martin. *The Shifts and the Shocks: What We've Learned—and Have Still to Learn—from the Financial Crisis.* New York: Penguin Press, 2014.

Zingales, Luigi. *A Capitalism for the People: Recapturing the Lost Genius of American Prosperity.* New York: Basic Books, 2012.

Zweig, Phillip L. *Wriston: Walter Wriston, Citibank, and the Rise and Fall of American Financial Supremacy.* New York: Crown Publishers, 1995.

INDEX